How To Use This Book

The second edition of *Teach Yourself TCP/IP in 14 Days* expands on the very popular first edition, bringing the information up-to-date and adding new topics to complete the coverage of TCP/IP. The book has been reorganized to make reading and learning easier, as well as to provide a more logical approach to the subject.

New material in this edition deals with installing, configuring, and testing a TCP/IP network of servers and clients. You will see how to easily set up UNIX, Linux, and Windows NT servers for all popular TCP/IP services, including Telnet, FTP, DNS, NIS, and NFS. On the client side, you will see how to set up DOS, Windows, Windows 95, and WinSock to interact with a server. Examples and tips throughout these sections make the process easy and clear.

Also added in this edition of *Teach Yourself TCP/IP in 14 Days* are new sections on DNS, NFS, and NIS. These network services have become popular with the growth of large TCP/IP networks, so we show you how to configure and use them all. A new section on the latest version of IP updates the treatment of the base protocols to 1996 standards.

Topics Covered in Detail in this Edition

- [ ] Standards and terminology
- [ ] Network architecture
- [ ] History of TCP/IP and the Internet
- [ ] IPng (IP version 6)
- [ ] Telnet and FTP
- [ ] Configuring servers and clients

Teach
Yourself
TCP/IP

in 14 days,
Second Edition

Teach Yourself
TCP/IP
in 14 Days,
Second Edition

Tim Parker

201 West 103rd Street
Indianapolis, Indiana 46290

This one is for my grandparents.
Eheu fugaces labuntur anni

Copyright © 1996 by Sams Publishing

SECOND EDITION

International Standard Book Number: 0-672-30885-1

Library of Congress Catalog Card Number: 95-72341

99 98 97 96   4 3 2

Interpretation of the printing code: the rightmost double-digit number is the year of the book's printing; the rightmost single-digit, the number of the book's printing. For example, a printing code of 96-1 shows that the first printing of the book occurred in 1996.

Composed in Agaramond and MCPdigital by Macmillan Computer Publishing

Printed in the United States of America

Trademarks

Publisher Richard K. Swadley
Publishing Team Leader Dean Miller
Managing Editor Cindy Morrow
Director of Marketing John Pierce
Assistant Marketing Managers Christina Perry
Rachel Wolfe

Acquisitions Editor
Grace Buechlein

Development Editor
Brian-Kent Proffitt

Production Editor
Mary Inderstrodt

Copy Editor
Angie Trzepacz

Technical Reviewers
John Jung
Angie Murdock

Editorial Coordinator
Bill Whitmer

Technical Edit Coordinator
Lynette Quinn or Lorraine
Schaffer

Resource Coordinator
Deborah Frisby

Editorial Assistants
Carol Ackerman
Andi Richter
Rhonda Tinch-Mize

Cover Designer
Tim Amrhein

Book Designer
Gary Adair

Copy Writer
Peter Fuller

Production Team Supervisor
Brad Chinn

Production
Chris Cleveland
Bruce Clingaman
Paula Lowell
Ian Smith
Andrew Stone

Indexer
Erika Millen

Overview

Contents

Preface

I first encountered TCP/IP a decade ago when a client lead me into a room with a bunch of UNIX-based computers, a stack of network boards, a roll of coaxial cable, and a pile of diskettes. My instructions were simple: Install a TCP/IP network that works. Unfortunately, there was no documentation along with the boards or software. A quick visit to the university library proved that few books were available on the subject; those that were left a lot to be desired. Eventually, through trial and error, I got the system working. In the process, I learned a great deal about the quirkiness of TCP/IP and UNIX.

TCP/IP is a family of protocols that covers a wide variety of tasks, all intertwined and interrelated in some way. There has been a steady increase in the number of TCP/IP networks as both the Internet and the UNIX operating systems have grown in popularity. UNIX and TCP/IP have been interwoven from the start of the protocol's history, which shows itself in the number of configuration files and architecture of TCP/IP. The last few years have seen TCP/IP implementations for almost every hardware platform and operating system available. Luckily, they are (almost) all compatible.

Several books have been written about TCP/IP, although none really suit the requirements for beginning users. There are a few excellent TCP/IP reference books that give precise details of the protocols, but they fail to give a solid overview—in easily understood terms—for newcomers. Finally the opportunity to write the TCP/IP book I'd like to have had 10 years ago came along. The result is now in your hands.

Two years ago when I wrote the first edition of *Teach Yourself TCP/IP in 14 Days,* I had no idea it would be as popular as it has turned out to be. The rapid growth of the Internet and TCP/IP as a networking protocol has obviously driven the demand for such books up, as is easily seen by the dozens of new arrivals on the bookshelf.

With the popularity of Windows 95 and the emergence of Windows NT as a replacement for UNIX servers, it became obvious that an update to this book to make it more timely would be beneficial. The core of the book remains the same as the first edition, although there are many new pages of material covering the Windows platforms and Linux. Many updates to existing material have been made, too, to make the book as timely as possible.

The organization of the book has been changed drastically since the first edition, driven mainly by my own use of the book as a teaching tool and determining a better order for students to read the material. Comments from readers through e-mail have also been embraced.

Since I wrote the first edition of this book, another 10 books have emerged from my computer, many for Sams. Sams' editorial and production staff are thanked again for their excellent work. I look forward to doing a third edition with them in another couple of years.

Hopefully you will find this edition of *Teach Yourself TCP/IP in 14 Days* readable, enjoyable, well-organized, and up-to-date. My thanks to all those who spent their hard-earned dollars on the first edition, and to all those who provided feedback. TCP/IP is not a scary subject, and I think you'll find this book both informative and enjoyable.

Acknowledgments

Writing books is supposed to get easier with practice. This is my ninth book, and although I no longer worry about grammar or writing style, this one had its own unique problems. Most of the problems hinge on the simple fact that explaining TCP/IP is impossible without getting into a fair level of detail, most of which is—simply put—quite dull. There is no easy way to spice up details of a complex communications protocol, but I have tried to make the subject as readable as possible.

TCP/IP is not a single protocol but a family of related protocols that perform dedicated tasks. Explaining these protocols means delving into detail without going to the point that the reader's eyes glaze over. It's a tricky line to tread, and I hope I've managed it to your satisfaction. This book covers everything you need to know as a newcomer to TCP/IP, while also providing enough information as you progress into the advanced levels. From there, the level of detail multiplies and the original design documents are the best sources of information.

This book took a lot of effort to complete, in part because of its lack of practical material. There was also a considerable amount of work from several people at Sams Publishing. The staff of editors at Sams have worked hard to produce a readable, well-presented book. They are to be thanked and congratulated for their efforts.

Several vendors kindly provided software for my use during the writing of this book. Thanks to the Santa Cruz Operation, FTP Software, NetManage, and Microsoft.

On a personal level, thanks go to my parents for understanding why I couldn't visit as often as I would have liked. Thanks also to Yvonne for tolerating all the late nights and weekends that were spent in front of a screen instead of with her. The result of all the effort is a book I am proud of and hope you find useful.

About the Author

Tim Parker started programming computers 20 years ago and began writing about programs five years later. Since then, he has published more than 500 articles and two dozen books on the subject. He has held roles as columnist and editor with some of the most popular computer magazines and newsletters.

Educated at the University of Toronto and the University of Ottawa, he pursued a doctoral degree in chemistry at the Ottawa-Carleton Institute for Graduate Work and Research. Along the way, computers became an integral part of his research. A desire to explain the cryptic world of computer science led him to his writing career. Although a freelance writing and programming career is not the most stable, Tim has never been short of work.

Tim was a founding columnist and reviewer for Computer Language Magazine, a columnist with UNIX Review, and has contributed to dozens of other magazines such as *UNIX World*, *Data Based Advisor, Compute!*, and *Microsystems Journal*. He is currently the technical editor of *SCO World* magazine, editor of the newsletter *UNIQUE: The UNIX Systems Information Source*, a frequent contributor to *UNIX Review* magazine, and a columnist with *MacLean-Hunter Publications*. He covers UNIX, DOS, and Macintosh platforms. His books on UNIX have been very well-received and are used in courses taught world-wide.

He is the president of his own consulting company, which specializes in technical writing and training, software development, and software quality testing. He is a pilot, scuba diver, and white-water kayaker. Tim currently lives in Kanata, Ontario with a temperamental network of too many PCs and workstations.

Tell Us What You Think!

As a reader, you are the most important critic and commentator of our books. We value your opinion and want to know what we're doing right, what we could do better, what areas you'd like to see us publish in, and any other words of wisdom you're willing to pass our way. You can help us make strong books that meet your needs and give you the computer guidance you require.

Do you have access to CompuServe or the World Wide Web? Then check out our CompuServe forum by typing GO SAMS at any prompt. If you prefer the World Wide Web, check out our site at http://www.mcp.com.

NOTE

If you have a technical question about this book, call the technical support line at (800) 571-5840, ext. 3668.

As the team leader of the group that created this book, I welcome your comments. You can fax, e-mail, or write me directly to let me know what you did or didn't like about this book—as well as what we can do to make our books stronger. Here's the information:

FAX: 317/581-4669

E-mail: opsys_mgr@sams.mcp.com

Mail: Dean Miller
          Comments Department
          Sams Publishing
          201 W. 103rd Street
          Indianapolis, IN 46290

Introduction

So you've just been told you are on a TCP/IP network, you are the new TCP/IP system administrator, or you have to install a TCP/IP system. But you don't know very much about TCP/IP. That's where this book comes in. You don't need any programming skills, and familiarity with operating systems is assumed. Even if you've never touched a computer before, you should be able to follow the material.

This book is intended for beginning through intermediate users and covers all the protocols involved in TCP/IP. Each protocol is examined in a fair level of detail to show how it works and how it interacts with the other protocols in the TCP/IP family. Along the way, this book shows you the basic tools required to install, configure, and maintain a TCP/IP network. It also shows you most of the user utilities that are available.

Because of the complex nature of TCP/IP and the lack of a friendly user interface, there is a lot of information to look at. Throughout the book, the role of each protocol is shown separately, as is the way it works on networks of all sizes. The relationship with large internetworks (like the Internet) is also covered.

Each chapter in the book adds to the complexity of the system, building on the material in the earlier chapters. Although some chapters seem to be unrelated to TCP/IP at first glance, all the material is involved in an integral manner with the TCP/IP protocol family. The last few chapters cover the installation and troubleshooting of a network.

By the time you finish this book, you will understand the different components of a TCP/IP system, as well as the complex acronym-heavy jargon used. Following the examples presented, you should be able to install and configure a complete TCP/IP network for any operating system and hardware platform.

The TCP/IP Protocol Family

Transport

Transmission Control Protocol (TCP): connection-based services
User Datagram Protocol (UDP): connectionless services

Routing

Internet Protocol (IP): handles transmission of information

Internet Control Message Protocol (ICMP): handles status messages for IP

Routing Information Protocol (RIP): determines routing

Open Shortest Path First (OSPF): alternate protocol for determining routing

Network Addresses

Address Resolution Protocol (ARP): determines addresses

Domain Name Service (DNS): determines addresses from machine names

Reverse Address Resolution Protocol (RARP): - determines addresses

User Services

Boot Protocol (BOOTP): starts up a network machine

File Transfer Protocol (FTP): transfers files

Telnet: allows remote logins

Gateway Protocols

Exterior Gateway Protocol (EGP): transfers routing information for external networks

Gateway-to-Gateway Protocol (GGP): transfers routing information between gateways

Interior Gateway Protocol (IGP): transfers routing information for internal networks

Others

Network File System (NFS): enables directories on one machine to be mounted on another

Network Information Service (NIS): maintains user accounts across networks

Remote Procedure Call (RPC): enables remote applications to communicate

Simple Mail Transfer Protocol (SMTP): transfers electronic mail

Simple Network Management Protocol (SNMP): sends status messages about the network

Chapter 1

Open Systems, Standards, and Protocols

Today I start looking at the subject of TCP/IP by covering some background information you will need to put TCP/IP in perspective, and to understand why the TCP/IP protocols were designed the way they are. This chapter covers some important information, including the following:

- [ ] What an open system is
- [ ] How an open system handles networking
- [ ] Why standards are required
- [ ] How standards for protocols like TCP/IP are developed
- [ ] What a protocol is
- [ ] The OSI protocols

You might be eager to get started with the nitty-gritty of the TCP/IP protocols, or to find out how to use the better-known services like FTP and Telnet. If you have a specific requirement to satisfy (such as how to transfer a file from one system to another), by all means use the Table of Contents to find the section you want. But if you want to really understand TCP/IP, you will need to wade through the material in this chapter. It's not complicated, although there are quite a few subjects to be covered. Luckily, none of it requires memorization; more often than not it is a matter of setting the stage for something else I discuss in the next week or so. So don't get too overwhelmed by this chapter!

Open Systems

This is a book about a family of protocols called TCP/IP, so why bother looking at open systems and standards at all? Primarily because TCP/IP grew out of the need to develop a standardized communications procedure that would inevitably be used on a variety of platforms. The need for a standard, and one that was readily available to anyone (hence *open*), was vitally important to TCP/IP's success. Therefore, a little background helps put the design of TCP/IP into perspective.

More importantly, open systems have become de rigueur in the current competitive market. The term *open system* is bandied around by many people as a solution for all problems (to be replaced occasionally by the term *client/server*), but neither term is usually properly used or understood by the people spouting them. Understanding what an open system really is and what it implies leads to a better awareness of TCP/IP's role on a network and across large internetworks like the Internet.

In a similar vein, the use of standards ensures that a protocol such as TCP/IP is the same on each system. This means that your PC can talk to a minicomputer running TCP/IP without special translation or conversion routines. It means that an entire network of different hardware and operating systems can work with the same network protocols. Developing a standard is not a trivial process. Often a single standard involves more than a single document describing a software system. A standard often involves the interrelationship of many different protocols, as does TCP/IP. Knowing the interactions between TCP/IP and the other components of a communications system is important for proper configuration and optimization, and to ensure that all the services you need are available and interworking properly.

What Is an Open System?

There are many definitions of open systems, and a single, concise definition that everyone is happy with is far from being accepted. For most people, an open system is best loosely defined as one for which the architecture is not a secret. The description of the architecture

has been published or is readily available to anyone who wants to build products for a hardware or software platform. This definition of an open system applies equally well to hardware and software.

When more than a single vendor begins producing products for a platform, customers have a choice. You don't particularly like Nocrash Software's network monitoring software? No problem, because FaultFree Software's product runs on the Nocrash hardware, and you like its fancy interface much better. You need a more colorful graphical front end to your Whizbang PC than the one Whizbang provides? Download one from Super Software through the Internet, and it works perfectly. The primary idea, of course, is a move away from proprietary platforms to one that is multivendor.

A decade ago, open systems were virtually nonexistent. Each hardware manufacturer had a product line, and you were practically bound to that manufacturer for all your software and hardware needs. Some companies took advantage of the captive market, charging outrageous prices or forcing unwanted configurations on their customers. The groundswell of resentment grew to the point that customers began forcing the issue. The lack of choice in software and hardware purchases is why several dedicated minicomputer and mainframe companies either went bankrupt or had to accept open system principles: their customers got fed up with relying on a single vendor. A good example of a company that made the adaptation is Digital Equipment Corporation (DEC). They moved from a proprietary operating system on their VMS minicomputers to a UNIX-standard open operating system. By doing that, they kept their customers happy, and they sold more machines. That's one of the primary reasons DEC is still in business today.

UNIX is a classic example of an open software platform. UNIX has been around for 30 years. The source code for the UNIX operating system was made available to anyone who wanted it, almost from the start. UNIX's source code is well understood and easy to work with, the result of 30 years of development and improvement. UNIX can be ported to run on practically any hardware platform, eliminating all proprietary dependencies. The attraction of UNIX is not the operating system's features themselves but simply that a UNIX user can run software from other UNIX platforms, that files are compatible from one UNIX system to another (except for disk formats), and that a wide variety of vendors sell products for UNIX.

The growth of UNIX pushed the large hardware manufacturers to the open systems principle, resulting in most manufacturers licensing the right to produce a UNIX version for their own hardware. This step let customers combine different hardware systems into larger networks, all running UNIX and working together. Users could move between machines almost transparently, ignorant of the actual hardware platform they were on. Open systems, originally of prime importance only to the largest corporations and governments, is now a key element in even the smallest company's computer strategy.

NOTE

Although UNIX is a copyrighted work now owned by X/Open, the details of the operating system have been published and are readily available to any developer who wants to produce applications or hardware that work with the operating system. UNIX is unique in this respect.

The term *open system networking* means many things, depending on whom you ask. In its broadest definition, open system networking refers to a network based on a well-known and understood protocol (such as TCP/IP) that has its standards published and readily available to anyone who wants to use them. Open system networking also refers to the process of networking open systems (machine-specific hardware and software) using a network protocol. It is easy to see why people want open systems networking, though. Three services are widely used and account for the highest percentage of network traffic: file transfer, electronic mail, and remote login. Without open systems networking, setting up any of these three services would be a nightmare.

File transfers enable users to share files quickly and efficiently, without excessive duplication or concerns about the transport method. Network file transfers are much faster than an overnight courier crossing the country, and usually faster than copying a file on a disk and carrying it across the room. File transfer is also extremely convenient, which not only pleases users but also eliminates time delays while waiting for material. A common open system governing file transfers means that any incompatibilities between the two machines transferring files can be overcome easily.

Electronic mail has mushroomed to a phenomenally large service, not just within a single business but worldwide. The Internet carries millions of messages from people in government, private industry, educational institutions, and private interests. Electronic mail is cheap (no paper, envelope, or stamp) and fast (around the world in 60 seconds or so). It is also an obvious extension of the computer-based world we work in. Without an open mail system, you wouldn't have anywhere near the capabilities you now enjoy.

Finally, remote logins enable a user who is based on one system to connect through a network to any other system that accepts him as a user. This can be in the next workgroup, the next state, or in another country. Remote logins enable users to take advantage of particular hardware and software in another location, as well as to run applications on another machine. Once again, without an open standard, this would be almost impossible.

1

Network Architectures

To understand networking protocols, it is useful to know a little about networks. A quick look at the most common network architectures will help later in this book when you read about network operations and routing. The term *network* usually means a set of computers and peripherals (printers, modems, plotters, scanners, and so on) that are connected together by some medium. The connection can be direct (through a cable) or indirect (through a modem). The different devices on the network communicate with each other through a predefined set of rules (the protocol).

The devices on a network can be in the same room or scattered through a building. They can be separated by many miles through the use of dedicated telephone lines, microwave, or a similar system. They can even be scattered around the world, again connected by a long-distance communications medium. The layout of the network (the actual devices and the manner in which they are connected to each other) is called the *network topology*.

Usually, if the devices on a network are in a single location such as a building or a group of rooms, they are called a local area network, or LAN. LANs usually have all the devices on the network connected by a single type of network cable. If the devices are scattered widely, such as in different buildings or different cities, they are usually set up into several LANs that are joined together into a larger structure called a wide area network, or WAN. A WAN is composed of two or more LANs. Each LAN has its own network cable connecting all the devices in that LAN. The LANs are joined together by another connection method, often high-speed telephone lines or very fast dedicated network cables called backbones, which I discuss in a moment.

One last point about WANs: they are often treated as a single entity for organizational purposes. For example, the ABC Software company might have branches in four different cities, with a LAN in each city. All four LANs are joined together by high-speed telephone lines. However, as far as the Internet and anyone outside the ABC Software company are concerned, the ABC Software WAN is a single entity. (It has a single domain name for the Internet. Don't worry if you don't known what a domain is at this point in time; it refers to a single entity for organizational purposes on the Internet, as you will see later.)

Local Area Networks

TCP/IP works across LANs and WANs, and there are several important aspects of LAN and WAN topologies you should know about. You can start with LANs and look at their topologies. Although there are many topologies for LANs, three topologies are dominant: bus, ring, and hub.

The Bus Network

The bus network is the simplest, comprising a single main communications pathway with each device attached to the main cable (bus) through a device called a transceiver or junction box. The bus is also called a backbone because it resembles a human spine with ribs emanating from it. From each transceiver on the bus, another cable (often very short) runs to the device's network adapter. An example of a bus network is shown in Figure 1.1.

Figure 1.1.

A schematic of a bus network showing the backbone with transceivers leading to network devices.

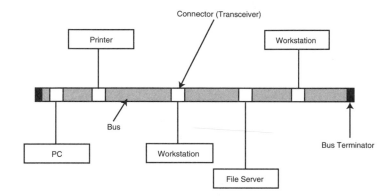

The primary advantage of a bus network is that it allows for a high-speed bus. Another advantage of the bus network is that it is usually immune to problems with any single network card within a device on the network. This is because the transceiver allows traffic through the backbone whether a device is attached to the junction box or not. Each end of the bus is terminated with a block of resistors or a similar electrical device to mark the end of the cable electrically. Each device on the pathway has a special identifying number, or address, that lets the device know that incoming information is for that device.

A bus network is seldom a straight cable. Instead, it is usually twisted around walls and buildings as needed. It does have a single pathway from one end to the other, with each end terminated in some way (usually with a resistor). Figure 1.1 shows a logical representation of the network, meaning it has simplified the actual physical appearance of the network into a schematic with straight lines and no real scale to the connections. A physical representation of the network would show how it goes through walls, around desks, and so on. Most devices on the bus network can send or receive data along the bus by packaging a message with the intended recipient's address.

A variation of the bus network topology is found in many small LANs that use Thin Ethernet cable (which looks like television coaxial cable) or twisted-pair cable (which resembles telephone cables). This type of network consists of a length of coaxial cable that snakes from machine to machine. Unlike the bus network in Figure 1.1, there are no transceivers on the bus. Instead, each device is connected into the bus directly using a T-shaped connector on

the network interface card, often using a connector called a BNC. The connector connects the machine to the two neighbors through two cables, one to each neighbor. At the ends of the network, a simple resistor is added to one side of the T-connector to terminate the network electrically.

A schematic of this type of network is shown in Figure 1.2. Each network device has a T-connector attached to the network interface card, leading to its two neighbors. The two ends of the bus are terminated with resistors.

Figure 1.2.

A schematic of a machine-to-machine bus network.

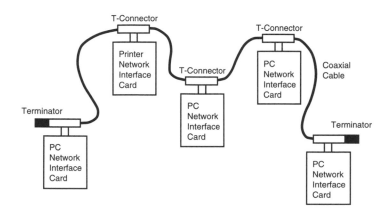

This machine-to-machine (also called peer-to-peer) network is not capable of sustaining the higher speeds of the backbone-based bus network, primarily because of the medium of the network cable. A backbone network can use very high-speed cables such as fiber optics, with smaller (and slower) cables from each transceiver to the device. A machine-to-machine network is usually built using twisted-pair or coaxial cable because these cables are much cheaper and easier to work with. Until recently, machine-to-machine networks were limited to a throughput of about 10 Mbps (megabits per second), although recent developments called 100VG AnyLAN and Fast Ethernet allow 100 Mbps on this type of network.

The advantage of this machine-to-machine bus network is its simplicity. Adding new machines to the network means installing a network card and connecting the new machine into a logical place on the backbone. One major advantage of the machine-to-machine bus network is also its cost: It is probably the lowest cost LAN topology available. The problem with this type of bus network is that if one machine is taken off the network cable, or the network interface card malfunctions, the backbone is broken and must be tied together again with a jumper of some sort or the network might cease to function properly.

The Ring Network

A ring network topology is often drawn as its name suggests, shaped like a ring. A typical ring network schematic is shown in Figure 1.3. You might have heard of a *token ring network* before, which is a ring topology network. You might be disappointed to find no physical ring architecture in a ring network, though.

Figure 1.3.

A schematic of a ring network.

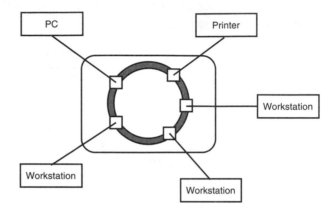

 NOTE

Despite the almost automatic assumption that a ring network has a backbone with the ends of the cable joined to form a loop, there is no real cabling ring at all. The ring name derives from the construction of the central control unit.

The term *ring* is a misnomer because ring networks don't have an unending cable like a bus network with the two terminators joined together. Instead, the ring refers to the design of the central unit that handles the network's message passing. In a token ring network, the central control unit is called a Media Access Unit, or MAU. The MAU has a ring circuit inside it (for which the network topology is named). The ring inside the MAU serves as the bus for devices to obtain messages.

The Hub Network

A hub network uses a main cable much like the bus network, which is called the *backplane*. The hub topology is shown in Figure 1.4. From the backplane, a set of cables leads to a hub, which is a box containing several ports into which devices are plugged. The cables to a connection point are often called *drops*, because they drop from the backplane to the ports.

Figure 1.4.

A schematic of a hub network.

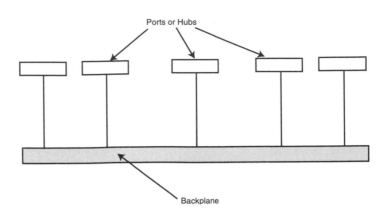

Hub networks can be very large, using a high-speed fiber optic backplane and slightly slower Ethernet drops to hubs from which a workgroup can be supported. The hub network can also be small, with a couple of hubs supporting a few devices connected together by standard Ethernet cables. The hub network is scaleable (meaning you can start small and expand as you need to), which is part of its attraction.

Hub networks have become popular for large installations, in part because they are easy to set up and maintain. They also can be the least expensive system in many larger installations, which adds to their attraction. The backplane can extend across a considerable distance just like a bus network, whereas the ports, or connection points, are usually grouped in a set placed in a box or panel. There can be many panels or connection boxes attached to the backplane.

Wide Area Networks

As I mentioned earlier, LANs can be combined into a large entity called a WAN. WANs are usually composed of LANs joined together by a high-speed link (such as a telephone line or dedicated cable). At the entrance to each LAN, one or more machines act as the link between the LAN and WAN: these are called gateways. I talk about gateways and the types of gateways used in a WAN in more detail on many of the following days, but for now you need to know only that a gateway is the interface between a LAN and a WAN. The same applies for any LAN that accesses the Internet: one machine usually acts as the gateway from the LAN to the Internet (which is really just a very large WAN).

Many terms other than *gateway* are also used. You will hear terms like *router* and *bridge*. They are all gateways, but they perform slightly different tasks. To understand their roles (which I mention many times in the next week's material), you need to take a quick look at how WANs are laid out.

LANs can be tied to a WAN through a gateway that handles the passage of data between the LAN and WAN backbone. In a simple layout, a router is used to perform this function. This is shown in Figure 1.5.

Figure 1.5.

A router connects a LAN to the backbone.

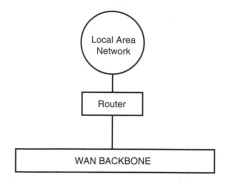

Another gateway device, called a bridge, is used to connect LANs using the same network protocol. Bridges are used only when the same network protocol (such as TCP/IP) is on both LANs. The bridge does not care which physical media is used. Bridges can connect twisted-pair LANs to coaxial LANs, for example, or act as an interface to a fiber optic network. As long as the network protocol is the same, the bridge functions properly.

If two or more LANs are involved in one organization and there is the possibility of a lot of traffic between them, it is better to connect the two LANs directly with a bridge instead of loading the backbone with the cross-traffic. This is shown in Figure 1.6.

Figure 1.6.

Using a bridge to connect two LANs.

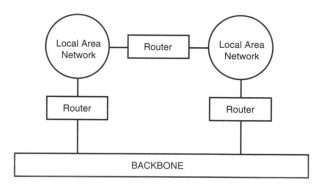

In a configuration using bridges between LANs, traffic from one LAN to another can be sent through the bridge instead of onto the backbone, providing better performance. For services such as Telnet and FTP, the speed difference between using a bridge and going through a router onto a heavily used backbone can be significant.

WANs are an important subject, and I look at them again in more detail on Day 13, "Managing and Troubleshooting TCP/IP."

Layers

Suppose you have to write a program that provides networking functions to every machine on your LAN. Writing a single software package that accomplishes every task required for communications between different computers would be a nightmarish task. Apart from having to cope with the different hardware architectures, simply writing the code for all the applications you desire would result in a program that was far too large to execute or maintain.

Dividing all the requirements into similar-purpose groups is a sensible approach, much as a programmer breaks code into logical chunks. With open systems communications, groups are quite obvious. One group deals with the transport of data, another with the packaging of messages, another with end-user applications, and so on. Each group of related tasks is called a *layer*.

 NOTE

> The layers of an architecture are meant to be stand-alone, independent entities. They usually cannot perform any observable task without interacting with other layers, but from a programming point of view they are self-contained.

Of course, some crossover of functionality is to be expected, and several different approaches to the same division of layers for a network protocol were proposed. One that became adopted as a standard is the Open Systems Interconnection Reference Model (which is discussed in more detail in the next section). The OSI Reference Model (OSI-RM) uses seven layers, as shown in Figure 1.7. The TCP/IP architecture is similar but involves only five layers, because it combines some of the OSI functionality in two layers into one. For now, though, consider the seven-layer OSI model.

The application, presentation, and session layers are all application-oriented in that they are responsible for presenting the application interface to the user. All three are independent of the layers below them and are totally oblivious to the means by which data gets to the application. These three layers are called the upper layers.

Figure 1.7.
The OSI Reference Model showing all seven layers.

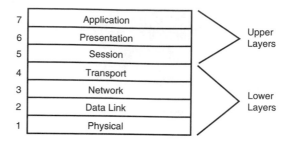

The lower four layers deal with the transmission of data, covering the packaging, routing, verification, and transmission of each data group. The lower layers don't worry about the type of data they receive or send to the application, but deal simply with the task of sending it. They don't differentiate between the different applications in any way.

The following sections explain each layer to help you understand the architecture of the OSI-RM (and later contrast it with the architecture of TCP/IP).

The Application Layer

The application layer is the end-user interface to the OSI system. It is where the applications, such as electronic mail, Usenet news readers, or database display modules, reside. The application layer's task is to display received information and send the user's new data to the lower layers.

In distributed applications, such as client/server systems, the application layer is where the client application resides. It communicates through the lower layers to the server.

The Presentation Layer

The presentation layer's task is to isolate the lower layers from the application's data format. It converts the data from the application into a common format, often called the *canonical representation.* The presentation layer processes machine-dependent data from the application layer into a machine-independent format for the lower layers.

The presentation layer is where file formats and even character formats (ASCII and EBCDIC, for example) are lost. The conversion from the application data format takes place through a "common network programming language" (as it is called in the OSI Reference Model documents) that has a structured format.

The presentation layer does the reverse for incoming data. It is converted from the common format into application-specific formats, based on the type of application the machine has instructions for. If the data comes in without reformatting instructions, the information might not be assembled in the correct manner for the user's application.

The Session Layer

The session layer organizes and synchronizes the exchange of data between application processes. It works with the application layer to provide simple data sets called *synchronization points* that let an application know how the transmission and reception of data are progressing. In simplified terms, the session layer can be thought of as a timing and flow control layer.

The session layer is involved in coordinating communications between different applications, letting each know the status of the other. An error in one application (whether on the same machine or across the country) is handled by the session layer to let the receiving application know that the error has occurred. The session layer can resynchronize applications that are currently connected to each other. This can be necessary when communications are temporarily interrupted, or when an error has occurred that results in loss of data.

The Transport Layer

The transport layer, as its name suggests, is designed to provide the "transparent transfer of data from a source end open system to a destination end open system," according to the OSI Reference Model. The transport layer establishes, maintains, and terminates communications between two machines.

The transport layer is responsible for ensuring that data sent matches the data received. This verification role is important in ensuring that data is correctly sent, with a resend if an error was detected. The transport layer manages the sending of data, determining its order and its priority.

The Network Layer

The network layer provides the physical routing of the data, determining the path between the machines. The network layer handles all these routing issues, relieving the higher layers from this issue.

The network layer examines the network topology to determine the best route to send a message, as well as figuring out relay systems. It is the only network layer that sends a message from source to target machine, managing other chunks of data that pass through the system on their way to another machine.

The Data Link Layer

The data link layer, according to the OSI reference paper, "provides for the control of the physical layer, and detects and possibly corrects errors that can occur." In practicality, the data link layer is responsible for correcting transmission errors induced during transmission (as opposed to errors in the application data itself, which are handled in the transport layer).

The data link layer is usually concerned with signal interference on the physical transmission media, whether through copper wire, fiber optic cable, or microwave. Interference is common, resulting from many sources, including cosmic rays and stray magnetic interference from other sources.

The Physical Layer

The physical layer is the lowest layer of the OSI model and deals with the "mechanical, electrical, functional, and procedural means" required for transmission of data, according to the OSI definition. This is really the wiring or other transmission form.

When the OSI model was being developed, a lot of concern dealt with the lower two layers, because they are, in most cases, inseparable. The real world treats the data link layer and the physical layer as one combined layer, but the formal OSI definition stipulates different purposes for each. (TCP/IP includes the data link and physical layers as one layer, recognizing that the division is more academic than practical.)

Terminology and Notations

Both OSI and TCP/IP are rooted in formal descriptions, presented as a series of complex documents that define all aspects of the protocols. To define OSI and TCP/IP, several new terms were developed and introduced into use; some (mostly OSI terms) are rather unusual. You might find the term *OSI-speak* used to refer to some of these rather grotesque definitions, much as *legalese* refers to legal terms.

To better understand the details of TCP/IP, it is necessary to deal with these terms now. You won't see all these terms in this book, but you might encounter them when reading manuals or online documentation. Therefore, all the major terms are covered here.

NOTE Many of the terms used by both OSI and TCP/IP might seem to have multiple meanings, but there is a definite attempt to provide a single, consistent definition for each word. Unfortunately, the user community is slow to adopt new terminology, so there is a considerable amount of confusion.

Packets

To transfer data effectively, many experiments have shown that creating a uniform chunk of data is better than sending characters singly or in widely varying sized groups. Usually these chunks of data have some information ahead of them (the *header*) and sometimes an indicator at the end (the *trailer*). These chunks of data are called *packets* in most synchronous communications systems.

The amount of data in a packet and the composition of the header can change depending on the communications protocol as well as some system limitations, but the concept of a packet always refers to the entire set (including header and trailer). The term *packet* is used often in the computer industry, sometimes when it shouldn't be.

WARNING

> You often see the word *packet* used as a generic reference to any group of data packaged for transmission. As an application's data passes through the layers of the architecture, each adds more information. The term *packet* is frequently used at each stage. Treat the term *packet* as a generalization for any data with additional information, instead of the specific result of only one layer's addition of header and trailer. This goes against the efforts of both OSI and the TCP governing bodies, but it helps keep your sanity intact!

Subsystems

A *subsystem* is the collective of a particular layer across a network. For example, if 10 machines are connected together, each running the seven-layer OSI model, all 10 application layers are the application subsystem, all 10 data link layers are the data link subsystem, and so on. As you might have already deduced, with the OSI Reference Model there are seven subsystems.

It is entirely possible (and even likely) that all the individual components in a subsystem will not be active at one time. Using the 10-machine example again, only three might have the data link layer actually active at any moment in time, but the cumulative of all the machines makes up the subsystem.

Entities

A layer can have more than one part to it. For example, the transport layer can have routines that verify checksums as well as routines that handle resending packets that didn't transfer correctly. Not all these routines are active at once, because they might not be required at any moment. The active routines, though, are called entities. The word *entity* was adopted in order to find a single term that could not be confused with another computer term such as module, process, or task.

N Notation

The notations N, N+1, N+2, and so on are used to identify a layer and the layers that are related to it. Referring to Figure 1.7, if the transport layer is layer N, the physical layer is N–3 and the presentation layer is N+2. With OSI, N always has a value of 1 through 7 inclusive.

One reason this notation was adopted was to enable writers to refer to other layers without having to write out their names every time. It also makes flow charts and diagrams of interactions a little easier to draw. The terms N+1 and N–1 are commonly used in both OSI and TCP for the layers above and below the current layer, respectively, as you will see.

To make things even more confusing, many OSI standards refer to a layer by the first letter of its name. This can lead to a real mess for the casual reader, because S-entity, 5-entity, and layer 5 all refer to the session layer.

N-Functions

Each layer performs N-functions. The functions are the different things the layer does. Therefore, the functions of the transport layer are the different tasks that the layer provides. For most purposes in this book, functions and entities mean the same thing.

N-Facilities

This uses the hierarchical layer structure to express the idea that one layer provides a set of facilities to the next higher layer. This is sensible, because the application layer expects the presentation layer to provide a robust, well-defined set of facilities to it. In OSI-speak, the (N+1)-entities assume a defined set of N-facilities from the N-entity.

Services

The entire set of N-facilities provided to the (N+1)-entities is called the N-service. In other words, the service is the entire set of N-functions provided to the next higher layer. Services might seem like functions, but there is a formal difference between the two. The OSI documents go to great lengths to provide detailed descriptions of services, with a "service definition standard" for each layer. This was necessary during the development of the OSI standard so that the different tasks involved in the communications protocol could be assigned to different layers, and so that the functions of each layer are both well-defined and isolated from other layers.

The service definitions are formally developed from the bottom layer (physical) upward to the top layer. The advantage of this approach is that the design of the N+1 layer can be based on the functions performed in the N layer, avoiding two functions that accomplish the same task in two adjacent layers.

An entire set of variations on the service name has been developed to apply these definitions, some of which are in regular use:

> An N-service user is a user of a service provided by the N layer to the next higher (N+1) layer.

> An N-service provider is the set of N-entities that are involved in providing the N layer service.

> An N-service access point (often abbreviated to N-SAP) is where an N-service is provided to an (N+1)-entity by the N-service provider.

> N-service data is the packet of data exchanged at an N-SAP.

> N-service data units (N-SDUs) are the individual units of data exchanged at an N-SAP (so that N-service data is made up of N-SDUs).

These terms are shown in Figure 1.8. Another common term is *encapsulation,* which is the addition of control information to a packet of data. The control data contains addressing details, checksums for error detection, and protocol control functions.

Figure 1.8.

Service providers and service users communicate through service access points.

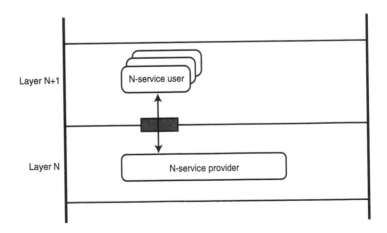

Making Sense of the Jargon

It is important to remember that all these terms are used in a formal description, because a formal language is usually the only method to adequately describe something as complex as a communications protocol. It is possible, though, to fit these terms together so that they make a little more sense when you encounter them. An example should help.

The session layer has a set of session functions. It provides a set of session facilities to the layer above it, the presentation layer. The session layer is made up of session entities. The presentation layer is a user of the services provided by the session layer (layer 5). A presentation entity is a user of the services provided by the session layer and is called a presentation service user.

The session service provider is the collection of session entities that are actively involved in providing the presentation layer with the session's services. The point at which the session service is provided to the presentation layer is the session service access point, where the session service data is sent. The individual bits of data in the session service data are called session service data units.

Confusing? Believe it or not, after a while you will begin to feel more comfortable with these terms. The important ones to know now are that a layer provides a set of entities through a service access point to the next higher layer, which is called the service user. The data is sent in chunks called service data, made up of service data units.

Queues and Connections

Communication between two parties (whether over a telephone, between layers of an architecture, or between applications themselves) takes place in three distinct stages: establishment of the connection, data transfer, and connection termination.

Communication between two OSI applications in the same layer is through queues to the layer beneath them. Each application (more properly called a service user) has two queues, one for each direction to the service provider of the layer beneath (which controls the whole layer). In OSI-speak, the two queues provide for simultaneous (or *atomic*) interactions between two N-service action points.

Data, called *service primitives,* is put into and retrieved from the queue by the applications (service users). A service primitive can be a block of data, an indicator that something is required or received, or a status indicator. As with most aspects of OSI, a lexicon has been developed to describe the actions in these queues:

> A *request primitive* is when one service submits a service primitive to the queue (through the N-SAP) requesting permission to communicate with another service in the same layer.

An *indication primitive* is what the service provider in the layer beneath the sending application sends to the intended receiving application to let it know that communication is desired.

A *response primitive* is sent by the receiving application to the layer beneath's service provider to acknowledge the granting of communications between the two service users.

A *confirmation primitive* is sent from the service provider to the final application to indicate that both applications on the layer above can now communicate.

An example might help clarify the process. Assume that two applications in the presentation layer want to communicate with each other. They can't do so directly (according to the OSI model), so they must go through the layer below them. These steps are shown in Figure 1.9.

Figure 1.9.

Two applications communicate through SAPs using primitives.

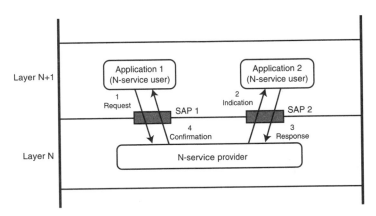

The first application sends a request primitive to the service provider of the session layer and waits. The session layer's service provider removes the request primitive from the inbound queue from the first application and sends an indication primitive to the second application's inbound queue.

The second application takes the indication primitive from its queue to the session service provider and decides to accept the request for connection by sending a positive response primitive back through its queue to the session layer. This is received by the session layer service provider, and a confirmation primitive is sent to the first application in the presentation layer. This is a process called *confirmed service* because the applications wait for confirmation that communications are established and ready.

OSI also provides for *unconfirmed service*, in which a request primitive is sent to the service provider, sending the indication primitive to the second application. The response and confirmation primitives are not sent. This is a sort of "get ready, because here it comes whether you want it or not" communication, often referred to as *send and pray.*

When two service users are using confirmed service to communicate, they are considered connected. Two applications are talking to each other, aware of what the other is doing with the service data. OSI refers to the establishment and maintenance of *state information* between the two, or the fact that each knows when the other is sending or receiving. OSI calls this *connection-oriented* or *connection-mode* communications.

Connectionless communication is when service data is sent independently, as with unconfirmed service. The service data is self-contained, possessing everything a receiving service user needs to know. These service data packets are often called *datagrams.* The application that sends the datagram has no idea who receives the datagram and how it is handled, and the receiving service users have no idea who sent it (other than information that might be contained within the datagram itself). OSI calls this *connectionless-mode.*

OSI (and TCP/IP) use both connected and connectionless systems between layers of their architecture. Each has its benefits and ideal implementations. All these communications are between applications (service users) in each layer, using the layer beneath to communicate. There are many service users, and this process is going on all the time. It's quite amazing when you think about it.

Standards

People don't question the need for rules in a board game. If you didn't have rules, each player could be happily playing as it suits them, regardless of whether their play was consistent with that of other players. The existence of rules ensures that each player plays the game in the same way, which might not be as much fun as a free-for-all. However, when a fight over a player's actions arises, the written rules clearly indicate who is right. The rules are a set of standards by which a game is played.

Standards prevent a situation arising where two seemingly compatible systems really are not. For example, 10 years ago when CP/M was the dominant operating system, the 5.25-inch floppy was used by most systems. But the floppy from a Kaypro II couldn't be read by an Osbourne I because the tracks were laid out in a different manner. A utility program could convert between the two, but that extra step was a major annoyance for machine users.

When the IBM PC became the platform of choice, the 5.25-inch format used by the IBM PC was adopted by other companies to ensure disk compatibility. The IBM format became a de facto standard, one adopted because of market pressures and customer demand.

Setting Standards

Creating a standard in today's world is not a simple matter. Several organizations are dedicated to developing the standards in a complete, unambiguous manner. The most important of these is the International Organization for Standardization, or ISO (often called the International Standardization Organization to fit their acronym, although this is incorrect). ISO consists of standards organizations from many countries who try to agree on international criterion. The American National Standards Institute (ANSI), British Standards Institute (BSI), Deutsches Institut fur Normung (DIN), and Association Francaise du Normalization (AFNOR) are all member groups. The ISO developed the Open Systems Interconnection (OSI) standard that is discussed throughout this book.

Each nation's standards organization can create a standard for that country, of course. The goal of ISO, however, is to agree on worldwide standards. Otherwise, incompatibilities could exist that wouldn't allow one country's system to be used in another. (An example of this is with television signals: the US relies on NTSC, whereas Europe uses PAL—systems that are incompatible with each other.)

Curiously, the language used for most international standards is English, even though the majority of participants in a standards committee are not from English-speaking countries. This can cause quite a bit of confusion, especially because most standards are worded awkwardly to begin with.

The reason most standards involve awkward language is that to describe something unambiguously can be very difficult, sometimes necessitating the creation of new terms that the standard defines. Not only must the concepts be clearly defined, but the absolute behavior is necessary too. With most things that standards apply to, this means using numbers and physical terms to provide a concrete definition. Defining a 2×4 piece of lumber necessitates the use of a measurement of some sort, and similarly defining computer terms requires mathematics.

Simply defining a method of communications, such as TCP/IP, would be fairly straightforward if it weren't for the complication of defining it for open systems. The use of an open system adds another difficulty because all aspects of the standard must be machine-independent. Imagine trying to define a 2×4 without using a measurement you are familiar with, such as inches, or if inches are adopted, it would be difficult to define inches in an unambiguous way (which indeed is what happens, because most units of length are defined with respect to the wavelength of a particular kind of coherent light).

Computers communicate through bits of data, but those bits can represent characters, numbers, or something else. Numbers could be integers, fractions, or octal representations. Again, you must define the units. You can see that the complications mount, one on top of the other.

To help define a standard, an abstract approach is usually used. In the case of OSI, the meaning (called the semantics) of the data transferred (the abstract syntax) is first dealt with, and the exact representation of the data in the machine (the concrete syntax) and the means by which it is transferred (transfer syntax) are handled separately. The separation of the abstract lets the data be represented as an entity, without concern for what it really means. It's a little like treating your car as a unit instead of an engine, transmission, steering wheel, and so on. The abstraction of the details to a simpler whole makes it easier to convey information. ("My car is broken" is abstract, whereas "the power steering fluid has all leaked out" is concrete.)

To describe systems abstractly, it is necessary to have a language that meets the purpose. Most standards bodies have developed such a system. The most commonly used is ISO's Abstract Syntax Notation One, frequently shortened to ASN.1. It is suited especially for describing open systems networking. Thus, it's not surprising to find it used extensively in the OSI and TCP descriptions. Indeed, ASN.1 was developed concurrently with the OSI standards when it became necessary to describe upper-layer functions.

The primary concept of ASN.1 is that all types of data, regardless of type, size, origin, or purpose, can be represented by an object that is independent of the hardware, operating system software, or application. The ASN.1 system defines the contents of a datagram protocol header—the chunk of information at the beginning of an object that describes the contents to the system. (Headers are discussed in more detail in the section titled "Protocol Headers" later in this chapter.)

Part of ASN.1 describes the language used to describe objects and data types (such as a data description language in database terminology). Another part defines the basic encoding rules that deal with moving the data objects between systems. ASN.1 defines data types that are used in the construction of data packets (datagrams). It provides for both structured and unstructured data types, with a list of 28 supported types.

NOTE

Don't be too worried about learning ASN.1 in this book. I refer to it in passing in only a couple of places. It is useful, though, to know that the language is provided for the formal definition of all the aspects of TCP/IP.

Internet Standards

When the Defense Advanced Research Projects Agency (DARPA) was established in 1980, a group was formed to develop a set of standards for the Internet. The group, called the Internet Configuration Control Board (ICCB) was reorganized into the Internet Activities Board (IAB) in 1983, whose task was to design, engineer, and manage the Internet.

In 1986, the IAB turned over the task of developing the Internet standards to the Internet Engineering Task Force (IETF), and the long-term research was assigned to the Internet Research Task Force (IRTF). The IAB retained final authorization over anything proposed by the two task forces.

The last step in this saga was the formation of the Internet Society in 1992, when the IAB was renamed the Internet Architecture Board. This group is still responsible for existing and future standards, reporting to the board of the Internet Society.

After all that, what happened during the shuffling? Almost from the beginning, the Internet was defined as "a loosely organized international collaboration of autonomous, interconnected networks," which supported host-to-host communications "through voluntary adherence to open protocols and procedures" defined in a technical paper called the Internet Standards, RFC 1310,2. That definition is still used today.

The IETF continues to work on refining the standards used for communications over the Internet through a number of working groups, each one dedicated to a specific aspect of the overall Internet protocol suite. There are working groups dedicated to network management, security, user services, routing, and many more things. It is interesting that the IETF's groups are considerably more flexible and efficient than those of, say, the ISO, whose working groups can take years to agree on a standard. In many cases, the IETF's groups can form, create a recommendation, and disband within a year or so. This helps continuously refine the Internet standards to reflect changing hardware and software capabilities.

Creating a new Internet standard (which happened with TCP/IP) follows a well-defined process, shown schematically in Figure 1.10. It begins with a request for comment (RFC). This is usually a document containing a specific proposal, sometimes new and sometimes a modification of an existing standard. RFCs are widely distributed, both on the network itself and to interested parties as printed documents. Important RFCs and instructions for retrieving them are included in the appendixes at the end of this book.

Figure 1.10.
*The process for adopting
a new Internet standard.*

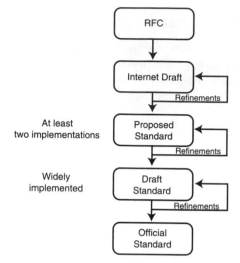

The RFC is usually discussed for a while on the network itself, where anyone can express their opinion, as well as in formal IETF working group meetings. After a suitable amount of revision and continued discussion, an *Internet draft* is created and distributed. This draft is close to final form, providing a consolidation of all the comments the RFC generated.

The next step is usually a *proposed standard,* which remains as such for at least six months. During this time, the Internet Society requires at least two independent and interoperable implementations to be written and tested. Any problems arising from the actual tests can then be addressed. (In practice, it is usual for many implementations to be written and given a thorough testing.)

After that testing and refinement process is completed, a *draft standard* is written, which remains for at least four months, during which time many more implementations are developed and tested. The last step—after many months—is the adoption of the standard, at which point it is implemented by all sites that require it.

Protocols

Diplomats follow rules when they conduct business between nations, which you see referred to in the media as protocol. Diplomatic protocol requires that you don't insult your hosts and that you do respect local customs (even if that means you have to eat some unappetizing dinners!). Most embassies and commissions have specialists in protocol, whose function is to ensure that everything proceeds smoothly when communications are taking place. The protocol is a set of rules that must be followed in order to "play the game," as career diplomats are fond of saying. Without the protocols, one side of the conversation might not really understand what the other is saying.

Similarly, computer protocols define the manner in which communications take place. If one computer is sending information to another and they both follow the protocol properly, the message gets through, regardless of what types of machines they are and what operating systems they run (the basis for open systems). As long as the machines have software that can manage the protocol, communications are possible. Essentially, a computer protocol is a set of rules that coordinates the exchange of information.

Protocols have developed from very simple processes ("I'll send you one character, you send it back, and I'll make sure the two match") to elaborate, complex mechanisms that cover all possible problems and transfer conditions. A task such as sending a message from one coast to another can be very complex when you consider the manner in which it moves. A single protocol to cover all aspects of the transfer would be too large, unwieldy, and overly specialized. Therefore, several protocols have been developed, each handling a specific task.

Combining several protocols, each with their own dedicated purposes, would be a nightmare if the interactions between the protocols were not clearly defined. The concept of a layered structure was developed to help keep each protocol in its place and to define the manner of interaction between each protocol (essentially, a protocol for communications between protocols!).

As you saw earlier, the ISO has developed a layered protocol system called OSI. OSI defines a protocol as "a set of rules and formats (semantic and syntactic), which determines the communication behavior of N-entities in the performance of N-functions." You might remember that N represents a layer, and an entity is a service component of a layer.

When machines communicate, the rules are formally defined and account for possible interruptions or faults in the flow of information, especially when the flow is connectionless (no formal connection between the two machines exists). In such a system, the ability to properly route and verify each packet of data (datagram) is vitally important. As discussed earlier, the data sent between layers is called a service data unit (SDU), so OSI defines the analogous data between two machines as a protocol data unit (PDU).

The flow of information is controlled by a set of actions that define the state machine for the protocol. OSI defines these actions as protocol control information (PCI).

Breaking Data Apart

It is necessary to introduce a few more terms commonly used in OSI and TCP/IP, but luckily they are readily understood because of their real-world connotations. These terms are necessary because data doesn't usually exist in manageable chunks. The data might have to be broken down into smaller sections, or several small sections can be combined into a large section for more efficient transfer. The basic terms are as follows:

Segmentation is the process of breaking an N-service data unit (N-SDU) into several N-protocol data units (N-PDUs).

Reassembly is the process of combining several N-PDUs into an N-SDU (the reverse of segmentation).

Blocking is the combination of several SDUs (which might be from different services) into a larger PDU within the layer in which the SDUs originated.

Unblocking is the breaking up of a PDU into several SDUs in the same layer.

Concatenation is the process of one layer combining several N-PDUs from the next higher layer into one SDU (like blocking except occurring across a layer boundary).

Separation is the reverse of concatenation, so that a layer breaks a single SDU into several PDUs for the next layer higher (like unblocking except across a layer boundary).

These six processes are shown in Figure 1.11.

Figure 1.11.

Segmentation, reassembly, blocking, unblocking, concatenation, and separation.

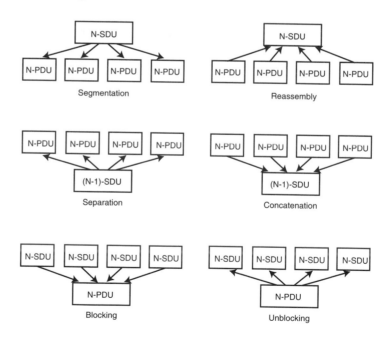

Finally, here is one last set of definitions that deal with connections:

> *Multiplexing* is when several connections are supported by a single connection in the next lower layer (so three presentation service connections could be multiplexed into a single session connection).

> *Demultiplexing* is the reverse of multiplexing, in which one connection is split into several connections for the layer above it.

> *Splitting* is when a single connection is supported by several connections in the layer below (so the data link layer might have three connections to support one network layer connection).

> *Recombining* is the reverse of splitting, so that several connections are combined into a single one for the layer above.

Multiplexing and splitting (and their reverses, demultiplexing and recombining) are different in the manner in which the lines are split. With multiplexing, several connections combine into one in the layer below. With splitting, however, one connection can be split into several in the layer below. As you might expect, each has its importance within TCP and OSI.

Protocol Headers

Protocol control information is information about the datagram to which it is attached. This information is usually assembled into a block that is attached to the front of the data it accompanies and is called a *header* or *protocol header*. Protocol headers are used for transferring information between layers as well as between machines. As mentioned earlier, the protocol headers are developed according to rules laid down in the ISO's ASN.1 document set.

When a protocol header is passed to the layer beneath, the datagram including the layer's header is treated as the entire datagram for that receiving layer, which adds its own protocol header to the front. Thus, if a datagram started at the application layer, by the time it reached the physical layer, it would have seven sets of protocol headers on it. These layer protocol headers are used when moving back up the layer structure; they are stripped off as the datagram moves up. An illustration of this is shown in Figure 1.12.

Figure 1.12.

*Adding each layer's
protocol header to user
data.*

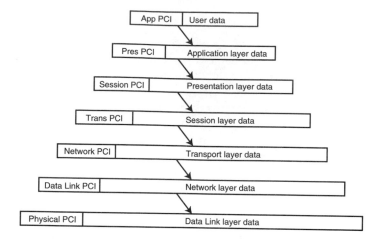

It is easier to think of this process as layers on an onion. The inside is the data that is to be sent. As it passes through each layer of the OSI model, another layer of onion skin is added. When it is finished moving through the layers, several protocol headers are enclosing the data. When the datagram is passed back up the layers (probably on another machine), each layer peels off the protocol header that corresponds to the layer. When it reaches the destination layer, only the data is left.

This process makes sense, because each layer of the OSI model requires different information from the datagram. By using a dedicated protocol header for each layer of the datagram, it is a relatively simple task to remove the protocol header, decode its instructions, and pass the rest of the message on. The alternative would be to have a single large header that contained all the information, but this would take longer to process. The exact contents of the protocol header are not important right now, but I examine them later when looking at the TCP protocol.

As usual, OSI has a formal description for all this, which states that the N-user data to be transferred is prepended with N-protocol control information (N-PCI) to form an N-protocol data unit (N-PDU). The N-PDUs are passed across an N-service access point (N-SAP) as one of a set of service parameters comprising an N-service data unit (N-SDU). The service parameters comprising the N-SDU are called N-service user data (N-SUD), which is prepended to the (N–1)PCI to form another (N–1)PDU.

For every service in a layer, there is a protocol for it to communicate to the layer below it (remember that applications communicate through the layer below, not directly). The protocol exchanges for each service are defined by the system, and to a lesser extent by the application developer, who should be following the rules of the system.

Protocols and headers might sound a little complex or overly complicated for the task that must be accomplished, but considering the original goals of the OSI model, it is generally acknowledged that this is the best way to go. (Many a sarcastic comment has been made about OSI and TCP that claim the header information is much more important than the data contents. In some ways this is true, because without the header the data would never get to its destination.)

Summary

Today's text has thrown a lot of terminology at you, most of which you will see frequently in the following chapters. In most cases, a gentle reminder of the definition accompanies the first occurrence of the term. To understand the relationships between the different terms, though, you might have to refer back to today's material.

You now have the basic knowledge to relate TCP/IP to the OSI's layered model, which will help you understand what TCP/IP does (and how it goes about doing it). The next chapter looks at the history of TCP/IP and the growth of the Internet.

Q&A

Q What are the three main types of LAN architecture? What are their primary characteristics?

A The three network architectures are bus, ring, and hub. There are others, but these three describe the vast majority of all LANs.

A bus network is a length of cable that has a connector for each device directly attached to it. Both ends of the network cable are terminated. A ring network has a central control unit called a Media Access Unit to which all devices are attached by cables. A hub network has a backplane with connectors leading through another cable to the devices.

Q What are the seven OSI layers and their responsibilities?

A The OSI layers (from the bottom up) are as follows:

Physical: Transmits data

Data Link: Corrects transmission errors

Network: Provides the physical routing information

Transport: Verifies that data is correctly transmitted

Session: Synchronizes data exchange between upper and lower layers

Presentation: Converts network data to application-specific formats

Application: End-user interface

Q **What is the difference between segmentation and reassembly, and concatenation and separation?**

A Segmentation is the breaking apart of a large N-service data unit (N-SDU) into several smaller N-protocol data units (N-PDUs), whereas reassembly is the reverse.

Concatenation is the combination of several N-PDUs from the next higher layer into one SDU. Separation is the reverse.

Q **Define multiplexing and demultiplexing. How are they useful?**

A Multiplexing is when several connections are supported by a single connection. According to the formal definition, this applies to layers (so that three presentation service connections could be multiplexed into a single session connection). However, it is a term generally used for all kinds of connections, such as putting four modem calls down a single modem line. Demultiplexing is the reverse of multiplexing, in which one connection is split into several connections.

Multiplexing is a key to supporting many connections at once with limited resources. A typical example is a remote office with twenty terminals, each of which is connected to the main office by a telephone line. Instead of requiring twenty lines, they can all be multiplexed into three or four. The amount of multiplexing possible depends on the maximum capacity of each physical line.

Q **How many protocol headers are added by the time an OSI-based e-mail application (in the application layer) has sent a message to the physical layer for transmission?**

A Seven, one for each OSI layer. More protocol headers can be added by the actual physical network system. As a general rule, each layer adds its own protocol information.

Workshop

1. Provide definitions for each of the following terms:

   packet

   subsystem

   entity

   service

   layer

   ISO

   ASN.1

2. What does each of the following primitives do?

   service primitive

   request primitive

   indication primitive

   response primitive

   confirmation primitive

3. What is a Service Access Point? How many are there per layer?

4. Explain the process followed in adopting a new Internet Standard for TCP/IP.

5. Use diagrams to show the differences between segmentation, separation, and blocking.

Chapter 2

TCP/IP and the Internet

Before proceeding into a considerable amount of detail about TCP/IP, the Internet, and the Internet Protocol (IP), it is worthwhile to try to complete a quick outline of TCP/IP. Then, as the details of each protocol are discussed individually, they can be placed in the broader outline more easily, thereby leading to a more complete understanding in the next two chapters.

Just what is TCP/IP? As you saw on Day 1, "Open Systems, Standards, and Protocols," it is a software-based communications protocol used in networking. Although the name TCP/IP implies that the entire scope of the product is a combination of two protocols—Transmission Control Protocol and Internet Protocol—the term TCP/IP refers not to a single entity combining two protocols, but a larger set of software programs that provides network services such as remote logins, remote file transfers, and electronic mail. TCP/IP provides a method for transferring information from one machine to another. A communications protocol should handle errors in transmission, manage the routing and delivery of data, and control the actual transmission by the use of predetermined status signals. TCP/IP accomplishes all of this.

TCP/IP is not a single product. It is a catch-all name for a family of protocols that use a similar behavior. Using the term TCP/IP usually refers to one or more protocols within the family, not just TCP and IP.

In the first chapter, you saw that the OSI Reference Model is composed of seven layers. TCP/IP was designed with layers as well, although they do not correspond one-to-one with the OSI-RM layers. You can overlay the TCP/IP programs on this model to give you a rough idea of where all the TCP/IP layers reside. I do that in a little more detail later in this chapter. Before that, I take a quick look at the TCP/IP protocols and how they relate to each other and show a rough mapping to the OSI layers.

Figure 2.1 shows the basic elements of the TCP/IP family of protocols. You can see that TCP/IP is not involved in the bottom two layers of the OSI model (data link and physical) but begins in the network layer, where the Internet Protocol (IP) resides. In the transport layer, the Transmission Control Protocol (TCP) and User Datagram Protocol (UDP) are involved. Above this, the utilities and protocols that make up the rest of the TCP/IP suite are built using the TCP or UDP and IP layers for their communications system.

Figure 2.1.

TCP/IP suite and OSI layers.

Telnet - Remote Login
FTP - File Transfer Protocol
SMTP - Simple Mail Transfer Protocol
X - X Windows System
Kerberos - Security
DNS - Domain Name System
ASN - Abstract Syntax Notation
SNMP - Simple Network Management Protocol

NFS - Network File Server
RPC - Remote Procedure Calls
TFTP - Transmission Control Protocol
TCP - Transmission Control Protocol
UDP- User Datagram Protocol
IP - Internet Protocol
ICMP - Internet Control Message Protocol

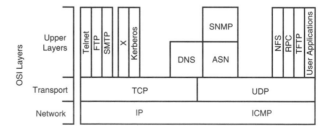

Figure 2.1 shows that some of the upper-layer protocols depend on TCP (such as Telnet and FTP), whereas some depend on UDP (such as TFTP and RPC). Most upper-layer TCP/IP protocols use only one of the two transport protocols (TCP or UDP), although a few, including DNS (Domain Name Service), can use both.

WARNING

A note of caution about TCP/IP: Despite the fact that TCP/IP is an open protocol, many companies have modified it for their own networking system. There can be incompatibilities because of these modifications, which, even though they might adhere to the official standards, might have other aspects that cause problems. Luckily, these types of changes are not rampant, but you should be careful when choosing a TCP/IP product to ensure its compatibility with existing software and hardware.

2

TCP/IP is dependent on the concept of clients and servers. This has nothing to do with a file server being accessed by a diskless workstation or PC. The term *client/server* has a simple meaning in TCP/IP: Any device that initiates communications is the client, and the device that answers is the server. The server is responding to (serving) the client's requests.

A Quick Overview of TCP/IP Components

To understand the roles of the many components of the TCP/IP protocol family, it is useful to know what you can do over a TCP/IP network. Then, once the applications are understood, the protocols that make it possible are a little easier to comprehend. The following list is not exhaustive but mentions the primary user applications that TCP/IP provides.

Telnet

The Telnet program provides a remote login capability. This lets a user on one machine log onto another machine and act as though he or she were directly in front of the second machine. The connection can be anywhere on the local network or on another network anywhere in the world, as long as the user has permission to log onto the remote system.

You can use Telnet when you need to perform actions on a machine across the country. This isn't often done except in a LAN or WAN context, but a few systems accessible through the Internet allow Telnet sessions while users play around with a new application or operating system.

File Transfer Protocol

File Transfer Protocol (FTP) enables a file on one system to be copied to another system. The user doesn't actually log in as a full user to the machine he or she wants to access, as with

Telnet, but instead uses the FTP program to enable access. Again, the correct permissions are necessary to provide access to the files.

Once the connection to a remote machine has been established, FTP enables you to copy one or more files to your machine. (The term *transfer* implies that the file is moved from one system to another but the original is not affected. Files are copied.) FTP is a widely used service on the Internet, as well as on many large LANs and WANs.

Simple Mail Transfer Protocol

Simple Mail Transfer Protocol (SMTP) is used for transferring electronic mail. SMTP is completely transparent to the user. Behind the scenes, SMTP connects to remote machines and transfers mail messages much like FTP transfers files. Users are almost never aware of SMTP working, and few system administrators have to bother with it. SMTP is a mostly trouble-free protocol and is in very wide use.

Kerberos

Kerberos is a widely supported security protocol. Kerberos uses a special application called an *authentication server* to validate passwords and encryption schemes. Kerberos is one of the more secure encryption systems used in communications and is quite common in UNIX.

Domain Name Service

Domain Name Service (DNS) enables a computer with a common name to be converted to a special network address. For example, a PC called Darkstar cannot be accessed by another machine on the same network (or any other connected network) unless some method of checking the local machine name and replacing the name with the machine's hardware address is available. DNS provides a conversion from the common local name to the unique physical address of the device's network connection.

Simple Network Management Protocol

Simple Network Management Protocol (SNMP) provides status messages and problem reports across a network to an administrator. SNMP uses User Datagram Protocol (UDP) as a transport mechanism. SNMP employs slightly different terms from TCP/IP, working with managers and agents instead of clients and servers (although they mean essentially the same thing). An agent provides information about a device, whereas a manager communicates across a network with agents.

Network File System

Network File System (NFS) is a set of protocols developed by Sun Microsystems to enable multiple machines to access each other's directories transparently. They accomplish this by using a distributed file system scheme. NFS systems are common in large corporate environments, especially those that use UNIX workstations.

Remote Procedure Call

The Remote Procedure Call (RPC) protocol is a set of functions that enables an application to communicate with another machine (the server). It provides for programming functions, return codes, and predefined variables to support distributed computing.

Trivial File Transfer Protocol

Trivial File Transfer Protocol (TFTP) is a very simple, unsophisticated file transfer protocol that lacks security. It uses UDP as a transport. TFTP performs the same task as FTP but uses a different transport protocol.

Transmission Control Protocol

Transmission Control Protocol (the TCP part of TCP/IP) is a communications protocol that provides reliable transfer of data. It is responsible for assembling data passed from higher-layer applications into standard packets and ensuring that the data is transferred correctly.

User Datagram Protocol

User Datagram Protocol (UDP) is a connectionless-oriented protocol, meaning that it does not provide for the retransmission of datagrams (unlike TCP, which is connection-oriented). UDP is not very reliable, but it does have specialized purposes. If the applications that use UDP have reliability checking built into them, the shortcomings of UDP are overcome.

Internet Protocol

Internet Protocol (IP) is responsible for moving the packets of data assembled by either TCP or UDP across networks. It uses a set of unique addresses for every device on the network to determine routing and destinations.

Internet Control Message Protocol

Internet Control Message Protocol (ICMP) is responsible for checking and generating messages on the status of devices on a network. It can be used to inform other devices of a failure in one particular machine. ICMP and IP usually work together.

TCP/IP History

The architecture of TCP/IP is often called the Internet architecture because TCP/IP and the Internet as so closely interwoven. In the last chapter, you saw how the Internet standards were developed by the Defense Advanced Research Projects Agency (DARPA) and eventually passed on to the Internet Society.

The Internet was originally proposed by the precursor of DARPA, called the Advanced Research Projects Agency (ARPA), as a method of testing the viability of packet-switching networks. (When ARPA's focus became military in nature, the name was changed.) During its tenure with the project, ARPA foresaw a network of leased lines connected by switching nodes. The network was called ARPANET, and the switching nodes were called Internet Message Processors, or IMPs.

The ARPANET was initially to be comprised of four IMPs located at the University of California at Los Angeles, the University of California at Santa Barbara, the Stanford Research Institute, and the University of Utah. The original IMPs were to be Honeywell 316 minicomputers.

The contract for the installation of the network was won by Bolt, Beranek, and Newman (BBN), a company that had a strong influence on the development of the network in the following years. The contract was awarded in late 1968, followed by testing and refinement over the next five years.

NOTE

Bolt, Beranek, and Newman (BBN) made many suggestions for the improvement of the Internet and the development of TCP/IP, for which their names are often associated with the protocol.

In 1971, ARPANET entered into regular service. Machines used the ARPANET by connecting to an IMP using the "1822" protocol—so called because that was the number of the technical paper describing the system. During the early years, the purpose and utility of the network was widely (and sometimes heatedly) discussed, leading to refinements and modifications as users requested more functionality from the system.

A commonly recognized need was the capability to transfer files from one machine to another, as well as the capability to support remote logins. Remote logins would enable a user in Santa Barbara to connect to a machine in Los Angeles over the network and function as though he or she were in front of the UCLA machine. The protocol then in use on the network wasn't capable of handling these new functionality requests, so new protocols were continually developed, refined, and tested.

Remote login and remote file transfer were finally implemented in a protocol called the Network Control Program (NCP). Later, electronic mail was added through File Transfer Protocol (FTP). Together with NCP's remote logins and file transfer, this formed the basic services for ARPANET.

By 1973, it was clear that NCP was unable to handle the volume of traffic and proposed new functionality. A project was begun to develop a new protocol. The TCP/IP and gateway architectures were first proposed in 1974. The published article by Cerf and Kahn described a system that provided a standardized application protocol that also used end-to-end acknowledgments.

Neither of these concepts were really novel at the time, but more importantly (and with considerable vision), Cerf and Kahn suggested that the new protocol be independent of the underlying network and computer hardware. Also, they proposed universal connectivity throughout the network. These two ideas were radical in a world of proprietary hardware and software, because they would enable any kind of platform to participate in the network. The protocol was developed and became known as TCP/IP.

A series of RFCs (Requests for Comment, part of the process for adopting new Internet Standards) was issued in 1981, standardizing TCP/IP version 4 for the ARPANET. In 1982, TCP/IP supplanted NCP as the dominant protocol of the growing network, which was now connecting machines across the continent. It is estimated that a new computer was connected to ARPANET every 20 days during its first decade. (That might not seem like much compared to the current estimate of the Internet's size doubling every year, but in the early 1980s it was a phenomenal growth rate.)

During the development of ARPANET, it became obvious that nonmilitary researchers could use the network to their advantage, enabling faster communication of ideas as well as faster physical data transfer. A proposal to the National Science Foundation led to funding for the Computer Science Network in 1981, joining the military with educational and research institutes to refine the network. This led to the splitting of the network into two different networks in 1984. MILNET was dedicated to unclassified military traffic, whereas ARPANET was left for research and other nonmilitary purposes.

ARPANET's growth and subsequent demise came with the approval for the Office of Advanced Scientific Computing to develop wide access to supercomputers. They created

NSFNET to connect six supercomputers spread across the country through T-1 lines (which operated at 1.544 Mbps). The Department of Defense finally declared ARPANET obsolete in 1990, when it was officially dismantled.

Berkeley UNIX Implementations and TCP/IP

TCP/IP became important when the Department of Defense started including the protocols as military standards, which were required for many contracts. TCP/IP became popular primarily because of the work done at UCB (Berkeley). UCB had been a center of UNIX development for years, but in 1983 they released a new version that incorporated TCP/IP as an integral element. That version—4.2BSD (Berkeley System Distribution)—was made available to the world as public domain software.

The popularity of 4.2BSD spurred the popularity of TCP/IP, especially as more sites connected to the growing ARPANET. Berkeley released an enhanced version (which included the so-called Berkeley Utilities) in 1986 as 4.3BSD. An optimized TCP implementation followed in 1988 (4.3BSD/Tahoe). Practically every version of TCP/IP available today has its roots (and much of its code) in the Berkeley versions.

NOTE   Despite the demise of Berkeley Software Distribution's UNIX version in 1993, the BSD and UCB developments are integral parts of TCP/IP and continue to be used as part of the protocol family's naming system.

OSI and TCP/IP

The adoption of TCP/IP didn't conflict with the OSI standards because the two developed concurrently. In some ways, TCP/IP contributed to OSI, and vice versa. Several important differences do exist, though, which arise from the basic requirements of TCP/IP which are:

- ☐ A common set of applications
- ☐ Dynamic routing
- ☐ Connectionless protocols at the networking level
- ☐ Universal connectivity
- ☐ Packet-switching

The differences between the OSI architecture and that of TCP/IP relate to the layers above the transport level and those at the network level. OSI has both the session layer and the presentation layer, whereas TCP/IP combines both into an application layer. The requirement for a connectionless protocol also required TCP/IP to combine OSI's physical layer and data link layer into a network level. TCP/IP also includes the session and presentation layers of the OSI model into TCP/IP's application layer. A schematic view of TCP/IP's layered structure compared with OSI's seven-layer model is shown in Figure 2.2. TCP/IP calls the different network level elements *subnetworks*.

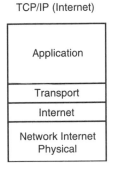

Figure 2.2.

The OSI and TCP/IP layered structures.

OSI Model

| Application |
| Presentation |
| Session |
| Transport |
| Network |
| Data Link |
| Physical |

TCP/IP (Internet)

| Application |
| Transport |
| Internet |
| Network Internet Physical |

NOTE

OSI and TCP/IP are not incompatible, but neither are they perfectly compatible. They both have a layered architecture, but the OSI architecture is much more rigorously defined, and the layers are more independent than TCP/IP's.

Some fuss was made about the network level combination, although it soon became obvious that the argument was academic, as most implementations of the OSI model combined the physical and link levels on an intelligent controller (such as a network card). The combination of the two layers into a single layer had one major benefit: It enabled a subnetwork to be designed that was independent of any network protocols, because TCP/IP was oblivious to the details. This enabled proprietary, self-contained networks to implement the TCP/IP protocols for connectivity outside their closed systems.

The layered approach gave rise to the name TCP/IP. The transport layer uses the Transmission Control Protocol (TCP) or one of several variants, such as the User Datagram Protocol (UDP). (There are other protocols in use, but TCP and UDP are the most common.) There is, however, only one protocol for the network level—the Internet Protocol (IP). This is what assures the system of universal connectivity, one of the primary design goals.

There is a considerable amount of pressure from the user community to abandon the OSI model (and any future communications protocols developed that conform to it) in favor of TCP/IP. The argument hinges on some obvious reasons:

- ☐ TCP/IP is up and running and has a proven record.
- ☐ TCP/IP has an established, functioning management body.
- ☐ Thousands of applications currently use TCP/IP and its well-documented application programming interfaces.
- ☐ TCP/IP is the basis for most UNIX systems, which are gaining the largest share of the operating system market (other than desktop single-user machines such as the PC and Macintosh).
- ☐ TCP/IP is vendor-independent.

Arguing rather strenuously against TCP/IP, surprisingly enough, is the U.S. government—the very body that sponsored it in the first place. Their primary argument is that TCP/IP is not an internationally adopted standard, whereas OSI has that recognition. The Department of Defense has even begun to move its systems away from the TCP/IP protocol set. A compromise will probably result, with some aspects of OSI adopted into the still-evolving TCP/IP protocol suite.

TCP/IP and Ethernet

For many people the terms TCP/IP and Ethernet go together almost automatically, primarily for historical reasons, as well as the simple fact that there are more Ethernet-based TCP/IP networks than any other type. Ethernet was originally developed at Xerox's Palo Alto Research Center as a step toward an electronic office communications system, and it has since grown in capability and popularity.

Ethernet is a hardware system providing for the data link and physical layers of the OSI model. As part of the Ethernet standards, issues such as cable type and broadcast speeds are established. There are several different versions of Ethernet, each with a different data transfer rate. The most common is Ethernet version 2, also called 10Base5, Thick Ethernet, and IEEE 802.3 (after the number of the standard that defines the system adopted by the Institute of Electrical and Electronic Engineers). This system has a 10 Mbps rate.

There are several commonly used variants of Ethernet, such as Thin Ethernet (called 10Base2), which can operate over thinner cable (such as the coaxial cable used in cable television systems), and Twisted-Pair Ethernet (10BaseT), which uses simple twisted-pair wires similar to telephone cable. The latter variant is popular for small companies because it is inexpensive, easy to wire, and has no strict requirements for distance between machines.

NOTE

It is usually easy to tell which type of Ethernet network is being used by checking the connector to a network card. If it has a telephone-style plug, it is 10BaseT. The cable for 10BaseT looks the same as telephone cable. If the network has a D-shaped connector with many pins in it, it is 10Base5. A 10Base2 network has a connector similar to a cable TV coaxial connector, except it locks into place. The 10Base2 connector is always circular.

The size of a network is also a good indicator. 10Base5 is used in large networks with many devices and long transmission runs. 10Base2 is used in smaller networks, usually with all the network devices in fairly close proximity. Twisted-pair (10BaseT) networks are often used for very small networks with a maximum of a few dozen devices in close proximity.

Ethernet and TCP/IP work well together, with Ethernet providing the physical cabling (layers one and two) and TCP/IP the communications protocol (layers three and four) that is broadcast over the cable. The two have their own processes for packaging information: TCP/IP uses 32-bit addresses, whereas Ethernet uses a 48-bit scheme. The two work together, however, because of one component of TCP/IP called the Address Resolution Protocol (ARP), which converts between the two schemes. (I discuss ARP in more detail later, in the section titled "Address Resolution Protocol.")

Ethernet relies on a protocol called Carrier Sense Multiple Access with Collision Detect (CSMA/CD). To simplify the process, a device checks the network cable to see if anything is currently being sent. If it is clear, the device sends its data. If the cable is busy (carrier detect), the device waits for it to clear. If two devices transmit at the same time (a collision), the devices know because of their constant comparison of the cable traffic to the data in the sending buffer. If a collision occurs, the devices wait a random amount of time before trying again.

The Internet

As ARPANET grew out of a military-only network to add subnetworks in universities, corporations, and user communities, it became known as the Internet. There is no single network called the Internet, however. The term refers to the collective network of subnetworks. The one thing they all have in common is TCP/IP as a communications protocol.

As described in the first chapter, the organization of the Internet and adoption of new standards is controlled by the Internet Advisory Board (IAB). Among other things, the IAB coordinates several task forces, including the Internet Engineering Task Force (IETF) and

Internet Research Task Force (IRTF). In a nutshell, the IRTF is concerned with ongoing research, whereas the IETF handles the implementation and engineering aspects associated with the Internet.

A body that has some bearing on the IAB is the Federal Networking Council (FNC), which serves as an intermediary between the IAB and the government. The FNC has an advisory capacity to the IAB and its task forces, as well as the responsibility for managing the government's use of the Internet and other networks. Because the government was responsible for funding the development of the Internet, it retains a considerable amount of control, as well as sponsoring some research and expansion of the Internet.

The Structure of the Internet

As mentioned earlier, the Internet is not a single network but a collection of networks that communicate with each other through gateways. For the purposes of this chapter, a *gateway* (sometimes called a *router*) is defined as a system that performs relay functions between networks, as shown in Figure 2.3. The different networks connected to each other through gateways are often called subnetworks, because they are a smaller part of the larger overall network. This does not imply that a subnetwork is small or dependent on the larger network. Subnetworks are complete networks, but they are connected through a gateway as a part of a larger internetwork, or in this case the Internet.

Figure 2.3.

Gateways act as relays between subnetworks.

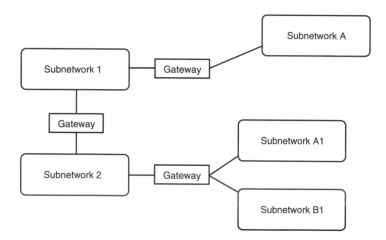

With TCP/IP, all interconnections between physical networks are through gateways. An important point to remember for later use is that gateways route information packets based on their destination network name, not the destination machine. Gateways are supposed to be completely transparent to the user, which alleviates the gateway from handling user applications (unless the machine that is acting as a gateway is also someone's work machine or a local network server, as is often the case with small networks). Put simply, the gateway's sole task is to receive a Protocol Data Unit (PDU) from either the internetwork or the local network and either route it on to the next gateway or pass it into the local network for routing to the proper user.

Gateways work with any kind of hardware and operating system, as long as they are designed to communicate with the other gateways they are attached to (which in this case means that it uses TCP/IP). Whether the gateway is leading to a Macintosh network, a set of IBM PCs, or mainframes from a dozen different companies doesn't matter to the gateway or the PDUs it handles.

NOTE
There are actually several types of gateways, each performing a different type of task. I look at the different gateways in more detail on Day 5, "Gateway and Routing Protocols."

In the United States, the Internet has the NFSNET as its backbone, as shown in Figure 2.4. Among the primary networks connected to the NFSNET are NASA's Space Physics Analysis Network (SPAN), the Computer Science Network (CSNET), and several other networks such as WESTNET and the San Diego Supercomputer Network (SDSCNET), not shown in Figure 2.4. There are also other smaller user-oriented networks such as the Because It's Time Network (BITNET) and UUNET, which provide connectivity through gateways for smaller sites that can't or don't want to establish a direct gateway to the Internet.

Figure 2.4.

The U.S. Internet network.

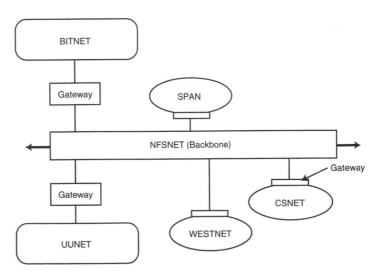

The NFSNET backbone is comprised of approximately 3,000 research sites, connected by T-3 leased lines running at 44.736 Megabits per second. Tests are currently underway to increase the operational speed of the backbone to enable more throughput and accommodate the rapidly increasing number of users. Several technologies are being field-tested, including Synchronous Optical Network (SONET), Asynchronous Transfer Mode (ATM), and ANSI's proposed High-Performance Parallel Interface (HPPI). These new systems can produce speeds approaching 1 Gigabit per second.

The Internet Layers

Most internetworks, including the Internet, can be thought of as a layered architecture (yes, even more layers!) to simplify understanding. The layer concept helps in the task of developing applications for internetworks. The layering also shows how the different parts of TCP/IP work together. The more logical structure brought about by using a layering process has already been seen in the first chapter for the OSI model, so applying it to the Internet makes sense. Be careful to think of these layers as conceptual only; they are not really physical or software layers as such (unlike the OSI or TCP/IP layers).

It is convenient to think of the Internet as having four layers. This layered Internet architecture is shown in Figure 2.5. These layers should not be confused with the architecture of each machine, as described in the OSI seven-layer model. Instead, they are a method of seeing how the internetwork, network, TCP/IP, and the individual machines work together. Independent machines reside in the subnetwork layer at the bottom of the architecture, connected together in a local area network (LAN) and referred to as the subnetwork, a term you saw in the last section.

Figure 2.5.

The Internet architecture.

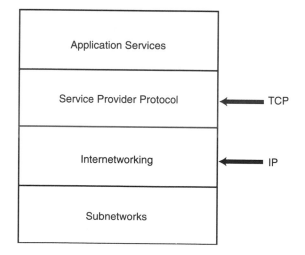

On top of the subnetwork layer is the internetwork layer, which provides the functionality for communications between networks through gateways. Each subnetwork uses gateways to connect to the other subnetworks in the internetwork. The internetwork layer is where data gets transferred from gateway to gateway until it reaches its destination and then passes into the subnetwork layer. The internetwork layer runs the Internet Protocol (IP).

The service provider protocol layer is responsible for the overall end-to-end communications of the network. This is the layer that runs the Transmission Control Protocol (TCP) and other protocols. It handles the data traffic flow itself and ensures reliability for the message transfer.

The top layer is the application services layer, which supports the interfaces to the user applications. This layer interfaces to electronic mail, remote file transfers, and remote access. Several protocols are used in this layer, many of which you will read about later.

To see how the Internet architecture model works, a simple example is useful. Assume that an application on one machine wants to transfer a datagram to an application on another machine in a different subnetwork. Without all the signals between layers (and simplifying the architecture a little), the process is shown in Figure 2.6. The layers in the sending and receiving machines are the OSI layers, with the equivalent Internet architecture layers indicated.

Figure 2.6.

Transfer of a datagram over an internetwork.

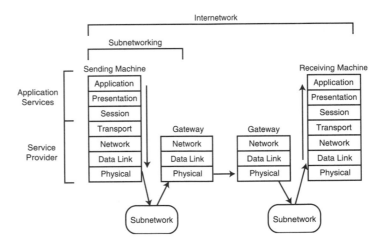

The data is sent down the layers of the sending machine, assembling the datagram with the Protocol Control Information (PCI) as it goes. From the physical layer, the datagram (which is sometimes called a *frame* after the data link layer has added its header and trailing information) is sent out to the local area network. The LAN routes the information to the gateway out to the internetwork. During this process, the LAN has no concern about the message contained in the datagram. Some networks, however, alter the header information to show the machines it has passed through, among other things.

From the gateway, the frame passes from gateway to gateway along the internetwork until it arrives at the destination subnetwork. At each step, the gateway analyzes the datagram's header to determine if it is for the subnetwork the gateway leads to. If not, it routes the datagram back out over the internetwork. This analysis is performed in the physical layer, eliminating the need to pass the frame up and down through different layers on each gateway. The header can be altered at each gateway to reflect its routing path.

When the datagram is finally received at the destination subnetwork's gateway, the gateway recognizes that the datagram is at its correct subnetwork and routes it into the LAN and eventually to the target machine. The routing is accomplished by reading the header information. When the datagram reaches the destination machine, it passes up through the layers, with each layer stripping off its PCI header and then passing the result on up. At long last, the application layer on the destination machine processes the final header and passes the message to the correct application.

If the datagram was not data to be processed but a request for a service, such as a remote file transfer, the correct layer on the destination machine would decode the request and route the file back over the internetwork to the original machine. Quite a process!

Internetwork Problems

Not everything goes smoothly when transferring data from one subnetwork to another. All manner of problems can occur, despite the fact that the entire network is using one protocol. A typical problem is a limitation on the size of the datagram. The sending network might support datagrams of 1,024 bytes, but the receiving network might use only 512-byte datagrams (because of a different hardware protocol, for example). This is where the processes of segmentation, separation, reassembly, and concatenation (explained in the last chapter) become important.

The actual addressing methods used by the different subnetworks can cause conflicts when routing datagrams. Because communicating subnetworks might not have the same network control software, the network-based header information might differ, despite the fact that the communications methods are based on TCP/IP. An associated problem occurs when dealing with the differences between physical and logical machine names. In the same manner, a network that requires encryption instead of clear-text datagrams can affect the decoding of header information. Therefore, differences in the security implemented on the subnetworks can affect datagram traffic. These differences can all be resolved with software, but the problems associated with addressing methods can become considerable.

Another common problem is the different networks' tolerance for timing problems. Time-out and retry values might differ, so when two subnetworks are trying to establish communication, one might have given up and moved on to another task while the second is still waiting patiently for an acknowledgment signal. Also, if two subnetworks are communicating properly and one gets busy and has to pause the communications process for a short while, the amount of time before the other network assumes a disconnection and gives up might be important. Coordinating the timing over the internetwork can become very complicated.

Routing methods and the speed of the machines on the network can also affect the internetwork's performance. If a gateway is managed by a particularly slow machine, the traffic coming through the gateway can back up, causing delays and incomplete transmissions for the entire internetwork. Developing an internetwork system that can dynamically adapt to loads and reroute datagrams when a bottleneck occurs is very important.

There are other factors to consider, such as network management and troubleshooting information, but you should begin to see that simply connecting networks together without due thought does not work. The many different network operating systems and hardware platforms require a logical, well-developed approach to the internetwork. This is outside the scope of TCP/IP, which is simply concerned with the transmission of the datagrams. The TCP/IP implementations on each platform, however, must be able to handle the problems mentioned.

Internet Addresses

Network addresses are analogous to mailing addresses in that they tell a system where to deliver a datagram. Three terms commonly used in the Internet relate to addressing: name, address, and route.

NOTE

The term *address* is often generically used with communications protocols to refer to many different things. It can mean the destination, a port of a machine, a memory location, an application, and more. Take care when you encounter the term to make sure you know what it is really referring to.

A *name* is a specific identification of a machine, a user, or an application. It is usually unique and provides an absolute target for the datagram. An *address* typically identifies where the target is located, usually its physical or logical location in a network. A *route* tells the system how to get a datagram to the address.

You use the recipient's name often, either specifying a user name or a machine name, and an application does the same thing transparently to you. From the name, a network software package called the *name server* tries to resolve the address and the route, making that aspect unimportant to you. When you send electronic mail, you simply indicate the recipient's name, relying on the name server to figure out how to get the mail message to them.

Using a name server has one other primary advantage besides making the addressing and routing unimportant to the end user: It gives the system or network administrator a lot of freedom to change the network as required, without having to tell each user's machine about any changes. As long as an application can access the name server, any routing changes can be ignored by the application and users.

Naming conventions differ depending on the platform, the network, and the software release, but following is a typical Ethernet-based Internet subnetwork as an example. There are several types of addressing you need to look at, including the LAN system, as well as the wider internetwork addressing conventions.

Subnetwork Addressing

On a single network, several pieces of information are necessary to ensure the correct delivery of data. The primary components are the physical address and the data link address.

The Physical Address

Each device on a network that communicates with others has a unique *physical address,* sometimes called the *hardware address.* On any given network, there is only one occurrence of each address; otherwise, the name server has no way of identifying the target device unambiguously. For hardware, the addresses are usually encoded into a network interface card, set either by switches or by software. With respect to the OSI model, the address is located in the physical layer.

In the physical layer, the analysis of each incoming datagram (or protocol data unit) is performed. If the recipient's address matches the physical address of the device, the datagram can be passed up the layers. If the addresses don't match, the datagram is ignored. Keeping this analysis in the bottom layer of the OSI model prevents unnecessary delays, because otherwise the datagram would have to be passed up to other layers for analysis.

The length of the physical address varies depending on the networking system, but Ethernet and several others use 48 bits in each address. For communication to occur, two addresses are required: one each for the sending and receiving devices.

The IEEE is now handling the task of assigning universal physical addresses for subnetworks (a task previously performed by Xerox, as they developed Ethernet). For each subnetwork,

2

the IEEE assigns an organization unique identifier (OUI) that is 24 bits long, enabling the organization to assign the other 24 bits however it wants. (Actually, two of the 24 bits assigned as an OUI are control bits, so only 22 bits identify the subnetwork. Because this provides 2^{22} combinations, it is possible to run out of OUIs in the future if the current rate of growth is sustained.)

The format of the OUI is shown in Figure 2.7. The least significant bit of the address (the lowest bit number) is the individual or group address bit. If the bit is set to 0, the address refers to an individual address; a setting of 1 means that the rest of the address field identifies a group address that needs further resolution. If the entire OUI is set to 1s, the address has a special meaning which is that all stations on the network are assumed to be the destination.

Figure 2.7.

Layout of the organiza-tion unique identifier.

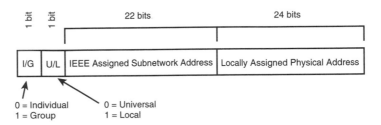

The second bit is the *local* or *universal* bit. If set to zero, it has been set by the universal administration body. This is the setting for IEEE-assigned OUIs. If it has a value of 1, the OUI has been locally assigned and would cause addressing problems if decoded as an IEEE-assigned address.

The remaining 22 bits make up the physical address of the subnetwork, as assigned by the IEEE. The second set of 24 bits identifies local network addresses and is administered locally. If an organization runs out of physical addresses (there are about 16 million addresses possible from 24 bits), the IEEE has the capacity to assign a second subnetwork address.

The combination of 24 bits from the OUI and 24 locally assigned bits is called a media access control (MAC) address. When a packet of data is assembled for transfer across an internetwork, there are two sets of MACs: one from the sending machine and one for the receiving machine.

The Data Link Address

The IEEE Ethernet standards (and several other allied standards) use another address called the link layer address (abbreviated as LSAP for link service access point). The LSAP identifies the type of link protocol used in the data link layer. As with the physical address, a datagram carries both sending and receiving LSAPs. The IEEE also enables a code that identifies the EtherType assignment, which identifies the upper layer protocol (ULP) running on the network (almost always a LAN).

Ethernet Frames

The layout of information in each transmitted packet of data differs depending on the protocol, but it is helpful to examine one to see how the addresses and related information are prepended to the data. This section uses the Ethernet system as an example because of its wide use with TCP/IP. It is quite similar to other systems as well.

A typical Ethernet frame (remember that a frame is the term for a network-ready datagram) is shown in Figure 2.8. The preamble is a set of bits that is used primarily to synchronize the communication process and account for any random noise in the first few bits that are sent. At the end of the preamble is a sequence of bits that is the start frame delimiter (SFD), which indicates that the frame follows immediately.

Figure 2.8.
The Ethernet frame.

Preamble	Recipient Address	Sender Address	Type	Data	CRC
64 bits	48 bits	48 bits	16 bits	Variable Length	32 bits

The recipient and sender addresses follow in IEEE 48-bit format, followed by a 16-bit type indicator that is used to identify the protocol. The data follows the type indicator. The Data field is between 46 and 1,500 bytes in length. If the data is less than 46 bytes, it is padded with 0s until it is 46 bytes long. Any padding is not counted in the calculation of the data field's total length, which is used in one part of the IP header. The next chapter covers IP headers.

At the end of the frame is the cyclic redundancy check (CRC) count, which is used to ensure that the frame's contents have not been modified during the transmission process. Each gateway along the transmission route calculates a CRC value for the frame and compares it to the value at the end of the frame. If the two match, the frame can be sent farther along the network or into the subnetwork. If they differ, a modification to the frame must have occurred, and the frame is discarded (to be later retransmitted by the sending machine when a timer expires).

In some protocols, such as the IEEE 802.3, the overall layout of the frame is the same, with slight variations in the contents. With 802.3, the 16 bits used by Ethernet to identify the protocol type are replaced with a 16-bit value for the length of the data block. Also, the data area itself is prepended by a new field.

IP Addresses

TCP/IP uses a 32-bit address to identify a machine on a network and the network to which it is attached. IP addresses identify a machine's connection to the network, not the machine itself—an important distinction. Whenever a machine's location on the network changes, the IP address must be changed, too. The IP address is the set of numbers many people see on their workstations or terminals, such as 127.40.8.72, which uniquely identifies the device.

IP (or Internet) addresses are assigned only by the Network Information Center (NIC), although if a network is not connected to the Internet, that network can determine its own numbering. For all Internet accesses, the IP address must be registered with the NIC.

There are four formats for the IP address, with each used depending on the size of the network. The four formats, called Class A through Class D, are shown in Figure 2.9. The class is identified by the first few bit sequences. The class can be determined from the first three (high-order) bits. In fact, in most cases, the first two bits are enough, because there are few Class D networks.

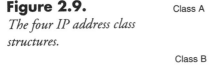

Figure 2.9.

The four IP address class structures.

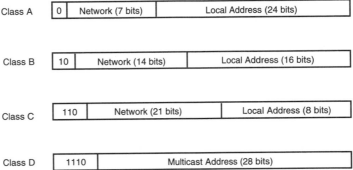

Class A	0	Network (7 bits)	Local Address (24 bits)
Class B	10	Network (14 bits)	Local Address (16 bits)
Class C	110	Network (21 bits)	Local Address (8 bits)
Class D	1110	Multicast Address (28 bits)	

Class A addresses are for large networks that have many machines. The 24 bits for the local address (also frequently called the host address) are needed in these cases. The network address is kept to 7 bits, which limits the number of networks that can be identified. Class B addresses are for intermediate networks, with 16-bit local or host addresses and 14-bit network addresses. Class C networks have only 8 bits for the local or host address, limiting the number of devices to 256. There are 21 bits for the network address. Finally, Class D networks are used for multicasting purposes, when a general broadcast to more than one device is required. The lengths of each section of the IP address have been carefully chosen to provide maximum flexibility in assigning both network and local addresses.

IP addresses are four sets of 8 bits, for a total 32 bits. You often represent these bits as separated by a period for convenience, so the IP address format can be thought of as network.local.local.local for Class A or network.network.network.local for Class C. The IP addresses are usually written out in their decimal equivalents, instead of the long binary strings. This is the familiar host address number that network users are used to seeing, such as 147.10.13.28, which would indicate that the network address is 147.10 and the local or host address is 13.28. Of course, the actual address is a set of 1s and 0s. The decimal notation used for IP addresses is properly called *dotted quad notation*—a bit of trivia for your next dinner party.

The IP addresses can be translated to common names and letters. This can pose a problem, though, because there must be some method of unambiguously relating the physical address, the network address, and a language-based name (such a tpci_ws_4 or bobs_machine). The section later in this chapter titled "The Domain Name Service" looks at this aspect of address naming.

From the IP address, a network can determine if the data is to be sent out through a gateway. If the network address is the same as the current address (routing to a local network device, called a *direct host*), the gateway is avoided, but all other network addresses are routed to a gateway to leave the local network (*indirect host*). The gateway receiving data to be transmitted to another network must then determine the routing from the data's IP address and an internal table that provides routing information.

As mentioned, if an address is set to all 1s, the address applies to all addresses on the network. (See the earlier section titled "The Physical Address.") The same rule applies to IP addresses, so that an IP address of 32 1s is considered a broadcast message to all networks and all devices. It is possible to broadcast to all machines in a network by altering the local or host address to all 1s, so that the address 147.10.255.255 for a Class B network (identified as network 147.10) would be received by all devices on that network (255.255 being the local addresses composed of all 1s), but the data would not leave the network.

WARNING

There are two contradictory ways to indicate broadcasts. The later versions of TCP/IP use 1s, but earlier BSD systems use 0s. This causes a lot of confusion. All the devices on a network must know which broadcast convention is used; otherwise, datagrams can be stuck on the network forever!

A slight twist is coding the network address as all 0s, which means the originating network or the local address being set to 0s, which refers to the originating device only (usually used only when a device is trying to determine its IP address). The all-zero network address format is used when the network IP address is not known but other devices on the network can still interpret the local address. If this were transmitted to another network, it could cause confusion! By convention, no local device is given a physical address of 0.

It is possible for a device to have more than one IP address if it is connected to more than one network, as is the case with gateways. These devices are called *multihomed,* because they have a unique address for each network they are connected to. In practice, it is best to have a dedicated machine for a multihomed gateway; otherwise, the applications on that machine can get confused as to which address they should use when building datagrams.

Two networks can have the same network address if they are connected by a gateway. This can cause problems for addressing, because the gateway must be able to differentiate which network the physical address is on. This problem is looked at again in the next section, showing how it can be solved.

Address Resolution Protocol

Determining addresses can be difficult because every machine on the network might not have a list of all the addresses of the other machines or devices. Sending data from one machine to another if the recipient machine's physical address is not known can cause a problem if there is no resolution system for determining the addresses. Having to constantly update a table of addresses on each machine would be a network administration nightmare. The problem is not restricted to machine addresses within a small network, because if the remote destination network addresses are unknown, routing and delivery problems will also occur.

The Address Resolution Protocol (ARP) helps solve these problems. ARP's job is to convert IP addresses to physical addresses (network and local) and in doing so, eliminate the need for applications to know about the physical addresses. Essentially, ARP is a table with a list of the IP addresses and their corresponding physical addresses. The table is called an *ARP cache*. The layout of an ARP cache is shown in Figure 2.10. Each row corresponds to one device, with four pieces of information for each device.

Figure 2.10.

The ARP cache address translation table layout.

	IF INDEX	PHYSICAL ADDRESS	IP ADDRESS	TYPE
Entry 1				
Entry 2				
Entry 3				
Entry n				

☐ IF Index: The physical port (interface)

☐ Physical Address: The physical address of the device

☐ IP Address: The IP address corresponding to the physical address

☐ Type: The type of entry in the ARP cache

Mapping Types

The mapping type is one of four possible values indicating the status of the entry in the ARP cache. A value of 2 means the entry is invalid; a value of 3 means the mapping is dynamic (the entry can change); a value of 4 means static (the entry doesn't change); and a value of 1 means none of the above.

When the ARP receives a recipient device's IP address, it searches the ARP cache for a match. If it finds one, it returns the physical address. If the ARP cache doesn't find a match for an IP address, it sends a message out on the network. The message, called an *ARP request,* is a broadcast that is received by all devices on the local network. (You might remember that a broadcast has all 1s in the address.) The ARP request contains the IP address of the intended recipient device. If a device recognizes the IP address as belonging to it, the device sends a reply message containing its physical address back to the machine that generated the ARP request, which places the information into its ARP cache for future use. In this manner, the ARP cache can determine the physical address for any machine based on its IP address.

Whenever an ARP request is received by an ARP cache, it uses the information in the request to update its own table. Thus, the system can accommodate changing physical addresses and new additions to the network dynamically without having to generate an ARP request of its own. Without the use of an ARP cache, all the ARP requests and replies would generate a lot of network traffic, which can have a serious impact on network performance. Some simpler network schemes abandon the cache and simply use broadcast messages each time. This is feasible only when the number of devices is low enough to avoid network traffic problems.

The layout of the ARP request is shown in Figure 2.11. When an ARP request is sent, all fields in the layout are used except the Recipient Hardware Address (which the request is trying to identify). In an ARP reply, all the fields are used.

2

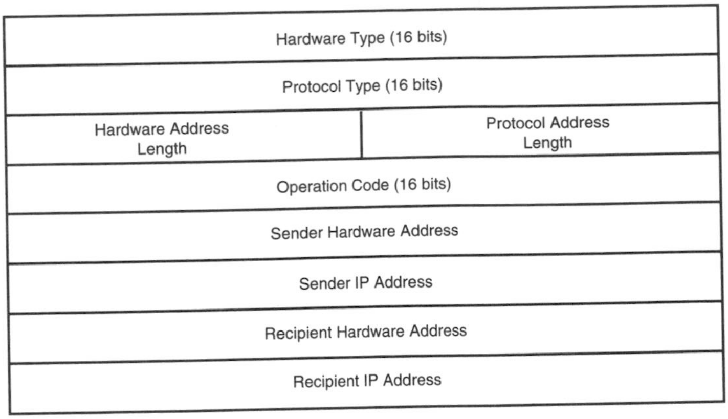

Figure 2.11.
The ARP request and
ARP reply layout.

Hardware Type (16 bits)	
Protocol Type (16 bits)	
Hardware Address Length	Protocol Address Length
Operation Code (16 bits)	
Sender Hardware Address	
Sender IP Address	
Recipient Hardware Address	
Recipient IP Address	

This layout, which is combined with the network system's protocols into a protocol data unit (PDU), has several fields. The fields and their purposes arc as follows:

☐ Hardware Type: The type of hardware interface

☐ Protocol Type: The type of protocol the sending device is using

☐ Hardware Address Length: The length of each hardware address in the datagram, given in bytes

☐ Protocol Address Length: The length of the protocol address in the datagram, given in bytes

☐ Operation Code (Opcode): The Opcode indicates whether the datagram is an ARP request or an ARP reply. If the datagram is a request, the value is set to 1. If it is a reply, the value is set to 2.

☐ Sender Hardware Address: The hardware address of the sending device

☐ Sender IP Address: The IP address of the sending device

☐ Recipient IP Address: The IP Address of the recipient

☐ Recipient Hardware Address: The hardware address of the recipient device

Some of these fields need a little more explanation to show their legal values and field usage. The following sections describe these fields in more detail.

The Hardware Type Field

The hardware type identifies the type of hardware interface. Legal values are as follows:

Type	Description
1	Ethernet
2	Experimental Ethernet
3	X.25
4	Proteon ProNET (Token Ring)
5	Chaos
6	IEEE 802.X
7	ARCnet

The Protocol Type Field

The protocol type identifies the type of protocol the sending device is using. With TCP/IP, these protocols are usually an EtherType, for which the legal values are as follows:

Decimal	Description
512	XEROX PUP
513	PUP Address Translation
1536	XEROX NS IDP
2048	Internet Protocol (IP)
2049	X.75
2050	NBS
2051	ECMA
2052	Chaosnet
2053	X.25 Level 3
2054	Address Resolution Protocol (ARP)
2055	XNS
4096	Berkeley Trailer
21000	BBN Simnet
24577	DEC MOP Dump/Load
24578	DEC MOP Remote Console
24579	DEC DECnet Phase IV
24580	DEC LAT
24582	DEC
24583	DEC
32773	HP Probe
32784	Excelan
32821	Reverse ARP
32824	DEC LANBridge
32823	AppleTalk

If the protocol is not EtherType, other values are allowed.

ARP and IP Addresses

Two (or more) networks connected by a gateway can have the same network address. The gateway has to determine which network the physical address or IP address corresponds with. The gateway can do this with a modified ARP, called the Proxy ARP (sometimes called Promiscuous ARP). A proxy ARP creates an ARP cache consisting of entries from both networks, with the gateway able to transfer datagrams from one network to the other. The gateway has to manage the ARP requests and replies that cross the two networks.

An obvious flaw with the ARP system is that if a device doesn't know its own IP address, there is no way to generate requests and replies. This can happen when a new device (typically a diskless workstation) is added to the network. The only address the device is aware of is the physical address set either by switches on the network interface or by software. A simple solution is the Reverse Address Resolution Protocol (RARP), which works the reverse of ARP, sending out the physical address and expecting back an IP address. The reply containing the IP address is sent by an RARP server, a machine that can supply the information. Although the originating device sends the message as a broadcast, RARP rules stipulate that only the RARP server can generate a reply. (Many networks assign more than one RARP server, both to spread the processing load and to act as a backup in case of problems.)

The Domain Name Service

Instead of using the full 32-bit IP address, many systems adopt more meaningful names for their devices and networks. Network names usually reflect the organization's name (such as tpci.com and bobs_cement). Individual device names within a network can range from descriptive names on small networks (such as tims_machine and laser_1) to more complex naming conventions on larger networks (such as hpws_23 and tpci704). Translating between these names and the IP addresses would be practically impossible on an Internet-wide scale.

To solve the problem of network names, the Network Information Center (NIC) maintains a list of network names and the corresponding network gateway addresses. This system grew from a simple flat-file list (which was searched for matches) to a more complicated system called the Domain Name Service (DNS) when the networks became too numerous for the flat-file system to function efficiently.

DNS uses a hierarchical architecture, much like the UNIX filesystem. The first level of naming divides networks into the category of subnetworks, such as com for commercial, mil for military, edu for education, and so on. Below each of these is another division that identifies the individual subnetwork, usually one for each organization. This is called the *domain name* and is unique. The organization's system manager can further divide the company's subnetworks as desired, with each network called a *subdomain*. For example, the system `merlin.abc_corp.com` has the domain name `abc_corp.com`, whereas the network `merlin.abc_corp` is a subdomain of `merlin.abc_corp.com`. A network can be identified with an *absolute name* (such as `merlin.abc_corp.com`) or a *relative name* (such as `merlin`) that uses part of the complete domain name.

Seven first-level domain names have been established by the NIC so far. These are as follows:

`.arpa`	An ARPANET-Internet identification
`.com`	Commercial company
`.edu`	Educational institution
`.gov`	Any governmental body
`.mil`	Military
`.net`	Networks used by Internet Service Providers
`.org`	Anything that doesn't fall into one of the other categories

The NIC also allows for a country designator to be appended. There are designators for all countries in the world, such as `.ca` for Canada and `.uk` for the United Kingdom.

DNS uses two systems to establish and track domain names. A *name resolver* on each network examines information in a domain name. If it can't find the full IP address, it queries a *name server*, which has the full NIC information available. The name resolver tries to complete the addressing information using its own database, which it updates in much the same manner as the ARP system (discussed earlier) when it must query a name server. If a queried name server cannot resolve the address, it can query another name server, and so on, across the entire internetwork.

There is a considerable amount of information stored in the name resolver and name server, as well as a whole set of protocols for querying between the two. The details, luckily, are not important to an understanding of TCP/IP, although the overall concept of the address resolution is important when understanding how the Internet translates between domain names and IP addresses.

Summary

In this chapter you have seen the relationship of OSI and TCP/IP layered architectures, a history of TCP/IP and the Internet, the structure of the Internet, Internet and IP addresses, and the Address Resolution Protocol. Using these concepts, you can now move on to look at the TCP/IP family of protocols in more detail.

The next chapter begins with the Internet Protocol (IP), showing how it is used and the format of its header information. The rest of the chapter covers gateway information necessary to piece together the rest of the protocols. Gateways are also revisited on Day 5.

Q&A

Q Explain the role of gateways in internetworks.

A Gateways act as a relay between networks, passing datagrams from network to network searching for a destination address. Networks talk to each other through gateways.

Q Expand the following TCP/IP protocol acronyms: DNS, SNMP, NFS, RPC, TFTP.

A DNS is the Domain Name Service, which allows a common name to be used instead of an IP address. SNMP is the Simple Network Management Protocol, used to provide information about devices. NFS is the Network File System, a protocol that allows machines to access other file systems as if they were part of their own. RPC is the Remote Procedure Call protocol that allows applications to communicate. TFTP is the Trivial File Transfer Protocol, a simple file transfer system with no security.

Q Name the Internet's advisory bodies.

A The Internet Advisory Board (IAB) controls the Internet. The Internet Engineering Task Force (IETF) handles implementations of protocols on the Internet, and the Internet Research Task Force (IRTF) handles research.

Q What does ARP do?

A The Address Resolution Protocol converts IP addresses to physical device addresses.

Q What are the four IP address classes and their structures?

A Class A for large networks: Network address is 7 bits; local address is 24 bits. Class B for midsize networks: Network address is 14 bits; local address is 16 bits. Class C for small networks: Network address is 21 bits; local address is 8 bits. Class D for multicast addresses, using 28 bits. Class D networks are seldom encountered.

Quiz

1. Draw the layered architectures of both the OSI Reference Model and TCP/IP. Show how the layers correspond in each diagram.

2. Show the layered Internet architecture, explaining each layer's purpose.

3. Show how a datagram is transferred from one network, through one or more gateways, to the destination network. In each device, show the layered architecture and how high up the layered structure the datagram goes.

4. Draw the IP header and an Ethernet frame, showing the number of bits used for each component. Explain each component's role.

5. Explain what an ARP cache is. What is its structure and why is it used?

2

Chapter 3

The Internet Protocol (IP)

Yesterday I looked at the history of TCP/IP and the Internet in some detail. Today I move on to the first of the two important protocol elements of TCP/IP: the Internet Protocol, the "IP" part of TCP/IP. A good understanding of IP is necessary to continue on to TCP and UDP, because the IP is the component that handles the movement of datagrams across a network. Knowing how a datagram must be assembled and how it is moved through the networks helps you understand how the higher-level layers work with IP. For almost all protocols in the TCP/IP family, IP is the essential element that packages data and ensures that it is sent to its destination.

This chapter contains, unfortunately, even more detail on headers, protocols, and messaging than you saw in the last couple of days. This level of information is necessary in order for you to deal with understanding the applications and their interaction with IP, as well as troubleshooting the system. Although I don't go into exhaustive detail, there is enough here that you can refer back to this chapter whenever needed.

As with many of the subjects I look at in this book, don't assume that this chapter covers everything there is to know about IP. There are many books written on IP alone, going into each facet of the protocol and its functionality. Luckily, most of the details are transparent to you, and there is little advantage gained in knowing it. For that reason, I simplify the subject a little, still providing enough detail for you to see how IP works and what it does.

Internet Protocol

The Internet Protocol (IP) is a primary protocol of the OSI model, as well as an integral part of TCP/IP (as the name suggests). Although the word "Internet" appears in the protocol's name, it is not restricted to use with the Internet. It is true that all machines on the Internet can use or understand IP, but IP can also be used on dedicated networks that have no relation to the Internet at all. IP defines a protocol, not a connection. Indeed, IP is a very good choice for any network that needs an efficient protocol for machine-to-machine communications, although it faces some competition from protocols like Novell NetWare's IPX on small to medium local area networks that use NetWare as a PC server operating system.

What does IP do? Its main tasks are addressing of datagrams of information between computers and managing the fragmentation process of these datagrams. The protocol has a formal definition of the layout of a datagram of information and the formation of a header composed of information about the datagram. IP is responsible for the routing of a datagram, determining where it will be sent, and devising alternate routes in case of problems.

Another important aspect of IP's purpose has to do with unreliable delivery of a datagram. Unreliable in the IP sense means that the delivery of the datagram is not guaranteed, because it can get delayed, misrouted, or mangled in the breakdown and reassembly of message fragments. IP has nothing to do with flow control or reliability: There is no inherent capability to verify that a sent message is correctly received. IP does not have a checksum for the data contents of a datagram, only for the header information. The verification and flow control tasks are left to other components in the layer model. (For that matter, IP doesn't even properly handle the forwarding of datagrams. IP can make a guess as to the best routing to move a datagram to the next node along a path, but it does not inherently verify that the chosen path is the fastest or most efficient route.) Part of the IP system defines how gateways manage datagrams, how and when they should produce error messages, and how to recover from problems that might arise.

In the first chapter, you saw how data can be broken into smaller sections for transmission and then reassembled at another location, a process called fragmentation and reassembly. IP provides for a maximum packet size of 65,535 bytes, which is much larger than most networks can handle, hence the need for fragmentation. IP has the capability to automatically divide a datagram of information into smaller datagrams if necessary, using the principles you saw in Day 1.

When the first datagram of a larger message that has been divided into fragments arrives at the destination, a *reassembly timer* is started by the receiving machine's IP layer. If all the pieces of the entire datagram are not received when the timer reaches a predetermined value, all the datagrams that have been received are discarded. The receiving machine knows the order in which the pieces are to be reassembled because of a field in the IP header. One consequence of this process is that a fragmented message has a lower chance of arrival than an unfragmented message, which is why most applications try to avoid fragmentation whenever possible.

IP is connectionless, meaning that it doesn't worry about which nodes a datagram passes through along the path, or even at which machines the datagram starts and ends. This information is in the header, but the process of analyzing and passing on a datagram has nothing to do with IP analyzing the sending and receiving IP addresses. IP handles the addressing of a datagram with the full 32-bit Internet address, even though the transport protocol addresses use 8 bits. A new version of IP, called version 6 or IPng (IP Next Generation) can handle much larger headers, as you will see toward the end of today's material in the section titled "IPng: IP Version 6."

The Internet Protocol Datagram Header

It is tempting to compare IP to a hardware network such as Ethernet because of the basic similarities in packaging information. Yesterday you saw how Ethernet assembles a frame by combining the application data with a header block containing address information. IP does the same, except the contents of the header are specific to IP. When Ethernet receives an IP-assembled datagram (which includes the IP header), it adds its header to the front to create a frame—a process called *encapsulation.* One of the primary differences between the IP and Ethernet headers is that Ethernet's header contains the physical address of the destination machine, whereas the IP header contains the IP address. You might recall from yesterday's discussion that the translation between the two addresses is performed by the Address Resolution Protocol.

NOTE

> Encapsulation is the process of adding something to the start (and sometimes the end) of data, just as a pill capsule holds the medicinal contents. The added header and tail give details about the enclosed data.

The datagram is the transfer unit used by IP, sometimes more specifically called an Internet datagram, or IP datagram. The specifications that define IP (as well as most of the other protocols and services in the TCP/IP family of protocols) define headers and tails in terms of words, where a word is 32 bits. Some operating systems use a different word length, although 32 bits per word is the more-often encountered value (some minicomputers and larger systems use 64 bits per word, for example). There are eight bits to a byte, so a 32-bit word is the same as four bytes on most systems.

The IP header is six 32-bit words in length (24 bytes total) when all the optional fields are included in the header. The shortest header allowed by IP uses five words (20 bytes total). To understand all the fields in the header, it is useful to remember that IP has no hardware dependence but must account for all versions of IP software it can encounter (providing full backward-compatibility with previous versions of IP). The IP header layout is shown schematically in Figure 3.1. The different fields in the IP header are examined in more detail in the following subsections.

Figure 3.1.

The IP header layout.

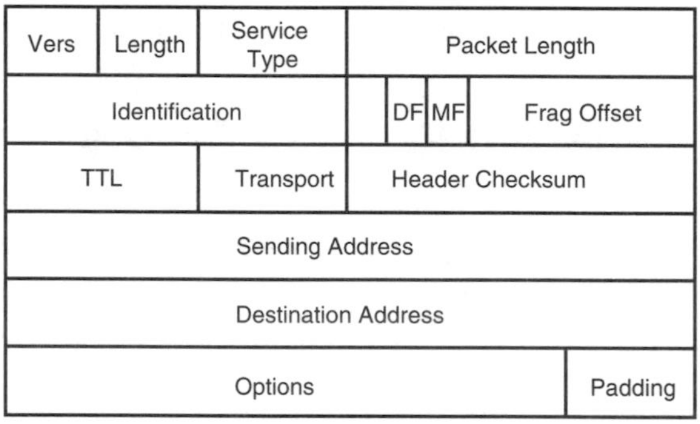

Version Number

This is a 4-bit field that contains the IP version number the protocol software is using. The version number is required so that the receiving IP software knows how to decode the rest of the header, which changes with each new release of the IP standards. The most widely used version is 4, although several systems are now testing version 6 (called IPng). The Internet and most LANs do not support IP version 6 at present.

Part of the protocol definition stipulates that the receiving software must first check the version number of incoming datagrams before proceeding to analyze the rest of the header and encapsulated data. If the software cannot handle the version used to build the datagram, the receiving machine's IP layer rejects the datagram and ignores the contents completely.

Header Length

This 4-bit field reflects the total length of the IP header built by the sending machine; it is specified in 32-bit words. The shortest header is five words (20 bytes), but the use of optional fields can increase the header size to its maximum of six words (24 bytes). To properly decode the header, IP must know when the header ends and the data begins, which is why this field is included. (There is no start-of-data marker to show where the data in the datagram begins. Instead, the header length is used to compute an offset from the start of the IP header to give the start of the data block.)

Type of Service

The 8-bit (1 byte) Service Type field instructs IP how to process the datagram properly. The field's 8 bits are read and assigned as shown in Figure 3.2, which shows the layout of the Service Type field inside the larger IP header shown in Figure 3.1. The first 3 bits indicate the datagram's precedence, with a value from 0 (normal) through 7 (network control). The higher the number, the more important the datagram and, in theory at least, the faster the datagram should be routed to its destination. In practice, though, most implementations of TCP/IP and practically all hardware that uses TCP/IP ignores this field, treating all datagrams with the same priority.

Figure 3.2.

The 8-bit Service Type field layout.

Precedence (3 bits)	Delay	Thru	Rel	Not used

The next three bits are 1-bit flags that control the delay, throughput, and reliability of the datagram. If the bit is set to 0, the setting is normal. A bit set to 1 implies low delay, high throughput, and high reliability for the respective flags. The last two bits of the field are not used. Most of these bits are ignored by current IP implementations, and all datagrams are treated with the same delay, throughput, and reliability settings.

For most purposes, the values of all the bits in the Service Type field are set to 0 because differences in precedence, delay, throughput, and reliability between machines are virtually nonexistent unless a special network has been established. Although these flags would be useful in establishing the best routing method for a datagram, no currently available UNIX-based IP system bothers to evaluate the bits in these fields. (Although it is conceivable that the code could be modified for high security or high reliability networks.)

Datagram Length (or Packet Length)

This field gives the total length of the datagram, including the header, in bytes. The length of the data area itself can be computed by subtracting the header length from this value. The size of the total datagram length field is 16 bits, hence the 65,535 bytes maximum length of a datagram (including the header). This field is used to determine the length value to be passed to the transport protocol to set the total frame length.

Identification

This field holds a number that is a unique identifier created by the sending node. This number is required when reassembling fragmented messages, ensuring that the fragments of one message are not intermixed with others. Each chunk of data received by the IP layer from a higher protocol layer is assigned one of these identification numbers when the data arrives. If a datagram is fragmented, each fragment has the same identification number.

Flags

The Flags field is a 3-bit field, the first bit of which is left unused (it is ignored by the protocol and usually has no value written to it). The remaining two bits are dedicated to flags called DF (Don't Fragment) and MF (More Fragments), which control the handling of the datagrams when fragmentation is desirable.

If the DF flag is set to 1, the datagram cannot be fragmented under any circumstances. If the current IP layer software cannot send the datagram on to another machine without fragmenting it, and this bit is set to 1, the datagram is discarded and an error message is sent back to the sending device.

If the MF flag is set to 1, the current datagram is followed by more packets (sometimes called *subpackets*), which must be reassembled to re-create the full message. The last fragment that is sent as part of a larger message has its MF flag set to 0 (off) so that the receiving device knows when to stop waiting for datagrams. Because the order of the fragments' arrival might not correspond to the order in which they were sent, the MF flag is used in conjunction with the Fragment Offset field (the next field in the IP header) to indicate to the receiving machine the full extent of the message.

Fragment Offset

If the MF (More Fragments) flag bit is set to 1 (indicating fragmentation of a larger datagram), the fragment offset contains the position in the complete message of the submessage contained within the current datagram. This enables IP to reassemble fragmented packets in the proper order.

Offsets are always given relative to the beginning of the message. This is a 13-bit field, so offsets are calculated in units of 8 bytes, corresponding to the maximum packet length of 65,535 bytes. Using the identification number to indicate which message a receiving datagram belongs to, the IP layer on a receiving machine can then use the fragment offset to reassemble the entire message.

Time to Live (TTL)

This field fragment gives the amount of time in seconds that a datagram can remain on the network before it is discarded. This is set by the sending node when the datagram is assembled. Usually the TTL field is set to 15 or 30 seconds.

The TCP/IP standards stipulate that the TTL field must be decreased by at least one second for each node that processes the packet, even if the processing time is less than one second. Also, when a datagram is received by a gateway, the arrival time is tagged so that if the datagram must wait to be processed, that time counts against its TTL. Hence, if a gateway is particularly overloaded and can't get to the datagram in short order, the TTL timer can expire while awaiting processing, and the datagram is abandoned.

If the TTL field reaches 0, the datagram must be discarded by the current node, but a message is sent back to the sending machine when the packet is dropped. The sending machine can then resend the datagram. The rules governing the TTL field are designed to prevent IP packets from endlessly circulating through networks.

Transport Protocol

This field holds the identification number of the transport protocol to which the packet has been handed. The numbers are defined by the Network Information Center (NIC), which governs the Internet. There are currently about 50 protocols defined and assigned a transport protocol number. The two most important protocols are ICMP (detailed in the section titled "Internet Control Message Protocol (ICMP)" later today), which is number 1, and TCP, which is number 6. The full list of numbers is not necessary here because most of the protocols are never encountered by users. (If you really want this information, it's in several RFCs mentioned in the appendixes.)

Header Checksum

The number in this field of the IP header is a checksum for the protocol header field (but not the data fields) to enable faster processing. Because the Time to Live (TTL) field is decremented at each node, the checksum also changes with every machine the datagram passes through. The checksum algorithm takes the ones-complement of the 16-bit sum of all 16-bit words.

This is a fast, efficient algorithm, but it misses some unusual corruption circumstances such as the loss of an entire 16-bit word that contains only 0s. However, because the data checksums used by both TCP and UDP cover the entire packet, these types of errors usually can be caught as the frame is assembled for the network transport.

Sending Address and Destination Address

These fields contain the 32-bit IP addresses of the sending and destination devices. These fields are established when the datagram is created and are not altered during the routing.

Options

The Options field is optional, composed of several codes of variable length. If more than one option is used in the datagram, the options appear consecutively in the IP header. All the options are controlled by a byte that is usually divided into three fields: a 1-bit copy flag, a 2-bit option class, and a 5-bit option number. The copy flag is used to stipulate how the option is handled when fragmentation is necessary in a gateway. When the bit is set to 0, the option should be copied to the first datagram but not subsequent ones. If the bit is set to 1, the option is copied to all the datagrams.

The option class and option number indicate the type of option and its particular value. At present, there are only two option classes set. (With only 2 bits to work with in the field, a maximum of four options could be set.) When the value is 0, the option applies to datagram or network control. A value of 2 means the option is for debugging or administration purposes. Values of 1 and 3 are unused. Currently supported values for the option class and number are given in Table 3.1.

Table 3.1. Valid option class and numbers for IP headers.

Option Class	Option Number	Description
0	0	Marks the end of the options list
0	1	No option (used for padding)
0	2	Security options (military purposes only)
0	3	Loose source routing
0	7	Activates routing record (adds fields)
0	9	Strict source routing
2	4	Timestamping active (adds fields)

3

Of most interest to you are options that enable the routing and timestamps to be recorded. These are used to provide a record of a datagram's passage across the internetwork, which can be useful for diagnostic purposes. Both these options add information to a list contained within the datagram. (The timestamp has an interesting format: It is expressed in milliseconds since midnight, Universal Time. Unfortunately, because most systems have widely differing time settings—even when corrected to Universal Time—the timestamps should be treated with more than a little suspicion.)

There are two kinds of routing indicated within the Options field: loose and strict. *Loose routing* provides a series of IP addresses that the machine must pass through, but it enables any route to be used to get to each of these addresses (usually gateways). *Strict routing* enables no deviations from the specified route. If the route can't be followed, the datagram is abandoned. Strict routing is frequently used for testing routes but rarely for transmission of user datagrams because of the higher chances of the datagram being lost or abandoned.

Padding

The content of the padding area depends on the options selected. The padding is usually used to ensure that the datagram header is a round number of bytes.

A Datagram's Life

To understand how IP and other TCP/IP layers work to package and send a datagram from one machine to another, I take a simplified look at a typical datagram's passage. When an application must send a datagram out on the network, it performs a few simple steps. First, it constructs the IP datagram within the legal lengths stipulated by the local IP implementation. The checksum is calculated for the data, and then the IP header is constructed. Next, the first hop (machine) of the route to the destination must be determined to route the datagram to the destination machine directly over the local network, or to a gateway if the internetwork is used. If routing is important, this information is added to the header using an option. Finally, the datagram is passed to the network for its manipulation of the datagram.

As a datagram passes along the internetwork, each gateway performs a series of tests. After the network layer has stripped off its own header, the gateway IP layer calculates the checksum and verifies the integrity of the datagram. If the checksums don't match, the datagram is discarded and an error message is returned to the sending device. Next, the TTL field is decremented and checked. If the datagram has expired, it is discarded and an error message is sent back to the sending machine. After determining the next hop of the route, either by analysis of the target address or from a specified routing instruction within the Options field of the IP header, the datagram is rebuilt with the new TTL value and new checksum.

3

If fragmentation is necessary because of an increase in the datagram's length or a limitation in the software, the datagram is divided, and new datagrams with the correct header information are assembled. If a routing or timestamp is required, it is added as well. Finally, the datagram is passed back to the network layer.

When the datagram is finally received at the destination device, the system performs a checksum calculation and—assuming the two sums match—checks to see if there are other fragments. If more datagrams are required to reassemble the entire message, the system waits, meanwhile running a timer to ensure that the datagrams arrive within a reasonable time. If all the parts of the larger message have arrived but the device can't reassemble them before the timer reaches 0, the datagram is discarded and an error message is returned to the sender. Finally, the IP header is stripped off, the original message is reconstructed if it was fragmented, and the message is passed up the layers to the upper layer application. If a reply was required, it is then generated and sent back to the sending device.

When extra information is added to the datagram for routing or timestamp recording, the length of the datagram can increase. Handling all these conditions is part of IP's forte, for which practically every problem has a resolution system.

Internet Control Message Protocol (ICMP)

As you have seen today and over the last two days, many problems can occur in routing a message from sender to receiver. The TTL timer might expire; fragmented datagrams might not arrive with all segments intact; a gateway might misroute a datagram, and so on. Letting the sending device know of a problem with a datagram is important, as is correctly handling error conditions within the network routing itself. The Internet Control Message Protocol (ICMP) was developed for this task.

ICMP is an error-reporting system. It is an integral part of IP and must be included in every IP implementation. This provides for consistent, understandable error messages and signals across the different versions of IP and different operating systems. It is useful to think of ICMP as one IP package designed specifically to talk to another IP package across the network: in other words, ICMP is the IP layer's communications system. Messages generated by ICMP are treated by the rest of the network as any other datagram, but they are interpreted differently by the IP layer software. ICMP messages have a header built in the same manner as any IP datagram, and ICMP datagrams are not differentiated at any point from normal data-carrying datagrams until a receiving machine's IP layer processes the datagram properly.

In almost all cases, error messages sent by ICMP are routed back to the original datagram's sending machine. This is because only the sender's and destination device's IP addresses are included in the header. Because the error doesn't mean anything to the destination device, the sender is the logical recipient of the error message. The sender can then determine from the ICMP message the type of error that occurred and establish how to best resend the failed datagram.

ICMP messages go through two encapsulations, as do all IP messages: incorporation into a regular IP datagram and then into the network frame. This is shown in Figure 3.3. ICMP headers have a different format than IP headers, though, and the format differs slightly depending on the type of message. However, all ICMP headers start with the same three fields: a message type, a code field, and a checksum for the ICMP message. Figure 3.4 shows the layout of the ICMP message.

Figure 3.3.

Two-step encapsulation of an ICMP message.

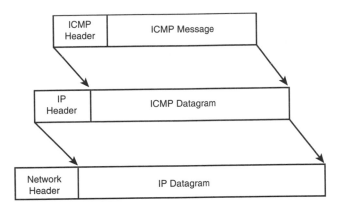

Figure 3.4.

The layout of an ICMP message.

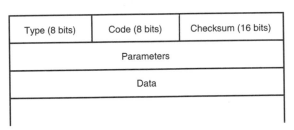

Usually, any ICMP message that is reporting a problem with delivery also includes the header and first 64 bits of the data field from the datagram for which the problem occurred. Including the 64 bits of the original datagram accomplishes two things. First, it enables the sending device to match the datagram fragment to the original datagram by comparison. Also, because most of the protocols involved are defined at the start of the datagram, the inclusion of the original datagram fragment allows for some diagnostics to be performed by the machine receiving the ICMP message.

The 8-bit Message Type field in the ICMP header (shown in Figure 3.4) can have one of the values shown in Table 3.2.

Table 3.2. Valid values for the ICMP Message Type field.

Value	Description
0	Echo Reply
3	Destination Not Reachable
4	Source Quench
5	Redirection Required
8	Echo Request
11	Time to Live Exceeded
12	Parameter Problem
13	Timestamp Request
14	Timestamp Reply
15	Information Request (now obsolete)
16	Information Reply (now obsolete)
17	Address Mask Request
18	Address Mask Reply

The Code field expands on the message type, providing a little more information for the receiving machine. The checksum in the ICMP header is calculated in the same manner as the normal IP header checksum.

The layout of the ICMP message is slightly different for each type of message. Figure 3.5 shows the layouts of each type of ICMP message header. The Destination Unreachable and Time Exceeded messages are self-explanatory, although they are used in other circumstances, too, such as when a datagram must be fragmented but the Don't Fragment flag is set. This results in a Destination Unreachable message being returned to the sending machine.

The Source Quench ICMP message is used to control the rate at which datagrams are transmitted, although this is a very rudimentary form of flow control. When a device receives a Source Quench message, it should reduce the transmittal rate over the network until the Source Quench messages cease. The messages are typically generated by a gateway or host that either has a full receiving buffer or has slowed processing of incoming datagrams because of other factors. If the buffer is full, the device is supposed to issue a Source Quench message for each datagram that is discarded. Some implementations issue Source Quench messages when the buffer exceeds a certain percentage to slow down reception of new datagrams and enable the device to clear the buffer.

3

Figure 3.5.

ICMP message header layouts.

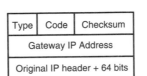

Type	Code	Checksum
Unused		
Original IP header + 64 bits		

Destination unreachable
Source Quench, Time Exceeded

Type	Code	Checksum
Ptr	Unused	
Original IP header + 64 bits		

Parameter Problem

Type	Code	Checksum
Gateway IP Address		
Original IP header + 64 bits		

Redirect

Type	Code	Checksum
Identifier	Sequence No.	
Original IP header + 64 bits		

Echo Request and Echo Reply

Type	Code	Checksum
Identifier	Sequence No.	
Originating Timestamp		

Timestamp Request

Type	Code	Checksum
Identifier	Sequence No.	
Originating Timestamp		
Receiving Timestamp		
Transmitting Timestamp		

Timestamp Reply

Type	Code	Checksum
Identifier	Sequence No.	

Information Request and Reply,
Address Mask Request

Type	Code	Checksum
Identifier	Sequence No.	
Address Mask		

Address Mask Reply

Redirection messages are sent to a gateway in the path when a better route is available. For example, if a gateway has just received a datagram from another gateway but on checking its datafiles finds a better route, it sends the Redirection message back to that gateway with the IP address of the better route. When a Redirection message is sent, an integer is placed in the code field of the header to indicate the conditions for which the rerouting applies. A value of 0 means that datagrams for any device on the destination network should be redirected. A value of 1 indicates that only datagrams for the specific device should be rerouted. A value of 2 implies that only datagrams for the network with the same type of service (read from one of the IP header fields) should be rerouted. Finally, a value of 3 reroutes only for the same host with the same type of service.

The Parameter Problem message is used whenever a semantic or syntactic error has been encountered in the IP header. This can happen when options are used with incorrect arguments. When a Parameter Problem message is sent back to the sending device, the Parameter field in the ICMP error message contains a pointer to the byte in the IP header that caused the problem. (See Figure 3.5.)

Echo request or reply messages are commonly used for debugging purposes. When a request is sent, a device or gateway down the path sends a reply back to the specified device. These request/reply pairs are useful for identifying routing problems, failed gateways, or network cabling problems. The simple act of processing an ICMP message also acts as a check of the network, because each gateway or device along the path must correctly decode the headers and then pass the datagram along. Any failure along the way could be with the implementation of the IP software. A commonly used request/reply system is the ping command. The ping command sends a series of requests and waits for replies.

Timestamp requests and replies enable the timing of message passing along the network to be monitored. When combined with strict routing, this can be useful in identifying bottlenecks. Address mask requests and replies are used for testing within a specific network or subnetwork.

IPng: IP Version 6

When IP version 4 (the current release) was developed, the use of a 32-bit IP address seemed more than enough to handle the projected use of the Internet. With the incredible growth rate of the Internet over the last few years, however, the 32-bit IP address might become a problem. To counter this limit, IP Next Generation, usually called IP version 6 (IPv6), is under development.

Several proposals for IPng implementation are currently being studied, the most popular of which are TUBA (TCP and UDP with Bigger Addresses), CATNIP (Common Architecture for the Internet), and SIPP (Simple Internet Protocol Plus). None of the three meet all the proposed changes for version 6, but a compromise or modification based on one of these proposals is likely.

What does IPng have to offer? The list of changes tells you the main features of IPng in a nutshell:

- [ ] 128-bit network address instead of 32-bit
- [ ] More efficient IP header with extensions for applications and options
- [ ] No header checksum
- [ ] A flow label for quality-of-service requirements
- [ ] Prevention of intermediate fragmentation of datagrams
- [ ] Built-in security for authentication and encryption

Next I look at IPng in a little more detail to show the changes that affect most users, as well as network programmers and network administrators. I start with a look at the IPng header. Remember that at present IPng is still under development and is not widely deployed except on test networks.

3

IPng Datagram

As mentioned earlier, the header for IPng datagrams has been modified over the earlier version 4 header. The changes are mostly to provide support for the new, longer 128-bit IP addresses and to remove obsolete and unneeded fields. The basic layout of the IPng header is shown in Figure 3.6. As you can see, there are quite a few changes from the IP header used in IP version 4. (Refer to Figure 3.1.)

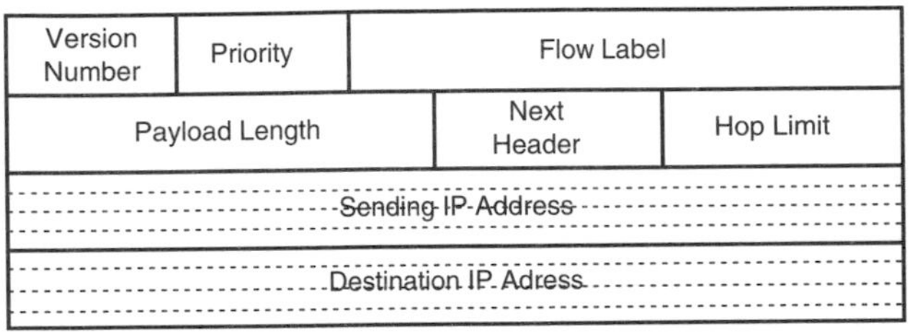

Figure 3.6.

The IPng header layout.

Version Number	Priority	Flow Label	
Payload Length		Next Header	Hop Limit
Sending IP Address			
Destination IP Adress			

The version number in the IP datagram header is 4 bits long and holds the release number (which is 6 with IPng). The Priority field is 4 bits long and holds a value indicating the datagram's priority. The priority is used to define the transmission order. The priority is set first with a broad classification, then a narrower identifier within each class. I look at the priority classification in a little more detail in a moment.

The Flow Label field is 24 bits long and is still in the development stage. It is likely to be used in combination with the source machine IP address to provide flow identification for the network. For example, if you are using a UNIX workstation on the network, the flow is different from another machine such as a Windows 95 PC. This field can be used to identify flow characteristics and provide some adjustment capabilities. The field can also be used to help identify target machines for large transfers, in which case a cache system becomes more efficient at routing between source and destination. Flow labels are discussed in more detail in the section titled "Flow Labels" later today.

The Payload Length field is a 16-bit field used to specify the total length of the IP datagram, given in bytes. The total length is exclusive of the IP header itself. The use of a 16-bit field limits the maximum value in this field to 65,535, but there is a provision to send large datagrams using an extension header (see the section titled "IP Extension Headers" later today).

The Next Header field is used to indicate which header follows the IP header when other applications want to piggy-back on the IP header. Several values have been defined for the Next Header field, as shown in Table 3.3.

Table 3.3. IP Next Header field values.

Value	Description
0	Hop-by-hop options
4	IP
6	TCP
17	UDP
43	Routing
44	Fragment
45	Interdomain Routine
46	Resource Reservation
50	Encapsulating Security
51	Authentication
58	ICMP
59	No Next Header
60	Destination Options

The Hop Limit field determines the number of hops the datagram can travel. With each forwarding, the number is decremented by 1. When the Hop Limit field reaches 0, the datagram is discarded, just as with IP version 4.

Finally, the Sending and Destination IP Addresses in 128-bit format are placed in the header. I look at the new IP address format in more detail in the section titled "128-Bit IP Addresses" later in this chapter.

Priority Classification

The Priority Classification field in the IPng header first divides the datagram into one of two categories: congestion controlled or noncongestion controlled. Noncongestion-controlled datagrams are always routed as a priority over congestion-controlled datagrams. There are subclassifications of noncongestion-controlled datagram priorities available for use, but none of the categories have been accepted as standard yet.

If the datagram is congestion controlled, it is sensitive to congestion problems on the network. If congestion occurs, the datagram can be slowed down and held temporarily in caches until the problem is alleviated. Beneath the broad congestion-controlled category are several subclasses that further refine the priority of the datagram. The subcategories of congestion-controlled priorities are given in Table 3.4.

3

Table 3.4. Priorities for congestion-controlled datagrams.

Value	Meaning
0	No priority specified
1	Background traffic
2	Unattended data transfer
3	Unassigned
4	Attended bulk transfer
5	Unassigned
6	Interactive traffic
7	Control traffic

Noncongestion-controlled traffic has priorities 8 through 15 available, but as I mentioned earlier, they are not defined.

Examples of each of the primary subcategories might help you see how the datagrams are prioritized. Routing and network management traffic that is considered highest priority is assigned category 7. Interactive applications such as Telnet and remote X sessions are assigned as interactive traffic (category 6). Transfers that are not time-critical (such as Telnet sessions) but are still controlled by an interactive application such as FTP are assigned as category 4. E-mail is usually assigned as category 2, whereas low-priority material such as news is set to category 1.

Flow Labels

As mentioned earlier, the Flow Label field new to the IPng header can be used to help identify the sender and destination of many IP datagrams. By employing caches to handle flows, the datagrams can be routed more efficiently. Not all applications can handle flow labels, in which case the field is set to a value of 0.

A simple example might help show the usefulness of the flow label field. Suppose a PC running Windows 95 is connected to a UNIX server on another network and is sending a large number of datagrams. By setting a specific value of the flow label for all the datagrams in the transmission, the routers along the way to the server can assemble entries in their routing caches that indicate which way to route each datagram with the same flow label. When subsequent datagrams with the same flow label arrive, the router doesn't have to recalculate the route; it can simply check the cache and extract the saved information from that. This speeds up the passage of the datagrams through each router.

To prevent caches from growing too large or holding stale information, IPng stipulates that the cache maintained in a routing device cannot be kept for more than six seconds. If a new datagram with the same flow label is not received within six seconds, the cache entry is removed. To prevent repeated values from the sending machine, the sender must wait six seconds before using the same flow label value for another destination.

IPng allows flow labels to be used to reserve a route for time-critical applications. For example, a real-time application that has to send several datagrams along the same route and needs as rapid a transmission as possible (such as is needed for video or audio, for example) can establish the route by sending datagrams ahead of time, being careful not to exceed the six second time-out on the interim routers.

128-Bit IP Addresses

Probably the most important aspect of IPng is its capability to provide for longer IP addresses. IPng increases the IP address from 32 bits to 128 bits. This enables an incredible number of addresses to be assembled, probably more than can ever be used.

The new IP addresses support three kinds of addresses: unicast, multicast, and anycast.

- [ ] Unicast addresses are meant to identify a particular machine's interface. This lets a PC, for example, have several different protocols in use, each with its own address. Thus, you could send messages specifically to a machine's IP interface address and not the NetBEUI interface address.

- [ ] A multicast address identifies a group of interfaces, enabling all machines in a group to receive the same packet. This is much like broadcasts in IP version 4, although with more flexibility for defining groups. Your machine's interfaces could belong to several multicast groups.

- [ ] An anycast address identifies a group of interfaces on a single multicast address. In other words, more than one interface can receive the datagram on the same machine.

The handling of fragmentation and reassembly is also changed with IPng to provide more capabilities for IP. Also proposed for IPng is an authentication scheme that can ensure that the data has not been corrupted between sender and receiver, as well as ensuring that the sending and receiving machines are who they claim they are.

IP Extension Headers

IPng has the provision to enable additional headers to be tacked onto the IP header. This might be necessary when a simple routing to the destination is not possible, or when special services such as authentication are required for the datagram. The additional information required is packaged into an extension header and appended to the IP header.

IPng defines several types of extension headers identified by a number placed in the Next Header field of the IP header. The currently accepted values and their meanings were shown in Table 3.3. Several extensions can be appended onto one IP header, with each extension's Next Header field indicating the next extension. Normally, the extension headers are appended in ascending numerical order. This makes it easier for routers to analyze the extensions, stopping the examination when it gets past router-specific extensions.

Hop-by-Hop Headers

Extension type 0 is hop-by-hop, which is used to provide IP options to every machine the datagram passes through. The options included in the hop-by-hop extension have a standard format of a Type value, a Length, and a Value (except for the Pad1 option, which has a single value set to 0 and no length or value field). Both the Type and Length fields are a single byte in length, whereas the Value field's length is variable and indicated by the length byte.

There are three types of hop-by-hop extensions defined so far, called Pad1, PadN, and Jumbo Payload. The Pad1 option is a single byte with a value of 0, no length, and no value. It is used to alter the order and position of other options in the header when necessary, dictated usually by an application. The PadN option is similar except it has N zeros placed in the Value field and a calculated value for the length.

The Jumbo Payload extension option is used to handle datagram sizes in excess of 65,535 bytes. The Length field in the IP header is limited to 16 bits, hence the limit of 65,535 for the datagram size. To handle larger datagram lengths, the IP header's Length field is set to 0, which redirects the routers to the extension to pick up a correct length value. The Length field can be defined in the extension header using 32 bits, which is in excess of 4 terabytes.

Routing Headers

A routing extension can be tacked onto the IP header when the sending machine wants to control the routing of the datagram instead of leaving it to the routers along the path. The routing extension can be used to give routes to the destination. The routing extension includes fields for each IP address along the desired route.

Fragment Headers

The fragment header can be appended to an IP datagram to enable a machine to fragment a large datagram into smaller parts. Part of the design of IPng was to prevent subsequent fragmentation, but in some cases fragmentation must be enabled in order to pass the datagram along the network.

Authentication Headers

The authentication header is used to ensure that no alteration was made to the contents of the datagram and that the datagram originated at the machine shown in the IP header. By default, IPng uses an authentication scheme called Message Digest 5 (MD5). Other authentication schemes can be used as long as both ends of the connection agree on the same scheme.

The authentication header consists of a security parameters index (SPI) that, when combined with the destination IP address, defines the authentication scheme. The SPI is followed by authentication data, which with MD5 is 16 bytes long. MD5 starts with a key (padded to 128 bits if it is shorter), then appends the entire datagram. The key is then tagged at the end, and the MD5 algorithm is run on the whole. To prevent problems with hop counters and the authentication header itself altering the values, they are zeroed for the purposes of calculating the authentication value. The MD5 algorithm generates a 128-bit value that is placed in the authentication header. The steps are repeated in reverse at the receiving end. Both ends must have the same key value, of course, for the scheme to work.

The datagram contents can be encrypted prior to generating authentication values using the default IPng encryption scheme, called Cipher Block Chaining (CBC), part of the Data Encryption Standard (DES).

Internet Protocol Support in Different Environments

The University of California at Berkeley was given a grant in the early 1980s to modify their UNIX operating system to include support for IP. The BSD4.2 UNIX release already offered support for TCP and IP, as well as the Simple Mail Transfer Protocol (SMTP) and Address Resolution Protocol (ARP), but with DARPA's funds, BSD4.3 was developed to provide more complete support.

The BSD4.2 support for IP was quite good prior to this grant, but it was limited to use in small local area networks only. To increase the capabilities of BSD UNIX's IP support, BSD added retransmission capabilities, Time to Live information, and redirection messages. Other features were added, too, enabling BSD4.3 to work with larger networks, internetworks (connections between different networks), and wide area networks connected by leased lines. This process brought the BSD UNIX system (and its licensees, such as Sun's SunOS) in line with the IP standards used on AT&T UNIX and other UNIX-based platforms.

With the strong support for IP among the UNIX community, it was inevitable that manufacturers of other software operating systems would start to produce software that allowed their machines to interconnect to the UNIX IP system. Most of the drive to produce IP versions for non-UNIX operating systems was not because of the Internet (which hadn't started its phenomenal growth at the time) but the desire to integrate the other operating systems into local area networks that used UNIX servers.

This section of today's material examines several hardware and software systems, focusing on the most widely used platforms, and shows the availability of IP (and entire TCP/IP suites) for those machines. Much of this is of interest only if you have the particular platform discussed (DEC VAX users tend not to care about interconnectivity to IBM SNA platforms, for example), so you can be selective about the sections you read. In some cases, I use one IP package from some of these platforms as an example and for screen captures later in this book.

MS-DOS

PCs came onto the scene when TCP/IP was already in common use, so it was not surprising to find interconnection software rapidly introduced. In many ways, the PC was a perfect platform as a stand-alone machine with access through a communications package to other larger systems. The PC was perfect for a client/server environment.

There are many PC-based versions of TCP/IP. The most widely used packages come from FTP Software, The Wollongong Group, and Beame and Whiteside Software, Inc. All the packages feature interconnection capabilities to other machines using TCP/IP, and most add other useful features such as FTP and mail routing.

FTP Software's PC/TCP is one of the most widely used. PC/TCP supports the major network interfaces: Packet Driver, IBM's Adapter Support Interface (ASI), Novell's Open Data Link Interface (ODI), and Microsoft/3Com's Network Driver Interface Specification (NDIS). All four LAN interfaces are discussed in more detail in the section titled "Local Area Networks" later today.

The design of PC/TCP covers all seven layers of the OSI model, developed in such a manner that components can be configured as required to support different transport mechanisms and applications. Typically, the Packet Driver, ASI, ODI, or NDIS module has a generic PC/TCP kernel on top of it, with the PC/TCP application on top of that.

PC/TCP enables the software to run both TCP/IP and another protocol, such as DECnet, Novell NetWare, or LAN Manager, simultaneously. This can be useful for enabling a PC to work within a small LAN workgroup, as well as within a larger network, without switching software.

Microsoft Windows

There are several TCP/IP products appearing for Microsoft's Windows 3.*x*, Windows for Workgroups, and Windows 95. Most of the early packages for Windows 3.*x* were ports of DOS products. Although these tend to work well, a totally Windows-designed product tends to have a slight edge in terms of integration with the Windows environment. Windows for Workgroups 3.11 has no inherent TCP/IP drives, but several products are available to add TCP/IP suites for this GUI, as well as Windows 3.1 and Windows 3.11.

One Windows 3.*x*-designed product is NetManage's Chameleon TCP/IP for Windows. Chameleon offers a complete port of TCP/IP and additional software utilities to enable a PC running Windows 3.*x* to integrate into a TCP/IP network. Chameleon offers terminal emulation, Telnet, FTP, electronic mail, DNS directory services, and NFS capabilities. There are several versions of Chameleon, depending on whether NFS is required.

Windows 95 has TCP/IP drivers included with the distribution software, but they are not loaded by default (NetWare's IPX/SPX is the default protocol for Windows 95). You must install and configure the TCP/IP product as a separate step after installing Windows 95 if you want to use IP on your network. You can see how this is done on Day 10, "Setting Up a Sample Network: Clients."

Windows NT

Windows NT is ideally suited for TCP/IP because it is designed to act as a server and gateway. Although Windows NT is not inherently multiuser, it does work well as a TCP/IP access device. Windows NT includes support for the TCP/IP protocols as a network transport, although the implementation does not include all the utilities usually associated with TCP/IP. TCP/IP can be chosen as the default protocol on a Windows NT machine when the operating system is installed.

Among the add-on products available for Windows NT, NetManage's Chameleon32 is a popular package. Similar to the Microsoft Windows version, Chameleon32 offers versions for NFS.

OS/2

IBM's OS/2 platform has a strong presence in corporations because of the IBM reputation and OS/2's solid performance. Not surprisingly, TCP/IP products are popular in these installations, as well. Although OS/2 differs from DOS in many ways, it is possible to run DOS-based ports of TCP/IP software under OS/2. A better solution is to run a native OS/2 application. Several TCP/IP OS/2-native implementations are available, including a TCP/IP product from IBM itself.

Macintosh

Except for versions of UNIX that run on the Macintosh, the Macintosh and UNIX worlds have depended on several different versions of TCP/IP to keep them connected. With many corporations now wanting their investment in Macintosh computers to serve double duty as X terminals onto UNIX workstation, TCP/IP for the Mac has become even more important.

Macintosh TCP products are available in several forms, usually as an add-on application or device driver for the Macintosh operating system. An alternative is Tenon Intersystems' MachTen product line, which enables a UNIX kernel and the Macintosh operating system to coexist on the same machine, providing compatibility between UNIX and the Macintosh file system and Apple events. TCP/IP is part of the MachTen product.

The AppleTalk networking system enables Macs and UNIX machines to interconnect to a limited extent, although this requires installation of AppleTalk software on the UNIX host—something many system administrators are reluctant to do. Also, because AppleTalk is not as fast and versatile as Ethernet and other network transports, this solution is seldom favored.

A better solution is simply to install TCP/IP on the Macintosh using one of several commercial packages available. Apple's own MacTCP software product can perform the basic services but must be coupled with software from other vendors for the higher layer applications. MacTCP also requires a Datagram Delivery Protocol to Internet Protocol (DDP-to-IP) router to handle the sending and receiving of DDP and IP datagrams.

Apple's MacTCP functions by providing the physical through transport layers of the architecture. MacTCP allows for both LocalTalk and Ethernet hardware and supports both IP and TCP, as well as several other protocols. Running on top of MacTCP is the third-party application, which uses MacTCP's function calls to provide the final application for the user. Functions such as Telnet and FTP protocols are supported with add-on software, too.

DEC

Digital Equipment Corporation's minicomputers were for many years a mainstay in scientific and educational research, so an obvious development for DEC and third-party software companies was to introduce IP software. Most DEC machines run either VMS or Ultrix (DEC's licensed version of UNIX). Providing IP capabilities to Ultrix was a matter of duplicating the code developed at Berkeley, but VMS was not designed for IP-type communications, relying instead on DEC's proprietary network software.

DEC's networking software is the Digital Network Architecture (DECnet). The first widely used version was DECnet Phase IV (introduced in 1982), which used industry-standard protocols for the lower layers but was proprietary in the upper layers. The 1987 release of DECnet Phase V provided a combined DECnet IV and OSI system that allowed new OSI protocols to be used within the DECnet environment.

DEC announced the ADVANTAGE-NETWORKS in 1991 as an enhancement of DECnet Phase V, adding support for the Internet Protocols. With the ADVANTAGE-NET-WORKS, users could choose between the older, DEC-specific DECnet, OSI, or IP schemes. ADVANTAGE-NETWORKS is DEC's attempt to provide interoperability, providing the DEC-exclusive DECnet system for LAN use, and the TCP/IP and OSI systems for WANs and system interconnection between different hardware types.

Users of VMS systems can connect to the UNIX environment in several ways. The easiest is to use a software gateway between the VMS machine and a UNIX machine. DEC's TCP/IP Services for VMS performs this function, as do several third-party software solutions, such as the Kermit protocol from Columbia University, Wollongong Group's WIN/TCP, and TGV's MultiNet. The advantage of the third-party communications protocol products such as Kermit is that they don't have to be connected to a UNIX machine, because any operating system that supports the communications protocol will work.

ADVANTAGE-NETWORKS users have more options available, many from DEC. Because the protocol is already embedded in the network software, it makes the most sense simply to use it as it comes, if it fits into the existing system architecture. Because of internal conversion software, ADVANTAGE-NETWORKS can connect from a DECnet machine using either the DECnet or the OSI protocols.

IBM's SNA

IBM's Systems Network Architecture (SNA) is in widespread use for both mainframes and minicomputers. Essentially all IBM equipment provides full support for IP and TCP, as well as many other popular protocols. Native IBM software is available for each machine, and several third-party products have appeared (usually at a lower cost than those offered by IBM).

The IBM UNIX version, AIX (which few people know stands for Advanced Interactive Executive), has the TCP/IP software built in, enabling any machine that can run AIX (from workstations to large minicomputers) to interconnect through IP with no additional software. The different versions of AIX have slightly different support, so users should check before blindly trying to connect AIX machines.

For large systems such as mainframes, IBM has the 3172 Interconnect Controller, which sits between the mainframe and a network. The 3172 is a hefty box that handles high-speed traffic between a mainframe channel and the network, off-loading the processing for the communications aspect from the mainframe processor. It can connect to Ethernet or token ring networks and through additional software to DEC's DECnet.

IBM mainframes running either MVS or VM can run software appropriately called TCP/IP for MVS and TCP/IP for VM. These products provide access from other machines running TCP/IP to access the mainframe operating system remotely, usually over a LAN. The software enables the calling machine (the client in a client/server scheme) to act as a 3270-series terminal to MVS or VM. FTP is provided for file transfers with automatic conversion from EBCDIC to ASCII. An interface to PROFS is available. Both TCP/IP software products support SMTP for electronic mail.

Local Area Networks

LANs are an obvious target for TCP/IP, because TCP/IP helps solve many interconnection problems between different hardware and software platforms. To run TCP/IP over a network, the existing network and transport layer software must be replaced with TCP/IP, or the two must be merged together in some manner so that the LAN protocol can carry TCP/IP information within its existing protocol (encapsulation).

Whichever solution is taken for the lower layer, a higher layer interface also must be developed, which resides in the equivalent of the data link layer, communicating between the higher layer applications and the hardware. This interface enables the higher layers to be independent of the hardware when using TCP/IP, which many popular LAN operating systems are not currently able to claim.

Three interfaces (which have been mentioned earlier today) are currently in common use. The Packet Driver interface was the first interface developed to meet these needs. 3Com Corporation and Microsoft developed the Network Driver Interface Specification (NDIS) for OS/2 and 3Com's networking software. NDIS provides a driver to communicate with the networking hardware and a protocol driver that acts as the interface to the higher layers. Novell's Open Data Link Interface (ODI) is similar to NDIS.

For single-vendor, PC-based networks, several dedicated TCP/IP packages are available, such as Novell's LAN WorkPlace, designed to enable any NetWare system to connect to a LAN using an interface hardware card and a software driver.

Summary

Today I started an in-depth look at the TCP/IP protocol family with the Internet Protocol. I covered what IP is and how it does its task of passing datagrams between machines. The construction of the IP datagram and the format of the IP header are shown in detail. The construction of the IP header is important to many TCP/IP family protocol members, so you can use this knowledge in later chapters. I also looked at the Internet Control Message Protocol (ICMP), an important aspect of the TCP/IP system.

The next chapter moves to the next-higher layer in the TCP/IP layered architecture and looks at the Transmission Control Protocol (TCP). I also look at the related User Datagram Protocol (UDP). TCP and UDP form the basis for all TCP/IP protocols.

Q&A

Q **Why does the IP header have a Time to Live field?**

A The easiest way to answer this is to consider what would happen without the field. A datagram with faulty information in the IP header could circulate around a network forever, forwarding from one gateway to another in search of a destination. With a Time to Live field, the number of bounces the datagram makes is limited. This has been proven to have an important effect on network traffic.

Q **Give a one-sentence description of ICMP.**

A ICMP is an error-reporting system that communicates between different IP-based devices, providing information about status changes and failed devices.

Q **What is a neighbor in the IP sense?**

A Neighbors are connected through a gateway. There is no physical restriction on the distance between neighbors. However, all neighbors share gateways.

Q **How is an ICMP message datagram constructed?**

A The ICMP message, which can include part of the datagram that causes an ICMP message to be generated, has an ICMP header attached to the front of it. This is then passed to IP, which encapsulates it within an IP header. Finally, a network header is added when the datagram is sent over the network.

Quiz

1. Explain why IP is important to the proper transmission of data.
2. Show the construction of the IP header and the meaning of each element within the header structure.
3. ICMP headers are quite small. Show the structure of a typical message header and the meaning of the bits within it.

3

Chapter 4

TCP and UDP

Yesterday's text examined the Internet Protocol (IP) in considerable detail. As you might remember, the Internet Protocol handles the lower-layer functionality. Today I look at the transport layer, where the Transmission Control Protocol (TCP) and User Datagram Protocol (UDP) come into play.

TCP is one of the most widely used transport layer protocols, expanding from its original implementation on the ARPANET to connecting commercial sites all over the world. On Day 1, "Open Systems, Standards, and Protocols," you looked at the OSI seven-layer model, which bears a striking resemblance to TCP/IP's layered model, so it is not surprising that many of the features of the OSI transport layer were based on TCP.

In theory, a transport layer protocol could be a very simple software routine, but TCP cannot be called simple. Why use a transport layer that is as complex as TCP? The most important reason depends on IP's unreliability. As you saw yesterday, IP does not guarantee delivery of a datagram; it is a connectionless system with no reliability. IP simply handles the routing of datagrams, and if problems occur, IP discards the packet without a second thought (generating an ICMP error message back to the sender in the process). The task of ascertaining the status of the datagrams sent over a network and handling the resending of information if parts have been discarded falls to TCP, which can be thought of as riding shotgun over IP.

Most users think of TCP and IP as a tightly knit pair, but TCP can be (and frequently is) used with other protocols without IP. For example, TCP or parts of it are used in the File Transfer Protocol (FTP) and the Simple Mail Transfer Protocol (SMTP), both of which do not use IP.

What Is TCP?

The Transmission Control Protocol provides a considerable number of services to the IP layer and the upper layers. Most importantly, it provides a connection-oriented protocol to the upper layers that enable an application to be sure that a datagram sent out over the network was received in its entirety. In this role, TCP acts as a message-validation protocol providing reliable communications. If a datagram is corrupted or lost, TCP usually handles the retransmission, rather than the applications in the higher layers.

 NOTE

> TCP is not a piece of software. It is a communications protocol. When you install a TCP stack on your machine, you are installing the TCP layer, and usually a lot more software to provide the rest of the TCP/IP services. TCP is used as a catch-all phrase for TCP/IP in many cases.

TCP manages the flow of datagrams from the higher layers to the IP layer, as well as incoming datagrams from the IP layer up to the higher level protocols. TCP has to ensure that priorities and security are properly respected. TCP must be capable of handling the termination of an application above it that was expecting incoming datagrams, as well as failures in the lower layers. TCP also must maintain a state table of all data streams in and out of the TCP layer. The isolation of all these services in a separate layer enables applications to be designed without regard to flow control or message reliability. Without the TCP layer, each application would have to implement the services themselves, which is a waste of resources.

TCP resides in the transport layer, positioned above IP but below the upper layers and their applications, as shown in Figure 4.1. TCP resides only on devices that actually process datagrams, ensuring that the datagram has gone from the source to the target machine. It does not reside on a device that simply routes datagrams, so there is usually no TCP layer in a gateway. This makes sense, because on a gateway the datagram has no need to go higher in the layered model than the IP layer.

Figure 4.1.
TCP provides end-to-end communications.

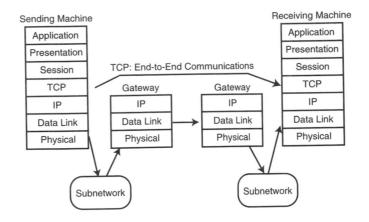

Because TCP is a connection-oriented protocol responsible for ensuring the transfer of a datagram from the source to destination machine (end-to-end communications), TCP must receive communications messages from the destination machine to acknowledge receipt of the datagram. The term *virtual circuit* is usually used to refer to the communications between the two end machines, most of which are simple acknowledgment messages (either confirmation of receipt or a failure code) and datagram sequence numbers.

Following a Message

To illustrate the role of TCP, it is instructive to follow a sample message between two machines. The processes are simplified at this stage, to be expanded on later today. The message originates from an application in an upper layer and is passed to TCP from the next higher layer in the architecture through some protocol (often referred to as an upper-layer protocol, or ULP, to indicate that it resides above TCP). The message is passed as a *stream*—a sequence of individual characters sent asynchronously. This is in contrast to most protocols, which use fixed blocks of data. This can pose some conversion problems with applications that handle only formally constructed blocks of data or insist on fixed-size messages.

TCP receives the stream of bytes and assembles them into TCP *segments*, or packets. In the process of assembling the segment, header information is attached at the front of the data. Each segment has a checksum calculated and embedded within the header, as well as a sequence number if there is more than one segment in the entire message. The length of the segment is usually determined by TCP or by a system value set by the system administrator. (The length of TCP segments has nothing to do with the IP datagram length, although there is sometimes a relationship between the two.)

If two-way communications are required (such as with Telnet or FTP), a connection (virtual circuit) between the sending and receiving machines is established prior to passing the segment to IP for routing. This process starts with the sending TCP software issuing a request for a TCP connection with the receiving machine. In the message is a unique number (called a socket number) that identifies the sending machine's connection. The receiving TCP software assigns its own unique socket number and sends it back to the original machine. The two unique numbers then define the connection between the two machines until the virtual circuit is terminated. (I look at sockets in a little more detail in a moment.)

After the virtual circuit is established, TCP sends the segment to the IP software, which then issues the message over the network as a datagram. IP can perform any of the changes to the segment that you saw in yesterday's material, such as fragmenting it and reassembling it at the destination machine. These steps are completely transparent to the TCP layers, however. After winding its way over the network, the receiving machine's IP passes the received segment up to the recipient machine's TCP layer, where it is processed and passed up to the applications above it using an upper-layer protocol.

If the message was more than one TCP segment long (not IP datagrams), the receiving TCP software reassembles the message using the sequence numbers contained in each segment's header. If a segment is missing or corrupt (which can be determined from the checksum), TCP returns a message with the faulty sequence number in the body. The originating TCP software can then resend the bad segment.

If only one segment is used for the entire message, after comparing the segment's checksum with a newly calculated value, the receiving TCP software can generate either a positive acknowledgment (ACK) or a request to resend the segment and route the request back to the sending layer.

The receiving machine's TCP implementation can perform a simple flow control to prevent buffer overload. It does this by sending a buffer size called a window value to the sending machine, following which the sender can send only enough bytes to fill the window. After that, the sender must wait for another window value to be received. This provides a handshaking protocol between the two machines, although it slows down the transmission time and slightly increases network traffic.

NOTE

The use of a sliding window is more efficient than a single block send and acknowledgment scheme because of delays waiting for the acknowledgment. By implementing a sliding window, several blocks can be sent at once. A properly configured sliding window protocol provides a much higher throughput.

4

As with most connection-based protocols, timers are an important aspect of TCP. The use of a timer ensures that an undue wait is not involved while waiting for an ACK or an error message. If the timers expire, an incomplete transmission is assumed. Usually an expiring timer before the sending of an acknowledgment message causes a retransmission of the datagram from the originating machine.

Timers can cause some problems with TCP. The specifications for TCP provide for the acknowledgment of only the highest datagram number that has been received without error, but this cannot properly handle fragmentary reception. If a message is composed of several datagrams that arrive out of order, the specification states that TCP cannot acknowledge the reception of the message until all the datagrams have been received. So even if all but one datagram in the middle of the sequence have been successfully received, a timer might expire and cause all the datagrams to be resent. With large messages, this can cause an increase in network traffic.

If the receiving TCP software receives duplicate datagrams (as can occur with a retransmission after a timeout or due to a duplicate transmission from IP), the receiving version of TCP discards any duplicate datagrams, without bothering with an error message. After all, the sending system cares only that the message was received—not how many copies were received.

TCP does not have a negative acknowledgment (NAK) function; it relies on a timer to indicate lack of acknowledgment. If the timer has expired after sending the datagram without receiving an acknowledgment of receipt, the datagram is assumed to have been lost and is retransmitted. The sending TCP software keeps copies of all unacknowledged datagrams in a buffer until they have been properly acknowledged. When this happens, the retransmission timer is stopped, and the datagram is removed from the buffer.

TCP supports a push function from the upper-layer protocols. A push is used when an application wants to send data immediately and confirm that a message passed to TCP has been successfully transmitted. To do this, a push flag is set in the ULP connection, instructing TCP to forward any buffered information from the application to the destination as soon as possible (as opposed to holding it in the buffer until it is ready to transmit it).

Ports and Sockets

All upper-layer applications that use TCP (or UDP) have a port number that identifies the application. In theory, port numbers can be assigned on individual machines, or however the administrator desires, but some conventions have been adopted to enable better communications between TCP implementations. This enables the port number to identify the type of service that one TCP system is requesting from another. Port numbers can be changed, although this can cause difficulties. Most systems maintain a file of port numbers and their corresponding service.

Typically, port numbers above 255 are reserved for private use of the local machine, but numbers below 255 are used for frequently used processes. A list of frequently used port numbers is published by the Internet Assigned Numbers Authority and is available through an RFC or from many sites that offer Internet summary files for downloading. The commonly used port numbers on this list are shown in Table 4.1. The numbers 0 and 255 are reserved.

Table 4.1. Frequently used TCP port numbers.

Port Number	Process Name	Description
1	TCPMUX	TCP Port Service Multiplexer
5	RJE	Remote Job Entry
7	ECHO	Echo
9	DISCARD	Discard
11	USERS	Active Users
13	DAYTIME	Daytime
17	Quote	Quotation of the Day
19	CHARGEN	Character generator
20	FTP-DATA	File Transfer Protocol—Data
21	FTP	File Transfer Protocol—Control
23	TELNET	Telnet
25	SMTP	Simple Mail Transfer Protocol
27	NSW-FE	NSW User System Front End
29	MSG-ICP	MSG-ICP
31	MSG-AUTH	MSG Authentication
33	DSP	Display Support Protocol
35		Private Print Servers
37	TIME	Time
39	RLP	Resource Location Protocol
41	GRAPHICS	Graphics
42	NAMESERV	Host Name Server
43	NICNAME	Who Is
49	LOGIN	Login Host Protocol
53	DOMAIN	Domain Name Server
67	BOOTPS	Bootstrap Protocol Server
68	BOOTPC	Bootstrap Protocol Client

4

Port Number	Process Name	Description
69	TFTP	Trivial File Transfer Protocol
79	FINGER	Finger
101	HOSTNAME	NIC Host Name Server
102	ISO-TSAP	ISO TSAP
103	X400	X.400
104	X400SND	X.400 SND
105	CSNET-NS	CSNET Mailbox Name Server
109	POP2	Post Office Protocol v2
110	POP3	Post Office Protocol v3
111	RPC	Sun RPC Portmap
137	NETBIOS-NS	NETBIOS Name Service
138	NETBIOS-DG	NETBIOS Datagram Service
139	NETBIOS-SS	NETBIOS Session Service
146	ISO-TP0	ISO TP0
147	ISO-IP	ISO IP
150	SQL-NET	SQL NET
153	SGMP	SGMP
156	SQLSRV	SQL Service
160	SGMP-TRAPS	SGMP TRAPS
161	SNMP	SNMP
162	SNMPTRAP	SNMPTRAP
163	CMIP-MANAGE	CMIP/TCP Manager
164	CMIP-AGENT	CMIP/TCP Agent
165	XNS-Courier	Xerox
179	BGP	Border Gateway Protocol

Each communication circuit into and out of the TCP layer is uniquely identified by a combination of two numbers, which together are called a socket. The socket is composed of the IP address of the machine and the port number used by the TCP software. Both the sending and receiving machines have sockets. Because the IP address is unique across the internetwork, and the port numbers are unique to the individual machine, the socket numbers are also unique across the entire internetwork. This enables a process to talk to another process across the network, based entirely on the socket number.

NOTE

TCP uses the connection (not the protocol port) as a fundamental element. A completed connection has two end points. This enables a protocol port to be used for several connections at the same time (multiplexing).

The last section examined the process of establishing a message. During the process, the sending TCP requests a connection with the receiving TCP, using the unique socket numbers. This process is shown in Figure 4.2. If the sending TCP wants to establish a Telnet session from its port number 350, the socket number would be composed of the source machine's IP address and the port number (350), and the message would have a destination port number of 23 (Telnet's port number). The receiving TCP has a source port of 23 (Telnet) and a destination port of 350 (the sending machine's port).

Figure 4.2.

Setting up a virtual circuit with socket numbers.

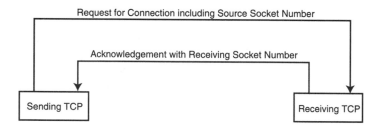

The sending and receiving machines maintain a port table, which lists all active port numbers. The two machines involved have reversed entries for each session between the two. This is called binding and is shown in Figure 4.3. The source and destination numbers are simply reversed for each connection in the port table. Of course, the IP addresses, and hence the socket numbers, are different.

Figure 4.3.

Binding entries in port tables.

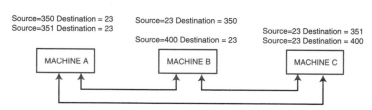

4

If the sending machine is requesting more than one connection, the source port numbers are different, even though the destination port numbers might be the same. For example, if the sending machine were trying to establish three Telnet sessions simultaneously, the source machine port numbers might be 350, 351, and 352, and the destination port numbers would all be 23.

It is possible for more than one machine to share the same destination socket—a process called multiplexing. In Figure 4.4, three machines are establishing Telnet sessions with a destination. They all use destination port 23, which is port multiplexing. Because the datagrams emerging from the port have the full socket information (with unique IP addresses), there is no confusion as to which machine a datagram is destined for.

Figure 4.4.
Multiplexing one destination port.

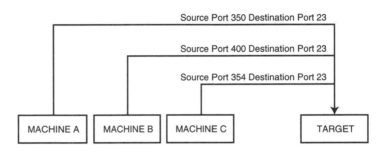

When multiple sockets are established, it is conceivable that more than one machine might send a connection request with the same source and destination ports. However, the IP addresses for the two machines are different, so the sockets are still uniquely identified despite identical source and destination port numbers.

TCP Communications with the Upper Layers

TCP must communicate with applications in the upper layer and a network system in the layer below. Several messages are defined for the upper-layer protocol to TCP communications, but there is no defined method for TCP to talk to lower layers (usually, but not necessarily, IP). TCP expects the layer beneath it to define the communication method. It is usually assumed that TCP and the transport layer communicate asynchronously.

The TCP to upper-layer protocol (ULP) communication method is well-defined, consisting of a set of service request primitives. The primitives involved in ULP to TCP communications are shown in Table 4.2.

Table 4.2. ULP-TCP service primitives.

Command	Parameters Expected
ULP to TCP Service Request Primitives	
ABORT	Local connection name
ACTIVE-OPEN	Local port, remote socket Optional: ULP timeout, timeout action, precedence, security, options
ACTIVE-OPEN-WITH-DATA	Source port, destination socket, data, data length, push flag, urgent flag Optional: ULP timeout, timeout action, precedence, security
ALLOCATE	Local connection name, data length
CLOSE	Local connection name
FULL-PASSIVE-OPEN	Local port, destination socket Optional: ULP timeout, timeout action, precedence, security, options
RECEIVE	Local connection name, buffer address, byte count, push flag, urgent flag
SEND	Local connection name, buffer address, data length, push flag, urgent flag Optional: ULP timeout, timeout action
STATUS	Local connection name
UNSPECIFIED-PASSIVE-OPEN	Local port Optional: ULP timeout, timeout action, precedence, security, options
TCP to ULP Service Request Primitives	
CLOSING	Local connection name
DELIVER	Local connection name, buffer address, data length, urgent flag
ERROR	Local connection name, error description
OPEN-FAILURE	Local connection name
OPEN-ID	Local connection name, remote socket, destination address
OPEN-SUCCESS	Local connection name

4

Command	Parameters Expected
TCP to ULP Service Request Primitives	
STATUS RESPONSE	Local connection name, source port, source address, remote socket, connection state, receive window, send window, amount waiting ACK, amount waiting receipt, urgent mode, precedence, security, timeout, timeout action
TERMINATE	Local connection name, description

Passive and Active Ports

TCP enables two methods to establish a connection: active and passive. An active connection establishment happens when TCP issues a request for the connection, based on an instruction from an upper-level protocol that provides the socket number. A passive approach takes place when the upper-level protocol instructs TCP to wait for the arrival of connection requests from a remote system (usually from an active open instruction). When TCP receives the request, it assigns a port number. This enables a connection to proceed rapidly, without waiting for the active process.

There are two passive open primitives. A specified passive open creates a connection when the precedence level and security level are acceptable. An unspecified passive open opens the port to any request. The latter is used by servers that are waiting for clients of an unknown type to connect to them.

TCP has strict rules about the use of passive and active connection processes. Usually a passive open is performed on one machine, while an active open is performed on the other, with specific information about the socket number, precedence (priority), and security levels.

Although most TCP connections are established by an active request to a passive port, it is possible to open a connection without a passive port waiting. In this case, the TCP that sends a request for a connection includes both the local socket number and the remote socket number. If the receiving TCP is configured to enable the request (based on the precedence and security settings, as well as application-based criteria), the connection can be opened. This process is looked at again in the section titled "TCP and Connections."

TCP Timers

TCP uses several timers to ensure that excessive delays are not encountered during communications. Several of these timers are elegant, handling problems that are not immediately obvious at first analysis. The timers used by TCP are examined in the following sections, which reveal their roles in ensuring that data is properly sent from one connection to another.

The Retransmission Timer

The retransmission timer manages retransmission timeouts (RTOs), which occur when a preset interval between the sending of a datagram and the returning acknowledgment is exceeded. The value of the timeout tends to vary, depending on the network type, to compensate for speed differences. If the timer expires, the datagram is retransmitted with an adjusted RTO, which is usually increased exponentially to a maximum preset limit. If the maximum limit is exceeded, connection failure is assumed, and error messages are passed back to the upper-layer application.

Values for the timeout are determined by measuring the average time that data takes to be transmitted to another machine and the acknowledgment received back, which is called the round-trip time, or RTT. From experiments, these RTTs are averaged by a formula that develops an expected value, called the smoothed round-trip time, or SRTT. This value is then increased to account for unforeseen delays.

The Quiet Timer

After a TCP connection is closed, it is possible for datagrams that are still making their way through the network to attempt to access the closed port. The quiet timer is intended to prevent the just-closed port from reopening again quickly and receiving these last datagrams.

The quiet timer is usually set to twice the maximum segment lifetime (the same value as the Time to Live field in an IP header), ensuring that all segments still heading for the port have been discarded. Typically, this can result in a port being unavailable for up to 30 seconds, prompting error messages when other applications attempt to access the port during this interval.

The Persistence Timer

The persistence timer handles a fairly rare occurrence. It is conceivable that a receive window might have a value of 0, causing the sending machine to pause transmission. The message to restart sending might be lost, causing an infinite delay. The persistence timer waits a preset time and then sends a one-byte segment at predetermined intervals to ensure that the receiving machine is still clogged.

The receiving machine resends the zero window-size message after receiving one of these status segments, if it is still backlogged. If the window is open, a message giving the new value is returned, and communications are resumed.

The Keep-Alive Timer and the Idle Timer

Both the keep-alive timer and the idle timer were added to the TCP specifications after their original definition. The keep-alive timer sends an empty packet at regular intervals to ensure that the connection to the other machine is still active. If no response has been received after sending the message by the time the idle timer has expired, the connection is assumed to be broken.

The keep-alive timer value is usually set by an application, with values ranging from 5 to 45 seconds. The idle timer is usually set to 360 seconds.

 NOTE

> TCP uses adaptive timer algorithms to accommodate delays. The timers adjust themselves to the delays experienced over a connection, altering the timer values to reflect inherent problems.

4

Transmission Control Blocks and Flow Control

TCP has to keep track of a lot of information about each connection. It does this through a Transmission Control Block (TCB), which contains information about the local and remote socket numbers, the send and receive buffers, security and priority values, and the current segment in the queue. The TCB also manages send and receive sequence numbers.

The TCB uses several variables to keep track of the send and receive status and to control the flow of information. These variables are shown in Table 4.3.

Table 4.3. TCP send and receive variables.

Variable Name	Description
	Send Variables
SND.UNA	Send Unacknowledged
SND.NXT	Send Next

continues

Table 4.3. continued

Variable Name	Description
	Send Variables
SND.WND	Send window
SND.UP	Sequence number of last urgent set
SND.WL1	Sequence number for last window update
SND.WL2	Acknowledgment number for last window update
SND.PUSH	Sequence number of last pushed set
ISS	Initial send sequence number
	Receive Variables
RCV.NXT	Sequence number of next received set
RCV.WND	Number of sets that can be received
RCV.UP	Sequence number of last urgent data
RCV.IRS	Initial receive sequence number

Using these variables, TCP controls the flow of information between two sockets. A sample connection session helps illustrate the use of the variables. It begins with Machine A wanting to send five blocks of data to Machine B. If the window limit is seven blocks, a maximum of seven blocks can be sent without acknowledgment. The SND.UNA variable on Machine A indicates how many blocks have been sent but are unacknowledged (5), and the SND.NXT variable has the value of the next block in the sequence (6). The value of the SND.WND variable is 2 (seven blocks possible, minus five sent), so only two more blocks could be sent without overloading the window. Machine B returns a message with the number of blocks received, and the window limit is adjusted accordingly.

The passage of messages back and forth can become quite complex as the sending machine forwards blocks unacknowledged up to the window limit, waiting for acknowledgment of earlier blocks that have been removed from the incoming cue, and then sending more blocks to fill the window again. The tracking of the blocks becomes a matter of bookkeeping, but with large window limits and traffic across internetworks that sometimes cause blocks to go astray, the process is, in many ways, remarkable.

TCP Protocol Data Units

As mentioned earlier, TCP must communicate with IP in the layer below (using an IP-defined method) and applications in the upper layer (using the TCP-ULP primitives). TCP also must communicate with other TCP implementations across networks. To do this, it uses Protocol Data Units (PDUs), which are called segments in TCP parlance.

The layout of the TCP PDU (commonly called the header) is shown in Figure 4.5.

Figure 4.5.

The TCP Protocol Data Unit.

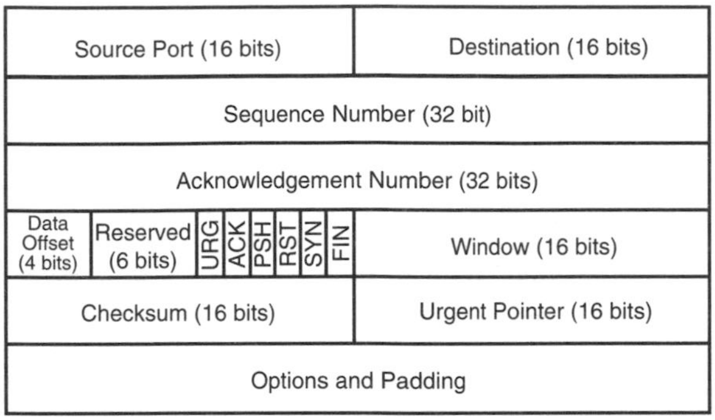

The different fields are as follows:

- [ ] **Source port:** A 16-bit field that identifies the local TCP user (usually an upper-layer application program).
- [ ] **Destination port:** A 16-bit field that identifies the remote machine's TCP user.
- [ ] **Sequence number:** A number indicating the current block's position in the overall message. This number is also used between two TCP implementations to provide the initial send sequence (ISS) number.
- [ ] **Acknowledgment number:** A number that indicates the next sequence number expected. In a backhanded manner, this also shows the sequence number of the last data received; it shows the last sequence number received plus 1.
- [ ] **Data offset:** The number of 32-bit words that are in the TCP header. This field is used to identify the start of the data field.
- [ ] **Reserved:** A 6-bit field reserved for future use. The 6 bits must be set to 0.
- [ ] **Urg flag:** If on (a value of 1), indicates that the urgent pointer field is significant.
- [ ] **Ack flag:** If on, indicates that the Acknowledgment field is significant.
- [ ] **Psh flag:** If on, indicates that the push function is to be performed.
- [ ] **Rst flag:** If on, indicates that the connection is to be reset.
- [ ] **Syn flag:** If on, indicates that the sequence numbers are to be synchronized. This flag is used when a connection is being established.
- [ ] **Fin flag:** If on, indicates that the sender has no more data to send. This is the equivalent of an end-of-transmission marker.

☐ **Window:** A number indicating how many blocks of data the receiving machine can accept.

☐ **Checksum:** Calculated by taking the 16-bit one's complement of the one's complement sum of the 16-bit words in the header (including pseudo-header) and text together. (A rather lengthy process required to fit the checksum properly into the header.)

☐ **Urgent pointer:** Used if the urg flag was set; it indicates the portion of the data message that is urgent by specifying the offset from the sequence number in the header. No specific action is taken by TCP with respect to urgent data; the action is determined by the application.

☐ **Options:** Similar to the IP header option field, this is used for specifying TCP options. Each option consists of an option number (one byte), the number of bytes in the option, and the option values. Only three options are currently defined for TCP:

    0 End of option list

    1 No operation

    2 Maximum segment size

☐ **Padding:** Filled to ensure that the header is a 32-bit multiple.

Following the PDU or header is the data. The Options field has one useful function: to specify the maximum buffer size a receiving TCP implementation can accommodate. Because TCP uses variable-length data areas, it is possible for a sending machine to create a segment that is longer than the receiving software can handle.

The Checksum field calculates the checksum based on the entire segment size, including a 96-bit pseudoheader that is prefixed to the TCP header during the calculation. The pseudoheader contains the source address, destination address, protocol identifier, and segment length. These are the parameters that are passed to IP when a send instruction is passed, and also the ones read by IP when delivery is attempted.

TCP and Connections

TCP has many rules imposed on how it communicates. These rules and the processes that TCP follows to establish a connection, transfer data, and terminate a connection are usually presented in state diagrams. (Because TCP is a state-driven protocol, its actions depend on the state of a flag or similar construct.) Avoiding overly complex state diagrams is difficult, so flow diagrams can be used as a useful method for understanding TCP.

Establishing a Connection

A connection can be established between two machines only if a connection between the two sockets does not exist, both machines agree to the connection, and both machines have adequate TCP resources to service the connection. If any of these conditions are not met, the connection cannot be made. The acceptance of connections can be triggered by an application or a system administration routine.

When a connection is established, it is given certain properties that are valid until the connection is closed. Typically, these are a precedence value and a security value. These settings are agreed upon by the two applications when the connection is in the process of being established.

In most cases, a connection is expected by two applications, so they issue either active or passive open requests. Figure 4.6 shows a flow diagram for a TCP open. The process begins with Machine A's TCP receiving a request for a connection from its ULP, to which it sends an active open primitive to Machine B. (Refer back to Table 4.2 for the TCP primitives.) The segment that is constructed has the Syn flag set on (set to 1) and has a sequence number assigned. The diagram shows this with the notation SYN SEQ 50, indicating that the Syn flag is on and the sequence number (Initial Send Sequence number, or ISS) is 50. (Any number could have been chosen.)

Figure 4.6.

Establishing a connection.

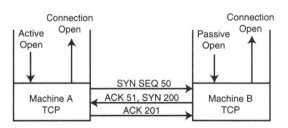

The application on Machine B has issued a passive open instruction to its TCP. When the SYN SEQ 50 segment is received, Machine B's TCP sends an acknowledgment back to Machine A with the sequence number of 51. Machine B also sets an ISS number of its own. The diagram shows this message as "ACK 51; SYN 200," indicating that the message is an acknowledgment with sequence number 51, it has the Syn flag set, and it has an ISS of 200.

Upon receipt, Machine A sends back its own acknowledgment message with the sequence number set to 201. This is "ACK 201" in the diagram. Then, having opened and acknowledged the connection, Machine A and Machine B both send connection open messages through the ULP to the requesting applications.

It is not necessary for the remote machine to have a passive open instruction, as mentioned earlier. In this case, the sending machine provides both the sending and receiving socket numbers, as well as precedence, security, and timeout values. It is common for two applications to request an active open at the same time. This is resolved quite easily, although it does involve a little more network traffic.

Data Transfer

Transferring information is straightforward, as shown in Figure 4.7. For each block of data received by Machine A's TCP from the ULP, TCP encapsulates it and sends it to Machine B with an increasing sequence number. After Machine B receives the message, it acknowledges it with a segment acknowledgment that increments the next sequence number (and hence indicates that it has received everything up to that sequence number). Figure 4.7 shows the transfer of two segments of information—one each way.

Figure 4.7.

Data transfers.

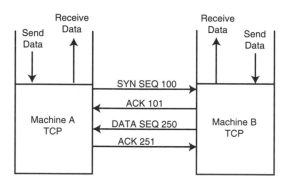

The TCP data transport service actually embodies six subservices:

- ☐ **Full duplex:** Enables both ends of a connection to transmit at any time, even simultaneously.

- ☐ **Timeliness:** The use of timers ensures that data is transmitted within a reasonable amount of time.

- ☐ **Ordered:** Data sent from one application is received in the same order at the other end. This occurs despite the fact that the datagrams might be received out of order through IP, because TCP reassembles the message in the correct order before passing it up to the higher layers.

- ☐ **Labeled:** All connections have an agreed-upon precedence and security value.

- ☐ **Controlled flow:** TCP can regulate the flow of information through the use of buffers and window limits.

- ☐ **Error correction:** Checksums ensure that data is free of errors (within the checksum algorithm's limits).

Closing Connections

To close a connection, one of the TCPs receives a close primitive from the ULP and issues a message with the Fin flag set on. This is shown in Figure 4.8. In the figure, Machine A's TCP sends the request to close the connection to Machine B with the next sequence number. Machine B then sends back an acknowledgment of the request and its next sequence number. Following this, Machine B sends the close message through its ULP to the application and waits for the application to acknowledge the closure. This step is not strictly necessary; TCP can close the connection without the application's approval, but a well-behaved system would inform the application of the change in state.

Figure 4.8.

Closing a connection.

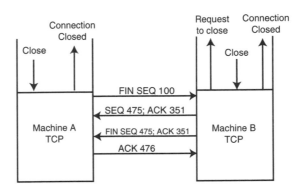

After receiving approval to close the connection from the application (or after the request has timed out), Machine B's TCP sends a segment back to Machine A with the Fin flag set. Finally, Machine A acknowledges the closure, and the connection is terminated.

An abrupt termination of a connection can occur when one side shuts down the socket. This can be done without any notice to the other machine and without regard to any information in transit between the two. Aside from sudden shutdowns caused by malfunctions or power outages, abrupt termination can be initiated by a user, an application, or a system monitoring routine that judges the connection worthy of termination. The other end of the connection might not realize that an abrupt termination has occurred until it attempts to send a message and the timer expires.

To keep track of all the connections, TCP uses a connection table. Each existing connection has an entry in the table that shows information about the end-to-end connection. The layout of the TCP connection table is shown in Figure 4.9.

Figure 4.9.

The TCP connection table.

	STATE	LOCAL ADDRESS	LOCAL PORT	REMOTE ADDRESS	REMOTE PORT
Connection 1					
Connection 2					
Connection 3					
Connection n					

The meaning of each column is as follows:

- ☐ **State:** The state of the connection (closed, closing, listening, waiting, and so on).
- ☐ **Local address:** The IP address for the connection. When in a listening state, this is set to `0.0.0.0`.
- ☐ **Local port:** The local port number.
- ☐ **Remote address:** The remote machine's IP address.
- ☐ **Remote port:** The port number of the remote connection.

User Datagram Protocol (UDP)

TCP is a connection-based protocol. There are times when a connectionless protocol is required, so UDP is used. UDP is used with both the Trivial File Transfer Protocol (TFTP) and the Remote Call Procedure (RCP). Connectionless communications don't provide reliability, meaning there is no indication to the sending device that a message has been received correctly. Connectionless protocols also do not offer error-recovery capabilities—which must be either ignored or provided in the higher or lower layers. UDP is much simpler than TCP. It interfaces with IP (or other protocols) without the bother of flow control or error-recovery mechanisms, acting simply as a sender and receiver of datagrams.

NOTE

UDP is connectionless; TCP is based on connections.

4

The UDP message header is much simpler than TCP's. It is shown in Figure 4.10. Padding can be added to the datagram to ensure that the message is a multiple of 16 bits.

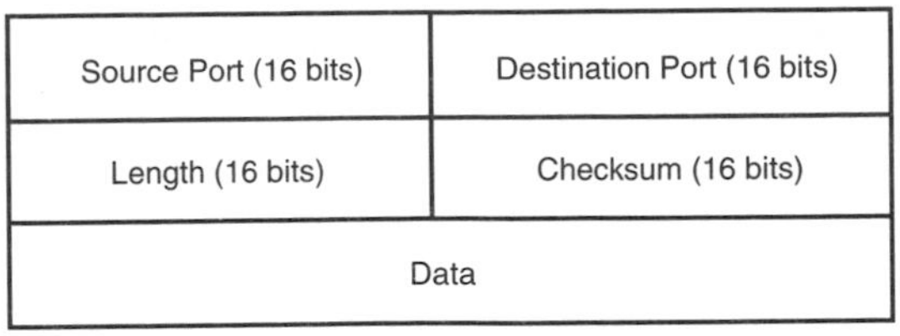

Figure 4.10.
The UDP header.

Source Port (16 bits)	Destination Port (16 bits)
Length (16 bits)	Checksum (16 bits)
Data	

The fields are as follows:

☐ **Source port:** An optional field with the port number. If a port number is not specified, the field is set to 0.

☐ **Destination port:** The port on the destination machine.

☐ **Length:** The length of the datagram, including header and data.

☐ **Checksum:** A 16-bit one's complement of the one's complement sum of the datagram, including a pseudoheader similar to that of TCP.

The UDP checksum field is optional, but if it isn't used, no checksum is applied to the data segment because IP's checksum applies only to the IP header. If the checksum is not used, the field should be set to 0.

Summary

Today, I looked at TCP in reasonable detail. Combined with the information in the last three days, you now have the theory and background necessary to better understand TCP/IP utilities, such as Telnet and FTP, as well as other protocols that use or closely resemble TCP/IP, such as SMTP and TFTP.

The details of TCP/IP are revisited later in this book, but you can now proceed to actually using TCP/IP and its toolset.

Q&A

Q **Define multiplexing and how it would be used to combine three source machines to one destination machine. Relate to port numbers.**

A Multiplexing was explained in some detail on Day 1. It refers to combining several connections into one. Three machines could each establish source ports to one machine using only one receiving port. The port numbers for the sending machines would all be different, but all three would use the same destination port number. This was shown in Figure 4.4.

Q What one word best describes the difference between TCP and UDP?

A Connections. TCP is connection-based, whereas UDP is connectionless.

Q What are port numbers and sockets?

A A port number is used to identify the type of service provided. A socket is the address of the port on which a connection is established. There is no inherent physical relationship between the two, although many machines assign certain sockets for particular services (port numbers).

Q Describe the timers used with TCP.

A The retransmission timer is used to control the resending of a datagram. The quiet timer is used to delay the reassignment of a port. The persistence timer is used to test a receive window. Keep-alive timers send empty data to keep a connection alive. The idle timer is the amount of time to wait for a disconnection to be terminated after no datagrams are received.

Q What are the six data transport subservices offered by TCP?

A The subservices are full duplex, timeliness, ordered, labeled, controlled flow, and error correction.

Workshop

The Workshop provides quiz questions to help you solidify your understanding of the material covered. Some Workshop sections of this book also contain exercises to provide you with experience in using what you have learned. Try to understand the quiz and exercise answers before continuing on to the next chapter. Answers are provided in Appendix F, "Answers to Quizzes."

Quiz

1. Draw a diagram showing the binding of port tables when three machines are sending information to each other.

2. Draw the TCP protocol data unit (PDU) and explain the meaning of each field.

3. Use a diagram to show the signals involved with two machines establishing a TCP connection. Then, show how data is transferred. Finally, show the termination process.

4. What is a TCP connection table? How is it used?

5. Draw the UDP header and explain the fields it contains.

6. What are the advantages of using UDP over TCP? When would you not want to use UDP?

Chapter 5

Gateway and Routing Protocols

TCP/IP functions perfectly well on a local area network, but its development was spurred by internetworks (more specifically by the Internet itself), so it seems logical that TCP/IP has an architecture that works well with internetwork operations. Today I examine these internetwork specifics in more detail by looking at the manner in which gateways transfer routing information between themselves.

The routing method used to send a message from its origin to destination is important, but the method by which the routing information is transferred depends on the role of the network gateways. There are special protocols developed specifically for different kinds of gateways, all of which function with TCP.

Gateways, Bridges, and Routers

To forward messages through networks, a machine's IP layer software compares the destination address of the message (contained in the Protocol Data Unit, or PDU) to the local machine's address. If the message is not for the local machine, the message is passed on to the next machine. Moving messages around small network is quite easy, but large networks and internetworks add to the complexity, requiring gateways, bridges, and routers, which try to establish the best method of moving the message to its destination.

Defining the meaning of these terms is relatively easy:

- A gateway is a device that performs routing functions, usually as a stand-alone device, that also can perform protocol translation from one network to another.
- A bridge is a network device that connects two or more networks that use the same protocol.
- A router is a network node that forwards datagrams around the network.

The gateway's protocol conversion capability is important (otherwise, the machine is no different from a bridge). Protocol conversion usually takes place in the lower layers, sometimes including the transport layer. Conversion can occur in several forms, such as when moving from a local area network format to Ethernet (in which case the format of the packet is changed) or from one proprietary file convention to another (in which case the file specifications are converted).

Bridges act as links between networks, which often have a bridge at either end of a dedicated communications line (such as a leased line) or through a packet system such as the Internet. There might be a conversion applied between bridges to increase the transmission speed. This requires both ends of the connection to understand a common protocol.

Routers operate at the network level, forwarding packets to their destination. Sometimes a protocol change can be performed by a router that has several delivery options available, such as Ethernet or serial lines.

A term you might occasionally see is *brouter,* a contraction of bridge and router. As you might expect, brouters perform the functions of both a bridge and a router, although sometimes not all functions are provided. The term brouter is often applied for any device that performs some or all of the functions of both a bridge and a router.

A term in common use when dealing with routes is *packet-switching.* A packet-switched network is one in which all transfers are based on a self-contained packet of data (like that of TCP/IP's datagrams). There are also message-switched (self-contained complete messages, as with UNIX's UUCP system) and line-switched (fixed or dedicated connections) networks, but these are rarely used with TCP/IP. Packet-switched networks tend to be faster overall than message-switched networks, but they are also considerably more complex.

Gateway Protocols

Gateway protocols are used to exchange information with other gateways in a fast, reliable manner. Using gateway protocols, transmission time over large internetworks has been shown to increase, although there is considerable support for the idea of having only one protocol across the entire Internet (which would eliminate gateway protocols in favor of TCP/IP throughout).

The Internet provides for two types of gateways: core and non-core. All core gateways are administered by the Internet Network Operations Center (INOC). Non-core gateways are not administered by this central authority but by groups outside the Internet hierarchy (who might still be connected to the Internet but administer their own machines). Typically, corporations and educational institutions use non-core gateways.

The origin of core gateways arose from the ARPANET, where each node was under the control of the governing agency. ARPANET called them *stub gateways*, whereas any gateway not under direct control (non-core in Internet terms) was called a *nonrouting gateway*. The move to the Internet and its proliferation of gateways required the implementation of the Gateway-to-Gateway Protocol (GGP), which was used between core gateways. The GGP was usually used to spread information about the non-core gateways attached to each core gateway, enabling routing tables to be built.

As the Internet grew, it became impossible for any one gateway to hold a complete map of the entire internetwork. This was solved by having each gateway handle only a specific section of the internetwork, relying on neighboring gateways to know more about their own attached networks when a message was passed. One problem that frequently occurred was a lack of information for complete routing decisions, so default routes were used.

Earlier in this book, the term *autonomous system* was introduced. An autonomous system is one in which the structure of the network it is attached to is not visible to the rest of the internetwork. Usually, a gateway leads into the network, so all traffic for that network must go through the gateway, which hides the internal structure of the local network from the rest of the internetwork.

If the local network has more than one gateway and they can talk to each other, they are considered interior neighbors. (The term interior neighbor is sometimes applied to the machines within the network, too, not just the gateways.) If the gateways belong to different autonomous systems, they are exterior gateways. Thus, when default routes are required, it is up to the exterior gateways to route messages between autonomous systems. Interior gateways are used to transfer messages into an autonomous system.

Within a network, the method of transferring routing information between interior gateways is usually the Routing Information Protocol (RIP) or the less common HELLO protocol, both of which are Interior Gateway Protocols (IGPs). These protocols are designed specifically for interior neighbors. On the Internet, messages between two exterior gateways are through the Exterior Gateway Protocol (EGP). RIP, HELLO, and EGP all rely on a frequent (every thirty seconds) transfer of information between gateways to update routing tables.

NOTE

The three gateway protocols are intertwined: EGP is used between gateways of autonomous systems, whereas the IGP's RIP and HELLO are used within the network itself. GGP is used between core gateways.

Why not use GGP for all internetwork communications, dropping the need for EGPs? The answer lies in the fact that core gateways that use GGP know about all the other core gateways on the internetwork. This simplifies their messaging and provides complete routing tables. However, core gateways usually lead into many complex networks of more autonomous networks, most of which the core gateways don't know about. However, the exterior gateways must know about all the networks directly connected to it, but not all the networks on the entire internetwork, so the routing tables and routing algorithms for a core and non-core gateway are different. This also means that messages can have different formats, because routing information for a non-core gateway has some connections that are hidden from other gateways.

It is possible for a large autonomous system to be composed of several subnetworks or areas, each of which communicates with the other areas through an IGP. Each subnetwork or area has a designated gateway, called a *border gateway*, or *border router*, to indicate that it is within an area. Border routers communicate with each other using IGP. A commonly encountered term is *boundary gateway*, which is the same as an exterior gateway or a path to another autonomous network. This is illustrated in Figure 5.1, which shows three subnetworks or areas that communicate with each other through boundary gateways or routers using IGP, and two exterior gateways (also called boundary gateways) that communicate with the rest of the internetwork using EGP.

Figure 5.1.

Interior and exterior gateways.

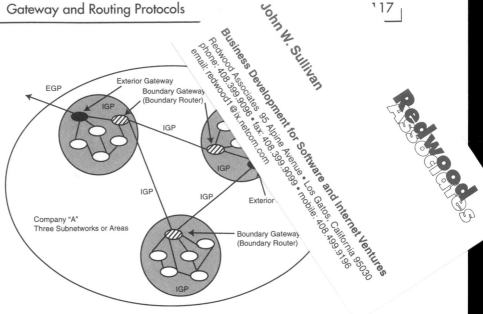

John W. Sullivan

Business Development for Software and Internet Ventures

Redwood Associates · 95 Alpine Avenue · Los Gatos, California 95030
phone: 408.399.9096 · fax: 408.399.9099 · mobile: 408.499.9196
email: redwood1@ix.netcom.com

Routing Daemons

To handle the routing tables, most UNIX systems use a daemon called routed. A few systems run a daemon called gated. Both routed and gated can exchange RIP messages with other machines, updating their route tables as necessary. The gated program can also handle EGP and HELLO messages, updating tables for the internetwork. Both routed and gated can be managed by the system administrator to select favorable routes, or to tag a route as not reliable.

The configuration information for gated and routed is usually stored as files named gated.cfg, gated.conf, or gated.cf. Some systems specify gated information files for each protocol, resulting in the files gated.egp, gated.hello, and gated.rip. A sample configuration file for EGP used by the gated process is shown here:

```
#     @gated.egp 4.1 Lachman System V STREAMS TCP  source
#   sample EGP config file

traceoptions general kernel icmp egp protocol ;
autonomoussystem 519 ;
rip no;
egp yes {
     group ASin 519 {
          neighbor  128.212.64.1 ;
     } ;
} ;
```

```
static {
     default gateway 128.212.64.1 pref 100 ;
} ;
propagate proto egp as 519 {
     proto rip gateway 128.212.64.1 {
          announce 128.212 metric 2 ;
     } ;
     proto direct {
          announce 128.212 metric 2 ;
     } ;
} ;
propagate proto rip {
     proto default {
          announce 0.0.0.0 metric 1 ;
     } ;
     proto rip {
          noannounce all ;
     } ;
} ;
```

The code above shows a number of configuration details. It starts with a number of options and the switch that turns EGP on and sets the neighbor IP address. This is followed by code that defines the way EGP behaves. Most of the details are of little interest and are seldom (if ever) modified by a user. Instead, configuration routines tend to manage this file's contents.

The UNIX system administrator also has a program called route that enables direct entry of routing table information. The information on a UNIX system regarding routing is usually stored in the file /etc/gateways.

It has become common practice to allow a default network Internet address of 0.0.0.0, which refers to a gateway on the network that should be capable of resolving an unknown address. (This is included in the previous sample configuration file as *proto default*.) The default route is used when the local machine cannot resolve the address properly. Because the routing tables on a gateway are usually more complete than those on a local machine, this helps send packets to their intended destination. If the default address gateway cannot resolve the address, an Internet Control Message Protocol (ICMP) error message is returned to the sender.

Routing

Routing refers to the transmission of a packet of information from one machine through another. Each machine that the packet enters analyzes the contents of the packet header and decides its action based on the information within the header. If the destination address of the packet matches the machine's address, the packet should be retained and processed by higher-level protocols. If the destination address doesn't match the machine's, the packet is forwarded further around the network. Forwarding can be to the destination machine itself, or to a gateway or bridge if the packet is to leave the local network.

5

Routing is a primary contributor to the complexity of packet-switched networks. It is necessary to account for an optimal path from source to destination machines, as well as to handle problems such as a heavy load on an intervening machine or the loss of a connection. The route details are contained in a routing table, and several sophisticated algorithms work with the routing table to develop an optimal route for a packet.

Creating a routing table and maintaining it with valid entries are important aspects of a protocol. Here are a few common methods of building a routing table:

☐ A fixed table is created with a map of the network, which must be modified and reread every time there is a physical change anywhere on the network.

☐ A dynamic table is used that evaluates traffic load and messages from other nodes to refine an internal table.

☐ A fixed central routing table is used that is loaded from the central repository by the network nodes at regular intervals or when needed.

Each method has advantages and disadvantages. The fixed table approach, whether located on each network node or downloaded at regular intervals from a centrally maintained fixed table, is inflexible and can't react to changes in the network topology quickly. The central table is better than the first option, simply because it is possible for an administrator to maintain the single table much more easily than a table on each node.

The dynamic table is the best for reacting to changes, although it does require better control, more complex software, and more network traffic. However, the advantages usually outweigh the disadvantages, and a dynamic table is the method most frequently used on the Internet.

Fewest-Hops Routing

Most networks and gateways to internetworks work on the assumption that the shortest route (in terms of machines traveled through) is the best way to route messages. Each machine that a message passes through is called a *hop*, so this routing method is known as *fewest hops*. Although experimentation has shown that the fewest-hops method is not necessarily the fastest method (because it doesn't take into account transmission speed between machines), it is one of the easiest routing methods to implement.

To provide fewest-hops routing, a table of the distance between any two machines is developed, or an algorithm is available to help calculate the number of hops required to reach a target machine. This is shown using the sample internetwork of gateways in Figure 5.2 and its corresponding table of distances between the gateways in the figure, which is shown in Table 5.1.

Figure 5.2.

An internetwork of gateways.

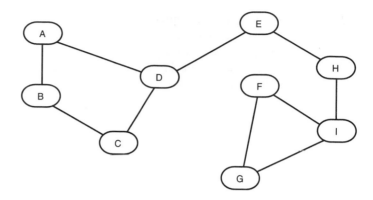

Table 5.1. Table of fewest hops from Figure 5.2.

	A	B	C	D	E	F	G	H	I
A		1	2	1	2	5	5	3	4
B	1		1	2	3	6	6	4	5
C	2	1		1	2	5	5	3	4
D	1	2	1		1	4	4	2	3
E	2	3	2	1		3	3	1	2
F	5	6	5	4	3		1	2	1
G	5	6	5	4	3	1		2	1
H	3	4	3	2	1	2	2		1
I	4	5	4	3	2	1	1	1	

When a message is to be routed using the fewest-hops approach, the table of distances is consulted, and the route with the fewest number of hops is selected. The message is then routed to the gateway that is closest to the destination network. When intermediate gateways receive the message, they perform the same type of table lookup and forward to the next gateway on the route.

There are several problems with the fewest-hops approach. If the tables of the gateways through which a message travels to its destination have different route information, it is conceivable that a message that left the source machine on the shortest route could end up following a more circuitous path because of differing tables in the intervening gateways. The fewest-hops method also doesn't account for transfer speed, line failures, or other factors that could affect the overall time to travel to the destination; it is merely concerned with the shortest apparent distance, assuming that all connections are equal. To accommodate these factors, another routing method must be used.

Type of Service Routing

This type of routing depends on the type of routing service available from gateway to gateway. This is called *type of service* (TOS) routing. It is also more formally called *quality of service* (QOS) by OSI. TOS includes consideration for the speed and reliability of connections, as well as security and route-specific factors.

To effect TOS routing, most systems use dynamic updating of tables that reflect traffic and link conditions. They also take into account current queue lengths at each gateway, because the fastest theoretical route might not matter if the message is backlogged in a queue. This information is obtained through the frequent transfer of status messages between gateways, especially when conditions deteriorate.

Dynamic updating of tables can have a disadvantage in that if tables are updated too frequently, a message might circulate through a section of the internetwork without proper routing to its destination, or proceed through a long and convoluted path. For this reason, dynamic updating occurs at regular but not too frequent intervals. To prevent stray datagrams from circulating on the internetwork too long, the Time to Live information in the IP message header is important.

NOTE

The IP header's Time to Live (TTL) field is very important to dynamic gateway routing protocols, which is why it is a mandatory field. Without it, datagrams could circulate throughout the network indefinitely.

5

The dynamic nature of TOS routing can sometimes cause a message's fragments to be routed in different ways to a destination. For example, if a long message of 10 datagrams is being sent by one route, but the routing tables are changed during transmission to reflect a backlog, the remainder of the datagrams might be sent via an alternate route. This doesn't matter, of course, because the receiving machine reassembles the message in the proper order as the datagrams are received.

Updating Gateway Routing Information

A somewhat simplified example of a dynamic update is useful at this stage. The exact communications protocols between gateways are examined in more detail later today.

Assume that two autonomous networks are connected to each other at two locations, as shown in Figure 5.3, with connections to different autonomous networks at other locations. The A–C connection and the B–D connection can both be used for routing from within the networks, depending on which is the optimal path. Gateway C has a copy of gateway A's routing table, and vice versa. Gateways B and D each have copies of the other's routing tables, as well. These copies are transmitted at intervals so the gateways can maintain an up-to-date picture of the connections available through the other gateway. The gateways use EGP to send the messages. (They would use GGP if they were core gateways.)

Figure 5.3.

Two interconnected networks.

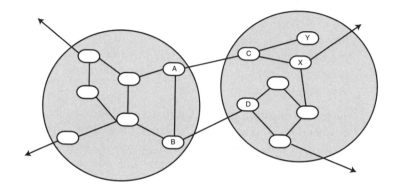

Suppose that a gateway link within one of the networks was broken due to a machine or connection failure, such as that between gateway C and machine X in Figure 5.3. Gateway C would find out about the problem through an IGP message and update its routing table to reflect the break, usually by putting the largest legal value for routing length in that entry. (Remember that IGP is a general term for any internal network protocol for gateway communications, such as RIP or HELLO.) Gateway C transfers its new copy of the routing table to gateway A.

Routing a message to machine Y would now be impossible through the C–X connection. However, because gateway A has the routing information from C, and it exchanges routing information with gateway B, which also exchanges with gateway D, any message passing through either D or B for machine Y could be rerouted up through gateway A, then C, and finally to Y. An EGP message between B–D and A–C would indicate that the new route costs less than the maximum value assigned going through C–X (which is broken), so the round-about transfer through the four gateways can be used.

EGP messages between gateways are usually sent whenever a connection problem exists and the routing information is set to its maximum (worst) value, or when a better connection alternative has been discovered for some reason. This can be because of an update from a remote gateway's routing table, or the addition of new connections, machines, or networks to the system. Whichever happens, an EGP message informs all the connected gateways of the changes.

The IGP and EGP Gateway Protocols

Gateways need to know what is happening to the rest of the network in order to route datagrams properly and efficiently. This includes not only routing information but also the characteristics of subnetworks. For example, if one gateway is particularly slow but is the only access method to a subnetwork, other gateways on the network can tailor the traffic to suit.

A GGP is used to exchange routing information between devices. It is important not to confuse routing information, which contains addresses, topology, and details on routing delays, with the algorithms used to make routing information. Usually the routing algorithms are fixed within a gateway and not modified. Of course, as the routing information changes, the algorithm adapts the chosen routes to reflect the new information.

GGPs are primarily for autonomous (self-complete) networks. An autonomous system uses gateways that are connected in one large network, such as one might find in a large corporation. Two kinds of gateways must be considered in an autonomous network. The gateways between smaller subnetworks help tie the small systems into the larger corporate network, but the gateways for each subnetwork are usually under the control of one system (usually in the IS department). These gateways are considered autonomous because the connections between gateways are constant and seldom change. These gateways communicate through an IGP.

Large internetworks like the Internet are not as static as corporate systems. Gateways can change constantly as the subsidiary networks make changes, and the communications routes between gateways are more subject to change, too. For widely spread companies, there might be gateways spread throughout the country (or the world) that are all part of the same corporate network but use the Internet to communicate. The communications between these gateways are slightly different than when they are all physically connected together. These gateways communicate through an EGP.

There are fewer rules governing IGPs than EGPs simply because the IGP can handle custom-developed applications and protocols within its local network. When the Internet is used for gateway-to-gateway communications, the messages must conform to the internetwork standards. Also, when connecting two subnetworks, it is possible to send only one message to the subnetwork gateway through EGP, which can then be duplicated, modified, and propagated to all gateways on the internal system using IGP. EGP has formalized rules governing its use.

Gateway-to-Gateway Protocol (GGP)

GGP is used for communications between core gateways. A recent improvement of the protocol, called SPREAD, is starting to be used but is not yet as common as GGP. Even if

GGP is phased out in favor of SPREAD, it is a useful illustration of gateway-to-gateway protocols.

GGP is a vector-distance protocol, meaning that messages tend to specify a destination (vector) and the distance to that destination. Vector-distance protocols are also called Bellman-Ford protocols, after the researchers who first published the idea. For a vector-distance protocol to be effective, a gateway must have complete information about all the gateways on the internetwork; otherwise, computing a distance with a fewest-hops type of protocol cannot succeed.

 NOTE

> You might recall from earlier today that core gateways have complete information about all other core gateways, so a vector-distance protocol works. Non-core gateways don't have a complete internetwork map, so GGP-type messages are not useful.

A gateway establishes its connections to other gateways by sending out messages, waiting for replies, and then building a table. This is initially accomplished when a gateway is installed and has no routing information at all. This aspect of communications is not defined within GGP but relies on network-specific messages. Once the initial table has been defined, GGP is used for all messages.

Connectivity with another gateway on the Internet is determined using the K-out-of-N method. In this procedure, a gateway sends an echo message to another gateway and waits for a reply. It repeats this every fifteen seconds. According to the Internet standards, if the gateway does not receive three (K) replies out of four (N) requests, the other gateway is considered down, or unusable, and routing messages are not sent to that gateway. This process can be repeated at regular intervals.

If a down gateway becomes active again, the Internet standards require two out of four echo messages to be acknowledged. This is called J-out-of-M, where J is two and M is four. The Internet-assigned values for J, K, M, and N can be changed for autonomous networks, but the standard defines the values for use on the Internet itself.

Each message between gateways has a sequence number that is incremented with each transmitted message. Each gateway tracks its own sequence number for sending to every other gateway it is connected to, as well as the incoming sequence numbers from that gateway. They are not necessarily the same, because more messages might flow one way than the other, although usually each message should have an acknowledgment or reply of some type.

Sequence numbers have important meanings for the messages and are not just for the sake of keeping an incremental count of the traffic volume. When a gateway receives a message from another gateway, it compares the sequence number in that message to the last received sequence number in its internal tables. If the latest message has a higher sequence number than the last message received, the gateway accepts the message and updates its sequence number to the latest received value. If the number was less than the last received sequence number, the message is considered old and is ignored, with an error message containing the just-received message sent back. This process is shown in Figure 5.4.

Figure 5.4.

Processing sequence numbers in GGP.

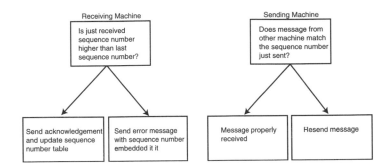

The receiving gateway acknowledges the received message by sending a return message that contains the sequence number of the just-received message. The other gateway compares that number with the number of its last sent message, and if they are the same, the gateway knows that the message was properly received. If the numbers do not match, the gateway knows an error occurred and transmits the message again.

When a message is ignored by the recipient gateway, the sending gateway receives a message with the sequence number of the ignored message. It can then determine which messages were skipped and adjust itself accordingly, resending messages that need to be sent.

The GGP message format is shown in Figure 5.5. After it is constructed, it is encapsulated into an IP datagram that includes source and target addresses. The first field is a message type, which is set to a value of 12 for routing information. The sequence number was discussed earlier and provides an incremental counter for each message. The Update field is set to a value of 0 unless the sending gateway wants a routing update for the provided destination address, in which case it is set to a value of 1. The Number of Distances field holds the number of groups of addresses contained in the current message.

For each distance group in the message, a distance value and the number of networks that can be reached at that distance are provided, followed by all the network address identifications. According to the GGP standard, not all the distances need to be reported, but the more information supplied, the more useful the message is to each gateway.

5

Figure 5.5.

The GGP message format.

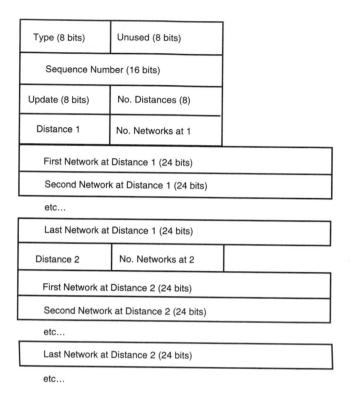

GGP does not deal with full Internet addresses specifically, so the host portion of the address does not necessarily have to be included in the address, although the network address is always provided. This can result in different lengths of addresses in the identification field (8, 16, or 24 bits, depending on the type of address).

Three other formats are used with GGP messages, as shown in Figure 5.6. The acknowledgment message uses the Type field to indicate whether the message is a positive acknowledgment (type is set to 2) or a negative acknowledgment (type is set to 10). The sequence number, as mentioned earlier today, is used to identify the message to which the acknowledgment applies.

The echo request and echo reply formats are passed between gateways to inform the gateways of status changes and to ensure the gateway is up. An echo request has the Type field set to the value 8, whereas an echo reply has the Type field set to a value of 0. Because the address of the sending gateway is embedded in the IP header, it is not duplicated in the GGP message. The remaining 24 bits of the message are unused.

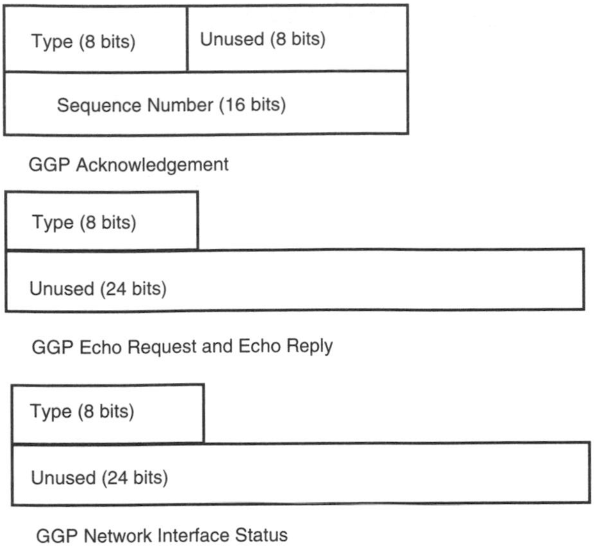

Figure 5.6.
Other GGP message formats.

Type (8 bits)	Unused (8 bits)
Sequence Number (16 bits)	

GGP Acknowledgement

Type (8 bits)
Unused (24 bits)

GGP Echo Request and Echo Reply

Type (8 bits)
Unused (24 bits)

GGP Network Interface Status

The network interface status message is used by a gateway to ensure that it is able to send and receive messages properly. This type of message can be sent to the originating gateway itself, with the type field set to a value of 9 and the IP address in the header set to the network interface's address.

The External Gateway Protocol (EGP)

As mentioned earlier, an EGP is used to transfer information between non-core neighboring gateways. Non-core gateways contain complete details about their immediate neighbors and the machines attached to them, but they lack information about the rest of the network. Core gateways know about all the other core gateways but often lack the details of the machines beyond a gateway.

EGP is usually restricted to information within the gateway's autonomous system. This prevents too much information from passing through the networks, especially when most of the information that relates to external autonomous systems would be unusable to another gateway. EGP therefore imposes restrictions on the gateways about the machines EGP passes routing information about.

5

Neighbors and EGP

Because EGP was developed to enable remote systems to exchange routing information and status messages, the protocol is heavily based in requests or commands followed by replies. The four EGP commands and their possible responses are shown in Table 5.2.

Table 5.2. EGP commands.

Command Name	Command Description	Response Name	Response Description
Request	Request that a neighbor become a gateway	Confirm/Refuse	Agree or refuse the request
Cease	Request the termination of a neighbor	Cease-Ack	Agree to termination
Hello	Request confirmation of routing to neighbor (neighbor reachability)	IHU	Confirms the routing
Poll	Request that the neighbor provide network information (network reachability)	Update	Provides network information

To understand Table 5.2 properly, you must understand the concept of *neighbor* to an internetwork. Gateways are neighbors if they share the same subnetwork. They might be gateways to the same network (such as the Internet) or work with different networks. When the two want to exchange information, they must first establish communications between each other; the two gateways are essentially agreeing to exchange routing information. This process is called *neighbor acquisition*.

WARNING

Neighbor doesn't mean the networks have to be next to each other. They are connected by a gateway, but the networks can be on different continents. The term neighbor has to do with connections, not geography.

5

The process of becoming neighbors is formal, because one gateway might not want to become a neighbor at that particular time (for any number of reasons, but usually because the gateway is busy). It begins with a Request, which is followed by either an acceptance (Confirm) or refusal (Refuse) from the second machine. If the two gateways are neighbors, either can break the relationship with a Cease message.

After two gateways become neighbors, they assure each other that they are still in contact by occasionally sending a Hello message, to which the second gateway responds with an IHU (I Heard You) message as soon as possible. These Hello/IHU messages can be sent at any time. With several gateways involved on a network, the number of Hello messages can become appreciable as the gateways continue to remain in touch. This process is called *neighbor reachability*.

The other message pair sent by EGP is network reachability, in which case one gateway sends a Poll message and expects an Update message in response. The response contains a list of networks that can be reached through that gateway, with a number representing the number of hops that must be made to reach the networks. By assembling the Update messages from different neighbors, a gateway can decide the best route to send a datagram.

Finally, an error message is returned whenever the gateway cannot understand an incoming EGP message.

EGP Messages

The layout of the different messages used by EGP are shown in Figure 5.7. The fields have the following meanings:

- [ ] The Version field holds the EGP version number of the sending machine (the current version is 2).
- [ ] The Type field identifies the type of EGP messages. There are 10 message types in EGP.
- [ ] The Code field contains a value that identifies the subtype of the message.
- [ ] The Status field is used with the Type and Code fields to reflect the current status of the gateway's state.
- [ ] The Checksum is calculated for the EGP message in the same manner as other TCP/IP headers.
- [ ] The System Number is an identification of the autonomous system that the sending gateway belongs to.
- [ ] The Sequence Number of the message is an incrementing counter for each message, also used to identify a reply to a previous message.

5

Figure 5.7.
EGP message format.

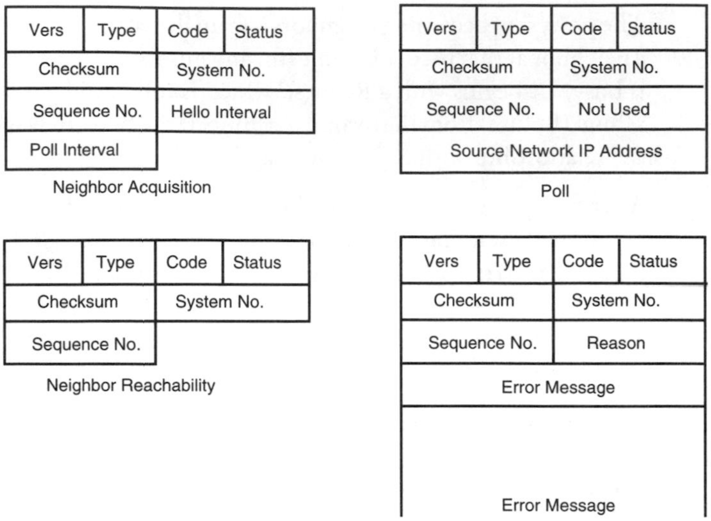

Vers	Type	Code	Status
Checksum		System No.	
Sequence No.		Hello Interval	
Poll Interval			

Neighbor Acquisition

Vers	Type	Code	Status
Checksum		System No.	
Sequence No.		Not Used	
Source Network IP Address			

Poll

Vers	Type	Code	Status
Checksum		System No.	
Sequence No.			

Neighbor Reachability

Vers	Type	Code	Status
Checksum		System No.	
Sequence No.		Reason	
Error Message			
Error Message			

The Reason field of the Error message can contain one of the following integers:

  0—Unspecified error
  1—Bad EGP header
  2—Bad EGP data field
  3—Reachability information not available
  4—Excessive polling
  5—No response received to a poll

Through a combination of the message Type, Code, and Status fields, the purpose and meaning of the EGP message can be more accurately determined. Table 5.3 shows all codes and status values.

Table 5.3. EGP messages.

Type	Description	Code	Description	Status	Description
1	Update	0		0	Indeterminate
				1	Up
				2	Down
				128	Unsolicited
2	Poll	0		0	Indeterminate
				1	Up
				2	Down

5

Type	Description	Code	Description	Status	Description
3	Neighbor Acquisition	0	Request	0	Not specified
		1	Confirm	1	Active mode
		2	Refuse	2	Passive mode
		3	Cease	3	Insufficient Resources
		4	Cease-Ack	4	Prohibited
				5	Shutting Down
				6	Parameter Problem
				7	Protocol Violation
5	Neighbor Reachability	0	Hello	0	Indeterminate
		1	I Heard You	1	Up
				2	Down
8	Error	0		0	Indeterminate
				1	Up
				2	Down
				128	Unsolicited

The Status field can indicate whether a gateway is up or down. In the down state, the gateway does not perform any routing. The Neighbor Acquisition status indicator can show whether the machine is active or passive. When passive, the gateway does not generate any Hello commands, but it responds to them. At least one neighbor has to be in the active state to issue the Hellos.

When a list of networks and their distances must be added to an EGP header, it is done in the format shown in Figure 5.8. The number of distances in the list is specified, followed by entries with the same format giving the distance (number of hops) to the gateway, the number of networks that can be reached through that gateway, and the network addresses. The number of internal and external gateways in the EGP header tells the gateway how many entries are in the list.

Using EGP, gateways can update each other and keep their routing tables current. A similar scheme is used for IGP, although the messages can be custom-designed by the network manager and application development team because they are not transmitted over the Internet.

Figure 5.8.

Routing information in an EGP header.

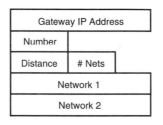

Neighbor Acquisition Messages

A Neighbor Acquisition message (Request, Confirm, and Refuse Acquisition message types) is sent when a neighbor is being checked for acquisition. The same message format is used whether the particular message is a request, a confirmation, or a refusal.

The type is set to a value of 3 to indicate that the message is a neighbor acquisition, and the Code field provides the details as to the type of Acquisition message, as shown in Table 5.4.

Table 5.4. EGP Acquisition message codes.

Code	Description
0	Request Acquisition
1	Confirm Acquisition
2	Refuse Acquisition
3	Cease
4	Cease Acknowledgment

The Status field in the Acquisition message header is set to one of eight possible values and is used to provide further information about the request. The valid Status field values are shown in Table 5.5.

Table 5.5. EGP Acquisition message Status values.

Status	Description
0	Unspecified; used when no other code is applicable
1	Active; indicates an active status mode
2	Passive; indicates a passive status mode
3	Insufficient resources available
4	Administratively prohibited
5	Going down either because of operator intervention or expiration of the t3 timer
6	Parameter error with incoming message
7	Protocol violation in incoming message or response message is incompatible with current machine state

The EGP Neighbor Acquisition message adds two new fields to the basic EGP message header. The 16-bit Hello Interval field specifies the minimum interval between Hello command pollings, in seconds. The 16-bit Poll Interval field specifies the minimum interval between Poll command pollings, again in seconds.

Neighbor Reachability Messages

The Neighbor Reachability messages are used to ensure that a neighbor that was previously acquired is still active and communicating. No extra fields are added to the basic EGP message format shown in Figure 5.7.

The Type field is set to a value of 5, but the Code field has a value of either 0 for a Hello message or 1 for an IHU (I Heard You) response. The Status field can have one of three values, shown in Table 5.6.

Table 5.6. EGP Neighbor Reachability Status field values.

Status	Description
0	Indeterminate; used when no other code is applicable
1	Neighbor is in an up state
2	Neighbor is in a down state

5

Poll Messages

The Poll messages are used to request network reachability information. An extra two fields are added to the basic EGP message format, which are a 16-bit field reserved for future use and a 32-bit IP Source Network field.

The Poll messages have the Type field set to a value of 2 and the Code field set to a value of 0. The Status field is set to one of the same three values used in the Reachability message, shown in Table 5.6.

The 16-bit Reserved field attached to the end of the basic EGP message format is ignored in the current versions of EGP. A 32-bit IP Source Network field is used to specify the IP address of the network about which the gateway is requesting reachability information.

Update Messages

Update messages are sent as a reply to a Poll message and provide information about network reachability. The format of the Update message is shown in Figure 5.9 and is similar to the GGP format discussed earlier.

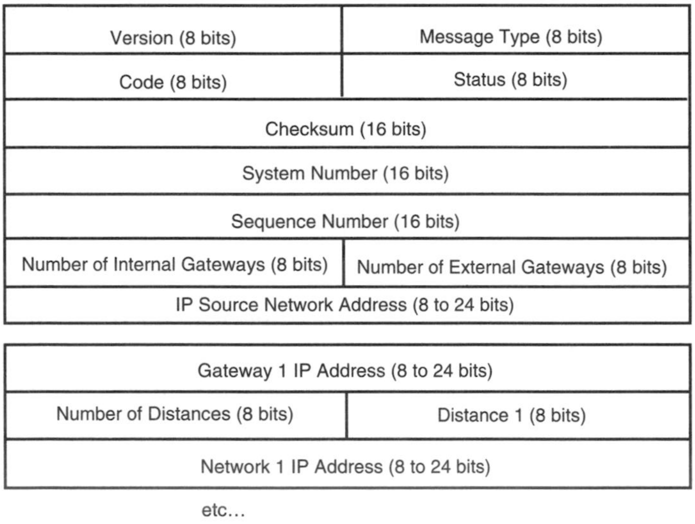

Figure 5.9.

EGP Update message format.

Version (8 bits)	Message Type (8 bits)
Code (8 bits)	Status (8 bits)
Checksum (16 bits)	
System Number (16 bits)	
Sequence Number (16 bits)	
Number of Internal Gateways (8 bits)	Number of External Gateways (8 bits)
IP Source Network Address (8 to 24 bits)	

Gateway 1 IP Address (8 to 24 bits)	
Number of Distances (8 bits)	Distance 1 (8 bits)
Network 1 IP Address (8 to 24 bits)	

etc...

The Type of an Update message is set to 1, and the Code is set to 0. The Status field is set to one of the values shown in Table 5.7. (The values are the same as those for Reachability and Poll messages except for the addition of one value.)

5

Table 5.7. EGP Update message Status field values.

Status	Description
0	Indeterminate; used when no other code is applicable
1	Neighbor is in an up state
2	Neighbor is in a down state
128	Unsolicited message

After the familiar EGP header information are three new fields. The number of internal gateways and number of external gateways fields specify the number of interior and exterior gateways that are reported in the message, respectively. The IP Source Network Address field contains the IP address of the network to which the information relates.

Following the three gateway summaries and the usual header are one or more sets of information about each gateway the current system is sending information about. These are called gateway blocks because each set of fields refers to one gateway. The first field is the gateway's IP address. The Number of Distances field provides the number of distances that are reported in the gateway block and the number of networks that lie at that distance. Then, for each distance specified, the IP network address of each network is provided. Many blocks of gateway information can be provided in an Update message.

Error Messages

The final EGP message is the Error message, which has the same format as the basic EGP message, with two fields attached. The 16-bit first field is reserved. Following this is a 96-bit field that contains the first 96 bits of the message that generated the error.

EGP to GGP Messages

Core gateways use GGP, and non-core gateways use EGP, so there must be some method for the two to communicate with each other to find out about hidden machines and networks that lie beyond their routing tables. This is shown in Figure 5.10, where gateway A is a core gateway leading from the internetwork to a network that has non-core gateways leading to two other networks. Another gateway on the internetwork does not have information about the networks and gateways past the core gateway, unless specifically updated about them through a request.

5

Figure 5.10.

Core and non-core gateways.

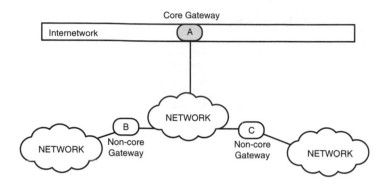

The Internet uses a method by which any autonomous (non-core) gateway can send reachability information to other systems, which must also go to at least one core gateway. If there is a larger autonomous network, one gateway usually assumes the responsibility for handling this reachability information. In Figure 5.10, gateway A is responsible for sending information about the three networks that lead from it, as well as the two non-core gateways.

EGPs use a polling process to keep themselves aware of their neighbors as they become active or go down, and to exchange routing and status information with all their neighbors. EGP is also a state-driven protocol, meaning that it depends on a state table containing values that reflect gateway conditions and a set of operations that must be performed when a state table entry changes. There are five states, as shown in Table 5.8.

Table 5.8. EGP states.

State	Description
0	Idle
1	Acquisition
2	Down
3	Up
4	Cease

The meanings of each of these EGP states follow:

☐ An idle state means the gateway is not involved in any activity and has no resources allocated to it. It usually responds to a message to initialize itself but ignores all other messages unless it switches to either the down or acquisition states.

☐ An acquisition state enables a gateway to transmit messages but not act as a full messaging gateway. It can receive messages and change to either down or idle states.

☐ The down state is when the gateway is not operational as far as polling operations are concerned. Messages are neither received nor generated.

☐ The up state is used whenever a gateway is processing and responding to all EGP messages it receives and can transmit messages.

☐ A gateway is in cease state when the gateway ceases all updating operations but can still send and receive Cease and Cease Acknowledgment messages.

All EGP messages fall into one of three categories: commands, responses, or indications. A command usually requires an action to be performed, whereas a response is a reply to a command to perform some action. An indication shows current status. Command-response signals are shown in Table 5.9.

Table 5.9. EGP commands and their responses.

Command	Response
Request	Confirm
Refuse	none
Error	none
Cease	Cease Ack
Error	none
Hello	IHU (I Heard You)
Error	none
Poll	Update
Error	none

EGP State Variables and Timers

As mentioned earlier, EGP is state-driven, which means that the current state of the system depends on the last message received, or the condition of one of the software timers. EGP maintains a state table with several parameters that can be referenced to determine actions. These values usually refer to delays between sending or receiving messages of a specific type. In addition, a set of timers is maintained for ensuring that intervals between events are reasonable. The EGP parameters and timers are shown in Table 5.10, using the names employed in the RFC that defines EGP.

Table 5.10. EGP parameters and timers.

Name	Description
M	Hello polling mode.
P1	Minimum interval acceptable between successive received Hello commands. Default is 30 seconds.
P2	Minimum interval acceptable between successive received Poll commands. Default is 120 seconds.
P3	Interval between Request or Cease command retransmissions. Default is 30 seconds.
P4	Interval during which the state variables are maintained without receiving an incoming message when in the up or down state. Default is one hour.
P5	Interval during which the state variables are maintained without receiving an incoming message when in the cease or acquisition state. Default is 2 minutes.
R	Receive sequence number.
S	Send sequence number.
T1	Interval between Hello command retransmissions.
T2	Interval between Poll command retransmissions.
T3	Interval during which reachability attempts are counted.
t1	Retransmission timer for Request, Hello, and Cease messages.
t2	Retransmission timer for Poll messages.
t3	Abort timer.

Many of the state parameters are set during the initial establishment of a connection between neighbors. The exceptions are the P1 through P5 values, which are established by the host system and are not modified by the neighbors. The send sequence number is determined only after a message has been received from the other gateway.

A full discussion of the changes between EGP states and the events that occur when a state change occurs is longer than this book and is not of relevance to this level of discussion. Therefore, the original RFC should be consulted for full state condition information. It is useful at this point simply to be aware of the state-driven nature of EGP and to understand that the state can be changed by a message reception, lack of a reply to a message, or expiration of a timer.

Interior Gateway Protocols (IGP)

There are several IGPs in use, none of which have proven themselves dominant. Usually, the choice of an IGP is made on the basis of network architecture and suitability to the network's software requirements. Earlier today, RIP and HELLO were mentioned. Both are examples of IGPs. Together with a third protocol called Open Shortest Path First (OSPF), these IGPs are now examined in more detail.

Both RIP and HELLO calculate distances to a destination, and their messages contain both a machine identifier and the distance to that machine. In general, messages tend to be long, because they contain many entries for a routing table. Both protocols are constantly connecting between neighbors to ensure that the machines are active and communicating, which can cause network traffic to build.

The Routing Information Protocol (RIP)

The Routing Information Protocol found wide use as part of the University of California at Berkeley's LAN software installations. Originally developed from two routing protocols created at Xerox's Palo Alto Research Center, RIP became part of UCB's BSD UNIX release, from which it became widely accepted. Since then, many versions of RIP have been produced, to the point where most UNIX vendors have their own enhanced RIP products. The basics are now defined by an Internet RFC.

RIP uses a broadcast technology (showing its LAN heritage). This means that the gateways broadcast their routing tables to other gateways on the network at regular intervals. This is also one of RIP's downfalls, because the increased network traffic and inefficient messaging can slow networks down compared to other IGPs. RIP tends to obtain information about all destinations in the autonomous system to which the gateways belong. Like GGP, RIP is a vector-distance system, sending a network address and distance to the address in its messages.

A machine in a RIP-based network can be either active or passive. If it is active, it sends its routing tables to other machines. Most gateways are active devices. A passive machine does not send its routing tables but can send and receive messages that affect its routing table. Most user-oriented machines (such as PCs and workstations) are passive devices. RIP employs the User Datagram Protocol (UDP) for messaging, employing port number 520 to identify messages as originating with RIP.

The format of a RIP message is shown in Figure 5.11. The message header is composed of three fields for the command (set to 1 if a request and 2 if a response), the version number of the RIP protocol, and an unused reserved field. The rest of the message contains address information. Each set begins with an identifier of the family protocol used (RIP is not specifically for the Internet's protocols, but if used on the Internet this value is set to 2) and a set of network IDs. There are 96 bits available for the network address, of which only a maximum of 32 are necessary for an Internet address. The last field is a metric value that usually identifies the number of hops to the network.

Figure 5.11.

RIP message format.

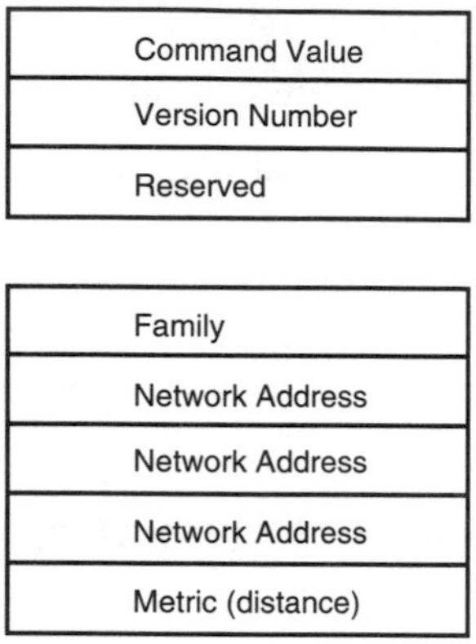

Command Value
Version Number
Reserved

Family
Network Address
Network Address
Network Address
Metric (distance)

A Request message is usually sent to another gateway when a routing update is needed. When a request is received, the system examines the message to check each network address provided. If its routing table has a distance to that network address, it is placed in the corresponding metric field in the response. If there is no entry in the local routing table, no value is returned. One convention in common use is to code the family as 1 and the metric field as 16. When this is received, the message is interpreted as a request for the entire routing table.

Each RIP-based machine in the network maintains a routing table, with an entry for each machine that it can communicate with. The table has entries for the target's IP address, its distance, the IP address of the next gateway in the path to the target, a flag to show whether the route has recently been updated, and a set of timers that control the route. The distance is expressed as a number of hops required to reach the target and has a value from 1 to 15. If the target is unreachable, a value of 16 is set.

The timers involved with RIP are devoted to each possible route in the routing table. A time-out timer is set when the route is initialized and each time the route is updated. If the timer expires (the default setting is 180 seconds) before another update, the route is considered unreachable. A second timer, called the garbage-collection timer, takes over after the time-out timer and marks when the route is completely expunged from the routing table. The garbage-collection timer has a default value of 120 seconds. If a request for a routing update is received after the time-out timer has expired but before the garbage-collection timer has expired, the entry for that gateway is sent but with the maximum value for the route value. After the garbage-collection timer has expired, the route is not sent at all.

A response timer triggers a set of messages every 30 seconds to all neighboring machines, in an attempt to update routing tables. These messages are composed of the machine's IP address and the distance to the recipient machine.

The HELLO Protocol

The HELLO protocol is used often, especially where TCP/IP installations are involved. It is different from RIP in that HELLO uses time instead of distance as a routing factor. This requires the network of machines to have reasonably accurate timing, which is synchronized with each machine. For this reason, the HELLO protocol depends on clock synchronization messages.

The format of a HELLO message is shown in Figure 5.12. The primary header fields are as follows:

☐ A checksum of the entire message
☐ The current date of the sending machine
☐ The current time of the sending machine
☐ A timestamp used to calculate round-trip delays
☐ An offset that points to the following entries
☐ The number of hosts that follow as a list

Figure 5.12.
HELLO message format.

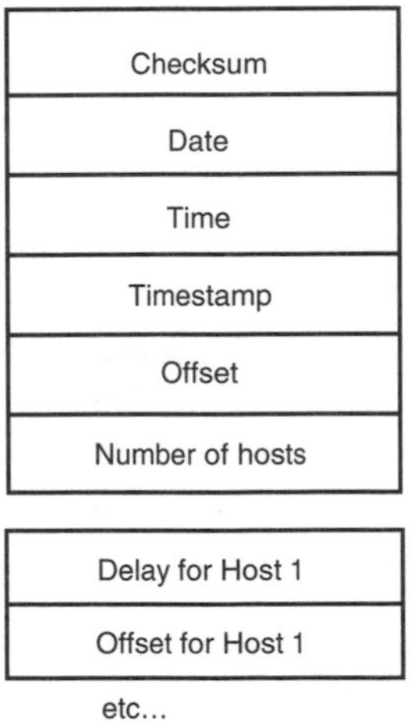

| Checksum |
| Date |
| Time |
| Timestamp |
| Offset |
| Number of hosts |

| Delay for Host 1 |
| Offset for Host 1 |

etc...

Following the header are several entries with a delay estimate to the machine and an offset, which is an estimate of the difference between the sending and receiving clocks. The offsets are important because HELLO is a time-critical protocol, so the offset enables correction between times on different machines.

The timestamp on messages is used by machines that the message passes through to calculate delays in the network. In this manner, a routing table based on realistic delivery times can be constructed.

The Open Shortest Path First (OSPF) Protocol

The Open Shortest Path First protocol was developed by the Internet Engineering Task Force, with the hope that it would become the dominant protocol within the Internet. In many ways, the name "shortest path" is inaccurate in describing this protocol's routing process (both RIP and HELLO use a shortest-path method—RIP based on distance and HELLO on time). A better description for the system would be "optimum path," in which several criteria are evaluated to determine the best route to a destination. The HELLO protocol is used for passing state information between gateways and for passing basic messages, whereas the Internet Protocol (IP) is used for the network layer.

OSPF uses the destination address and type of service (TOS) information in an IP datagram header to develop a route. From a routing table that contains information about the topology of the network, an OSPF gateway (more formally called a *router* in the RFC, although both terms are interchangeable) determines the shortest path using cost metrics, which factor in route speed, traffic, reliability, security, and several other aspects of the connection. Whenever communications must leave an autonomous network, OSPF calls this external routing. The information required for an external route can be derived from both OSPF and EGP.

There are two types of external routing with OSPF. A Type 1 route involves the same calculations for the external route as for the internal. In other words, the OSPF algorithms are applied to both the external and internal routes. A Type 2 route uses the OSPF system only to calculate a route to the gateway of the destination system, ignoring any routes of the remote autonomous system. This has an advantage in that it can be independent of the protocol used in the destination network, which eliminates a need to convert metrics.

OSPF enables a large autonomous network to be divided into smaller areas, each with its own gateway and routing algorithms. Movement between the areas is over a backbone, or the parts of the network that route messages between areas. Care must be taken to avoid confusing OSPF's areas and backbone terminology with those of the Internet, which are similar but do not mean precisely the same thing. OSPF defines several types of routers or gateways:

5

☐ An internal router is one for which all connections belong to the same area, or one in which only backbone connections are made.

☐ A border router is a router that does not satisfy the description of an internal router (it has connections outside an area).

☐ A backbone router has an interface to the backbone.

☐ A boundary router is a gateway that has a connection to another autonomous system.

OSPF is designed to enable gateways to send messages to each other about internetwork connections. These routing messages are called *advertisements*, which are sent through HELLO update messages. Four types of advertisements are used in OSPF:

☐ A Router Links advertisement provides information on a local router's (gateway) connections in an area. This message is broadcast throughout the network.

☐ A Network Links advertisement provides a list of routers that are connected to a network. It is also broadcast throughout the network.

☐ A Summary Links advertisement contains information about routes outside the area. It is sent by border routers to their entire area.

☐ An Autonomous System Extended Links advertisement contains information on routes in external autonomous systems. It is used by boundary routers but covers the entire system.

OSPF maintains several tables for determining routes, including the protocol data table (the high-level protocol in use in the autonomous system), the area data table or backbone data table (which describes the area), the interface data table (information on the router-to-network connections), the neighbor data table (information on the router-to-router connections), and a routing data table (which contains the route information for messages). Each table has a structure of its own, the details of which are not needed for this level of discussion. Interested readers are referred to the RFC for complete specifications.

OSPF Packets

As mentioned earlier, OSPF uses IP for the network layer. The OSPF specifications provide for two reserved multicast addresses: one for all routers that support OSPF (224.0.0.5) and one for a designated router and a backup router (224.0.0.6). The IP protocol number 89 is reserved for OSPF. When IP sends an OSPF message, it uses the protocol number and a Type of Service (TOS) field value of 0. Usually, the IP precedence field is set higher than normal IP messages, also.

OSPF uses two header formats. The primary OSPF message header format is shown in Figure 5.13. Note that the fields are not shown in their scale lengths in this figure for illustrative purposes. The Version Number field identifies the version of the OSPF protocol in use (currently version 1). The Type field identifies the type of message and might contain a value from those shown in Table 5.11.

Figure 5.13.

OSPF message header format.

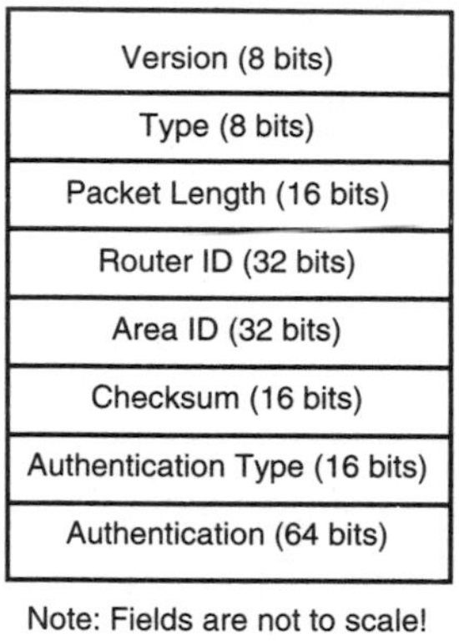

| Version (8 bits) |
| Type (8 bits) |
| Packet Length (16 bits) |
| Router ID (32 bits) |
| Area ID (32 bits) |
| Checksum (16 bits) |
| Authentication Type (16 bits) |
| Authentication (64 bits) |

Note: Fields are not to scale!

Table 5.11. OSPF header Type values.

Type	Description
1	Hello
2	Database description
3	Link state request
4	Link state update
5	Link state acknowledgment

The Packet Length field contains the length of the message, including the header. The Router ID is the identification of the sending machine, and the Area ID identifies the area the sending machine is in. The Checksum field uses the same algorithm as IP to verify the entire message, including the header.

The Authentication Type (AUType) field identifies the type of authentication to be used. There are currently only two values for this field: 0 for no authentication, and 1 for a password. The Authentication field contains the value that is used to authenticate the message, if applicable.

The second header format used by OSPF is for Link State advertisements only; it is shown in Figure 5.14. All Link State advertisements use this format, which identifies each advertisement to all routers. This header mirrors the topologic table.

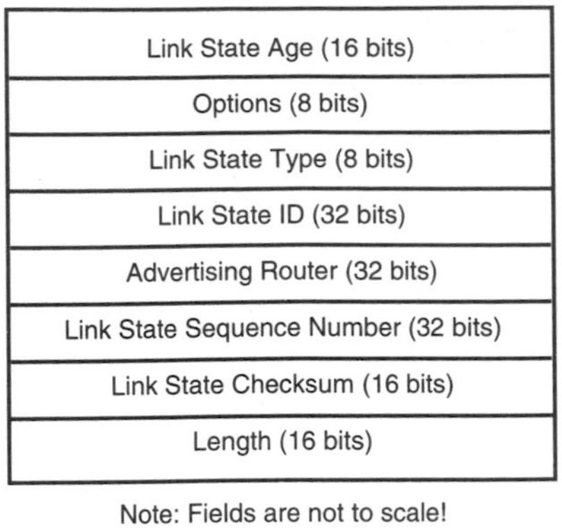

Figure 5.14.

OSPF Link State advertisement header format.

Link State Age (16 bits)
Options (8 bits)
Link State Type (8 bits)
Link State ID (32 bits)
Advertising Router (32 bits)
Link State Sequence Number (32 bits)
Link State Checksum (16 bits)
Length (16 bits)

Note: Fields are not to scale!

The Link State Age field contains the number of seconds since the Link State advertisement originated. The Options field contains any IP Type of Service (TOS) features supported by the sending machine. The Link State Type identifies the type of link advertisement, using one of the values shown in Table 5.12. The value in the Link State Type field further defines the format of the advertisement.

Table 5.12. Link State advertisement header Type values.

Value	Description
1	Router links (router to area)
2	Network links (router to network)
3	Summary link (information on the IP network)
4	Summary link (information on autonomous system border router)
5	AS external link (external to autonomous system)

The Link State ID field identifies which portion of the internetwork is described in the advertisement. The value depends on the Link State Type field and can contain IP addresses for networks or router IDs. The Advertising Router field identifies the originating router. The Link State Sequence Number is an incrementing number used to prevent old or duplicate packets from being interpreted. The Checksum field uses an IP algorithm for the entire message, including the header. Finally, the Length field contains the size of the advertisement, including the header.

5

HELLO Packets

Both types of OSPF headers are further encapsulated by the HELLO protocol, which is used for messaging between neighboring routers. The information in the HELLO header sets the parameters for the connection. The entire HELLO packet format is shown in Figure 5.15.

Figure 5.15.

OSPF HELLO packet format.

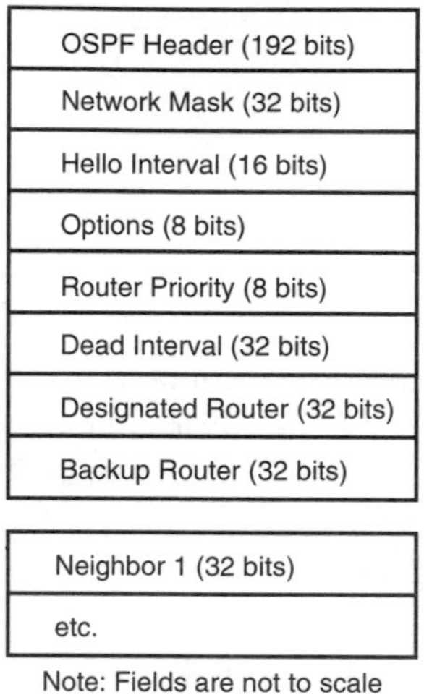

OSPF Header (192 bits)
Network Mask (32 bits)
Hello Interval (16 bits)
Options (8 bits)
Router Priority (8 bits)
Dead Interval (32 bits)
Designated Router (32 bits)
Backup Router (32 bits)

Neighbor 1 (32 bits)
etc.

Note: Fields are not to scale

After the OSPF header is the Network Mask field, which is dependent on the interface. The Hello Interval is the number of seconds between subsequent Hello packets from the same router. The Options field is for IP's Type of Service supported values. The Router Priority field defines whether the router can be designated as a backup. If the field has a 0 value, the router cannot be defined as a backup. The Dead Interval is the number of seconds before a router is declared to be down and unavailable. The Designated and Backup Router fields hold the addresses of the designated and backup routers, if there are any. Finally, each neighbor has a set of fields that contain the address of each router that has recently (within the time specified by the Dead Interval) sent HELLO packets over the network.

When this type of message is received by another router and it has been validated as containing no errors, the neighbor information can be processed into the neighbor data table.

Another message that is used to initialize the database of a router is the database description packet. It contains information about the topology of the network (either in whole or in part). To provide database description packet service, one router is set as the master, and the other is the slave. The master sends the database description packets, and the slave acknowledges them with database description responses.

The format of the database description packet is shown in Figure 5.16. After the OSPF header is a set of unused bits, followed by three 1-bit flags. When the I (initial) bit is set to 0, it indicates that this packet is the first in a series of packets. The M (more) bit, when set to 1, means that more database description packets follow this one. The MS (master/slave) bit indicates the master/slave relationship. When it has a value of 1 it means that the router that sent the packet is the master. A 0 indicates that the sending machine is the slave. The Data Descriptor Sequence Number is an incrementing counter. The rest of the packet contains Link State advertisements as seen in Figure 5.14.

Figure 5.16.
The database description packet layout.

OSPF Header (192 bits)			
Unused (29 bits)	1	M	MS
Data Descriptor Sequence Number (32)			
Database Information 1			

Link State Request and Update Packets

The Link State Request packet asks for information about a topological table from a database, whereas the Update packet can provide topological information of the types shown in Table 5.11. The Request packet is usually sent when an entry in the router's topological table is corrupted, missing, or out of date. The format of the Link State Request packet is shown in Figure 5.17. The Link State Request packet contains the OSPF header and a block of three repeating fields for the Link State Type, Link State ID, and Advertising Router.

Figure 5.17.
OSPF Link State Request packet format.

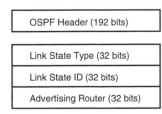

OSPF Header (192 bits)

Link State Type (32 bits)
Link State ID (32 bits)
Advertising Router (32 bits)

Note: Fields are not to scale!

The Link State Update packet has four formats, depending on the link state type: router links, network links, summary links, or autonomous systems external links. The Router Links advertisement packet is sent to neighbors periodically and contains fields for each router link and the type of service provided in each link, as shown in Figure 5.18.

5

Figure 5.18.

OSPF Router Links advertisement packet format.

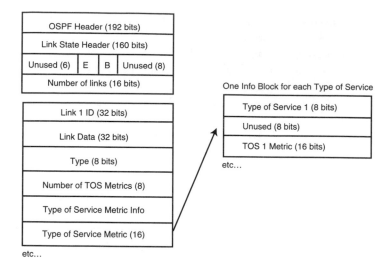

After the OSPF header and the Link State advertisement header are two single bit flags surrounded by 6- and 8-bit unused fields. The E (external) flag, when set to 1, indicates that the router is an autonomous systems (AS) boundary router. The B (border) flag, when set to 1, indicates that the router is an area border router. Following the unused 8-bit area is a field for the number of links (advertisements) in the message. Following this, the links are provided in sequence, one link to a block.

Each Link State advertisement block in the Router Links advertisement packet has a field for the Link ID (the type of router, although the value is dependent on the Type field later in the block), the Link Data (whose value is an IP address or a network mask, depending on the Type field's setting), the Type field (a value of 1 indicates a connection to another router, 2 a connection to a transit network, and 3 a connection to a stub network), and the Number of TOS field, which shows the number of metrics for the link (at least one must be provided, which is called TOS 0). Then, a repeating block is appended for each TOS, providing the type and the metric.

The other three formats available are the Network Links advertisement, Summary Links advertisement, and Autonomous Systems (AS) External Links advertisement. The fields have all been described earlier in this section.

The last packet involved in OSPF is the Link State acknowledgment packet, which is required when a Link State advertisement has been received correctly. The fields following the OSPF header are for the Link State Type, Link ID, Advertising Router ID, Link State Sequence Number, Link State Checksum value, and Link State Age, all of which have been mentioned earlier.

5

Summary

Today I looked at the gateway protocols used within the TCP/IP family specifically, as well as those in general use on the Internet and most networks. Gateways are a critical component for forwarding information from one network to another. Without gateways, each machine on the network would require a full map of every other machine on the internetwork.

As I have shown, there are several protocols of importance, depending on the role of the gateway. I also looked at the use of bridges, routers, and brouters in a network, and the role that each of these can play. With this material, I can leave the subject of gateways. Except for some message passing and administration material, you now know all you need about gateway protocols used with TCP/IP.

Q&A

Q What is a boundary gateway?

A A boundary gateway sits between two networks within a larger internetwork, as would be found in a large corporation. The boundary gateways mark the edges (or boundaries) of each LAN, passing message to other LANs within the larger internetwork. Boundary gateways do not communicate with the networks outside the organization. This task is performed by exterior gateways.

Q How are sequence numbers used to control status messages within GGP? Explain for both the sending and receiving gateways.

A The sending gateway sends packets with an incrementing sequence number. The destination gateway receives each packet and echoes back the sequence number in a message. If the destination gateway receives the next packet with a sequence number that does not follow the one last received, an error message is returned to the sender with the sequence number of the last packet in it. If the sequence number is correct, an acknowledgment is sent. As the sending gateway receives packets back from the destination, it compares the sequence number in the packet to its own internal counter. If the sequence number in the destination machine's packet does not match, the packet that would have been next in sequence from the last correctly received packet is resent.

Q What is a core gateway?

A A core gateway is one that resides as an interface between a network and the internetwork. A non-core gateway is between two LANs that are not connected to the larger internetwork.

5

Q Protocol conversion takes place in which of the following: gateways, routers, bridges, or brouters?

A Gateways perform protocol conversion. They have to because they can join two dissimilar network types. Some recent routers and brouters are capable of protocol conversion.

Q What are the three types of routing table?

A Routing tables can be fixed (a table that is modified manually every time there is a change), dynamic (one that modifies itself based on network traffic), or fixed central (one downloaded at intervals from a central repository, which can be dynamic).

Quiz

1. Define the roles of gateways, routers, bridges, and brouters.
2. What is a packet-switched network?
3. What is the difference between interior and exterior neighbor gateways?
4. What are the advantages and disadvantages of the three types of routing tables?
5. What is the HELLO protocol used for?

5

Chapter 6

Telnet and FTP

In the last five days you have seen the architecture of TCP/IP, as well as both the Internet Protocol and the Transmission Control Protocol in considerable detail. Building on these two protocols is a layer of application-layer protocols that are commonly associated with TCP/IP. Today I look at the most common application layer protocols: Telnet, File Transfer Protocol (FTP), Trivial File Transfer Protocol (TFTP), and Simple Mail Transfer Protocol (SMTP), as well as a suite of tools called the Berkeley r-utilities.

To cover all four protocols in complete detail would require several hundred pages, so today I examine the protocols' most important aspects, including their purposes, their relations to TCP and IP, their control codes and behavior, and their typical usage. Each of the four application layer protocols has advantages that make it ideally suited for a particular purpose. I hope that by the end of the day you will understand why they are used and how they fit into the TCP/IP world.

Telnet

The Telnet (telecommunications network) program is intended to provide a remote login or virtual terminal capability across a network. In other words, a user on machine A should be able to log into machine B anywhere on the network, and as far as the user is concerned, it appears that the user is seated in front of machine B. The Telnet service is provided through TCP's port number 23. (See Table 4.1 or Appendix D, "Well-Known Port Numbers," for the TCP port numbers.) The term Telnet is used to refer to both the program and the protocol that provide these services.

Telnet was developed because at one time the only method of enabling one machine to access another machine's resources (including hard drives and programs stored there) was to establish a link using communications devices such as modems or networks into dedicated serial ports or network adapters. This is a little more complicated than might appear at first glance because of the wide diversity of terminals and computers, each with their own control codes and terminal characteristics. When directly connected to another machine, the machine's CPU must manage the translation of terminal codes between the two, which puts a hefty load on the CPU. With several remote logins active, a machine's CPU can spend an inordinate amount of time managing the translations. This is especially a problem with servers that can handle many connections at once: If each had to be handled with full terminal translation, the server CPU could be bogged down just performing this function.

Telnet alleviates this problem by embedding the terminal characteristic sequences within the Telnet protocol. When two machines communicate using Telnet, Telnet itself can determine and set the communications and terminal parameters for the session during the connection phase. The Telnet protocol includes the capability not to support a service that one end of the connection cannot handle. When a connection has been established by Telnet, both ends have agreed upon a method for the two machines to exchange information, taking the load off the server CPU for a sizable amount of this work.

Usually, Telnet involves a process on the server that accepts incoming requests for a Telnet session. On UNIX systems, this process is called `telnetd`. On Windows NT and other PC-based operating systems, a Telnet Server program is usually involved. The client (the end doing the calling) runs a program, usually called `telnet`, that attempts the connection to the server. A relative of the `telnet` program is the program `rlogin`, which is common on UNIX machines and which I look at later today; see the section titled "The Berkeley Utilities."

6

NOTE

The `rlogin` program provides almost identical functionality to Telnet and adds support for the UNIX environment. Many machines, especially UNIX workstations, act as both client and server simultaneously, enabling a user to log into other machines on the network and other users to log into the user's machine.

Telnet Connections

The Telnet protocol uses the concept of a *network virtual terminal,* or NVT, to define both ends of a Telnet connection. Each end of the connection (each NVT) has a logical keyboard and printer. The logical printer can display characters, and the logical keyboard can generate characters. The logical printer is usually a terminal screen, whereas the logical keyboard is usually the user's keyboard, although it could be a file or other input stream. These terms are also used in the File Transfer Protocol (FTP) and Simple Mail Transfer Protocol (SMTP). Figure 6.1 illustrates the NVT and logical keyboard and printer.

Figure 6.1.

A network virtual terminal for Telnet.

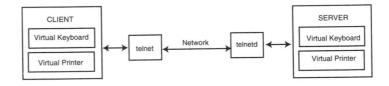

The Telnet protocol treats the two ends of the connection as NVTs. The two programs at either end (`telnet` and `telnetd` for a UNIX server) manage the translation from virtual terminals to actual physical devices. The concept of virtual terminals enables Telnet to interconnect to any type of device, as long as a mapping is available from the virtual codes to the physical device. One advantage of this approach is that some physical devices cannot support all operations, so the virtual terminal does not have those codes. When the two ends are establishing the connection, the lack of these codes is noted, and sequences that would use them are ignored. This process is straightforward: One end asks whether the function is supported, and the other replies either positively or negatively. If it is supported, the necessary codes are sent. The list of supported functions is covered quickly in this manner.

When a connection is established through Telnet, `telnetd` (or whatever program is acting as the Telnet server) starts a process on the server for running applications. Every keystroke in a Telnet session must go through several different processes, as shown in Figure 6.2. Each keystroke goes through `telnet`, `telnetd`, and the applications that are used during the Telnet session. Some applications want to communicate through a terminal device, so the remote system runs a pseudo-TTY driver that acts like a terminal to the application. If a windowed interface such as X or Motif is used on the host and remote machines, the systems must be instructed to enable windowing information to be passed back and forth; otherwise, the remote machine tries to open the windows on the server.

Figure 6.2.

A Telnet connection.

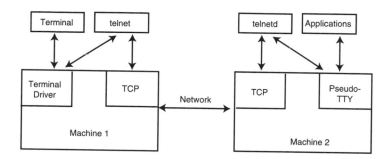

To start Telnet, you must provide either the name or the IP address of the machine to be connected with. The name can be used only if the system has a means of resolving the name into its IP address, such as with the Domain Name Service. A port name can usually be used to connect to a specific service, but this is used infrequently. For example, to connect to a machine with the IP address 205.150.89.1, you would enter this command:

```
telnet 205.150.89.1
```

If the system had the name darkstar, which was resolvable into its IP address, you could issue this command:

```
telnet darkstar
```

If no name, address, or port is specified, Telnet enters its command mode and waits for specific instructions. When the connection is established, a user ID and password are requested. You can log in with any user ID that is valid on the remote system (it does not have to be the same user ID you have on the local system). A typical connection to a UNIX server looks like this:

```
telnet 205.150.89.1
Trying...
Connected to tpci
Escape character is '^]'.
HP-UX tpci A.09.01 A 9000/720 (ttys2)
login: tparker
password: xxxxxxxx
$
```

As you can see in the preceding code, Telnet tried to connect to the remote system, told you it was connected, then set up the communications parameters between the two systems. When that was done, the login prompt was displayed (as on any UNIX terminal), followed by a password request. If the login and password are enabled, the UNIX shell prompt (a dollar sign) is shown to indicate that the remote machine is now active.

WARNING

You can use a machine name as part of the Telnet command only if the system has a means of resolving the name to its IP address. If not, no connection is established, although Telnet might remain in command mode. To exit, use Ctrl+D or the break sequence displayed as part of the start-up message.

You can enter Telnet's command mode at any time, usually by using the Ctrl+] key combination. (Press Ctrl and the right bracket key.) If you are currently connected to an active session when you enter command mode, Telnet waits for you to issue a command, execute it, and then return to the session automatically. Command mode lets you enter commands relative to the client (the machine you are physically in front of) instead of the server. You might need to do this to change directories or run a local application, for example.

Once the connection is successfully established, your session behaves as though you were on the remote machine, with all valid commands of that operating system. All instructions are relative to the server, so a directory command shows the current directory on the server, not the client. To see the client's directory, you would have to enter command mode. A sample Telnet login and logout session, calling from one UNIX workstation (merlin) to a server (tpci_hpws4, a name that can be resolved by the name server) follows:

```
merlin> telnet tpci_hpws4
Trying...
Connected to tpci_hpws4.
Escape character is '^]'.
HP-UX tpci_hpws4 A.09.01 A 9000/720 (ttys2)
login: tparker
password: xxxxxxxx
tpci_hpws4-1> pwd
/u1/tparker
tpci_hpws4-2> cd docs
tpci_hpws4-3> pwd
/u1/tparker/docs
tpci_hpws4-2> <Ctrl+d>
Connection closed by foreign host.
merlin>
```

Once you are connected to the remote machine, the session behaves exactly as if you were on that machine. To log out of the remote session, simply issue the logout command (in the previous example, the UNIX Ctrl+D combination), and you are returned to your local machine. The `telnet` program is useful when you are on an under powered machine or terminal and you want to use another machine's processing capabilities, or if another machine has a particular tool that you don't want to load on your local machine.

Telnet utilities are available for many different operating systems. Figure 6.3 shows a Windows for Workgroups Telnet application (part of a larger TCP/IP application suite from NetManage called ChameleonNFS, which I look at in much more detail on Day 10, "Setting Up a Sample Network: Clients") logging into an SCO UNIX server. Even when the local machine has a graphical interface such as Windows, you can most likely connect to remote machines using a character-based interface.

Figure 6.3.

Using Telnet from a Windows for Workgroups machine.

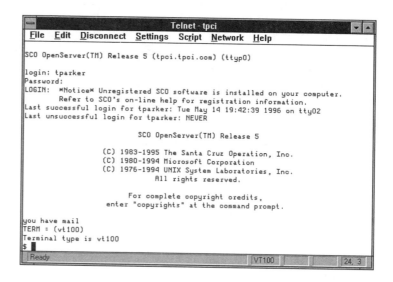

If the calling and receiving workstations use a graphical user interface (GUI) such as Motif or X, and you want to use them instead of a character-based interface, you must instruct both ends to use the local terminal for windowing (because you can't see a window on the remote terminal). Locally, a program is run that instructs the operating system to enable other machines to display directly onto the screen, and the remote must have an instruction to redirect windowing commands to the local screen. Many UNIX systems perform this function like this:

```
tpci_server-1> xhost +
tpci_server-2> telnet tpci_hpws4
Trying...
Connected to tpci_hpws4.
```

```
Escape character is '^]'.
HP-UX tpci_hpws4 A.09.01 A 9000/720 (ttys2)
login: tparker
password: xxxxxxxx
tpci_hpws4-1> setenv DISPLAY tpci_server:0.0
tpci_hpws4-2> <Ctrl+d>
Connection closed by foreign host.
tpci_server-3>
```

The UNIX xhost + instruction tells the local machine to enable the remote system to control windows on the local screen (which it normally is not allowed to do). The instruction setenv DISPLAY *machine_name* executed on the remote UNIX machine sets the UNIX shell environment variable DISPLAY to the local screen. Whenever a window must be opened (as when a Motif application is run), the windowing appears on the local screen, and the processing is conducted on the remote. These examples are for UNIX, but a similar sequence works on other machines and GUIs.

Complete applications that provide this capability to run local X and Motif windows on a Windows, Windows 95, or Windows NT machine are available from several commercial vendors. For example, Figure 6.4 shows an application running on a remote server called mandel that draws Mandelbrot figures. The server has been instructed to display the window on the local Windows for Workgroups machine using an X client package for Windows machines. The server passes all information about the size, position, and colors of the window, as well as instructions for drawing the contents to the local X client. The window appears on the Windows for Workgroups machine exactly as it would on the UNIX server.

Figure 6.4.
*Using an X client to show
UNIX X windows
on a PC.*

6

Telnet Commands

Several service options are available when a Telnet session is established. Their values can be changed during the course of a Telnet session if both ends agree (one end might be prevented from enabling or disabling a service because of administrator or resource settings). There are four verbs used by the Telnet protocol to offer, refuse, request, and prevent services: `will`, `won't`, `do`, and `don't`, respectively. The verbs are designed to be paired (`will`/`won't` and `do`/`don't`). To illustrate how these are used, consider the following Telnet session, which has the display of these verbs turned on using the `telnet` command `toggle options`:

```
tpci_server-1> telnet
telnet> toggle options
Will show option processing.
telnet> open tpci_hpws4
Trying...
Connected to tpci_hpws4.
Escape character is '^]'.
SENT do SUPPRESS GO AHEAD
SENT will TERMINAL TYPE (don't reply)
SEND will NAWS (don't reply)
RCVD do 36 (reply)
sent won't 36 (don't reply)
RECD do TERMINAL TYPE (don't reply)
RCVD will SUPPRESS GO AHEAD (don't reply)
RCVD do NAWS (don't reply)
Sent suboption NAWS 0 80 (80) 0 37 (37)
Received suboption Terminal type - request to send.
RCVD will ECHO (reply)
SEND do ECHO (reply)
RCVD do ECHO (reply)
SENT won't ECHO (don't reply)
HP-UX tpci_hpws4 A.09.01 A 9000/720 (ttys2)
login:
```

NOTE The Telnet commands are used by the protocol, not by users (although you can issue them during a Telnet session, but this is usually used only for diagnostic purposes). There are no inherent Telnet user commands, other than the command mode toggle, because Telnet's role is to connect you to a remote system and let you use it directly.

A partial set of Telnet command codes is shown in Table 6.1. Additional codes are used to represent printer functions such as horizontal and vertical tabs and form feeds, but these have been left off the table for brevity's sake. Part of the Telnet command code set includes six terminal functions (IP, AO, AYT, EC, EL, and GA) that are common across most terminal definitions, so they are formally defined in the Telnet standard.

Table 6.1. Telnet command codes.

Code	Value	Description
Abort Output (AO)	245	Runs process to completion but does not send the output
Are you there (AYT)	246	Queries the other end to ensure that an application is functioning
Break (BRK)	243	Sends a break instruction
Data Mark	242	Data portion of a Sync
Do	253	Asks for the other end to perform or an acknowledgment that the other end is to perform
Don't	254	Demands that the other end stop performing or confirms that the other end is no longer performing
Erase Character (EC)	247	Erases a character in the output stream
Erase Line (EL)	248	Erases a line in the output stream
Go Ahead (GA)	249	Indicates permission to proceed when using half-duplex (no echo) communications
Interpret as Command (IAC)	255	Interprets the following as a command
Interrupt Process (IP)	244	Interrupts, suspends, aborts, or terminates the process
NOP	241	No operation
SB	250	Subnegotiation of an option
SE	240	End of the subnegotiation
Will	251	Instructs the other end to begin performing or confirms that this end is now performing
Won't	252	Refuses to perform or rejects the other end performing

Telnet commands are sent in a formal package called a *command,* as shown in Figure 6.5. Typically the commands contain two or three bytes: the Interpret as Command (IAC) instruction, the command code being sent, and any optional parameter to the command. The options supported by Telnet are shown in Table 6.2.

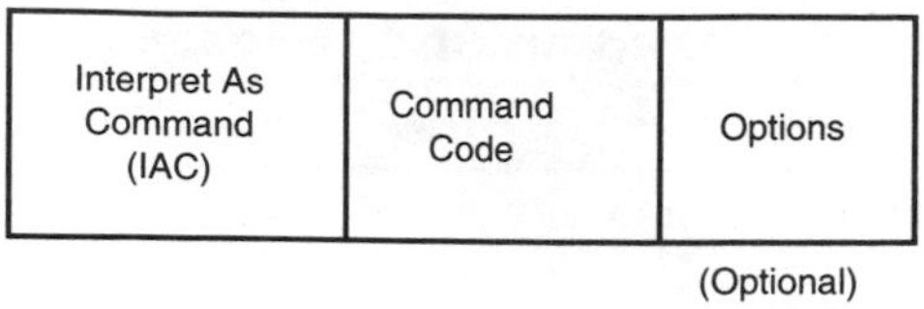

Figure 6.5.
*The Telnet command
structure.*

Interpret As Command (IAC)	Command Code	Options

(Optional)

Table 6.2. Supported Telnet option codes.

Code	Description
0	Binary transmission
1	Echo
2	Reconnection
3	Suppress Go Ahead (GA)
4	Approximate message size negotiation
5	Status
6	Timing mark
7	Remote controlled transmission and echo
8	Output line width
9	Output page length
10	Output carriage-return action
11	Output horizontal tab stop setting
12	Output horizontal tab stop action
13	Output form feed action
14	Output vertical tab stop setting
15	Output vertical tab stop action
16	Output line feed action
17	Extended ASCII characters
18	Logout
19	Bytes macro
20	Data entry terminal
21	SUPDUP
22	SUPDUP output
23	Send location
24	Terminal type
25	End of Record

6

Code	Description
26	TACACS user identification
27	Output marking
28	Terminal location number
29	3270 regime
30	X.3 PAD (Packet assembly and disassembly)
31	Window size

If you refer to the previous code listing with the options toggled on, some of the commands can be understood more clearly now. For example, will ECHO (which would be transmitted as values 255 251 1) instructs the other end to begin echoing back characters it receives. The command won't ECHO (the command would be 255 252 1) indicates that the sender will not echo back characters or wants to stop echoing.

NOTE The use of ASCII characters and small tables of commands and options make it relatively easy to follow Telnet communications.

TN3270

Many mainframes use EBCDIC, whereas most smaller machines rely on ASCII. This can cause a problem when trying to Telnet from EBCDIC-based machines to ASCII-based machines and vice versa, because the codes being transferred are not accurate. To correct this, a Telnet application called TN3270 was developed, which provides translation between the two formats.

When TN3270 is used to connect between two machines, Telnet itself establishes the initial connection, and then one end sets itself up for translation. If an ASCII machine is calling an EBCDIC machine, the translation between the two formats is conducted at the EBCDIC (server) end unless there is a gateway between them, in which case the gateway can perform the translation.

Many TCP/IP application suites that include a Telnet program also include a TN3270 program. For example, Figure 6.6 shows a TN3270 window from the NetManage ChameleonNFS suite in the process of connecting to a mainframe EBCDIC-based machine. The mainframe's IP address is used to initiate the connection.

6

Figure 6.6.

*TN3270 provides
conversion between
ASCII and EBCDIC.*

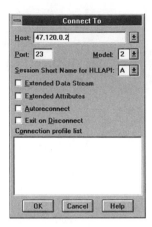

File Transfer Protocol (FTP)

File Transfer Protocol, usually called FTP, is a utility for managing files across machines without having to establish a remote session with Telnet. FTP enables you to transfer files back and forth, manage directories, and access electronic mail. FTP is not designed to enable access to another machine to execute programs, but it is the best utility for file transfers.

FTP uses two TCP channels. TCP port 20 is the data channel, and port 21 is the command channel. FTP is different from most other TCP/IP application programs in that it does use two channels, enabling simultaneous transfer of FTP commands and data. It also differs in one other important aspect: FTP conducts all file transfers in the foreground, instead of the background. In other words, FTP does not use spoolers or queues, so you are watching the transfer process in real time. By using TCP, FTP eliminates the need to worry about reliability or connection management, because FTP can rely on TCP to perform these functions properly.

In FTP parlance, the two channels that exist between the two machines are called the *protocol interpreter,* or PI, and the *data transfer process,* or DTP. The PI transfers instructions between the two implementations using TCP command channel 21, and the DTP transfers data on TCP data channel 20. This is shown in Figure 6.7.

FTP is similar to Telnet in that it uses a server program that runs continuously and a separate program that is executed on the client. On UNIX systems, these programs are named `ftpd` and `ftp`, respectively (similar to `telnetd` and `telnet`).

Figure 6.7.
FTP channel connections.

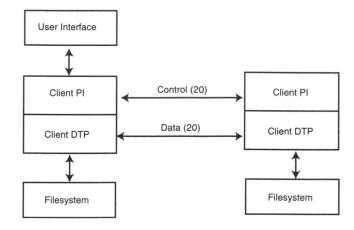

FTP Commands

Before looking at how you can use FTP to transfer files, you should look at the commands behind the protocol itself. As with Telnet's commands, these are for the protocol's use only and should not be used by a user (although administrators sometimes use the FTP commands for debugging and diagnostic purposes).

FTP's internal protocol commands are four-character ASCII sequences terminated by a newline character. Some of the codes require parameters after them. One primary advantage to using ASCII characters for commands is that a user can observe the command flow and understand it easily. This helps considerably in the debugging process. Also, it enables a knowledgeable user to communicate directly with the FTP server component (ftpd).

FTP commands used by the protocol are summarized in Table 6.3. These commands provide for the connection process, password checking, and the actual file transfers. These are not to be confused with the commands available to a user.

Table 6.3. FTP internal commands.

Command	Description
ABOR	Abort previous command
ACCT	User account ID
ALLO	Allocate storage for forthcoming operation
APPE	Append incoming data to an existing file
CDUP	Change to parent directory
CWD	Change working directory

continues

Table 6.3. continued

Command	Description
DELE	Delete file
HELP	Retrieve information
LIST	Transfer list of directories
MKD	Make a directory
MODE	Set transfer mode
NLST	Transfer a directory listing
NOOP	No operation
PASS	User password
PASV	Request a passive open
PORT	Port address
PWD	Display current directory
QUIT	Terminate the connection
REIN	Terminate and restart a connection
REST	Restart marker (restart transfer)
RETR	Transfer copy of file
RMD	Remove a directory
RNFR	Old pathname for rename command
RNTO	New pathname for rename command
SITE	Provides service specifics
SMNT	Mount a file system
STAT	Returns status
STOR	Accept and store data
STOU	Accept data and store under different name
STRU	File structure
SYST	Query to determine operating system
TYPE	Type of data
USER	User ID

FTP also uses simple return codes to indicate transfer conditions. Each return code is a three-digit number, the first of which signifies a successful execution (the first digit is 1, 2, or 3) or a failure. (The first digit is 4 or 5.) The second and third digits specify the return code or error condition in more detail. The FTP return codes are shown in Table 6.4 and Table 6.5. The third-digit codes are not included here because there are many of them and they vary between implementations.

Table 6.4. FTP reply code first digits.

First Digit	Description
1	Action initiated. Expect another reply before sending a new command.
2	Action completed. Can send a new command.
3	Command accepted but on hold due to lack of information.
4	Command not accepted or completed. Temporary error condition exists. Command can be reissued.
5	Command not accepted or completed. Reissuing the command will result in the same error (don't reissue).

Table 6.5. FTP reply code second digits.

Second Digit	Description
0	Syntax error or illegal command
1	Reply to request for information
2	Reply that refers to connection management
3	Reply for authentication command
4	Not used
5	Reply for status of server

FTP enables file transfers in several formats, which are usually system-dependent. The majority of systems (including UNIX systems) have only two modes: text and binary. Some mainframe installations add support for EBCDIC, whereas many sites have a local type designed for fast transfers between local network machines. (The local type might use 32- or 64-bit words.)

Text transfers use ASCII characters separated by carriage-return and newline characters, whereas binary enables transfer of characters with no conversion or formatting. Binary mode is faster than text and also enables for the transfer of all ASCII values (necessary for nontext files). On most systems, FTP starts in text mode, although many system administrators now set FTP to binary mode as a default for their users' convenience. FTP cannot transfer file permissions, because these are not specified as part of the protocol.

6

WARNING

> Before transferring files with FTP, make sure you are using the correct transfer mode. Transferring a binary file as ASCII results in garbage! Check with your system administrator if you are unsure of the mode, or watch the messages FTP returns to see the mode used.

FTP Connections

FTP is usually started with the name or address of the target machine. As with Telnet, the name must be resolvable into an IP address for the command to succeed. The target machine can also be specified from the FTP command line. For example, to connect to the IP address 205.150.89.5, you would issue this command:

```
ftp 205.150.89.5
```

When FTP connects to the destination, you must be able to log into the system as a valid user (as you do when connecting through Telnet). Some systems enable an anonymous or guest login for FTP file transfers (usually using your login name as a password as a record of your access; see the section titled "Anonymous FTP Access"), but most require you to have regular access to the machine. The following extract shows the login process as a user provides a login and password for the remote machine:

```
ftp tpci_hpws4
Connected to tpci_hpws4.
220 tpci_hpws4 FTP server
Name (tpci_hpws4:tparker):
331 Password required for tparker.
Password:
230 User tparker logged in.
Remote system type is UNIX.
Using binary mode to transfer files.
```

On large networks where a system such as Yellow Pages (YP) or Network Information Services (NIS) is used, FTP logins are usually permitted on most machines. If YP or NIS is not employed, you must be in the valid users file to obtain FTP access. As with Telnet, you can log into the remote with a different user ID from your local machine login. To transfer files, you must have the proper permissions on the remote, if file permissions are provided for by the operating system.

After logging into another machine using FTP, you are not actually on the remote machine. You are still logically on the client, so all instructions for file transfers and directory movement must be with respect to your local machine, not the remote one. Note that this is the opposite of Telnet (a distinction that causes considerable confusion among newcomers to FTP and Telnet).

WARNING

Remember that all references to files and directories are relative to the machine that initiated the FTP session. If you are not careful, you can accidentally overwrite existing files.

The process followed by FTP when a connection is established is as follows:

1. **Login:** Verifies the user ID and password.
2. **Define directory:** Identifies the starting directory.
3. **Define file transfer mode:** Defines the type of transfer.
4. **Start data transfer:** Enables user commands.
5. **Stop data transfer:** Closes the connection.

These steps are performed in sequence for each connection. A user has several commands available to control FTP; the most frequently used commands are summarized in Table 6.6.

Table 6.6. FTP user commands.

FTP Command	Description
ascii	Switch to ASCII transfer mode
binary	Switch to binary transfer mode
cd	Change directory on the server
close	Terminate the connection
del	Delete a file on the server
dir	Display the server directory
get	Fetch a file from the server
hash	Display a pound character for each block transmitted
help	Display help
lcd	Change directory on the client
mget	Fetch several files from the server
mput	Send several files to the server
open	Connect to a server
put	Send a file to the server
pwd	Display the current server directory
quote	Supply an FTP command directly
quit	Terminate the FTP session

6

Using FTP is similar to Telnet, except that all movements of files are relative to the client. Therefore, putting a file is moving it from the client to the server, whereas getting a file is the reverse. A sample FTP session follows:

```
tpci_hpws1-1> ftp tpci_hpws4
Connected to tpci_hpws4.
220 tpci_hpws4 FTP server (Version 1.7.109.2 Tue Jul 28 23:32:34 GMT 1992)
 ready.
Name (tpci_hpws4:tparker):
331 Password required for tparker.
Password:
230 User tparker logged in.
Remote system type is UNIX.
Using binary mode to transfer files.
ftp> pwd
257 "/u1/tparker" is current directory.
ftp> get mandelfile1.gif
remote: mandelfile1.gif local: mandelfi.gif
200 PORT command successful
150 Opening BINARY mode data connection for mandelfile1.gif
226 File transfer complete
1192834 bytes sent in 0.89 seconds
ftp> <Ctrl+d>
tpci_hpws1-2>
```

In this short sample, I transferred a file called mandelfile1.gif from a UNIX machine (the server) to the local machine (the client). You might have noticed that the filename was truncated automatically by the server to fit the DOS filesystem naming conventions. Also, note that I used binary mode (which was the system default). If the default had been ASCII mode, I would have just transferred over a megabyte of total garbage that couldn't be used for anything.

A debugging option is available from the command line by adding -d to the command. This displays the command channel instructions. Instructions from the client are shown with an arrow as the first character, whereas instructions from the server have three digits in front of them. A PORT in the command line indicates the address of the data channel on which the client is waiting for the server's reply. If no PORT is specified, channel 20 (the default value) is used. Unfortunately, the progress of data transfers cannot be followed in the debugging mode. A sample session with the debug option enabled is shown here:

6

```
tpci_hpws1-1> ftp -d
ftp> open tpci_hpws4
Connected to tpci_hpws4.
220 tpci_hpws4 FTP server Name (tpci_hpws4:tparker):
--> USER tparker
331 Password required for tparker.
Password:
--> PASS qwerty5
230 User tparker logged in.
--> SYST
215 UNIX Type: L8
Remote system type is UNIX.
--> Type I
200 Type set to I.
Using binary mode to transfer files.
ftp> ls
--> PORT 47,80,10,28,4,175
200 PORT command successful.
--> TYPE A
200 Type set to A.
--> LIST
150 Opening ASCII mode data connection for /bin/ls.
total 4
-rw-r-----  1 tparker  tpci    2803  Apr 29 10:46 file1
-rw-rw-r--  1 tparker  tpci    1286  Apr 14 10:46 file5_draft
-rwxr-----  2 tparker  tpci   15635  Mar 14 23:23 test_comp_1
-rw-r-----  1 tparker  tpci      52  Apr 22 12:19 xyzzy
Transfer complete.
--> TYPE I
200 Type set to I.
ftp> <Ctrl+d>
tpci_hpws1-2>
```

You might notice in the previous code how the mode changes from binary to ASCII to send the directory listing, and then back to binary (the system default value). You can see how the two systems communicate to display the status messages that appear without the debugging option active.

When FTP is used in a graphical user environment, you might be able to use a GUI-based tool. For example, NetManage's ChameleonNFS provides the FTP utility shown in Figure 6.8. In this case, the NFS client on the Windows for Workgroups machine has connected to a UNIX server. The Local side of the window shows the Windows machine, and the Remote side of the window shows the UNIX box's current filesystem contents. When using a GUI-based utility like this one, you can use the mouse and various buttons to transfer files back and forth between machines.

Figure 6.8.
Many operating systems have a GUI-based FTP client.

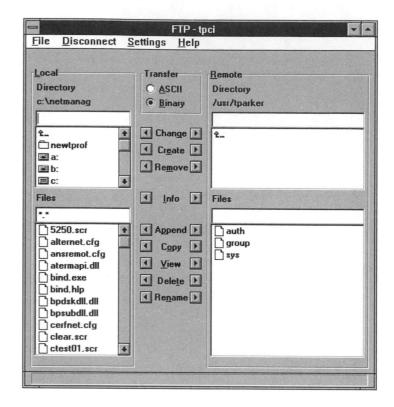

FTP Third-Party Transfers

FTP enables a transfer to occur through a third machine positioned between the client and the server. This procedure is known as a *third-party transfer* and is sometimes necessary to obtain proper permissions to access the remote machine. Figure 6.9 shows the schematic of a third-party transfer, with the control connection made through a third machine.

Figure 6.9.
A third-party FTP transfer.

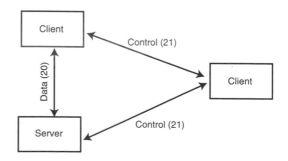

6

When setting up a third-party connection, the client opens the control connections between the remote machine and the second client that handles the control channel. Only the control channel goes through the second client, whereas the data channel goes directly between the two ends.

When a transfer request is submitted, it is transferred through the second client, which checks permissions and then forwards the request to the server. The data transfer can take place directly, because the permissions were checked on the control channel.

Anonymous FTP Access

FTP requires a user ID and password to enable file transfer capabilities, but there is a more liberal method of enabling general access to a file or directory, called *anonymous FTP*. Anonymous FTP removes the requirement for a login account on the remote machine, usually enabling the login anonymous with a password of either guest or the user's actual login name. The following session shows the use of an anonymous FTP system:

```
tpci_hpws4-1> ftp uofo.edu
Connected to uofo.edu.
220 uofo.edu FTP server (Version 1.7.109.2 Tue Jul 28 23:32:34 GMT 1992) ready.
Name (uofo:username): anonymous
331 Guest login ok, send userID as password.
Password: tparker
230 Guest login ok, access restrictions apply.
ftp> <Ctrl+d>
tpci_hpws4-2>
```

If the remote system is set to enable anonymous logins, you are prompted for a password and then given a warning about access limitations. If there is a file on the remote system you require, a get command transfers it. Anonymous FTP sites are becoming common, especially with the popularity of the Internet.

FTP Servers

Most UNIX machines act as FTP servers by default. To provide FTP server facilities, they run the daemon ftpd when the operating system is booted. The daemon is usually handled by the UNIX inetd process. When you start using inetd, the inetd daemon watches the TCP command port (channel 21) for an arriving request for a connection, then starts ftpd to service that request. If you want to ensure that your UNIX or Linux system can handle FTP requests, make sure the ftpd daemon can be started when needed by inetd by checking the inetd configuration file (usually /etc/inetd.config or /etc/inetd.conf) for a line that looks like this:

```
ftp stream  tcp  nowait  root  /usr/etc/ftpd   ftpd -l
```

If this line doesn't exist, you should add it. With most UNIX systems this line is already in the inetd configuration file, although it might be commented out, in which case you should remove the comment symbol.

Windows, Windows for Workgroups, and Windows 95 all lack an FTP server program as part of their distribution software (although Windows 95 does have an FTP client), so you have to add a commercial package. Many commercial TCP/IP suites include an FTP server process. Figure 6.10 shows the NetManage ChameleonNFS program group, which includes an FTP server program you can use as an example for Windows for Workgroups and Windows 3.x machines.

Figure 6.10.

The NetManage FTP Server dialog handles the FTP server process.

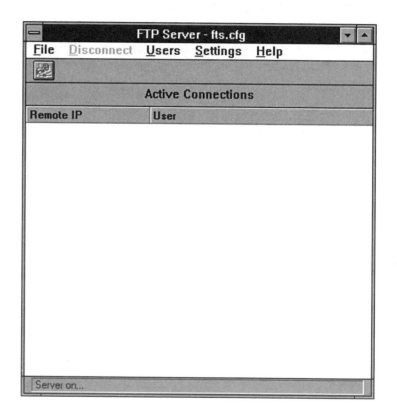

To start the NetManage FTP Server software, double-click the FTP server icon in the NetManage program group. A dialog, shown in Figure 6.10, appears. The FTP server process is now active, and anyone on another machine on your local area network can now connect to your machine, assuming they have access.

Access to your FTP service is controlled through the user lists maintained by the FTP Server package. Selecting the Users menu option from the NetManage FTP Server dialog opens the Users dialog, shown in Figure 6.11. This lets you add user names to your system. If another user on a different machine tries to connect to your FTP server software, the server verifies that their login name and password match the name and password you enter in this dialog. This lets you set up a list of users who can transfer files to and from your system, as long as the FTP server is running.

Figure 6.11.

Access to your machine is controlled through the FTP Server Users dialog.

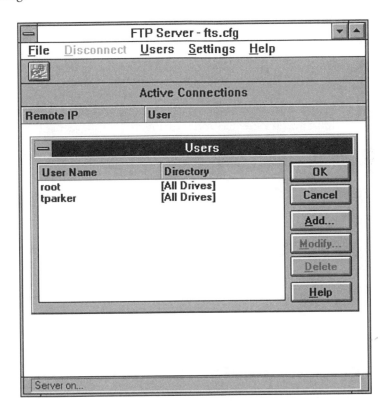

If you are running an FTP server process, it is often a good idea to create a directory just for FTP. Many users prefer to create a directory called public, which is where all files to be transferred in and out of the local system are placed. This lets you prevent accidental deletion or transfer of files in other directories on your system, as well as providing you with the opportunity to filter incoming material for suitability, viruses, and so on. If you use a transfer directory, check it regularly and make sure all users who have access to your system can work only in that directory.

If you want to provide an anonymous or guest account for users on your LAN or any other network that can connect to your machine, you should set up an account with either no password or a simple password like guest. It is very important to restrict the areas a guest or anonymous login can use.

As mentioned earlier, Windows 95 is supplied with client FTP software but not an FTP server. You can use other aspects of Windows 95 as a file transfer system, such as file and print sharing over any existing network, but these do not use FTP. If you want to set up an FTP server on your Windows 95 machine, you have to install third-party commercial software for this purpose.

A popular Windows 95 FTP server package called FTP Serv-U was written by Rob Beckers and is provided as shareware. An executable file called Serv-U starts the server. To control access to your Windows 95 system, you can set up logins using the Serv-U Users menu option. This displays a screen that lets you add logins and passwords, as well as the directories and drives the user has access to. Figure 6.12 shows the Edit User/Group dialog with a user being added. When a user from another system logs into your Windows 95 machine, they are asked for a login and password.

Figure 6.12.

Set up all users of your FTP server with the Edit User/Group dialog.

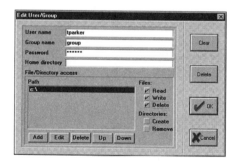

Trivial File Transfer Protocol (TFTP)

The Trivial File Transfer Protocol (TFTP) is one of the simplest file transfer protocols in use. It differs from FTP in two primary ways: It does not log onto the remote machine, and it uses the User Datagram Protocol (UDP) connectionless transport protocol instead of TCP. By using UDP, TFTP does not monitor the progress of the file transfer, although it does have to employ more complex algorithms to ensure proper data integrity. By avoiding logging onto the remote, user access and file permission problems are avoided. TFTP uses the TCP port identifier number 69, even though TCP is not involved in the protocol.

TFTP has few advantages over FTP. It is not usually used for file transfers between machines where FTP could be used instead, although TFTP is useful when a diskless terminal or workstation is involved. Typically, TFTP is used to load applications and fonts into these machines, as well as for bootstrapping. TFTP is necessary in these cases because the diskless machines cannot execute FTP until they are fully loaded with an operating system. TFTP's small executable size and memory requirements make it ideal for inclusion in a bootstrap, where the system requires only TFTP, UDP, and a network driver, all of which can be provided in a small EPROM.

TFTP handles access and file permissions by imposing restraints of its own. On most UNIX systems, for example, a file can be transferred only if it is accessible to all users on the remote (both read and write permissions are set). Because of the lax access regulations, most system administrators impose more control over TFTP (or ban its use altogether); otherwise, it is quite easy for a knowledgeable user to access or transfer files that could constitute a security violation.

TFTP transfers can fail for many reasons, because practically any kind of error encountered during a transfer operation causes a complete failure. TFTP does support some basic error messages, but it cannot handle simple errors such as insufficient resources for a file transfer or even a failure to locate a requested file.

TFTP Commands

The important instructions in TFTP's command set are shown in Table 6.7. The TFTP command set is similar to FTP's, but it differs in several important aspects because of the connectionless aspect of the protocol. Most noticeable is the connect command, which simply determines the remote's address instead of initiating a connection.

Table 6.7. TFTP's command set.

TFTP Command	Description
binary	Uses binary mode for transfers
connect	Determines the remote's address
get	Retrieves a file from the remote
put	Transfers a file to the remote
trace	Displays protocol codes
verbose	Displays all information

TFTP enables both text and binary transfers, as does FTP. As with both Telnet and FTP, TFTP uses a server process (tftpd on a UNIX system) and an executable, usually called tftp. A sample TFTP session on a UNIX host is shown here, with full trace options and binary transfers turned on:

```
tpci_hpws1-1> tftp
tftp> connect tpci_hpws4
tftp> trace
Packet tracing on.
tftp> binary
Binary mode on.
tftp> verbose
Verbose mode on.
tftp> status
Connected to tpci_hpws4.
Mode: octet Verbose: on Tracing: on
Rexmt-interval: 5 seconds, Max-timeout: 25 seconds
tftp> get /usr/rmaclean/docs/draft1
getting from tpci_hpws4:/usr/rmaclean/docs/draft1 to /tmp/draft1 [octet]
sent RRQ <file=/usr/rmaclean/docs/draft1, mode=octet>
received DATA <block1, 512 bytes>
send ACK <block=1>
received DATA <block2, 512 bytes>
send ACK <block=3>
received DATA <block4, 128 bytes>
send ACK <block=3>
Received 1152 bytes in 0.2 second 46080 bits/s]
tftp> quit
tpci_hpws1-2>
```

In the session above, you can see that the trace and verbose commands turn on the echoing of the instructions flowing between the two machines during a file transfer. Every time a block of data is sent after the get command is issued (the send ACK instruction shown on the session above), a received instruction is returned to acknowledge the ACK.

TFTP is available on all UNIX systems as well as in TCP/IP suites for other operating systems. Figure 6.13 shows the TFTP utility from ChameleonNFS, which lets you enter the remote host name, the remote and local filenames, and the type of transfer you want. The file transfer is then performed in the background using UDP.

Figure 6.13.

Using TFTP to transfer a file.

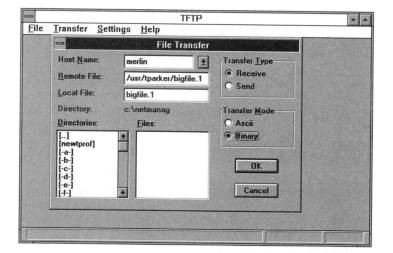

TFTP Packets

TFTP uses UDP as a transport protocol, so TFTP can use the UDP header to encapsulate TFTP protocol information. TFTP uses the UDP source and destination port fields to set the two ends of the connection. It accomplishes this by the use of *TFTP Transfer Identifiers,* or TIDs, which are created by TFTP and passed to UDP, which then places them in the headers.

As with Telnet and FTP, TFTP uses port binding, where the sending machine selects a TID, and the remote is set to port number 69 (TFTP's port number). The remote machine responds with an acknowledgment of a connection request, a source port of 69, and the destination TID sent in the request.

TFTP uses five types of Protocol Data Units, which are referred to as packets in the TFTP lexicon. These packets are listed in Table 6.8. Their layout is shown in Figure 6.14. Error messages supported by TFTP are shown in Table 6.9.

Figure 6.14.
TFTP packet layouts.

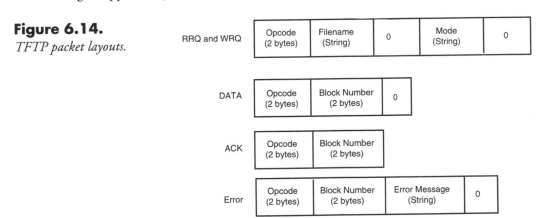

Table 6.8. TFTP Protocol Data Unit codes.

Code	OpCode	Description
ACK	4	Acknowledgment
DATA	3	Send Data
Error	5	Error
RRQ	1	Read request
WRQ	2	Write request

6

Table 6.9. TFTP error messages and codes.

Code	Description
0	Not defined
1	File not found
2	Permissions prevent access
3	Disk full or allocation limit exceeded
4	Illegal TFTP operation requested
5	Unknown transfer number

The layouts for both RRQ and WRQ packets have a Mode field, which indicates the type of transfer. There are three modes currently available to TFTP:

☐ **NetASCII:** Standard ASCII codes.

☐ **Byte:** 8-bit bytes and binary information.

☐ **Mail:** Indicates that the destination is a user, not a file (information is transferred as NetASCII).

The last block in all packets contains between 0 and 511 bytes of data, labeled 0 in Figure 6.14. This pads out the block of data to 512 bytes.

The communications process used by TFTP begins with the client sending an RRQ or WRQ request to the server through UDP. As part of the request, a transaction number, the filename, and a code to identify the transmission mode to be used are specified. The transaction number is used to identify future transactions in the sequence.

Because there is no connection between the two, the client sets a timer and waits for a reply from the server. If one doesn't arrive before the timer expires, another request is sent. After an ACK is received, a DATA packet is transmitted, for which another ACK or an ERROR is received. If there are several packets to be transferred, they are constructed so they have a length of 512 bytes and an incrementing sequence number. The process terminates when a DATA packet with a length of less than 512 bytes is received by the server. For each packet sent, TFTP waits for an acknowledgment before sending the next, a system known as a *flip-flop protocol.*

Simple Mail Transfer Protocol (SMTP)

The Simple Mail Transfer Protocol (SMTP) is the defined Internet method for transferring electronic mail. SMTP is similar to FTP in many ways, including the same simplicity of operation. SMTP uses TCP port number 25.

6

Most UNIX systems use programs called `sendmail` or `mmdf` to implement SMTP (as well as several other mail protocols). The `sendmail` program, for example, acts as both a client and a server, usually running in the background as a daemon. Users do not interact with `sendmail` directly but use a front-end mail program such as `mail`, `mailx`, or `Mail`. These mail system interfaces pass the message to `sendmail` for forwarding.

SMTP uses spools or queues. When a message is sent to SMTP, it places it in a queue. SMTP attempts to forward the message from the queue whenever it connects to remote machines. If it cannot forward the message within a specified time limit, the message is returned to the sender or removed.

SMTP Commands

SMTP data transmissions use a simple format. All the message text is transferred as 7-bit ASCII characters. The end of the message is indicated by a single period on a line by itself. If for some reason a line in the message begins with a period, a second one is added by the protocol to avoid confusion with the end-of-message indicator.

SMTP has a simple protocol command set, listed in Table 6.10. Using these protocol elements, mail is transferred with a minimum of effort.

Table 6.10. The SMTP protocol command set.

Command	Description
DATA	Message text
EXPN	Expansion of a distribution list
HELO	Use in connection establishment to exchange identifiers
HELP	Request for help
MAIL	The sender's address
NOOP	No operation
RCPT	The message destination address (more than one can be provided)
RSET	Terminate the current transaction
SAML	Send a message to the user's terminal and send mail
SEND	Send a message to the user's terminal
SOML	Either send a message to the user's terminal or send mail
TURN	Change the sending direction (reverse sending and receiving roles)
VRFY	Verify the user name

When a connection is established, the two SMTP systems exchange authentication codes. Following this, one system sends a MAIL command to the other to identify the sender and provide information about the message. The receiving SMTP returns an acknowledgment, after which a RCPT is sent to identify the recipient. If more than one recipient at the receiver location is identified, several RCPT messages are sent, but the message itself is transmitted only once. After each RCPT there is an acknowledgment. A DATA command is followed by the message lines, until a single period on a line by itself indicates the end of the message. The connection is closed with a QUIT command.

The sender and recipient address fields use standard Internet formats, involving the user name and domain name (such as tparker@tpci.com). The domain can be replaced by other information if a direct connection is established, or if there is a forwarding machine in the path. SMTP uses the Domain Name Service (DNS) for all addresses.

The Berkeley Utilities

The University of California at Berkeley was instrumental in the development of TCP/IP and contributed many utility programs to the application tool set. These are usually known by the term *Berkeley r-Utilities*. They are called r-utilities because they all start with the letter r (for remote). Most of the utilities are UNIX-specific, although they have since all been ported to other operating systems.

The `hosts.equiv` and `.rhosts` Files

To enable machines to communicate correctly over networks, access rights for machines and users must be set. Usually, when logging into another machine, a user must supply a user ID and a password. When you log into many machines, retyping this information can be tedious and time-consuming. It can also be a security problem, because it is easy to write a program that monitors network connections for this information. A way to enable fast access without actually logging in and preventing interception of passwords is clearly useful in some cases.

The system administrator can decide that all login names used on other machines whose names are in the file `hosts.equiv` are allowed access on the local machine. This enables a protocol that queries a machine for access to check the `hosts.equiv` file for the requesting machine's name, and if it is found, to grant access to the user on the remote machine. The user has the same access rights as on his or her home machine.

If the protocol doesn't find an entry in the `hosts.equiv` file, it can check another file maintained in a user's home directory, called `.rhosts`. A user can control who has access to their login name with the file `.rhosts` in their home directory, enabling other users to log in as if they were that user. The .rhosts file must be owned by the user (or root) and not allow write access to all users (on a UNIX system, the other permission cannot be write). An .rhosts file consists of a line for each user to be allowed into the home directory. The line consists of a machine name and a login name. A sample .rhosts file is shown here:

```
tpci_hpws1 rmaclean
tpci_hpws1 bsmallwood
tpci_hpws3 ychow
tpci_hpws3 bsmallwood
tpci_hpws4 glessard
tpci_hpws4 bsmallwood
tpci_sunws1 chatton
merlin tparker
merlin ahoyt
merlin lrainsford
```

This file allows user bsmallwood to log in from three different machines.

rlogin

The rlogin command (for *remote login*) enables a user to log into another machine. It is very similar in functionality to Telnet, although the protocol is much simpler. There is a background program running on the server called rlogind, and the program rlogin resides on the client.

The rlogin protocol begins a session by sending three character strings, separated by 0s. The first string is the user's login ID (on the client), the second string is the login name for the server (usually but not always the same as the login name on the client), and the third string is the login name and transmission rate of the user's terminal (such as wyse60/19200). When received on the server, the strings can be converted to environment variables (such as UNIX's TERM terminal variable). You cannot log into the remote machine with a different user ID, because the system does not prompt for the login name. It does prompt for a password, however.

After the login process is completed, rlogin doesn't use any protocol. Every character you type on the client machine is sent to the server, whereas every server-generated character is displayed on your console. The only exit to your local machine is by closing the connection by using Ctrl+D or entering the escape character on a line by itself. By default, the escape character is a tilde (~).

Some versions of rlogin enable a shell escape, a temporary suspension of the rlogin session and a return to the operating system, by using ~!.

rsh

The rsh utility (remote shell) lets you execute commands on a remote machine. As with most Berkeley utilities, a background process called rshd is involved. Executing a command on a remote machine is a matter of adding rsh and the machine name to the front of the command line, such as rsh tpci_hpws3 who or rsh tpci_sunws1 tar xvf /dev/rct0 (using UNIX examples). The rsh utility depends on the presence of either hosts.equiv or .rhosts to enable login; otherwise, access is not granted.

The rsh utility is not a shell in the sense that it does not interpret commands like the UNIX C shell or Bourne shell. Instead, a command entered is sent to the server's standard input and output, executing the command as a local process through the TCP connection. The primary advantage of this is that a shell script that executes on your local machine can be submitted to the remote machine with no modification, where it runs just as if it were local (except using the remote's file system). Unfortunately, any return codes generated by the remote system are not sent back to your local machine. Also, most screen-oriented applications do not function properly, because they have no terminal output to write to.

rcp

The Berkeley rcp (remote copy) command is similar to the UNIX cp command, except that it works across the network. The command syntax and option lists for rcp are the same as cp, although a machine name is usually specified as part of the filename by the addition of the machine name followed by a colon (see the following examples). Even recursive copying of directories is supported (a useful and attractive feature of rcp that isn't available under FTP or TFTP). The rcp program acts as both server and client, initiated when a request arrives.

```
rcp tpci_hpws4:/user/tparker/doc/draft1 .

rcp file2 merlin:/u1/bsmallwood/temp/file2

rcp -r merlin:/u2/tparker/tcp_book tpci_server/tcp_book

rcp merlin:/u1/ychow/iso9000_doc tpci_server:/u1/iso/doc1/iso_doc_from_ychow

rcp file4 tparker@tpci.com:new_info
```

As the examples indicate, the filenames at both the local and remote machines are specified, with standard UNIX conventions supported. The third example shows a file being transferred from one machine to another, neither of which is the machine from which the command is initiated. The last example shows the use of a full DNS-style name for the destination address.

6

The rcp utility is a faster method of transferring files than FTP, although rcp requires access permission through an .rhosts file (not hosts.equiv). Without an entry in this file, access is refused and FTP or TFTP must be used.

rwho

The rwho (remote who) command uses the rwhod daemon to display a list of users on the network. It shows all network users, compiled from a regularly sent packet of information from all running rwhod programs. The frequency of this packet broadcast is system-dependent but is usually in the order of every one to three minutes. When an rwhod program receives a broadcast from another machine, it places it in a system file for future use. (The file on a UNIX system is called /usr/spool/rwho.)

When a machine has not sent a broadcast message within a time limit (usually eleven minutes), it is assumed that the machine has disconnected from the network, and all users listed as active on that machine in the system file are ignored. The rwhod program drops a user ID from its broadcast if nothing has been entered at the user's terminal in the last hour.

The output from an rwho request is shown in the following example. For each user, it shows their login name, their machine and terminal name, and the time and date of their login.

```
bsmallwood merlin:tty2p       Feb 29 09:01
etreijs    tpci_hpws2:tty01   Feb 29 12:12
rmaclean   goofus:tty02       Feb 28 23:52
tparker    merlin:tty01       Feb 29 11:43
ychow      prudie:tty2a       Feb 28 11:37
```

The rcp program has one major problem on large networks: The continuous sending of update packets by each machine creates a considerable amount of network traffic. For this reason, some implementations directly request the user names only when an rwho request is received.

ruptime

The ruptime utility displays a list of all machines on the network, their status, the number of active users, current load, and elapsed time since the system was booted. The program uses the same information as the rwho command.

A sample output from a ruptime command follows:

```
merlin      up     3:15,12 users, load 0.90, 0.50, 0.09
prudie      down   9:12
tpci_hpws1  up    11:05, 3 users, load 0.10, 0.10, 0.00
tpci_hpws2  up    23:59, 5 users, load 0.30, 0.25, 0.08
tpci_hpws3  down   6:45
tpci_hpws4  up     9:05, 1 user,  load 0.12, 0.05, 0.01
```

6

rexec

The rexec (remote execution) program is a holdover from earlier versions of the UNIX operating system. It was designed to enable remote execution of a command through a server process called rexecd. The utility uses the dedicated TCP port number 512.

The protocol used by rexec is very similar to rsh, except that an encrypted password is sent with the request and there is a full login process. The rexec utility is seldom used because rsh is a faster and more convenient method for executing a command remotely.

Summary

Today I looked at the primary application protocols that use TCP/IP, as well as the Berkeley utilities. Now that you can see how protocols work on top of the TCP and IP protocols, the layered structure of TCP/IP becomes more pronounced. Future days' texts build on this information.

Q&A

Q What is the purpose of Telnet and FTP?

A Telnet provides a remote login capability, whereas FTP enables you to transfer files across the network.

Q What channels (port numbers) are used by Telnet, FTP, and SMTP?

A Telnet uses port number 23. FTP uses port number 21 for the control information and port number 20 for data. SMTP uses port number 25.

Q When you issue a get command in FTP, is it moving a file from the local to remote, or vice versa?

A FTP commands are relative to the remote, so a get command moves a file from the local to the remote.

Q How does TFTP differ from FTP?

A TFTP does not require logging in. It sends a request over UDP. With FTP, you must log into the destination either directly or through a third-party device.

Q Does rlogin differ from telnet?

A The rlogin program was developed earlier and for most users has no difference. There are some version dependencies with some releases of rlogin, reflecting its earlier (and less full-featured) origins.

6

Workshop

If you have access to a Telnet or FTP session, try logging into a remote machine and transferring files back and forth. Try to recognize that Telnet does everything relative to the local machine, whereas FTP is relative to the remote.

Quiz

1. Explain what a network virtual terminal is.
2. Draw diagrams showing two- and three-party FTP sessions, indicating the port numbers used by each machine.
3. Why would you want to enable anonymous FTP access? Are there any reasons for disallowing it?
4. TFTP enables files to be transferred without logging in. What problems can this cause?
5. What are the Berkeley Utilities?

6

Chapter 7

TCP/IP Configuration and Administration Basics

Although TCP/IP works transparently for the user, occasionally communications seem to be slow and TCP/IP is suspected as the cause. Most users are impatient and expect things to happen right away, so delays for any reason lead to frustration. Rather than sit and wait, most users like to be able to verify that a connection to a remote machine is active and a delay is caused by network traffic instead of a system failure. At the least, most users would like to understand why a session is progressing slowly.

TCP/IP has several utility programs that provide status information and performance statistics. Also available are several debugging programs and options to enable a developer or knowledgeable user to trace a problem. This chapter examines the basic set of these tools. Although TCP/IP is a standard, there are many different implementations of the protocol family. Most versions have the basic toolset discussed today, although some might alter names and output to their own liking.

WARNING

All network addresses and machine names in this chapter are chosen at random and do not represent any particular network. Because the network addresses used might correspond to a real network, you should not use them in any experimentation, or you might incur the wrath of a system administrator!

Not all the commands shown in this chapter are available to regular users (as opposed to system administrators) on all systems, although some system administrators do enable some access to the utilities for checking connection and TCP/IP status. The commands are presented here to show the debugging and diagnostic capabilities available to the TCP/IP user and administrator. The commands are not covered in exhaustive detail but are intended to complete the TCP/IP picture for you. Many of these programs and utilities are seen again later in this book when I set up a sample TCP/IP network.

Configuration Files

Several files are involved in the complete specification of network addresses and configuration for TCP/IP. For illustrative purposes, a UNIX system is used as the standard here, although a few other operating systems are mentioned as appropriate. Other operating systems use different filenames, but the purpose of the files is usually the same. You might have to check with your operating system documentation to identify the files used for each purpose.

UNIX allows comments on every line of these configuration files, as long as they are prefaced by a pound sign (#). If you see this character in your own system's configuration files, you should note that it is not part of an entry. With many operating systems, the default configuration files have many entries, most of which are commented out until the system administrator removes the comments.

WARNING

You might not be able to examine the files or run the utilities mentioned in this chapter because of security restrictions. If you edit the configuration files, make sure you do not make any unintentional changes! Make backups of all the files before you make any changes to your systems.

7

Symbolic Machine Names: `/etc/hosts`

Whenever a symbolic name is used as a target address by an application, there must be some method to resolve that name into a network address. An ASCII file is commonly used with the symbolic names matched to network addresses. This does not apply when the Yellow Pages (YP), Network Information Services (NIS), or the Domain Name Service (DNS) are used; they use their own configuration files.

On UNIX systems, the file `/etc/hosts` is used to hold the network addresses, as well as one special connection called the *loopback* (which is examined later in this chapter in the section titled "The Loopback Driver"). The loopback connection address is usually listed as the machine name `loopback` or `localhost`.

The file `/etc/hosts` consists of the network address in one column, separated from the symbolic name in another. The network addresses can be specified in decimal, octal, or hexadecimal format (although decimal is the most common). More than one symbolic name can be specified on a line by separating the names with either space characters or tabs. The `/etc/hosts` file can be as long as necessary to contain all the symbolic names used on the local machine; they do not need to be presented in any order. A sample UNIX `/etc/hosts` file is as follows:

```
# network host addresses
127.0.0.1           localhost local tpci_server
157.40.40.1         tpci_sco1
157.40.40.2         tpci_sco2
157.40.40.3         tpci_hpws1
157.40.40.0         tpci_server tpci_main tpci
47.80.157.36        bnr.ca BNR bnr
191.13.123.4        kitty_cat
205.150.89.1        roy_maclean big_roy
210.24.47.128       bobs_machine
```

As you can see, the file is made up of two columns. The first column gives the IP address of a machine, and the second (separated by one or more whitespace characters) gives the machine's name. If several names can be used to identify the remote machine, they are listed on the same line, separated by whitespace. For example, the remote machine with IP address `205.150.89.1` can be addressed as either `roy_maclean` or `big_roy`. Whenever either of those names is used in a command (such as an FTP or Telnet application), this file is used to match to the proper IP address.

A system or network administrator can update the `/etc/hosts` file at any time, and changes are effective immediately (so the machine doesn't have to be rebooted to effect the changes). Whenever a symbolic name is specified by a user or an application, the `/etc/hosts` file is always searched first for a matching name, and the proper address is read from the same line.

7

Most TCP/IP implementations on other platforms have a similar type of file to resolve IP addresses from symbolic names. NetManage ChameleonNFS running on a Windows 3.*x* machine, for example, uses a Host Table to match names and IP addresses. The Host Table, shown in Figure 7.1, is a graphical front-end to a file equivalent to /etc/hosts on a UNIX machine.

Figure 7.1.

ChameleonNFS uses a Host Table to match symbolic names and IP addresses.

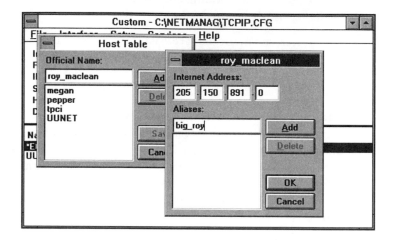

Network Names: /etc/networks

Networks can be addressed by a symbolic name, just as machines are. To resolve the network names, another file is used that contains the corresponding network address. Typically, this file isn't accessed often, because few users want to address an entire network within their application. The network name resolution file's most common use is to specify the local network's name.

UNIX systems usually use the file /etc/networks to specify symbolic network names. The format of the file provides a network symbolic name, its network address, and any alias that might be used, in much the same format as the /etc/hosts table is used for specific machines. A sample /etc/networks file is shown here:

```
# local network names
tpci       146.1           tpci_network   tpci_local
bnr        47.80           BNR bnr.ca
tmn        123.2.21
unique     89.123.23       UNIQUE
sco        132.147         SCO
loopback   127             localhost
```

The /etc/networks file layout is a little different from /etc/hosts in that the usual network name is given in the first column, followed by the IP network address, and then any aliases.

The last entry in this example file gives the loopback name. The first entry specifies the local machine name, its network address, and any name variants. Using this file, an application that wanted to reach the network called UNIQUE could use that name and let the operating system resolve it to the IP network address 89.123.23.

Many implementations of TCP/IP on other platforms don't bother with a network name resolution file like this. Part of the reason is that the /etc/networks file has little use on a UNIX platform, and many single-user operating systems don't require the type of versatility a multiuser operating system like UNIX must supply to an entire network.

Network Protocols: /etc/protocols

Protocol numbers are used to identify the transport protocol to the receiving machine to enable proper decoding of the information within the datagram. With TCP/IP, the protocol number is embedded in the Internet Protocol header. A configuration file is usually used to identify all the transport protocols available on the system and their respective protocol numbers.

UNIX systems use the /etc/protocols file for this purpose. Usually, this file is not modified by the administrator but is maintained by the system and updated automatically as part of the installation procedure when new TCP/IP software or services are added. The /etc/protocols file contains the protocol name, its number, and any alias that might be used for that protocol. A sample /etc/protocols file is shown here:

```
#
# Internet (IP) protocols
#
ip      0       IP      # internet protocol, pseudo protocol number
icmp    1       ICMP    # internet control message protocol
igmp    2       IGMP    # internet group management protocol
ggp     3       GGP     # gateway-gateway protocol
tcp     6       TCP     # transmission control protocol
egp     8       EGP     # Exterior-Gateway Protocol
pup     12      PUP     # PARC universal packet protocol
udp     17      UDP     # user datagram protocol
hello   63      HELLO   # HELLO Routing Protocol
ospf    89      OSPF    # Open Shortest Path First Routing Protocol
```

In this /etc/protocols file, the IP protocol is assigned protocol 0, and TCP is protocol 6. The values in this table should not be changed from their default values except when special network conditions mandate a change. If new TCP/IP services are added to the UNIX system this file resides on, new entries are made to this file by the application installation routine.

There are usually no equivalents of the /etc/protocols file on other operating systems because they assume that the standard transport number is used for each protocol.

Network Services: `/etc/services`

The final common configuration file used on most UNIX systems identifies the existing network services. As with the `/etc/protocols` file, this file is not usually modified by an administrator but is maintained by software as it is installed or configured.

The UNIX network services file is `/etc/services`. The file is in ASCII format consisting of the service name, a port number, and the protocol type. The port number and protocol type are separated by a slash. The port numbers for TCP/IP usually follow the conventions mentioned in the previous chapters. Any optional service alias names follow after the port numbers. A short extract from a sample `/etc/services` file (the file is usually quite lengthy) is shown here:

```
# network services
echo     7/tcp
echo     7/udp
discard  9/tcp    sink  null
discard  9/udp    sink  null
ftp      21/tcp
telnet   23/tcp
smtp     25/tcp    mail mailx
tftp     69/udp
# specific services
login    513/tcp
who      513/udp   whod
```

Setting the Hostname

TCP/IP requires that each machine on the network have an IP address. Usually, each machine also has a unique symbolic name; otherwise, the IP address must be used for all connections to that machine. Most operating systems have a simple program that identifies the name of the local machine. UNIX systems have the utility hostname for this purpose, as well as the uname program, which can give the node name with the command uname -n. The uname utility is usually supported in System V and compatible operating systems only.

The hostname is sometimes saved in a separate file that is read when the operating system starts up, or it can be read from one of the configuration files mentioned previously. The hostname is used by most protocols on the system and by many TCP/IP applications, so it is important for proper system operation. The hostname can sometimes be changed by editing the system file that contains the name and then rebooting the machine, although many operating systems provide a utility program to ensure that this process is performed correctly.

On many UNIX systems, the hostname and uname commands echo back the local machine name, as the following sample session shows:

```
$ hostname
tpci_sco4.tpci.com
$ uname -n
tpci_sco4
```

On the SCO UNIX system used in this example, the hostname command returns the fully qualified domain name, whereas the uname command provides the local machine name only. On a Hewlett-Packard workstation running HP-UX, both commands return only the local machine name. The exact behavior of the hostname and uname commands is therefore quite dependent on the implementation.

On a Linux system, for example, the hostname command can be used to not only show the current host name setting but also to change it when used with the -S (for set) option. For example, the command

```
hostname -S willow.tree.com
```

changes the local fully qualified domain name to willow.tree.com. Not all versions of Linux support the -S option of the hostname command.

Most TCP/IP suites for other operating systems use a simpler method of setting the host name. For example, on a Windows 3.x machine the NetManage ChameleonNFS package uses the dialog shown in Figure 7.2 to quickly set the hostname.

Figure 7.2.
ChameleonNFS uses this dialog to set the host-name.

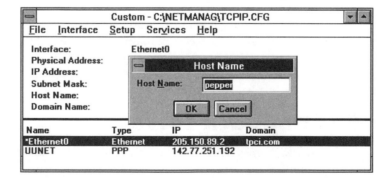

Windows NT has TCP/IP services built into the basic distribution. On a Windows NT system, the hostname is specified through the Network dialog opened from the Control Panel, as shown in Figure 7.3. Both the Windows NT and Windows 3.x systems enable a change in the hostname to be made effective immediately, although a system reboot is recommended to clear all configuration information held in memory.

7

Figure 7.3.

Setting the hostname through the Windows NT Network Control Panel.

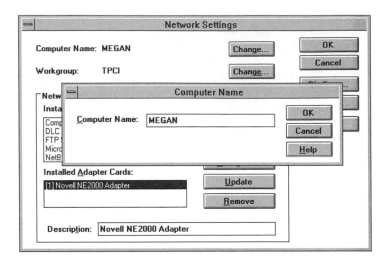

A potential problem can occur when the local machine is *multihomed,* or based in several networks with a different name and IP address for each network. The single name in the configuration file in such an installation might not provide enough information to permit proper routing over all the connected networks. This problem is seldom encountered, but it does require the system administrator to set the hostname for each network carefully.

Aside from the simple machine name query shown, the hostname system is a full protocol that enables access to the Network Information Center (NIC) tables to verify addresses and obtain information about the network, gateways, and hosts. It uses TCP port number 101 to connect to the NIC. This type of access is usually restricted to the network administrator.

The Loopback Driver

The *loopback driver* is probably the most fundamental and often-used diagnostic available to an administrator. A loopback driver acts as a virtual circuit, enabling outgoing information to be immediately rerouted back to an input. This enables testing of the machine's circuits by eliminating any external influences, such as the network itself, gateways, or remote machines. By convention, each machine uses the IP address 127.0.0.1 for the loopback driver (also called the localhost IP address).

Every system should have a loopback driver in place whether the machine is on a network or not. This is because some applications insist on having an IP address they can access to function properly. Many license servers on a UNIX machine have this requirement, for example. Although the need for a loopback driver isn't important for non-networked Windows and similar operating system machines, a loopback driver is always installed with a TCP/IP suite.

NOTE By using a loopback driver, an administrator can be sure that the local machine is working properly and that any failures are from further out. Also, some applications insist on having a loopback driver IP address in order to function properly.

Loopback drivers are usually embedded as part of the operating system kernel, or sometimes as an add-on utility program. Most multiuser systems employ an embedded loopback driver. UNIX is a good example: Within the kernel is a device driver specifically designed to act as a loopback driver. The loopback driver is almost always added automatically when the operating system is installed, but a few UNIX-based operating systems, including several versions of Linux, don't perform this function, and the loopback driver must be added manually by the system administrator. As previously mentioned, several configuration files on the system contain the address of the loopback's connection, such as /etc/hosts.

Using the loopback driver to reroute the output stream, the network interface card (usually an Ethernet card) is bypassed. The loopback driver is useful for testing TCP/IP software installations, because it immediately shows any problems with the local configuration. This can be done before the machine is physically connected to the network or even before the networking hardware and software are installed. For example, you can use the loopback driver to test your TCP/IP configuration before it is connected to a network by using the ping command with the local hostname or IP address, as the following example shows:

```
# ping -c5 localhost
PING localhost (127.0.0.1): 56 data bytes
64 bytes from localhost (127.0.0.1): icmp_seq=0 ttl=64 time=10 ms
64 bytes from localhost (127.0.0.1): icmp_seq=1 ttl=64 time=0 ms
64 bytes from localhost (127.0.0.1): icmp_seq=2 ttl=64 time=0 ms
64 bytes from localhost (127.0.0.1): icmp_seq=3 ttl=64 time=0 ms
64 bytes from localhost (127.0.0.1): icmp_seq=4 ttl=64 time=0 ms

--- localhost ping statistics ---
5 packets transmitted, 5 packets received, 0% packet loss
round-trip min/avg/max = 0/2/10 ms
# ping -c5 127.0.0.1
PING 127.0.0.1 (127.0.0.1): 56 data bytes
64 bytes from localhost (127.0.0.1): icmp_seq=0 ttl=64 time=0 ms
64 bytes from localhost (127.0.0.1): icmp_seq=1 ttl=64 time=0 ms
64 bytes from localhost (127.0.0.1): icmp_seq=2 ttl=64 time=0 ms
64 bytes from localhost (127.0.0.1): icmp_seq=3 ttl=64 time=0 ms
64 bytes from localhost (127.0.0.1): icmp_seq=4 ttl=64 time=0 ms

--- 127.0.0.1 ping statistics ---
5 packets transmitted, 5 packets received, 0% packet loss
round-trip min/avg/max = 0/0/0 ms
```

7

In the preceding example I used the ping command with the -c option to specify five pings, first with the local hostname (which /etc/hosts resolves to the IP address 127.0.0.1) and then with the IP address itself. If either command had failed, it would indicate a problem with either the /etc/hosts file (if the name localhost could not be resolved) or with the TCP/IP installation (if both commands failed).

Managing ARP

The arp program manages entries in the system's Address Resolution Protocol (ARP) tables. You may recall that ARP provides the link between the IP address and the underlying physical address. For more information, see Day 2, "TCP/IP and the Internet."

Using arp (or its equivalent in other operating systems), the administrator can create, modify, or delete entries in the ARP table. Typically, this has to be performed whenever a machine's network address changes (either because of a change in the network hardware or because of a physical move).

The arp program differs considerably between implementations and is seldom used by users, so examples of its use are left to the operating system's configuration and administration documentation.

Using `ifconfig`

The ifconfig program, or one like it, enables an administrator to activate and deactivate network interfaces, as well as to configure them. Access to the ifconfig program is generally restricted to a superuser or network administrator. Changes to the configuration can usually be made only before the system is fully operational (such as in single-user mode on a UNIX system). When issued, ifconfig essentially instructs the network layer of the kernel to work with the specified network interface by assigning an IP address, then issuing a command to make the interface active on the system. Only when the interface is active can the operating system kernel send and receive data through the interface.

The ifconfig program enables a network administrator to perform several useful functions on most operating systems:

> Activate or deactivate an interface
> Activate or deactivate ARP on an interface
> Activate or deactivate debugging mode on an interface
> Assign a broadcast address
> Assign a subnetwork mask
> Assign a routing method

Examining all the options available to ifconfig would require several dozen pages. Because this material is rarely used and differs with each implementation, administrators are referred to their operating system documentation. As an example, the Linux version of the ifconfig command uses this general format:

```
ifconfig interface_type IP_Address
```

interface_type is the interface's device driver name (such as lo for loopback, ppp for PPP, and eth for Ethernet), and IP_Address is the IP address used by that interface.

When used with only the name of an interface, ifconfig usually returns information about the current state of the interface, as shown in the following example. In this example, a query of both an Ethernet card (called ec0) and the loopback driver (called lo0) is performed. The status flags of the interface are followed by the Internet address, the broadcast address, and optionally a network mask, which defines the Internet address used for address comparison when routing.

```
tpci_sco1-12> ifconfig ec0
ec0: flags=807<UP,BROADCAST,DEBUG,ARP>
     inet 146.8.12.15 netmask fffff00 broadcast
146.8.12.15
tpci_sco1-13> ifconfig lo0
lo0: flags=49<UP,LOOPBACK,RUNNING>
     inet 127.0.0.1 netmask ff000000
```

The preceding example shows that the Ethernet connection ec0 is active (UP), able to transmit broadcasts (BROADCAST), and is in debugging mode (DEBUG). Also, the ARP protocol is active (ARP). You may recall that a broadcast message is sent to all machines on the local network by setting the host ID address to all 1s.

Once the ifconfig command has been run and an interface is active, many operating systems require the route command to be issued to add or remove routes in the kernel's routing table. This is needed to enable the local machine to find other machines. The general format of the route command on a UNIX or Linux system is this:

```
route add|del IP_Address
```

Either add or del is specified to add or remove the route from the kernel's routing table, and IP_Address is the remote route being affected.

The current contents of the kernel's routing table can be displayed on some systems by entering the command route by itself on the command line. For example, on a Linux system that is set up only with the loopback driver, you see an output like this:

```
$ route
Kernel Routing Table
Destination     Gateway    Genmask      Flags  MSS  Window  Use Iface
loopback        *          255.0.0.0    U      1936 0        16  lo
```

The important columns are the destination name, which shows the name of the configured target (in this case only `loopback`), the mask to be used (`Genmask`), and the interface (`Iface`, in this case `/dev/lo`). You can force `route` to display the IP addresses instead of symbolic names by using the `-n` option:

```
$ route -n
Kernel Routing Table
Destination     Gateway    Genmask     Flags  MSS  Window  Use Iface
127.0.0.1       *          255.0.0.0   U      1936 0        16  lo
```

Not all UNIX and Linux versions show this type of output from the `route` command.

The use of the `ifconfig` and `route` programs can be shown in the setup of a Slackware Linux system's Ethernet connection. To make the Ethernet interface active, the `ifconfig` command is issued with the Ethernet device name (`eth0` on a Slackware Linux system) and the local IP address. For example, the command

```
ifconfig eth0 147.123.20.1
```

sets up the local machine with the IP address `147.123.20.1`. The interface is the Ethernet device `/dev/eth0`. The interface can then be checked with the `ifconfig` command using the interface name:

```
$ ifconfig eth0
eth0    Link encap 10Mps: Ethernet Hwaddr
        inet addr 147.123.20.1 Bcast 147.123.1.255 Mask 255.255.255.0
        UP BROADCAST RUNNING  MTU 1500 Metric 1
        RX packets:0 errors:0 dropped:0 overruns:0
        TX packets:0 errors:0 dropped:0 overruns:0
```

You may notice in the output that the broadcast address was set based on the local machine's IP address. This is used by TCP/IP to access all machines on the local area network at once. The Message Transfer Unit (MTU) size is usually set to the maximum value of 1500 (for Ethernet networks).

Next, an entry is added to the kernel routing tables to let the kernel know about the local machine's network address. The IP address that is used with the `route` command is not your local machine's IP address, but that of the network as a whole without the local identifier. To set the entire local area network at once, the `-net` option of the route command is used. In the case of the IP addresses shown earlier, the command would be this:

```
route add -net 147.123.20.0
```

This adds all the machines on the network identified by the network address `147.123.20` to the kernel's list of accessible machines. An alternative method is to use the `/etc/networks` file. Once the route has been added to the kernel routing tables, it can be tested with the `ping` command.

The `inetd` **Daemon**

The `inetd` program is a holdover from the early days of TCP/IP UNIX development. When a UNIX machine was started, it would activate TCP/IP and immediately accept connections at its ports, spawning a process for each. This could result in many identical processes, one for each available port.

To control the processes better, the `inetd` program was developed to handle the port connections itself, offloading that task from the server. The primary difference is that `inetd` creates a process for each connection that is established, whereas the server creates a process for each port (which leads to many unused processes).

On many systems, some of the test programs and status information utilities are run through `inetd`. Typically, services like `echo`, `discard`, and `time` use `inetd`.

The `inetd` program uses a configuration file usually called `/etc/inetd.cfg`, `/etc/inetd.conf`, or `/etc/inetd.cf` on UNIX systems. An extract of a sample `/etc/inetd.cfg` file is shown in the following code:

```
#       @(#)inetd.conf      5.2 Lachman System V STREAMS TCP  source
#
#       System V STREAMS TCP - Release 4.0
ftp         stream    tcp    nowait    NOLUID    /etc/ftpd       ftpd
telnet      stream    tcp    nowait    NOLUID    /etc/telnetd    telnetd
shell       stream    tcp    nowait    NOLUID    /etc/rshd       rshd
login       stream    tcp    nowait    NOLUID    /etc/rlogind    rlogind
exec        stream    tcp    nowait    NOLUID    /etc/rexecd     rexecd
finger      stream    tcp    nowait    nouser    /etc/fingerd    fingerd
comsat      dgram     udp    wait      root      /etc/comsat     comsat
ntalk       dgram     udp    wait      root      /etc/talkd      talkd
echo        stream    tcp    nowait    root      internal
discard     stream    tcp    nowait    root      internal
chargen     stream    tcp    nowait    root      internal
daytime     stream    tcp    nowait    root      internal
time        stream    tcp    nowait    root      internal
echo        dgram     udp    wait      root      internal
discard     dgram     udp    wait      root      internal
chargen     dgram     udp    wait      root      internal
daytime     dgram     udp    wait      root      internal
time        dgram     udp    wait      root      internal
```

The columns show the service name (which corresponds to an entry in the services file, such as `/etc/services`), the socket type (`stream`, `raw`, or `datagram`), the protocol name, whether `inetd` can accept further connections at the same port immediately (`nowait`) or must wait for the server to finish (`wait`), the login that owns the service, the server program name, and any optional parameters needed for the server program.

The configuration file is read when the server is booted and every time a hang-up signal is received from an application. This enables dynamic changes to the file, because any modifications would be read and registered on the next file read.

7

The `netstat` Command

The `netstat` program or a similar utility provides comprehensive information about the local system and its TCP/IP implementation. This is the program most commonly used by administrators to quickly diagnose a problem with TCP/IP. The actual information and its format supplied by the `netstat` utility differs with the operating system implementation, but it usually supplies the following important summaries, each of which is covered in more detail later:

> Communications end points
> Network interface statistics
> Information on the data buffers
> Routing table information
> Protocol statistics

On some systems, information about the interprocess communications and other protocol stacks might be appended. The information to be displayed can usually be toggled with a command-line option. The output from a typical UNIX installation that uses the `netstat` command is shown in the next few sections, which discuss `netstat` and its output in more detail. The output and meaning might be different with other operating systems, but the general purpose of the diagnostic tool remains the same.

Communications End Points

The `netstat` command with no options provides information on all active communications end points. To display all end points (active and passive), `netstat` uses the `-a` option.

The output is formatted into columns showing the protocol (`Proto`), the amount of data in the receive and send queues (`Recv-Q` and `Send-Q`), the local and remote addresses, and the current state of the connection. A truncated sample output is shown here:

```
$ netstat -a
Active Internet connections (including servers)
Proto Recv-Q Send-Q Local Address          Foreign Address        (state)
ip        0      0  *.*                     *.*
tcp       0   2124  tpci.login              merlin.1034            ESTABL.
tcp       0      0  tpci.1034               prudie.login           ESTABL.
tcp   11212      0  tpci.1035               treijs.1036            ESTABL.
tcp       0      0  tpci.1021               reboc.1024             TIME_WAIT
tcp       0      0  *.1028                  *.*                    LISTEN
tcp       0      0  *.*                     *.*                    CLOSED
tcp       0      0  *.6000                  *.*                    LISTEN
tcp       0      0  *.listen                *.*                    LISTEN
tcp       0      0  *.1024                  *.*                    LISTEN
```

```
tcp       0       0   *.sunrpc            *.*                  LISTEN
tcp       0       0   *.smtp              *.*                  LISTEN
tcp       0       0   *.time              *.*                  LISTEN
tcp       0       0   *.echo              *.*                  LISTEN
tcp       0       0   *.finger            *.*                  LISTEN
tcp       0       0   *.exec              *.*                  LISTEN
tcp       0       0   *.telnet            *.*                  LISTEN
tcp       0       0   *.ftp               *.*                  LISTEN
tcp       0       0   *.*                 *.*                  CLOSED
udp       0       0   *.60000             *.*
udp       0       0   *.177               *.*
udp       0       0   *.1039              *.*
udp       0       0   *.1038              *.*
udp       0       0   localhost.1036      localhost.syslog
udp       0       0   *.1034              *.*
udp       0       0   *.*                 *.*
udp       0       0   *.1027              *.*
udp       0       0   *.1026              *.*
udp       0       0   *.sunrpc            *.*
udp       0       0   *.1025              *.*
udp       0       0   *.time              *.*
udp       0       0   *.daytime           *.*
udp       0       0   *.chargen           *.*
udp       0       0   *.route             *.*
udp       0       0   *.*                 *.*
```

NOTE

The output shown for the `netstat` commands in this section is from an SCO UNIX system. Each implementation of `netstat` is slightly different, so the output columns might change, and different options might be needed to obtain each type of report. Check with your system documentation for more details about your `netstat` implementation.

In the preceding example, there are three active TCP connections, as identified by the state ESTABL. One has data being sent (as shown in the Send-Q column), and another has incoming data in the queue. The network names and port numbers of the connection ends are shown whenever possible. An asterisk (*) means there is no end point associated with that address yet.

One connection is waiting to be hung up, identified by TIME_WAIT in the state column. After 30 seconds, these sessions are terminated and the connection freed. Any row with LISTEN as the state has no connection at the moment, and is waiting. There is no state column for UDP sessions because they do not have an end-to-end connection (as discussed on Day 5, "Gateway and Routing Protocols"). A CLOSED entry in the output shows that the connection is closed but hasn't switched over to LISTEN yet.

7

Network Interface Statistics

The behavior of the network interface (such as the network interface card) can be determined with the -i option to the netstat command. This information quickly shows an administrator whether there are major problems with the network connection.

The netstat -i command displays the name of the interface, the maximum number of characters a packet can contain (Mtu), the network and host addresses or names, the number of input packets (Ipkts), input errors (Ierrs), output packets (Opkts), output errors (Oerrs), and number of collisions (Collis) experienced in the current sampling session. The collisions column has relevance only for a networking system that enables packet collisions, such as Ethernet. A sample output from a netstat -i command is shown here:

```
$ netstat -i
Name   Mtu    Network     Address      Ipkts    Ierrs Opkts   Oerrs Collis
ec0    1500   tpci        merlin          34    0     125     0     0
lan0   1497   47.80       tpci_hpws4   11625    0     11625   0     0
lo0    8232   loopback    localhost      206    0     206     0     0
```

An administrator can obtain more specific information about one interface by using the -I option with a device name and a time interval, specified in seconds, such as netstat -I ec0 30, to obtain specific information about the behavior of the ec0 (Ethernet) interface over the last 30 seconds.

Data Buffers

Information about the data buffers can be obtained with the netstat command's -m option. Monitoring the behavior of the buffers is important, because they directly impact the performance of TCP/IP. The output of the netstat -m command differs depending on the version of UNIX in use, reflecting the different implementations of the TCP/IP code.

The netstat -m command output from a System V-based UNIX version is shown in the following code example. Entries are provided for the streamhead, queue, message descriptor table (mblks), data descriptor table (dblks), and the different classes of data descriptor tables. The columns show the number of blocks configured (config) and currently allocated (alloc), the number of columns free (free), the total number of blocks in use (total), the maximum number of blocks that were in use at one time (max), and the number of times a block was not available (fail).

```
$ netstat -m
streams allocation:
              config    alloc    free    total     max    fail
streams         292       79     213      233      80      0
queues         1424      362    1062      516     368      0
mblks          5067      196    4871     3957     206      0
dblks          4054      196    3858     3957     206      0
```

```
class 0,    4 bytes     652      50     602      489      53      0
class 1,   16 bytes     652       2     650      408       4      0
class 2,   64 bytes     768       6     762     2720      14      0
class 3,  128 bytes     872     105     767      226     107      0
class 4,  256 bytes     548      21     527       36      22      0
class 5,  512 bytes     324      12     312       32      13      0
class 6, 1024 bytes     107       0     107        1       1      0
class 7, 2048 bytes      90       0      90        7       1      0
class 8, 4096 bytes      41       0      41       38       1      0
total configured streams memory: 1166.73KB
streams memory in use: 44.78KB
maximum streams memory used: 58.57KB
```

For the administrator, the failure column is important. It should always show 0s. If a larger
number appears, that resource has been overtaxed and the number of blocks assigned to that
resource should be increased (followed by a kernel rebuild and a reboot of the system to affect
the changes).

Routing Table Information

Routing tables are continually updated to reflect connections to other machines. To obtain
information about the routing tables, the netstat -r and -rs options are used. (The latter
generates statistics about the routing tables.)

The output from netstat -r and netstat -rs commands are shown in the following code
example. The columns show the destination machine, the address of the gateway to be used,
a flag to show whether the route is active (U) and whether it leads to a gateway (G) or a machine
(H for host), a reference counter (Refs) that specifies how many active connections can use
that route simultaneously, the number of packets that have been sent over the route (Use),
and the interface name.

```
$ netstat -r
Routing tables
Destination        Gateway          Flags    Refs      Use  Interface
localhost          localhost        UH          4       10  lo0
merlin             localhost        UH          2        2  ec0
treijs             hoytgate         UG          0        0  ec0
47.80              bcarh736         U          12    21029  lan0
tpci sco4-57> netstat -rs
routing:
           0 bad routing redirects
           0 dynamically created routes
           0 new gateways found unreachable
           2 destinations found unreachable
         122 uses of a wildcard route
           0 routes marked doutbful
           0 routes cleared of being doubtful
           0 routes deleted
```

7

Protocol Statistics

Statistics about the overall behavior of network protocols can be obtained with the netstat
-s command. This usually provides summaries for IP, ICMP, TCP, and UDP. The output
from this command is useful for determining where an error in a received packet was located,
which then leads the user to isolate whether that error was caused by a software or network
problem.

Issuing the netstat -s command provides a verbose output. A sample output is shown in the
following code. The entries are self-explanatory.

```
tpci_sco4-67> netstat -s
ip:
     183309 total packets received
     0 bad header checksums
     0 with size smaller than minimum
     0 with data size < data length
     0 with header length < data size
     0 with data length < header length
     0 with unknown protocol
     13477 fragments received
     0 fragments dropped (dup or out of space)
     0 fragments dropped after timeout
     0 packets reassembled
     0 packets forwarded
     0 packets not forwardable
     75 no routes
     0 redirects sent
     0 system errors during input
     309 packets delivered
     309 total packets sent
     0 system errors during output
     0 packets fragmented
     0 packets not fragmentable
     0 fragments created
icmp:
     1768 calls to icmp_error
     0 errors not generated because old message was icmp
     Output histogram:
          destination unreachable: 136
     0 messages with bad code fields
     0 messages < minimum length
     0 bad checksums
     0 messages with bad length
     Input histogram:
          destination unreachable: 68
     0 message responses generated
     68 messages received
     68 messages sent
     0 system errors during output
```

```
tcp:
    9019 packets sent
            6464 data packets (1137192 bytes)
            4 data packets (4218 bytes) retransmitted
            1670 ack-only packets (918 delayed)
            0 URG only packets
            0 window probe packets
            163 window update packets
            718 control packets
                24 resets
    9693 packets received
            4927 acks (for 74637 bytes)
            37 duplicate acks
            0 acks for unsent data
            5333 packets (1405271 bytes) received in-sequence
            23 completely duplicate packets (28534 bytes)
            0 packets with some dup. data (0 bytes duped)
            38 out-of-order packets (5876 bytes)
            0 packets (0 bytes) of data after window
            0 window probes
            134 window update packets
            0 packets received after close
            0 discarded for bad checksums
            0 discarded for bad header offset fields
            0 discarded because packet too short
            0 system errors encountered during processing
        224 connection requests
        130 connection accepts
        687 connections established (including accepts)
        655 connections closed (including 0 drops)
        24 embryonic connections dropped
        0 failed connect and accept requests
        0 resets received while established
        5519 segments updated rtt (of 5624 attempts)
        5 retransmit timeouts
            0 connections dropped by rexmit timeout
        0 persist timeouts
        0 keepalive timeouts
            0 keepalive probes sent
            0 connections dropped by keepalive
        0 connections lingered
            0 linger timers expired
            0 linger timers cancelled
            0 linger timers aborted by signal
udp:
        0 incomplete headers
        0 bad data length fields
        0 bad checksums
        68 bad ports
        125 input packets delivered
        0 system errors during input
        268 packets sent
```

7

The ping Utility

The ping (Packet Internet Groper) utility is used to query another system to ensure that a connection is still active. (You may recall the ruptime utility from yesterday, which also does this. However, ruptime waits five minutes before trying the remote, and you may want to know right away if the connection is active.) The ping command is available on most operating systems that implement TCP/IP.

The ping program operates by sending out an Internet Control Message Protocol (ICMP) echo request. If the destination machine's IP software receives the ICMP request, it issues an echo reply immediately. The sending machine continues to send an echo request until the ping program is terminated with a break sequence (Ctrl+C or the Delete key in UNIX). After termination, ping displays a set of statistics. A sample ping session is shown here:

```
$ ping merlin
PING merlin: 64 data bytes
64 bytes from 142.12.130.12: icmp_seq=0.  time=20.  ms
64 bytes from 142.12.130.12: icmp_seq=1.  time=10.  ms
64 bytes from 142.12.130.12: icmp_seq=2.  time=10.  ms
64 bytes from 142.12.130.12: icmp_seq=3.  time=20.  ms
64 bytes from 142.12.130.12: icmp_seq=4.  time=10.  ms
64 bytes from 142.12.130.12: icmp_seq=5.  time=10.  ms
64 bytes from 142.12.130.12: icmp_seq=6.  time=10.  ms
--- merling PING Statistics ---
7 packets transmitted, 7 packets received, 0% packet loss
round-trip (ms) min/avg/max = 10/12/20
```

An alternate method to invoke ping is to provide the number of times you want it to query the remote. Also, you could provide a packet length as a test. The following example instructs ping to use 256 data byte packets and try five times. Using ping to send large packets is one method of determining the network's behavior with large packet sizes, especially when fragmentation must occur. The ping program is also useful for monitoring response times of the network, by observing the reply time on packets sent as the network load (or the machine load) changes. This information can be very useful in the optimization of TCP/IP.

```
$ ping merlin 256 5
PING merlin: 256 data bytes
256 bytes from 142.12.130.12: icmp_seq=0.  time=20.  ms
256 bytes from 142.12.130.12: icmp_seq=1.  time=10.  ms
256 bytes from 142.12.130.12: icmp_seq=2.  time=10.  ms
256 bytes from 142.12.130.12: icmp_seq=3.  time=20.  ms
256 bytes from 142.12.130.12: icmp_seq=4.  time=10.  ms
--- merling PING Statistics ---
5 packets transmitted, 5 packets received, 0% packet loss
round-trip (ms) min/avg/max = 10/13/20
```

Some older implementations of ping simply reply with a message that the system at the other end is active. (The message is of the form x is alive.) To obtain the verbose messages shown previously, the -s option must be used.

The ping program is useful for diagnostics because it provides four important pieces of information: whether the TCP/IP software is functioning correctly; whether a local network device can be addressed (validating its address); whether a remote machine can be accessed (again validating the address and testing the routing); and verifying the software on the remote machine.

Most non-UNIX TCP/IP implementations provide ping utilities as part of their suite. For example, Figure 7.4 shows the NetManage ChameleonNFS ping utility. The Chameleon ping sends only a single ICMP packet instead of a continuous stream, but is useful for verifying that a remote machine is responding.

Figure 7.4.

ChameleonNFS uses a ping *utility to send a single packet.*

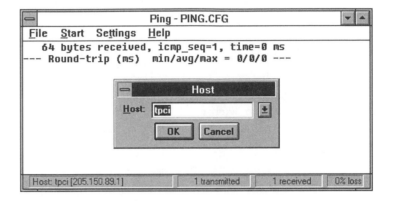

Windows 95 has a ping utility built into the distribution software, but it is DOS-based and doesn't use the Windows 95 GUI. Figure 7.5 shows the Windows 95 ping utility used to ping another machine on the network.

Figure 7.5.

The Windows 95 ping *utility is DOS-based.*

7

Tracing a Connection

There is a tracing option built into TCP/IP. When simpler methods have failed, this option can be used to trace a problem. To activate the trace, a system call is sent to the end point that turns on a flag. Most TCP/IP implementations enable the tracing option to be turned on from the command line using the -d (debug) option. When tracing is turned on, all activities are echoed to a buffer or to the screen, depending on the system configuration.

The output from the TCP/IP tracing option is examined using the program trpt (trace report). A specific connection can be specified, or all behavior passing through TCP/IP can be displayed. The output from trpt is verbose and of little interest to most users.

Summary

This chapter has shown you the basic administration programs used with TCP/IP, as well as the configuration files that are necessary in order to use symbolic names. Although this information is not likely to be used by most users, knowing the available tools and the type of diagnostics that can be produced is useful in better understanding TCP/IP.

Q&A

Q All the TCP/IP protocols available to you are listed in a system configuration file. Which file is this?

A All TCP/IP protocols are listed in /etc/ protocols. The file lists the protocol name and the corresponding protocol number.

Q What is a loopback driver used for?

A The loopback driver is a virtual circuit within the host machine, avoiding all contact with the physical network itself. The most common use of a loopback driver is as a diagnostic. By sending data to the loopback driver, you can make sure the protocols are working correctly on your machine. Without this capability, it would be difficult to separate network problems and software configuration problems.

Q What does the following excerpt from a netstat -a command tell you?

```
A  Proto  Recv-Q  Send-Q  Local Address      Foreign Address      (state)
   ip        0       0     *.*                *.*
   tcp       0    1024     tpci.login         merlin.1034          ESTABL.
   tcp    8756       0     tpci.1035          treijs.1036          ESTABL.
   tcp       0       0     tpci.1021          reboc.1024           TIME_WAIT
   tcp       0       0     *.1028             *.*                  LISTEN
   tcp       0       0     *.6000             *.*                  LISTEN
```

This extract shows there are two established TCP connections (to `merlin.1034` and `treijs.1036`), one of which is sending information and the other receiving. The connection to `reboc.1024` is waiting to hang up. There are two ports waiting for a connection.

Q **What is the utility `ping` used for?**

A The `ping` utility is used to query another system. It sends an ICMP message to the remote and waits for a reply. The `ping` command is very useful for testing connections.

Q **What command gives you overall statistics about the network protocols running on your system?**

A One of the best summaries is obtained with the `netstat -s` command.

7

Chapter 8

TCP/IP and Networks

In the previous seven days you have seen TCP/IP and its associated protocols covered in considerable depth. It is now time to begin looking at TCP/IP in a broader sense. Today you learn how TCP/IP can operate with other protocols in a networked system. You also learn about protocols that don't use TCP/IP but are commonly encountered.

It is useful to understand how TCP/IP operates in conjunction with other protocols so that the management of TCP/IP is clearer (you learn about managing a TCP/IP network in the next few days). You might find that some material today is repeated from earlier days, or rephrased slightly to present a different approach to the subject. In a sense, today acts as a summary, albeit an incomplete one, of the TCP/IP system as a whole.

To round out the day, I look at the miscellaneous optional services provided through TCP/IP. Most are dedicated to a simple task, but they do serve their purpose well and use TCP/IP, hence their inclusion here.

TCP/IP and Other Protocols

TCP/IP is not often found as a sole protocol. It is usually one of several protocols used in any given network. Therefore, the interactions between TCP/IP (and its associated protocols) and the other protocols that might be working with it must be understood. It is easiest to begin looking at this subject from a local area network point of view and then expand that view to cover internetworks.

The layers of a TCP/IP protocol, as well as most other OSI-model protocols, are designed to be independent of each other, enabling mixing of protocols. When a message is to be sent over the network to a remote machine, each protocol layer builds on the packet of information sent from the layer above, adding its own header and then passing the packet to the next lower layer. After being received over the network (packaged in whatever network format is required), the receiving machine passes the packet back up the layers, removing the header information one layer at a time.

Replacing any layer in the protocol stack requires that the new protocols can internetwork with the other layers, as well as perform all the required functions of that layer (for example, duplicating the services of the replaced protocol). Also, performing duplicate operations in more than one layer (redundant operations) should be avoided for obvious reasons.

To examine the internetworking of the layers and the substitution or addition of others, a simple installation can be used as a starting point. Figure 8.1 shows a simple layered architecture using TCP and IP with the Ethernet network. Figure 8.1 also shows the assembly of Ethernet packets as they pass from layer to layer.

Figure 8.1.

A simple layered architecture.

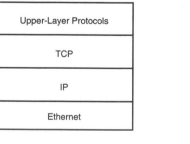

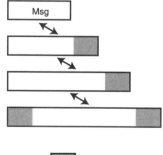

Header or Tail

As you saw earlier in this book, the process begins with a message of some form from an Upper Layer Protocol (ULP), which itself is passing a message from an application. As the message is passed to TCP, it adds its own header information and passes to the IP layer, which does the same. When the IP message is passed to the Ethernet layer, Ethernet adds its own information at the front and back of the message and sends the message out over the network.

NOTE
> The operating system itself is not a single layer but runs throughout the entire layered architecture with connections to each layer. The interfaces between each layer's protocols differ depending on the host machine, but it is convenient to ignore the operating system's influence for simplicity.

Although this simple model might seem ideal, in practice it has a few problems. Most importantly, it requires IP to interface directly with the Ethernet layer. This interface is not a clean one; it has many connections that break from the ideal layered architecture.

LAN Layers

To expand on the layered system requires a better understanding of the interfaces to the network layer in a LAN. Figure 8.2 shows an expanded layer architecture for a LAN. This type of architecture applies for collision sense multiple access (CSMA) and collision detect (CD) networks such as Ethernet.

Figure 8.2.

Network architecture.

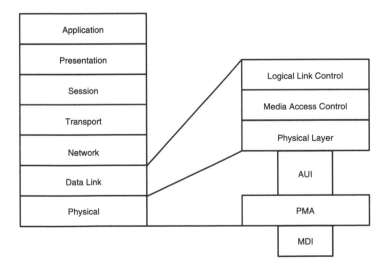

The LAN involves some additional layers. The Logical Link Control (LLC) layer is an interface between the IP layer and the network layers. There are several kinds of LLC configurations, but it is sufficient at this point to know its basic role as a buffer between the network and IP layers, either as a simple system for a connectionless service or as an elaborate system for a connection-based service. LLC is usually used with the High-Level Data Link Control (HDLC) link standard. For connectionless service, this uses an *unnumbered*

information (UI) message frame, whereas connection-based services can use the *asynchronous balanced mode* (ABM) message frame, both supported by HDLC. The configuration of LLC with respect to TCP/IP is important.

The Media Access Control (MAC) layer was mentioned briefly on Day 2, "TCP/IP and the Internet." MAC is responsible for managing traffic on the network, such as collision detection and transmission times. It also handles timers and retransmission functions. MAC is independent of the network medium but is dependent on the protocol used on the network.

The physical layer in the network architecture is composed of several services. The Attachment Unit Interface (AUI) provides an attachment between the machine's physical layer and the network medium. Typically, the AUI is where the network ports or jacks are located.

The Medium Attachment Unit (MAU) is composed of two parts: the Physical Medium Attachment (PMA) and the Medium Dependent Interface (MDI), both of which can be considered as separate parts as shown in the figure. The MAU is responsible for managing the connection of the machine to the LAN medium itself, as well as providing basic data integrity checking and network medium monitoring. The MAU has functions that check the signal quality from the network and test routines for verifying the network's correct operation.

When these layers are added to the layered architecture for a protocol stack, the IP-Ethernet layer is separated. This is shown in Figure 8.3. This type of configuration is more common than the one shown in Figure 8.1 and is usually called the IP/802 configuration (because Ethernet is defined by the IEEE 802 specification).

Figure 8.3.
TCP/IP with LLC/MAC.

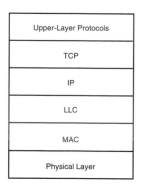
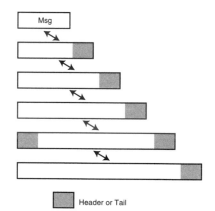

The IP/802 LAN can be connectionless using a simple form of LLC called LLC Type 1, which supports unnumbered information (UI). The LLC and MAC layers help separate IP from the physical layer. More headers are added to the message packet, but these have useful information. The LLC header has both source and destination service access points (SAP) in it to identify the layers above.

UDP is frequently used instead of TCP in this type of network. UDP is not as complex as TCP, so the entire network's complexity is reduced. However, UDP has no message integrity functionality built in, so a different form of LLC (called LLC Type 2) is used that implements these functions. LLC Type 2 provides the data integrity functionality that TCP usually provides, such as sequencing, transfer window management, and flow control. The disadvantage is that these functions are now below the IP layer, instead of above it. In case of fatal problems with the LLC layer, this can result in problems that must be dealt with in the application layer itself.

NOTE

> The differences between TCP and LLC Type 1 versus UDP and LLC Type 2 must be carefully weighed by a system administrator. The TCP/LLC 1 combination is more complex than UDP/LLC 2 but offers excellent reliability and integrity, whereas UDP/LLC 2 is better for high-throughput networks. In some cases, UDP/LLC 2 results in duplicated functions, because the LLC versions differ considerably among vendors.

NetBIOS and TCP/IP

A popular PC-oriented network operating system is NetBIOS, which can be cleanly integrated with TCP/IP. Figure 8.4 shows the network architecture for this kind of LAN. NetBIOS resides above the TCP or UDP protocol, although it usually has solid links into that layer (so the two layers cannot be cleanly separated). NetBIOS acts to connect applications together in the upper layers, providing messaging and resource allocation.

Three Internet port numbers are allocated for NetBIOS. These are for the NetBIOS name service (port 137), datagram service (port 138), and session service (port 139). There is also the provision for a mapping between Internet's Domain Name Service (DNS) and the NetBIOS Name Server (NBNS). (DNS is covered in detail on Day 11, "DNS.") The NetBIOS Name Server is used to identify PCs that operate in a NetBIOS area. In the interface between NetBIOS and TCP, a mapping between the names is used to produce the DNS name.

Figure 8.4.

The NetBIOS network architecture.

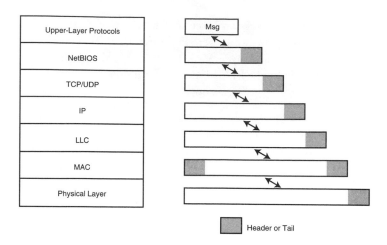

IP can be configured to run above NetBIOS, eliminating TCP or UDP entirely and running NetBIOS as a connectionless service. In this case, NetBIOS takes over the functions of the TCP/UDP layer, and the upper-layer protocols must have the data integrity, packet sequencing, and flow control functions. This is shown in Figure 8.5. In this architecture, NetBIOS encapsulates IP datagrams. Strong mapping between IP and NetBIOS is necessary so that NetBIOS packets reflect IP addresses. (To do this, NetBIOS codes the names as IP.*nnn.nnn.nnn.nnn*.)

Figure 8.5.

Running IP above NetBIOS.

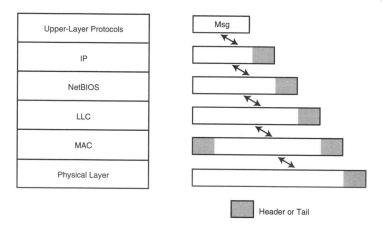

This type of network requires that the upper-layer protocols (ULPs) handle all the necessary features of the TCP protocol, but the advantage is that the network architecture is simple and efficient. For some networks, this type of approach is well suited, although the development of suitable ULPs can be problematic at times.

XNS and TCP/IP

The Xerox Network System (XNS) was widely used in the past and still retains a reasonable percentage of network use. XNS is popular because Xerox released the code to the public domain, hence making it a cost-effective network system. In most cases, XNS protocols were designed to work with Xerox's Ethernet, as well. XNS now appears in several commercial network software packages.

XNS can use IP, as shown in Figure 8.6. The Sequenced Packet Protocol (SPP) is above the IP layer, providing some TCP function, although it is not as complete a protocol. In the ULP layer is the Courier protocol, which provides presentation and session layer services.

Figure 8.6.

The XNS network architecture.

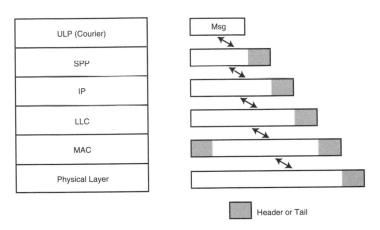

XNS uses the term *Internet Transport Protocols* to refer to the set of protocols used, including IP. Among the protocols is the Routing Information Protocol (RIP) and an error protocol similar to the Internet Control Message Protocol (ICMP).

IPX and UDP

Novell's NetWare networking product has a protocol similar to IP called the Internet Packet Exchange (IPX), which is based on Xerox's XNS. The IPX architecture is shown in Figure 8.7. IPX usually uses UDP for a connectionless protocol, although TCP can be used when combined with LLC Type 1.

Figure 8.7.

The IPX network architecture.

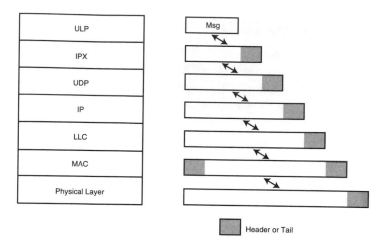

The stacking of the layers (with IPX above UDP) ensures that the UDP and IP headers are not affected, with the IPX information encapsulated as part of the usual message process. As with other network protocols, a mapping is necessary between the IP address and the IPX addresses. IPX uses network and host numbers of 4 and 6 bytes, respectively. These are converted as they are passed to UDP.

It is possible to reconfigure the network to use IPX networks by using TCP instead of UDP and substituting the connectionless LLC Type 1 protocol. This results in the architecture shown in Figure 8.8. When using this layer architecture, IP addresses are mapped using ARP.

Figure 8.8.

An IPX-based network architecture.

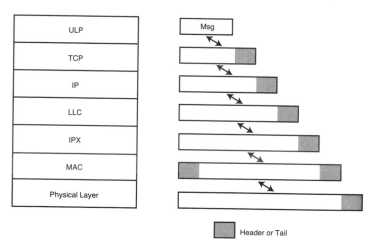

ARCnet and TCP/IP

ARCnet is widely used for LANs and has an Internet RFC for using it with IP. The architecture is similar to that of the IPX-based network but with ARCnet replacing IPX, as shown in Figure 8.9. Messages passed down from IP are encapsulated into ARCnet datagrams.

Figure 8.9.

The ARCnet-based network architecture.

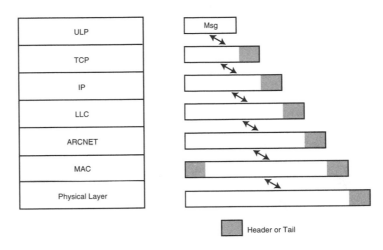

A special placement of the IP datagram behind the client data area of the ARCnet header ensures that IP compatibility is maintained if the message must pass out of the ARCnet network (through a converter). IP addresses are mapped to ARCnet addresses using ARP. The protocol also supports RARP to some extent.

FDDI Networks

The Fiber Distributed Data Interface (FDDI) is an ANSI-defined, high-speed network that uses fiber-optic cable as a transport medium. FDDI is gaining string support because of the high throughput that can be achieved. For TCP/IP, FDDI uses a layered architecture like the other networks discussed. FDDI differs slightly from other media in that there are two sublayers for the physical layer.

FDDI's addressing scheme is similar to other Ethernet networks, requiring a simple mapping, as seen with the Ethernet system. IP and ARP can both be used over FDDI. IP is used with the LLC Type 1 connectionless service.

The frame size for FDDI is set to 4500 bytes, including the header and other framing information. After that is taken into account, there are 4470 bytes available for data. (The Internet RFC for FDDI defines 4096 bytes for data and 256 bytes for header layers above the MAC layer.) This large packet size can cause problems for some gateways, so routing for FDDI packets must be carefully chosen to prevent truncation or corruption of the packet by a gateway that can't handle the large frame size. In case of doubt, FDDI packets should be reduced in size to 576 data bytes.

X.25 and IP

X.25 networks modify the network architecture by using an OSI TP4 layer on top of IP, and the X.25 Packet Layer Procedures (PLP) layer below IP. This is shown in Figure 8.10. TP4 is a TCP-like protocol that does not use port identifiers. The destination and source fields in the header are the *transport service access points* (TSAPs). TP4 is more complex than TCP, which sometimes works against it.

Figure 8.10.
The X.25-based network architecture.

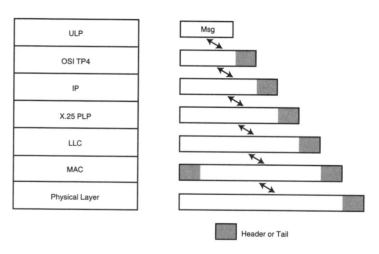

X.25 is not often used on a LAN, but it is used as a connection to a packet-switched network. An Internet RFC defines the rules for X.25 IP-based packet switching, including the limits for IP datagram sizes (576 bytes) and virtual circuits.

ISDN and TCP/IP

The Integrated Services Digital Network (ISDN) provides packet-switched TCP/IP networks. The architecture is shown in Figure 8.11. IP is not in the stack because it is usually incorporated into CLNP. (Both TCP and IP can be used with ISDN instead of OSI TP4 and CLNP, but the ISDN versions are optimized for that network.)

Figure 8.11.
The ISDN-based network architecture.

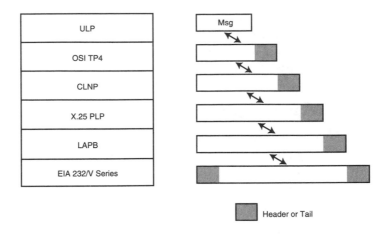

| ULP |
| OSI TP4 |
| CLNP |
| X.25 PLP |
| LAPB |
| EIA 232/V Series |

Msg

▢ Header or Tail

ISDN uses a more complex architecture than most networks, replacing gateways and routers with *terminal adapters* and *ISDN nodes.* These perform the equivalent functions but have a more rigid (and complex) internal architecture. The details are not relevant here, so the interested reader is referred to a good ISDN book.

Switched Multi-Megabit Data Services and IP

The Switched Multi-Megabit Data Services (SMDS) system is a public, packet-switched, connectionless service that provides high throughput with large packet sizes (up to 9188 data bytes). SMDS uses a subscriber-to-network and network-to-subscriber access mechanism for flow control. SMDS works with IP by interfacing the SMDS to the LLC layer.

SMDS using IP supports multiple logical IP subnetworks (LISs), which can be managed separately but treated as a single unit by SMDS. This method requires all the subnetworks to have the same IP address. The architecture of the SMDS layers is quite complex, so they are not covered in detail here. SMDS uses LLC Type 1 frames.

Asynchronous Transfer Mode (ATM) and BISDN

Two new protocols for high-speed internetworks that are becoming popular are Asynchronous Transfer Mode (ATM) and Broadband ISDN (BISDN). The architecture on the user's machine is similar to the TCP/IP architectures discussed earlier, although additional layers can be added to provide new services, such as video and sound capabilities.

The router, gateway, or other device that accesses the high-speed network is more complex as well. Called a *terminal adapter* (as with ISDN), it provides a sophisticated interface between user layers and adaptation layers, which are application-specific. From the terminal adapter, traffic is passed to the ATM service, which provides switching and multiplexing services.

Windows 95 and TCP/IP

Because Windows 95 is supposed to become the dominant operating system on PC machines running a DOS or Windows operating system, it is worth taking a quick look at how Windows 95 integrates networking software into its kernel. The approach used by Windows 95 is similar to that of Windows NT and OS/2, so the knowledge is useful for many operating systems on common client devices in today's LANs.

Windows 95 refines the network architecture used in Windows for Workgroups and Windows NT, resulting in better performance and reliability, as well as catering to the demands of different network requirements such as multiple protocol support. Because Windows 95 supports many different network protocols in 16- and 32-bit Virtual Mode Driver (VxD) versions, the architecture must provide the flexibility to accommodate a number of structures.

The Windows 95 architecture is layered; a layered architecture is the most common networking structure (such as OSI and TCP/IP). The network architecture used in Windows 95 is known as Microsoft's Windows Open Services Architecture (WOSA). WOSA was developed to enable applications to work with several different network types, and it includes a set of interfaces designed to enable coexistence of several network components.

The networking software components of Windows 95 are shown in their respective layers in Figure 8.12. Many of the network components are familiar from earlier versions of Windows for Workgroups, Windows NT, or other operating systems and communications protocols. I look at each layer in the Windows 95 architecture in a little more detail so that the function of each component is better understood. Because 32-bit applications are becoming dominant with Windows 95 and Windows NT, I'll look at them in this section. Older 16-bit applications are treated slightly differently, but the principles are the same.

Figure 8.12.
*The Windows 95
networking software
architecture showing the
components.*

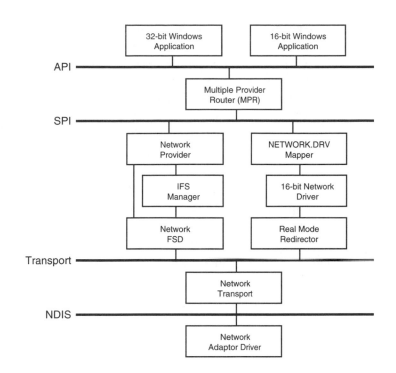

☐ **API:** The standard Win32 Application Programming Interface (API, the same
system used with Windows NT). The API handles remote file operations and
remote resources (printers and other devices). The Win32 APIs are used for
programming applications.

☐ **Multiple Provider Router (MPR):** The MPR routes all network operations for
Windows 95, as well as implementing network functions common to all network
types. Win32 APIs communicate directly with the MPR, although some can be
routed straight through. The MPR is a 32-bit protected mode DLL.

☐ **Network Provider:** The network provider implements the network service
provider interface. Only the MPR can communicate with the network provider.
The network provider is a 32-bit protected mode DLL.

☐ **IFS Manager:** The IFS Manager routes filesystem requests to the proper filesystem
driver (FSD). The IFS Manager can be called directly by network providers.

☐ **Network Filesystem Driver (FSD):** The FSD implements the particular remote
filesystem characteristics. The FSD can be used by the IFS Manager when the
filesystem of the local and remote machines match. The FSD is a 32-bit protected
mode VxD (virtual device driver).

☐ **Network Transport:** The network transport is a VxD that implements the device-specific network transport protocol. Multiple network transports can be active at a time. The network FSD interfaces with the network transport, usually with a one-to-one mapping, although that is not necessarily the case.

☐ **Network Driver Interface Specification (NDIS):** A vendor-independent software specification that defines interactions between the network transport and device driver. Windows 95 supports both 32-bit and 16-bit NDIS versions.

☐ **Network Adapter Driver:** The network adapter driver VxD controls the actual network hardware device. NDIS communicates with the driver, which sends packets over the network. Windows 95 uses Media Access Control (MAC) drivers.

One of the key features of Windows 95 is the inclusion of support for multiple concurrent protocols. The default protocol is NetWare's IPX/SPX. Also included are NetBIOS and NetBEUI drivers, and a complete 32-bit VxD for TCP/IP. All these drivers are plug-and-play enabled, allowing dynamic loading and unloading.

Windows 95's support for multiple protocols is achieved through the Network Driver Interface Specification (NDIS), which is a superset of the NDIS used in Windows for Workgroups and Windows NT. The NDIS 3.1 driver has three parts: the protocol itself (which can be implemented by third-party vendors) and protocol manager, the MAC or mini-port, and the mini-port wrapper. The NDIS protocol manager loads and unloads protocols as needed.

The version of NDIS included with Windows 95 adds plug-and-play enhancements and new mini-drivers. The plug-and-play capability is added to the protocol manager and the Media Access Control (MAC) layer, letting network drivers load and unload dynamically. The mini-driver (which is compatible with the mini-driver models used in Windows NT 3.5) decreases the amount of code that must be written to support a network adapter.

Windows 95 enables support for many network servers concurrently. This is an improvement over Windows for Workgroups 3.11, which enabled only its own network and one additional network. The server support of Windows 95 is provided by the Network Provider Interface (NPI). Using multiple network protocols at the same time, you can set up a Windows 95 machine to use TCP/IP for UNIX networks, and NetBEUI or IPX/SPX for local PC networks, if you want. Alternatively, as you see on Day 10, "Setting Up a Sample Network: Clients," you can set Windows 95 to be a pure TCP/IP-based machine.

8

Optional TCP/IP Services

TCP/IP networks offer a number of optional services that users and applications can use. All these optional services have strict definitions for their protocols. These optional services and their assigned port numbers are shown in Table 8.1.

Table 8.1. Optional TCP/IP services.

Service	Port	Description
Active Users	11	Returns the names of all users on the remote system
Character Generator	19	Returns all printable ASCII characters
Daytime	13	Returns the date and time, day of the week, and month of the year
Discard	9	Discards all received messages
Echo	7	Returns any messages
Quote of the Day	17	Returns a quotation
Time	37	Returns the time since January 1, 1900 (in seconds)

Active Users

The Active Users service returns a message to the originating user that contains a list of all users currently active on the remote machine. The behavior of the TCP and UDP versions is the same. When requested, the Active Users service monitors port 11 and, upon establishment of a connection, responds with a list of the currently active users and then closes the port. UDP sends a datagram, and TCP uses the connection itself.

Character Generator

The Character Generator service is designed to send a set of ASCII characters. Upon receipt of a datagram (the contents of which are ignored), the Character Generator service returns a list of all printable ASCII characters. The behavior of the TCP and UDP versions of the Character Generator are slightly different.

The TCP Character Generator monitors port 19, and upon connection ignores all input and sends a stream of characters back until the connection is broken. The order of characters is fixed. The UDP Character Generator service monitors port 19 for an incoming datagram (remember, UDP doesn't create connections) and responds with a datagram containing a random number of characters. Up to 512 characters can be sent.

Although this service might seem useless, it does have diagnostic purposes. It can ensure that a network can transfer all 95 printable ASCII characters properly, and it can also be used to test printers for their capability to print all the characters.

Daytime

The Daytime service returns a message with the current date and time. The format it uses is the day of the week, month of the year, day of the month, time, and the year. Time is specified in a *HH*:*MM*:*SS* format. Each field is separated by spaces to enable parsing of the contents.

Both TCP and UDP versions monitor port 13 and, upon receipt of a datagram, return the message. The Daytime service can be used for several purposes, including setting system calendars and clocks to minimize variations. It also can be used by applications.

Discard

The Discard service simply discards everything it receives. TCP waits for a connection on port 9, whereas UDP receives datagrams through that port. Anything incoming is ignored. No responses are sent.

The Discard service might seem pointless, but it can be useful for routing test messages during system setup and configuration. It can also be used by applications in place of a discard service of the operating system (such as /dev/null in UNIX).

Echo

The Echo service returns whatever it receives. It is called through port 7. With TCP, it simply returns whatever data comes down the connection, whereas UDP returns an identical datagram (except for the source and destination addresses). The echoes continue until the port connection is broken or no datagrams are received.

The Echo service provides very good diagnostics about the proper functioning of the network and the protocols themselves. The reliability of transmissions can be tested this way, too. Turnaround time from sending to receiving the echo provides useful measurements of response times and latency within the network.

8

Quote of the Day

The Quote of the Day service does as its name implies. It returns a quotation from a file of quotes, randomly selecting one a day when a request arrives on port 17. If a source file of quotations is not available, the service fails.

Time

The Time service returns the number of seconds that have elapsed since January 1, 1990. Port 37 is used to list a request (TCP) or receive an incoming datagram (UDP). When a request is received, the time is sent as a 32-bit binary number. It is up to the receiving application to convert the number to a useful figure.

The Time service is often used for synchronizing network machines or for setting clocks within an application.

Using the Optional Services

As already mentioned, the optional services can be accessed from an application. Users can directly access their service of choice (assuming it is supported) by using Telnet. A simple example is shown here:

```
$ telnet merlin 7
Trying...
Connected to merlin.tpci.com
Escape character is '^T'.
This is a message
This is a message
Isn't this exciting?
Isn't this exciting?
<Ctrl+T>
$ telnet merlin 13
Trying...
Connected to merlin.tpci.com
Escape character is '^T'.
Tues Jun 21 10:16:45 1994
Connection closed.
$ telnet merlin 19
!"#$%&'()*+,-./0123456789:;<=>?@ABCDEFGHIJKLMNOPQRSTUVWXYZ[[\]^_abcdefg
"#$%&'()*+,-./0123456789:;<=>?@ABCDEFGHIJKLMNOPQRSTUVWXYZ[[\]^_abcdefgh
#$%&'()*+,-./0123456789:;<=>?@ABCDEFGHIJKLMNOPQRSTUVWXYZ[[\]^_abcdefghi
$%&'()*+,-./0123456789:;<=>?@ABCDEFGHIJKLMNOPQRSTUVWXYZ[[\]^_abcdefghij
%&'()*+,-./0123456789:;<=>?@ABCDEFGHIJKLMNOPQRSTUVWXYZ[[\]^_abcdefghijk
&'()*+,-./0123456789:;<=>?@ABCDEFGHIJKLMNOPQRSTUVWXYZ[[\]^_abcdefghijkl
'()*+,-./0123456789:;<=>?@ABCDEFGHIJKLMNOPQRSTUVWXYZ[[\]^_abcdefghijklm
<Ctrl+T>
$
```

In this example, a connection to port 7 starts an Echo session. Everything typed by the user is echoed back immediately, unchanged. Then a connection to port 13 provides the Daytime service, showing the current date and time. The connection is broken by the service once the data is sent. Finally, the Character Generator is started. Both the Echo and Character Generator services were terminated with the Telnet break sequence of Ctrl+T.

Summary

I covered a lot of material in this chapter, mostly about the way TCP/IP can interact with other networking systems and protocols. By combining TCP/IP with existing networks, the advantages of both can be gained, as well as offering compatibility with a wide range of TCP-based devices.

I have also looked at several protocols that round out the TCP/IP family. These are mostly basic services, but they are essential to the proper operation of a TCP/IP-based network.

Q&A

Q What is the role of the Media Access Control (MAC) layer in a network architecture?

A The MAC layer handles traffic for the network, including collisions and timers. The MAC is independent of the network's physical medium, but its exact role and implementation depend on the network protocols.

Q What is the difference between LLC Type 1 and LLC Type 2?

A Logical Link Control (LLC) Type 1 is a simpler form that supports unnumbered information, designed for TCP. LLC Type 2 is for UDP and offers message integrity functionality.

Q What is XNS?

A XNS is the Xerox Network System, a networking design that Xerox released to the public domain. Because XNS is essentially free, it has gained a lot of support. XNS supports Ethernet.

Q What is ISDN?

A The Integrated Services Digital Network is a packet-switched, high-speed network that supports broadband (many channel) communications.

8

Q Why is a simple network protocol like the Character Generator supported?

A As simple as it may be, the Character Generator protocol (and many others like it) is used for basic tasks and queries that would require much more complex coding and operations when performed as part of a larger protocol. The Character Generator protocol is useful for testing communications. It is small, fast, easy to implement, and easy to understand.

Quiz

1. What components make up a Medium Attachment Unit (MAU) and what are their roles?

2. What is FDDI? Why is it popular?

3. What is the role of the Discard service?

4. The Time protocol is often used by network devices. What is its role?

5. Does the presence of a second network protocol (like IPX) affect the basic TCP/IP protocol suite's operations?

Chapter **9**

Setting Up a Sample Network: Servers

During the past eight days I have looked at several aspects of the TCP/IP protocol family. Now it's time to look at how you can actually set up TCP/IP on a network. This chapter explains how the servers for a TCP/IP network are configured, and the next chapter examines client machines. In both chapters, I try to cover a wide range of machines and operating systems.

In this chapter I look at how to set up four different types of servers: a Santa Cruz Operation (SCO) OpenServer 5 machine, a Linux machine, a Windows NT machine, and a Sun SPARCstation 5. All four servers are connected to the sample network, and any of them can be accessed by a client machine or other servers. Don't be too concerned if I am not going to use your particular version of UNIX, because most of the details of TCP/IP configuration are either identical or very similar across all UNIX versions. Usually all that changes is the directory name for some of the configuration files.

As you know from earlier in this book, UNIX and TCP/IP are intertwined closely because the original implementations of TCP/IP were for UNIX systems. TCP/IP was developed for the BSD UNIX version that originated at the University of California at Berkeley, and much of the language of TCP/IP is hooked into the BSD versions. Most UNIX systems have moved away from BSD UNIX and have embraced System V Release 4, originally developed at AT&T and now owned by the Open Software Foundation. SCO UNIX and SunSoft Solaris 2.4, both of which I use in this chapter, use the System V Release 4 version of UNIX, which provides some backward compatibility with BSD UNIX.

In the next chapter I expand the coverage of TCP/IP on the sample network by looking at client implementations. I look specifically at how you can implement TCP/IP for DOS, Windows 3.x, and Windows 95. Any of the operating systems mentioned in this chapter can act as clients to any of the servers, as well.

Most of the material covered in this chapter is familiar if you have read through the book in order. Some of it is summarized and shown again for quick reference, as well as for those who read the chapters out of order. If you get lost, you can consult the index for a pointer to more information.

The Sample Network

For this chapter I designed a dedicated TCP/IP network to show the steps you must follow to set up, configure, and test a TCP/IP implementation. The sample network relies on several servers, although many networks have only one. Also, I use several different types of servers to show you how they can be configured, whereas most real networks are not this diverse. All the machines are connected over an Ethernet network. In all, the sample network has four servers and three clients.

Each of the seven machines on the network has its own name and IP address. For this sample network, the IP address mask has been randomly chosen as 147.120. The names of the machines have been chosen from my pets, although any unique name would do, of course. The sample network configuration is shown in Figure 9.1. Bear in mind that this network is constructed to show the different types of operating systems I examine in today's and tomorrow's material; it is unlikely that a real network would have such an odd mix of servers and clients.

The physical setup of the network is undertaken first. It involves installing a network interface card in each machine (except the SPARCstation, which has the network card as part of the motherboard). On each system you must ensure that any jumpers for interrupt vectors and memory I/O addresses do not conflict with any other card on that system. (Some of the cards are software programmable; some are set by jumpers or DIP switches.) All the boards used in this system are from different manufacturers to show the independent nature of the TCP/IP network.

Figure 9.1.

The sample TCP/IP network.

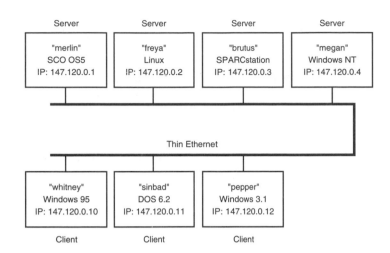

Cable must be run between all the machines, connecting the network interface cards together. In the case of Ethernet, the cables must be properly terminated. The sample network uses thin Ethernet, which closely resembles television coaxial cable. BNC Thin Ethernet connectors resemble a T, with cables attached to both ends of the T and the stem connected to the network card. Two of the machines form the ends of the cable and require a terminating resistor as part of their T. The SPARCstation normally uses an RJ45 connector (which looks like a wide telephone connector, so I used a transceiver to convert it to BNC).

To test the physical network, it is easiest to wait until a couple of machines have had their basic software configuration completed. All the machines on the network do not have to be active, as long as the network cable is contiguous from end to end and each BNC connector is attached to a network card to provide electrical termination. If problems are found when the network is tested, the physical network is the first item to check. Some network monitoring devices can supply integrity information prior to installing the network, but these devices are not usually available to system administrators who are just beginning their installation, or who have a small number of machines to maintain (primarily because the network testers tend to be expensive).

Configuring TCP/IP Software

This section follows through the configuration of the TCP/IP software. The discussion applies equally to the UNIX, Windows, and DOS machines on the sample network (as it would to any other type of machine, such as a Macintosh). Filenames can change with different operating systems, but the general approach remains valid.

Most operating systems and TCP/IP software packages provide several utilities, including menu-driven scripts that help automate the installation process of the TCP/IP applications. Some operating systems (notably older UNIX systems) still require manual configuration of several files using a text editor. To configure TCP/IP software properly, you must know several pieces of information before you start. The necessary information you need for each machine on the network follows:

- ☐ **Domain name:** The name the entire network will use.
- ☐ **System name:** The unique name of each local machine.
- ☐ **IP address:** The full address of each machine.
- ☐ **Driver type:** Each interface to the network must be associated with a device driver, instructing the operating system how to talk to the device.
- ☐ **Broadcast address:** The address used for network-wide broadcasts.
- ☐ **Netmask:** The network mask that uniquely identifies the local network.
- ☐ **Hardware network card configuration information:** The interrupt vector and memory address of the network card.

The system domain name is necessary if the network is to be connected to other machines outside the local network. Domain names can be invented by the system administrator. If, however, the network is to interface with Internet or one of its service providers, the domain name should be approved by the Internet Network Information Center (InterNIC). Creating and registering a new domain is as simple as filling out a form (and recently, paying a small administration fee). Domain names usually reflect the company name, with the extension identifying the type of organization. The sample network uses the name tpci.com.

As seen earlier in this book, the machine name is used for symbolic naming of a machine instead of forcing the full IP address to be specified. The system name must be unique on the local network. Other networks might have machines with the same name, but their network masks are different, so there is no possible confusion during packet routing. In most cases, system names are composed of eight characters (or less) and are usually all lowercase characters (in keeping with UNIX tradition for lowercase). The system name can be a mix of characters and numbers. Larger organizations tend to number their machines, and small companies give their machines more familiar names.

The device driver instructs the operating system how to communicate with the network interface (usually either a network card or a serial port). Each interface has its own specific device driver. Most operating systems have device drivers included in their distribution software, although some require software supplied with the network card. Generic drivers are available for most network cards on bulletin board systems.

9

With most operating systems, there are limits to the number of similar devices that are supported. SCO UNIX, for example, enables up to four Ethernet cards, two Token Ring adapters, four Serial Line Internet Protocol (SLIP) lines, and four Point-to-Point Protocol (PPP) lines. These limits should be enough for a machine on any network!

The network card configuration must be known in order to install the device driver properly. Network cards usually have several configuration settings, depending on the system for which they are designed. For the PC-based machines in the sample network, each card must have a unique interrupt vector (called an IRQ) and a unique I/O memory address. IRQ and address settings on many of the newer network boards are software-configurable, making the installation and configuration much easier.

Most network cards come with default settings that might conflict with other cards in the system. Users must carefully check for conflicts, resorting to a diagnostic program if available. UNIX users have several utilities available, depending on the operating system. SCO UNIX and most System V Release 4 operating systems have the utility hwconfig, which shows the current hardware configuration. The following example shows the hwconfig output and the output from the command with the -h option to provide long formatting with headers (making it is easier to read):

```
$ hwconfig
name=fpu vec=13 dma=- type=80387
name=serial base=0x3F8 offset=0x7 vec=4 dma=- unit=0 type=Standard nports=1
name=serial base=0x2F8 offset=0x7 vec=3 dma=- unit=1 type=Standard nports=1
name=floppy base=0x3F2 offset=0x5 vec=6 dma=2 unit=0 type=96ds15
name=floppy vec=- dma=- unit=1 type=135ds18
name=console vec=- dma=- unit=vga type=0 12 screens=68k
name=adapter base=0x2C00 offset=0xFF vec=11 dma=- type=arad ha=0 id=7 fts=st
name=nat base=0x300 offset=0x20 vec=7 dma=- type=NE2000 addr=00:00:6e:24:1e:3e
name=tape vec=- dma=- type=S ha=0 id=4 lun=0 ht=arad
name=disk vec=- dma=- type=S ha=0 id=0 lun=0 ht=arad fts=stdb
name=Sdsk vec=- dma=- cyls=1002 hds=64 secs=32
$
$ hwconfig -h
device          address       vec  dma  comment
======          =======       ===  ===  =======
fpu             -             13   -    type=80387
serial          0x3f8-0x3ff   4    -    unit=0 type=Standard nports=1
serial          0x2f8-0x2ff   3    -    unit=1 type=Standard nports=1
floppy          0x3f2-0x3f7   6    2    unit=0 type=96ds15
floppy          -             -    -    unit=1 type=135ds18
console         -             -    -    unit=vga type=0 12 screens=68k
adapter         0x2c00-0x2cff 11   -    type=arad ha=0 id=7 fts=st
nat             0x300-0x320   7    -    type=NE2000 addr=00:00:6e:24:1e:3e
tape            -             -    -    type=S ha=0 id=4 lun=0 ht=arad
disk            -             -    -    type=S ha=0 id=0 lun=0 ht=arad fts=stdb
Sdsk            -             -    -    cyls=1002 hds=64 secs=32
```

This output is from the SCO UNIX servers set up for the sample network. It has the network Ethernet card already configured as device nat, which uses IRQ 7 (shown under the vec or interrupt vector column). The nat line also shows the memory address as 300–320 (hexadecimal) and the device driver as NE2000 (a Novell NetWare-compatible driver). The address and vec columns show no conflicts between the settings used for the Ethernet card and other devices on the system. (The adapter entry is for a high-speed SCSI-2 card, which controls both the tape and the Sdsk device, the primary SCSI hard drive. All other entries should be self-explanatory.)

DOS users can use the Microsoft Diagnostic utility, MSD.EXE, or one of several third-party tools such as Central Point PC Tools or The Norton Utilities to display IRQ vectors and memory addresses in use by the system. Some software even indicates which vectors and addresses are available for use.

There is no need to have the same IRQ and memory address for each card on the network, because the network itself doesn't care about these settings. The IRQ and memory addresses are required for the machine to communicate with the network interface card only. The sample network used a different IRQ and memory address for each machine.

IRQ and memory addresses are usually set on the network interface card itself using either jumpers on pins or a DIP-switch block. The documentation accompanying the card should provide all the information necessary for setting these values. Some recently introduced network interface cards can be configured through software, enabling the settings to be changed without removing the card from the system. This can be very handy when a user is unsure of the best settings for the card.

The IP address is a 32-bit number that must be unique for each machine. If the network is to be connected to the Internet, the IP address must be assigned by the NIC (it is usually given to you when you register your domain name). Even if no access to the Internet is expected, arbitrarily assigning an IP address can cause problems when messages are passed with other networks. If the network is not connected to the outside world, a system administrator can ignore the NIC's numbering system and adopt any IP address. It is worthwhile, however, to consider future expansion and connection to other networks.

As you might recall, the NIC has four classes of IP addresses in use depending on the size of the network. Each class has some addresses that are restricted. These are shown in Table 9.1. Most networks are Class B, although a few large corporations require Class A networks.

Table 9.1. The NIC IP address classes.

Class	Network Mask Bytes	Number of Hosts per Network	Valid Addresses
A	1	16,777,216	`1.0.0.1 to 126.255.255.254`
B	2	65,534	`128.0.0.1 to 191.255.255.254`
C	3	254	`224.0.0.0 to 255.255.255.254`
D	reserved		

The network mask is the IP address stripped of its network identifiers, leaving only the local machine address. For a Class A network, this strips one byte, whereas a Class B network strips two bytes (leaving two). The small Class C network strips three bytes as the network mask, leaving one byte to identify the local machine (hence the limit of 254 machines on the network). The sample network is configured as a Class B machine with the randomly chosen IP address network mask of `147.120` (not NIC-assigned).

The broadcast address identifies packets that are to be sent to all machines on the local network. Because a network card usually ignores any incoming packets that don't have its specific IP address in them, a special broadcast address can be set that the card can intercept in addition to locally destined messages. The broadcast address has the host portion (the local machine identifiers) set to either all 0s or all 1s, depending on the convention followed. For convenience, the broadcast address's network mask is usually the same as the local network mask.

Broadcast addresses might seem simple because there are only two possible settings. Such addresses, however, commonly cause problems because conflicting settings are used on a network. BSD UNIX used the convention of all 0s for releases 4.1 and 4.2, whereas 4.3BSD and SVR4 (System V Release 4) UNIX moved to all 1s for the broadcast address. The Internet standard specifies all 1s as the broadcast address. If problems are encountered on the network with broadcasts, check all the configurations to ensure they are using the same setting. The sample network uses an all 1s mask for its broadcast address.

The steps followed for configuring TCP/IP are straightforward, generally following the information required for each machine. The configuration steps are as follows:

- **Link drivers:** TCP/IP must be linked to the operating system's kernel or loaded during the boot stage to enable TCP/IP.
- **Add host information:** Provide a list of all machines (hosts) on the network (used for name resolution).
- **Establish routing tables:** Provide the information for routing packets properly if name resolution isn't sufficient.

- ☐ **Set user access:** Configure the system to enable access in and out of the network, as well as establishing permissions.
- ☐ **Remote device access:** Configure the system for access to remote printers, scanners, CD-ROM carousels, and other shared network devices.
- ☐ **Configure the name domain server:** If using a distributed address lookup system such as Berkeley Internet Name Domain Server (BIND) or NIS, complete the name server files. (This step is necessary only if you are using BIND or a similar service.)
- ☐ **Tune system for performance:** Because a system running TCP/IP has different behavior than one without TCP/IP, some system tuning is usually required.
- ☐ **Configure NFS:** If the Network File System (NFS) is to be used, configure both the file system and the user access.
- ☐ **Anonymous FTP:** If the system is to enable anonymous FTP access, configure the system and public directories for this service.

You will use these steps (not necessarily in the sequence given) as the individual machines on the network are configured. The processes are different with each operating system, but the overall approach remains the same.

UNIX TCP/IP Configuration

Most UNIX TCP/IP operating systems rely on several files for configuration. These are summarized in Table 9.2. Remember that filenames can change with different implementations of the UNIX operating system, but the configuration information is consistent. I look at each of these files in more detail when I look at specific operating systems later today. These files apply only to UNIX usually; Windows NT, for example, uses a different set of tables.

Table 9.2. TCP/IP UNIX configuration files.

File	Description
/etc/hosts	Hostnames
/etc/networks	Network names
/etc/services	List of known services
/etc/protocols	Supported protocols
/etc/hosts.equiv	List of trusted hosts
/etc/ftpusers	List of unwelcome FTP users
/etc/inetd.conf	List of servers started by inetd

9

For the sample network, modifying these files on any of the three UNIX servers (SCO UNIX, Linux, and SPARCstation) is quite easy. An ASCII text editor is all that is required. Verifying the contents is usually quite simple, too, because the tables on one machine are very similar to those on other machines, except for a few entries.

Configuring SCO UNIX

SCO UNIX and SCO OpenServer 5 include several configuration utilities to help provide information for TCP/IP and to link the driver into the kernel correctly. This does not eliminate the need to edit the many configuration files manually and supply information about the other machines on the network. Most of the information in this section, although specific to SCO UNIX, is generally applicable to most UNIX operating systems, especially SVR4-compliant versions.

Most UNIX-based networks have a main server machine that starts the network processes. This machine is sometimes called a *super server,* because any machine that runs network processes and accepts requests from other machines is a server. UNIX uses the process inetd (Internet daemon) as the master server for all network processes that are to be activated (usually contained in a single file called inetd.conf). Hardware configuration requires linking information about the network card and protocol to the operating system kernel. The configuration is sometimes called a *chain.* The process is usually automated by a script file, requiring users to provide the interrupt vector number, the I/O memory address, and the type of card. The device driver for that network card is then rebuilt into the kernel so the driver is active whenever the system boots.

On SCO UNIX systems, a utility called netconfig is used, prompting the user for the three pieces of information (IRQ, address, and card type) and then rebuilding the kernel. Under SCO OpenServer 5, you can perform the same tasks through a GUI-driven utility that performs the same tasks. This process is repeated for each network card on the machine. (The sample network has only one card in each machine, which is the most common configuration.) When started, the SCO UNIX netconfig program presents you with this screen:

```
$ netconfig
Currently configured chains:
   1. nfs->sco_tcp
      nfs       SCO NFS Runtime System for SCO Unix
      sco_tcp   SCO TCP/IP for UNIX
   2. sco_tcp->lo0
      sco_tcp   SCO TCP/IP for UNIX
      lo0       SCO TCP/IP Loopback driver
Available options:
   1. Add a chain
   2. Remove a chain
   3. Reconfigure an element in a chain
   q. Quit
Select option: Please enter a value between 1 and 3 ('q' to quit):
```

Because a TCP/IP device driver is being added, option 1 (Add a chain) is selected. Some users confuse the first configured chain in the list with a TCP/IP driver for the network and attempt to reconfigure it. The first driver listed in the previous output is a default value for NFS and should be left alone. It has nothing to do with the addition of a TCP/IP network card. The second chain listed in the configuration is the loopback driver, which should be created automatically for all SCO systems when the operating system software is installed.

After indicating that a new chain is to be added, the system asks for the type of chain:

```
Num     Name        Description
  1.    lmxc        SCO LAN Manager Client
  2.    nfs         SCO NFS Runtime System for SCO UNIX
  3.    sco_ipx     SCO IPX/SPX for UNIX
  4.    sco_tcp     SCO TCP/IP for UNIX
Select top level of chain to Add or 'q' to quit:
```

Option 4 is chosen because you are installing TCP/IP. LAN Manager and IPX/SPX are used for integration with DOS-based networks. The NFS Runtime System is added later if NFS is to be used on the network. I look at configuring NFS in more detail on Day 12, "NFS and NIS."

The netconfig utility then presents a list of several dozen network interface cards for which the system has default values. If the card installed in the system is shown, the entry for the card is chosen. If the card is not on the list, a compatible entry must be found. This sometimes requires digging through the network interface card's documentation for emulation or compatible values, or contacting the manufacturer. Drivers are usually available for Ethernet cards.

The system then prompts for the IRQ the card is set for, followed by the memory address. After these are entered, the operating system creates the necessary entries in its internal configuration files to include the device driver for the network card. As a final step, the system asks if the user wants to rebuild and relink the kernel. This must be done if the new drivers are to be effective. After a system reboot, the drivers are active and can be tested with a ping command.

You can ping the localhost first, followed by the IP address you have assigned for the SCO machine. This does not test the network connection, because the operating system doesn't bother using the network card when pinging itself. The test does, however, verify that the IP address is set properly and that the TCP/IP software is embedded in the operating system kernel. An example of this type of ping testing looks like this:

```
# ping -c5 localhost
PING localhost (127.0.0.1): 56 data bytes
64 bytes from localhost (127.0.0.1): icmp_seq=0 ttl=64 time=10 ms
64 bytes from localhost (127.0.0.1): icmp_seq=1 ttl=64 time=0 ms
64 bytes from localhost (127.0.0.1): icmp_seq=2 ttl=64 time=0 ms
64 bytes from localhost (127.0.0.1): icmp_seq=3 ttl=64 time=0 ms
64 bytes from localhost (127.0.0.1): icmp_seq=4 ttl=64 time=0 ms
```

```
-- localhost ping statistics --
5 packets transmitted, 5 packets received, 0% packet loss
round-trip min/avg/max = 0/2/10 ms
# ping -c5 147.120.0.1
PING 147.120.0.1 (147.120.0.1): 56 data bytes
64 bytes from merlin (147.120.0.1): icmp_seq=0 ttl=64 time=0 ms
64 bytes from merlin (147.120.0.1): icmp_seq=1 ttl=64 time=0 ms
64 bytes from merlin (147.120.0.1): icmp_seq=2 ttl=64 time=0 ms
64 bytes from merlin (147.120.0.1): icmp_seq=3 ttl=64 time=0 ms
64 bytes from merlin (147.120.0.1): icmp_seq=4 ttl=64 time=0 ms

-- 147.120.0.1 ping statistics --
5 packets transmitted, 5 packets received, 0% packet loss
round-trip min/avg/max = 0/0/0 ms
```

In the preceding example, issued on the server merlin with IP address 147.120.0.1, I used the ping command with the -c option to specify how many packets to send. As you can see, both the localhost and IP address responded properly, indicating that the TCP/IP software is properly loaded and the IP address is recognized.

As you saw earlier today, UNIX TCP/IP networking software relies on several files for configuration. These were summarized in Table 9.2. You can look at each of these files now with respect to the SCO UNIX server on the sample network.

The /etc/hosts file contains the names of the other machines on the network and their network addresses. The file looks like this:

```
#       @(#)hosts    1.2 Lachman System V STREAMS TCP   source
#       SCCS IDENTIFICATION
127.0.0.1            localhost tpci
147.120.0.1          merlin merlin.tpci.com
147.120.0.2          freya freya.tpci.com
147.120.0.3          brutus brutus.tpci.com
147.120.0.4          megan megan.tpci.com_
147.120.0.10         whitney whitney.tpci.com
147.120.0.11         sinbad sinbad.tpci.com
147.120.0.12         pepper pepper.tpci.com
```

Each line contains the local machine name and its full name with the domain so that either version is recognized by the operating system. As new machines are added to the network, new lines are added to the file. The local machine has two entries in the file: one for the local name and one for localhost.

The /etc/networks file holds a list of network names and their addresses. This is an optional file as far as most TCP/IP installations are concerned, and most system administrators use it only when the users need it. The /etc/networks file lets you name networks in the same way as machines. The following example shows some of the SCO network machines as well as two networks that the local machines frequently connect to. Using the name maclean_net as part of a machine identifier supplied by a user is now possible because the operating system can resolve it to its IP address through this file.

```
#       @(#)networks 1.2 Lachman System V STREAMS TCP  source
#       SCCS IDENTIFICATION
loopback     127
sco          132.147
sco-hq       132.147.128
sco-mfg      132.147.64
sco-engr     132.147.192
sco-slip     132.147.32
sco-tcplab   132.147.160
sco-odtlab   132.147.1
maclean_net  147.50.1
bnr.ca       47
```

On Day 6 "Telnet and FTP," you examined the /etc/services file. It includes information about all the TCP and UDP services supported by the system. For the sample network and most small networks, the default values are acceptable. These entries are changed only if a service is being removed from TCP/IP, such as to prevent Telnet access. The file looks like this:

```
#       @(#)services 5.1 Lachman System V STREAMS TCP  source
#
#    System V STREAMS TCP - Release 4.0
# Network services, Internet style
#
echo         7/tcp
echo         7/udp
discard      9/tcp       sink null
discard      9/udp       sink null
systat       11/tcp      users
daytime      13/tcp
daytime      13/udp
netstat      15/tcp
qotd         17/tcp      quote
chargen      19/tcp      ttytst source
chargen      19/udp      ttytst source
ftp          21/tcp
telnet       23/tcp
smtp         25/tcp      mail
time         37/tcp      timserver
time         37/udp      timserver
rlp          39/udp      resource      # resource location
nameserver   42/tcp      name          # IEN 116
whois        43/tcp      nicname
domain       53/tcp      nameserver    # name-domain server
domain       53/udp      nameserver
mtp          57/tcp                    # deprecated
bootps       67/udp      bootps        # bootp server
bootpc       68/udp      bootpc        # bootp client
tftp         69/udp
rje          77/tcp      netrjs
finger       79/tcp
link         87/tcp      ttylink
supdup       95/tcp
```

```
hostnames          101/tcp       hostname           # usually from sri-nic
tsap               102/tcp       osi-tp0 tp0
#csnet-cs          105/?
pop                109/tcp       postoffice
sunrpc             111/tcp
sunrpc             111/udp
auth               113/tcp       authentication
sftp               115/tcp
uucp-path          117/tcp
nntp               119/tcp       readnews untp      # USENET News Transfer Protocol
ntp                123/tcp
ntp                123/udp
nb-ns              137/udp          nbns netbios-nameservice
nb-ns              137/tcp          nbns netbios-nameservice
nb-dgm             138/udp          nbdgm netbios-datagram
nb-dgm             138/tcp          nbdgm netbios-datagram
nb-ssn             139/tcp          nbssn netbios-session
snmp               161/udp
snmp-trap          162/udp
bgp                179/tcp
#
# UNIX specific services
#
exec               512/tcp
biff               512/udp       comsat
login              513/tcp
who                513/udp       whod
shell              514/tcp       cmd                # no passwords used
syslog             514/udp
printer            515/tcp       spooler            # line printer spooler
talk               517/udp
ntalk              518/udp
efs                520/tcp                          # for LucasFilm
route              520/udp       router routed      # 521 also
timed              525/udp       timeserver
tempo              526/tcp       newdate
courier            530/tcp       rpc
conference         531/tcp       chat
netnews            532/tcp       readnews
netwall            533/udp                          # -for emergency broadcasts
uucp               540/tcp       uucpd              # uucp daemon
remotefs           556/tcp       rfs_server rfs     # Brunhoff remote filesystem
pppmsg             911/tcp                          # PPP daemon
listen             1025/tcp      listener RFS remote_file_sharing
nterm              1026/tcp      remote_login network_terminal
ingreslock         1524/tcp
```

The /etc/hosts.equiv file controls access from other machines. The /etc/ftpusers file prevents unauthorized logins with specific user names. Both files are examined in more detail in the sections later today titled "User Equivalence" and "Anonymous FTP."

The /etc/inetd.conf file, mentioned earlier, controls the processes started by the inetd daemon when the system boots. The default inetd.conf file is fine for the sample system and seldom requires modification. The file appears as follows:

```
#        @(#)inetd.conf    5.2 Lachman System V STREAMS TCP  source
#
#     System V STREAMS TCP - Release 4.0
#
#        SCCS IDENTIFICATION
ftp        stream    tcp   nowait    NOLUID    /etc/ftpd       ftpd
telnet     stream    tcp   nowait    NOLUID    /etc/telnetd    telnetd
shell      stream    tcp   nowait    NOLUID    /etc/rshd       rshd
login      stream    tcp   nowait    NOLUID    /etc/rlogind    rlogind
exec       stream    tcp   nowait    NOLUID    /etc/rexecd     rexecd
finger     stream    tcp   nowait    nouser    /etc/fingerd    fingerd
#uucp      stream    tcp   nowait    NOLUID    /etc/uucpd      uucpd
# Enabling this allows public read files to be accessed via TFTP.
#tftp      dgram     udp   wait      nouser    /etc/tftpd      tftpd
comsat     dgram     udp   wait      root      /etc/comsat     comsat
ntalk      dgram     udp   wait      root      /etc/talkd      talkd
#bootps    dgram     udp   wait      root      /etc/bootpd     bootpd
echo       stream    tcp   nowait    root      internal
discard    stream    tcp   nowait    root      internal
chargen    stream    tcp   nowait    root      internal
daytime    stream    tcp   nowait    root      internal
time       stream    tcp   nowait    root      internal
echo       dgram     udp   wait      root      internal
discard    dgram     udp   wait      root      internal
chargen    dgram     udp   wait      root      internal
daytime    dgram     udp   wait      root      internal
time       dgram     udp   wait      root      internal
smtp       stream    tcp   nowait    mmdf      /usr/mmdf/chans/smtpd smtpd /usr/
                                               mmdf/chans/smtpsrvr smtp
```

With the files set up as shown and the daemons properly loading, TCP/IP and UDP should both be active and available. Most operating systems require a reboot after any changes to the kernel or some configuration files, so modifications to the TCP/IP files should be followed by system resets.

When the system boots, the TCP/IP daemons should be listed in the startup messages shown on the console. Any errors in the daemon startups are shown on the display or mailed to the system administrator. Usually, these error messages are cryptic but at least indicate the presence of a problem (which is better than you worrying about configuration information when the daemon is at fault).

Configuring Linux

Linux is a public domain UNIX version that has become very popular. In this section I configure the SlakWare release of Linux on the sample network. Many other Linux versions use the same TCP/IP configuration process as SlakWare, but you should check your version's release notes for any changes. Linux is a combination of BSD UNIX and SVR4 UNIX, but most of the configuration files for TCP/IP are identical to those for SCO UNIX and Solaris 2.4. Before you start configuring the TCP/IP files, though, you need to check a few details on your Linux system.

Most networked versions of Linux rely on the /proc filesystem, which must be created and mounted before networking can be configured and tested. Most Linux versions automatically create the /proc filesystem when the operating system is installed, so you shouldn't have to do anything more than make sure it is properly mounted by the kernel. The /proc filesystem is essentially a quick interface point for the kernel to obtain network information, as well maintaining important tables that are usually kept in the subdirectory /proc/net, which is created by the network installation routine.

If the /proc filesystem is not created by your Linux kernel, you have to rebuild the kernel and select the /proc option. Change to the source directory (such as /usr/src/Linux) and run the configuration routine with this command:

```
make config
```

When you are asked if you want the procfs support, answer yes. If you do not get asked about the /proc filesystem support, and the /proc directory is not created on your filesystem, you need to upgrade your kernel to support networking.

You can make sure the /proc filesystem is mounted automatically on your Linux system by examining the startup code for the kernel. To force the /proc filesystem to be mounted automatically, modify the /etc/fstab file and add the mount command there. Check the entries in /etc/fstab to see if there is a line like this:

```
none   /proc   proc   defaults
```

If no such line exists, you should add it to the contents of the /etc/fstab file using an ASCII editor.

Another step you must take before configuring TCP/IP under Linux is to set the hostname. To set the hostname, use this command:

```
hostname name
```

The *name* is the system name you want for your local machine. If a hostname is not already set, you can set the full domain name using this command:

```
hostname freya.tpci.com
```

This sets the hostname to freya on the sample network. When you set the local machine's name with the hostname command, an entry is usually made in the /etc/hosts file. You should verify that your machine name appears in that file.

The next step in configuring TCP/IP on your Linux machine is to make the network interface accessible. This is done with the ifconfig command. When run, ifconfig essentially makes the network layer of the kernel work with the network interface by giving it an IP address. When the interface is active, the kernel can send and receive data through the interface.

There are several interfaces you need to set up for your Linux machine, including the loopback driver (if it is not already created) and the Ethernet interface. The `ifconfig` command is used for each interface in turn. The general format of the `ifconfig` command is this:

```
ifconfig interface_type IP_Address
```

The `interface_type` is the interface's device driver name (such as `lo` for loopback and `eth` for Ethernet). The `IP_Address` is the IP address used by that interface.

When the `ifconfig` command has been run and the interface is active, you can use the `route` command to add or remove routes in the kernel's routing table. This is needed to enable the local machine to find other machines. The general format of the `route` command is this:

```
route add¦del IP_Address
```

Either `add` or `del` is specified to add or remove the route from the kernel's routing table, and `IP_Address` is the remote route being affected.

You can display the current contents of the kernel's routing table at any time by entering the command `route` all by itself on the command line. For example, if your system is set up with only the loopback driver, you see an output like this:

```
$ route
Kernel Routing Table
Destination     Gateway     Genmask     Flags   MSS   Window   Use Iface
loopback          *         255.0.0.0    U      1936   0        16  lo
```

The important columns are the destination name, which shows the name of the configured target (in this case, `loopback`), the mask to be used (`Genmask`), and the interface (`Iface`, in this case `/dev/lo`). You can force `route` to display IP addresses instead of symbolic names by using the `-n` option:

```
$ route -n
Kernel Routing Table
Destination     Gateway     Genmask     Flags   MSS   Window   Use Iface
127.0.0.1         *         255.0.0.0    U      1936   0        16  lo
```

A typical Linux network configuration includes a couple of interfaces. The loopback interface should exist on every machine. Once the loopback driver is configured, you can add the Ethernet driver for the network. You begin by installing the loopback driver.

The loopback interface should exist on every machine. The loopback interface always has the IP address `127.0.0.1`, so the `/etc/hosts` file should have an entry for this interface. The loopback driver might have been created by the kernel during software installation, so check the `/etc/hosts` file for a line similar to this:

```
localhost  127.0.0.1
```

If the line exists, the loopback driver is in place. Make sure the line doesn't have a pound sign ahead of it, which would comment it out. You can also use the `ifconfig` utility to display all the information it knows about the loopback driver. Use this command:

```
ifconfig lo
```

You should see several lines of information about the loopback driver. If you get an error message, the loopback driver does not exist.

If the loopback interface is not in the `/etc/hosts` file, you need to create it with the `ifconfig` command. The command

```
ifconfig lo 127.0.0.1
```

creates the necessary line in `/etc/hosts`.

Next you should add the loopback driver to the kernel routing tables with one of these two commands:

```
route add 127.0.0.1
```

or

```
route add localhost
```

It doesn't matter which command you use because they both refer to the same thing. The command essentially tells the kernel that it can use the route to address `127.0.0.1` or to the name `localhost`.

As a quick check that all is correct with the loopback driver, you can use the `ping` command to check the routing. If you issue either of these two commands:

```
ping localhost
```

or

```
ping 127.0.0.1
```

you should see output like this:

```
PING localhost: 56 data bytes
64 bytes from 127.0.0.1: icmp_seq=0.  ttl=255 time=1 ms
64 bytes from 127.0.0.1: icmp_seq=1.  ttl=255 time=1 ms
64 bytes from 127.0.0.1: icmp_seq=2.  ttl=255 time=1 ms
64 bytes from 127.0.0.1: icmp_seq=3.  ttl=255 time=1 ms
64 bytes from 127.0.0.1: icmp_seq=4.  ttl=255 time=1 ms
64 bytes from 127.0.0.1: icmp_seq=5.  ttl=255 time=1 ms
64 bytes from 127.0.0.1: icmp_seq=6.  ttl=255 time=1 ms
64 bytes from 127.0.0.1: icmp_seq=7.  ttl=255 time=1 ms
^C
-- localhost PING Statistics --
7 packets transmitted, 7 packets received, 0% packet loss
round-trip (ms) min/avg/max = 1/1/1
```

9

The `ping` command's progress was interrupted by the user by issuing a Ctrl+C after seven transmissions. You can let as many transmissions as you want go by. If you get no replies from the `ping` command, then the address `127.0.0.1` or the name `localhost` wasn't recognized and you should check the configuration files and `route` entry again.

If the configuration files look correct and the `route` command was accepted properly, but the `ping` command still doesn't produce the proper results, you have a more serious problem. In some cases, the network kernel is not properly configured and the entire process must be conducted again. Sometimes a mismatch in versions of kernel drivers and network utilities can cause hang-ups with the `ping` routine, as well.

Next, you need to add the Ethernet drivers to the kernel. You can perform the same configuration process with the Ethernet driver. To begin, you set up the Ethernet interface using `ifconfig`. To make the interface active, use the `ifconfig` command with the Ethernet device name and your local IP address. For example, use the command

```
ifconfig eth0 147.120.0.2
```

to set up the local machine with the IP address `147.120.0.2`. The interface is to the Ethernet device `/dev/eth0`. You don't have to specify the network mask with the `ifconfig` command because it deduces the proper value from the IP address entered. If you want to provide the network mask value explicitly, append it to the command line with the keyword `netmask`:

```
ifconfig eth0 147.120.0.2 netmask 255.255.255.0
```

You can then check the interface with the `ifconfig` command using the interface name:

```
$ ifconfig eth0
eth0        Link encap 10Mps: Ethernet Hwaddr
            inet addr 147.123.20.1 Bcast 147.123.1.255 Mask 255.255.255.0
            UP BROADCAST RUNNING  MTU 1500 Metric 1
            X packets:0 errors:0 dropped:0 overruns:0
            TX packets:0 errors:0 dropped:0 overruns:0
```

You might have noticed in the output from the command that the broadcast address was set based on the local machine's IP address. This is used by TCP/IP to access all machines on the local area network at once. The Message Transfer Unit (MTU) size is usually set to the maximum value of 1500 supported by Ethernet networks.

Next, you need to add an entry to the kernel routing tables that lets the kernel know about the local machine's network address. That lets it send data to other machines on the same network. The IP address that is used with the `route` command to do this is not your local machine's IP address, but that of the network as a whole without the local identifier. To set the entire local area network at once, the `-net` option of the `route` command is used. In the case of the IP addresses shown previously, the command would be as follows:

```
route add -net 147.120.0
```

This adds all the machines on the network identified by the network address 147.120.0 to the kernel's list of accessible machines. If you didn't do it this way, you would have to manually enter the IP address of each machine on the network. An alternative method is to use the /etc/networks file, which can contain a list of network names and their IP addresses. If you have an entry in the /etc/networks file for a network called maclean_net, you could add the entire network to the routing table with this command:

```
route add maclean_net
```

Once the route has been added to the kernel routing tables, you can try the Ethernet interface out by pinging another machine, such as the SCO server you configured earlier.

Now you can configure the files used by TCP/IP, as you did for the SCO UNIX system configured earlier. Because many of the details of these files are identical to those shown in the SCO UNIX section, I skip a lot of the details here.

The /etc/hosts file is used to hold the network addresses and symbolic names, as well as the loopback driver. The loopback connection address is usually listed as the machine name loopback or localhost. The /etc/hosts file consists of the network address in one column and the symbolic name in another. Although the network addresses can be specified in decimal, octal, or hexadecimal format, decimal is the most commonly used form (and use of the others can be downright confusing). You can specify more than one symbolic name on a line by separating the names with white space characters (spaces or tabs). The Linux server /etc/hosts file on the sample network looks like this (remember that the Linux server is called freya and has an IP address of 147.120.0.2):

```
# network host addresses
127.0.0.1             localhost tpci
147.120.0.2           freya freya.tpci.com
147.120.0.1           merlin merlin.tpci.com
147.120.0.3           brutus brutus.tpci.com
147.120.0.4           megan megan.tpci.com_
147.120.0.10          whitney whitney.tpci.com
147.120.0.11          sinbad sinbad.tpci.com
147.120.0.12          pepper pepper.tpci.com
```

This file is essentially identical to that of the SCO UNIX server, because all the machines on the network have the same names and addresses. Because the localhost name is set to freya, the Linux server knows which entry in the file refers to itself.

The file /etc/protocols identifies all the transport protocols available on the Linux server and gives their respective protocol numbers. All systems have this file, although some entries might be commented out to prevent unwanted intrusion or abuse. With Linux the /etc/protocols file is not usually modified by the administrator. Instead, the file is maintained by the networking software and updated automatically as part of installation procedures. The file contains the protocol name, its number, and any alias that can be used for that protocol. The /etc/protocols file from the Linux server is shown here:

```
# protocols
ip      0     IP   # internet protocol, pseudo protocol number
icmp    1     ICMP # internet control message protocol
igmp    2     IGMP # internet group multicast protocol
ggp     3     GGP  # gateway-gateway protocol
tcp     6     TCP  # transmission control protocol
pup     12    PUP  # PARC universal packet protocol
udp     17    UDP  # user datagram protocol
idp     22    IDP  # WhatsThis?
raw     255   RAW  # RAW IP interface
```

The exact contents of the /etc/protocols file on your system might differ a little from the file shown here, but the protocol numbers and names are probably the same. There might be additional protocols listed, depending on your version of Linux and networking software.

The last TCP/IP configuration file used on most Linux systems identifies existing network services. This is /etc/services. As with the /etc/protocols file, this file is not usually modified by an administrator but is maintained by software when installed or configured. The /etc/services file is in ASCII format and consists of the service name, a port number, and the protocol type. The port number and protocol type are separated by a slash. Any optional service alias names follow. A short extract from a sample /etc/services file (the file is usually quite lengthy) is shown next:

```
# network services
echo      7/tcp
echo      7/udp
discard   9/tcp     sink   null
discard   9/udp     sink   null
ftp       21/tcp
telnet    23/tcp
smtp      25/tcp    mail mailx
tftp      69/udp
# specific services
login     513/tcp
who       513/udp   whod
```

Most /etc/services files have many more lines, because a wide number of TCP/IP services are supported by most versions of Linux. Because you never have to worry about the contents of this file, you don't need to check each entry.

Configuring Solaris

SunSoft Solaris 2.4 is a System V Release 4 version of UNIX, so it is configured very much like the SCO UNIX system configured earlier. The Ethernet interface and drivers are linked into the kernel when the operating system is loaded, so none of the device configuration should have to be modified. When the Solaris operating system is loaded, part of the configuration procedure asks for the name of the server and its IP address (in the sample network the name is brutus and the IP address is 147.120.0.3).

These settings are then placed in the /etc/hosts file. You can use any ASCII editor to enter the rest of the machines on the sample network to complete the /etc/hosts file, as shown here:

```
#
# Internet Host Table
#
127.0.0.1            localhost
147.120.0.3          brutus brutus.tpci.com loghost
147.120.0.1          merlin merlin.tpci.com
147.120.0.2          freya freya.tpci.com
147.120.0.4          megan megan.tpci.com_
147.120.0.10         whitney whitney.tpci.com
147.120.0.11         sinbad sinbad.tpci.com
147.120.0.12         pepper pepper.tpci.com
```

The /etc/networks file on the SPARCstation server is similar to that on the SCO UNIX machine:

```
loopback      127
sco           132.147
sco-hq        132.147.128
sco-mfg       132.147.64
sco-engr      132.147.192
sco-slip      132.147.32
sco-tcplab    132.147.160
sco-odtlab    132.147.1
maclean_net   147.50.1
bnr.ca        47
```

In some cases, additional entries might exist for backward-compatibility reasons. You can add as many entries as you want to the /etc/networks file.

As with Linux, the /etc/services and /etc/protocols files are left alone, because they are supplied with all the configuration details already entered. These files can be modified if you need to disable a particular service (for security reasons, for example), but in most cases they are best left unmodified.

The SPARCstation was supplied with an RJ45 connector to the Ethernet network, so I used a transceiver to convert from RJ45 to a BNC connector. Passing through the transceiver converts the Ethernet connection to the mode you need. I could have wired the entire network with RJ45 connectors, but I would then need a hub to connect all the RJ45 connectors to (as I discussed on Day 1, "Open Systems, Standards, and Protocols").

After the SPARCstation is connected to the network, you can try pinging a remote machine. If you get a proper response, all is well and you can move on to configuring other machines. If there is a problem with ping, you have to verify that all the files are correct, that the IP address is valid, and that the network transceiver is functioning properly.

Configuring Windows NT Server

Windows NT is available in both server and workstation versions. Today I configure the server version for the sample network. I use Windows NT Server 3.51 on the sample system although Windows NT 4.0 performs in almost exactly the same way. (Windows NT 4.0 was still in beta as this book was being written; the only changes noticeable were because of the GUI modifications to resemble the Windows 95 GUI.) Although TCP/IP is provided with Windows NT, it is not installed as the default network protocol. Instead, IPX/SPX and NetBEUI are installed as default protocols. To configure TCP/IP, you need to extract the TCP/IP software from the distribution media if it hasn't already been installed.

You can check for the presence of the TCP/IP software by opening the Network Settings window inside the Control Panel. This window is shown in Figure 9.2. The scroll list in the bottom left corner has a list of all installed components. If it does not include an entry such as TCP/IP Protocol, the TCP/IP software is not installed. To install the TCP/IP software, click the Add Software button on the Network Settings window.

Figure 9.2.

The Windows NT Network Settings screen shows all the components that are installed.

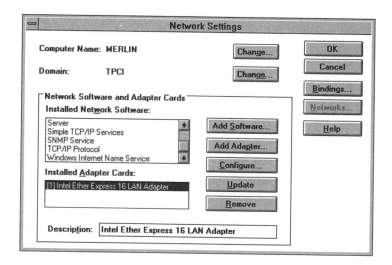

When you select Add Software, the system checks for all the installed and available components (which can take some time), then displays the windows shown in Figure 9.3. After selecting TCP/IP to be installed, you can select the specific TCP/IP components and any other TCP/IP services you want to install from the window shown in Figure 9.4.

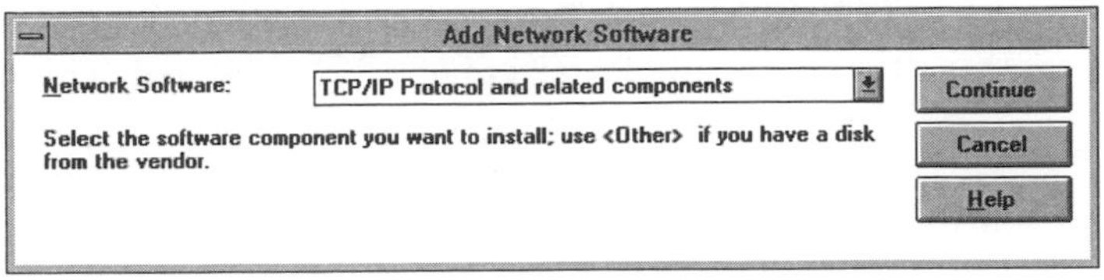

Figure 9.3.

You can add the TCP/IP software to your Windows NT system through this window.

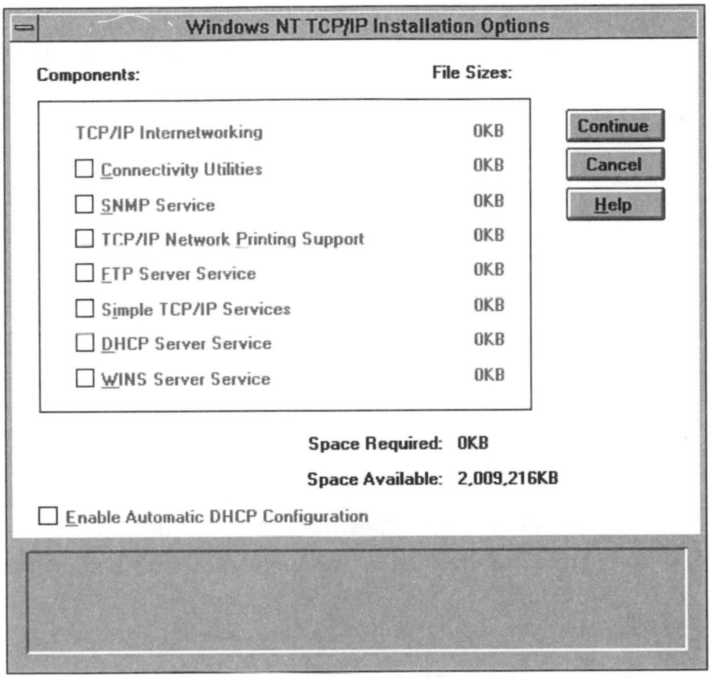

Add Network Software	
Network Software: [TCP/IP Protocol and related components ▼]	Continue
Select the software component you want to install; use <Other> if you have a disk from the vendor.	Cancel
	Help

Figure 9.4.

Select the components of the Windows NT TCP/IP software that you want to install from this window.

Windows NT TCP/IP Installation Options

Components:	File Sizes:	
TCP/IP Internetworking	0KB	Continue
☐ Connectivity Utilities	0KB	Cancel
☐ SNMP Service	0KB	Help
☐ TCP/IP Network Printing Support	0KB	
☐ FTP Server Service	0KB	
☐ Simple TCP/IP Services	0KB	
☐ DHCP Server Service	0KB	
☐ WINS Server Service	0KB	

Space Required: 0KB

Space Available: 2,009,216KB

☐ Enable Automatic DHCP Configuration

9

The server version of Windows NT offers several TCP/IP configuration options and extra services. Those shown in Figure 9.4 include the following:

- ☐ **TCP/IP Internetworking:** These must be installed for TCP/IP to function. It includes the drivers for TCP, IP, UDP, and ARP, as well as several other protocols like ICMP. PPP and SLIP are also provided through this option.

- ☐ **Connectivity Utilities:** Utilities like `finger`, `ping`, `telnet`, and many others. These should be installed with all TCP/IP configurations.

- ☐ **SNMP Service:** The SNMP drivers used to enable the server or workstation to be administered remotely. This option should be used if your Windows NT machine is to be managed by a remote UNIX workstation. The SNMP Service is also required if you want to run the Performance Monitor and obtain TCP/IP behavior statistics.

- [ ] **TCP/IP Network Printing:** Enables network printers (those attached directly to the network cables instead of a PC) to be used. This option can also be used if you want to send all print requests on this machine to another machine for handling, such as a UNIX print server.

- [ ] **FTP Server Service:** If you want to use FTP to transfer files from Windows NT, this service must be loaded.

- [ ] **Simple TCP/IP Services:** Offers specialty services like Daytime, Echo, and Quote that are used by some applications. If you are using UNIX workstations on the same network, these services probably should be supported by the Windows NT machine.

- [ ] **DHCP Server Service:** Installs the DHCP server software. If you want to use DHCP on your network, you need a DHCP server.

- [ ] **WINS Server:** If WINS is to be used on your network, install the server software.

Clicking the OK button begins the installation process, with Windows NT prompting you for the distribution CD-ROM or disks as needed. After the TCP/IP software is installed, you have to reboot the machine and then the Network Settings window should show the TCP/IP protocols in place.

If you installed a network adapter when the Windows NT operating system software was loaded, the network adapter card should also show in the list of installed components in the Network Settings window. If you need to add a network adapter card to the system, it can be added through the Network Settings window, too. The Add Adapter button starts the installation routine, which prompts for the type of network adapter card, then the settings on the card for IRQ and memory address. After the network card has been configured, the drivers are loaded by Windows NT, then a system reboot makes the card available.

The Network Settings window lets you configure each component of the TCP/IP software installed on the Windows NT server. You can change the machine name and domain name from the Network Settings window by clicking the Change button next to those items at the top of the screen. Only an administrator can change the machine and domain names.

If you highlight TCP/IP Protocol in the Network Settings window, then click the Configure button, you see the TCP/IP Configuration window shown in Figure 9.5. This lets you provide the IP address of the local machine (assuming it is not assigned through the use of another service like DHCP or WINS). If you are using a DHCP or WINS server (other than the machine you are configuring now), the IP address of that server should be entered on this screen.

9

Figure 9.5.
The IP address of the local machine is entered in this window.

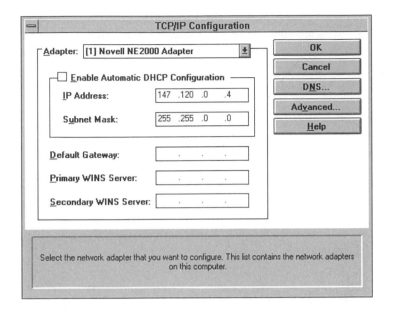

If you are using DNS on your network, select the DNS button in the TCP/IP Configuration window. This displays the DNS Configuration window. This window lets you specify the hostname and domain name of the DNS server as well as any specifics about the DNS server search order. If you are not using DNS, you can leave this window as it is. Because you are not setting up a DNS server at the moment, you can leave this window alone. Finally, the Advanced button on the TCP/IP Configuration window lets you select subnet masks and gateway IP addresses, if necessary.

From the Network Settings window, you should check the network bindings to make sure TCP/IP is used for communications over the local area network. Select the Bindings button on the Network Settings window to display the Network Bindings window, shown in Figure 9.6.

Figure 9.6.
The Network Bindings window shows all network bindings configured on the system.

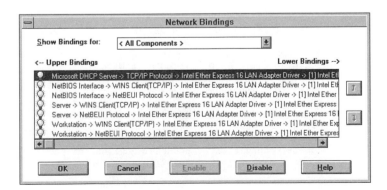

If TCP/IP is properly configured, you see the TCP/IP protocol bound to the network adapter card. The binding should be enabled, as shown by a yellow lightbulb to the left of the binding name. If it is not enabled, click the Enable button at the bottom of the window. If other protocols, such as IPX/SPX, are bound to the same network card and enabled but not needed, you should disable them. Only leave the bindings that you need enabled.

After the configuration information has been verified, you should click Update or OK and allow Windows NT to complete the configuration for you. You might have to provide the source disks or CD-ROM if new software is necessary. After the configuration is complete, you need to reboot the machine to effect any changes.

To verify that the configuration is working properly, you should run the ping command and try pinging another machine on the network. The ping utility is DOS-based and can usually be found under WINNT35\SYSTEM32. Start a DOS session and issue the ping command, followed by a known IP address. If the remote is successfully pinged, your installation and configuration are working.

Testing the Server Configurations

Testing the TCP/IP configuration on any of the four configured servers is straightforward. Begin by using ping on each machine to ensure that the software is talking to the network hardware. Unfortunately, a successful ping of the local machine does not always mean the network is being accessed properly; it simply means the network software is processing the request. To test the network interface itself, ping the other machines on the network. In the following example, merlin is the localhost and sinbad is a DOS machine running ftp Software's PC/TCP (which you see tomorrow):

```
$ ping merlin
PING localhost (147.120.0.1): 56 data bytes
64 bytes from localhost (147.120.0.1): icmp_seq=0 ttl=255 time=0 ms
64 bytes from localhost (147.120.0.1): icmp_seq=1 ttl=255 time=0 ms
64 bytes from localhost (147.120.0.1): icmp_seq=2 ttl=255 time=0 ms
64 bytes from localhost (147.120.0.1): icmp_seq=3 ttl=255 time=0 ms
64 bytes from localhost (147.120.0.1): icmp_seq=4 ttl=255 time=0 ms
-- localhost ping statistics --
5 packets transmitted, 5 packets received, 0% packet loss
round-trip min/avg/max = 0/0/0 ms
$ ping sinbad
PING sinbad (147.120.0.11): 56 data bytes
64 bytes from localhost (147.120.0.1): icmp_seq=0 ttl=255 time=20 ms
64 bytes from localhost (147.120.0.1): icmp_seq=1 ttl=255 time=20 ms
64 bytes from localhost (147.120.0.1): icmp_seq=2 ttl=255 time=50 ms
64 bytes from localhost (147.120.0.1): icmp_seq=3 ttl=255 time=30 ms
64 bytes from localhost (147.120.0.1): icmp_seq=4 ttl=255 time=40 ms
-- pepper ping statistics --
5 packets transmitted, 5 packets received, 0% packet loss
round-trip min/avg/max = 20/32/50 ms
```

The first test shows that the software is configured properly. The command to ping merlin resulted in a conversion within the /etc/hosts file to recognize the instruction as the localhost entry. After verifying the local connection, the remote machine is tried. The successful round-trip of the packets indicates that the remote is working properly, and that the network is functional. Of course, this works only if the remote machine has been loaded with TCP/IP software and is active.

If the localhost ping command failed, the software was probably configured incorrectly, or the hardware was not accessed properly. First, check the connectors on the network cards, because they have an annoying habit of working loose. Next, check the network configuration (IRQ, address, and type of adapter), followed by the configuration files, as shown earlier. If everything looks correct and the remote machine answers its own ping command properly, there is a problem with software compatibility.

The netstat network status command is useful for monitoring the network's performance and detecting problems. TCP/IP system administrators frequently use the options -i, -m, and -s. See Day 13, "Managing and Troubleshooting TCP/IP," for more troubleshooting information.

A common problem is the lack of enough STREAMS buffers, which causes a process to hang or a connection to terminate for no apparent reason. The size of the STREAMS buffer and its current status can be checked with the command netstat -m:

```
$ netstat -m
streams allocation:
                       config   alloc   free    total    max    fail
streams                  292      78     214      145     79      0
queues                  1424     360    1064      327    364      0
mblks                   5077     197    4880     3189    206      0
dblks                   4062     197    3865     3167    205      0
class 0,     4 bytes     652      51     601      357     53      0
class 1,    16 bytes     652       1     651      284      3      0
class 2,    64 bytes     768       8     760     2158     15      0
class 3,   128 bytes     872     104     768      237    106      0
class 4,   256 bytes     548      21     527       90     22      0
class 5,   512 bytes     324      12     312       13     13      0
class 6,  1024 bytes     107       0     107        1      1      0
class 7,  2048 bytes      98       0      98        1      1      0
class 8,  4096 bytes      41       0      41       26      1      0
total configured streams memory: 1183.09KB
streams memory in use: 44.66KB
maximum streams memory used: 58.28KB_
```

The number in the fail column should be 0 in each row; otherwise, there is a problem with the amount of buffer allocated. To change the number of STREAMS buffers allocated, kernel variables must be changed and the kernel relinked. As a general rule, if there are problems with the existing STREAMS buffer sizes, increase the number by 50 percent. If that doesn't solve the problem, increase by another 50 percent.

To fully test the TCP/IP system, use Telnet or FTP to log in and transfer files from machine to machine. Because these two utilities are the most common users of TCP/IP (unless NIS or NFS are active), they help show any problems with the port assignments, services provided, or name mapping.

Pseudo ttys

Most UNIX systems support pseudo ttys (false terminals) to enable external machines to use Telnet and rlogin for access to the local machine. Without a pseudo tty, the remote machine cannot establish a session.

The SCO UNIX system, for example, configures 32 pseudo ttys by default, which should be plenty for small and moderate sized networks. (Remember that 32 pseudo ttys enable 32 sessions from remote users.) Adding or deleting pseudo ttys can be done through a configuration utility or, in the case of SCO UNIX, with the mkdev ptty command. There is no useful advantage gained by drastically reducing the number of pseudo ttys on small networks. Pseudo ttys should be reconfigured after TCP/IP has been installed and is working correctly.

User Equivalence

User equivalence lets a user rlogin to another machine with the same account information, without entering a password. This is helpful when a user must log into another machine frequently, avoiding the login process for speed and reducing the number of processes running on the remote.

To permit user equivalence, UNIX requires that the user exists on both machines and that entries in two configuration files match. The /etc/passwd file, which controls overall access to the machine, must have an entry for the user's login name on both machines. One of two configuration files also must have information about the user.

If the file .rhosts is used, user equivalence is established only for accounts specifically named in the file. The .rhosts file usually resides in the root directory and has one entry per line, specifying the remote machine name and the user ID. An .rhosts file looks like this:

```
# .rhosts file for brutus.com
merlin tparker
merlin ychow
merlin bsmallwood
pepper etreijs
pepper tparker
freya rmaclean
```

With this configuration, the user `tparker`, on remote machine `merlin`, could log in to the local machine as `tparker` only. A user can allow access to an account by another by creating a `.rhosts` file in his or her home directory.

If the file `hosts.equiv` is used (which usually resides in the `/etc` directory), user equivalence is valid for any account on both machines except `root`. If the file `hosts.equiv` contained only a machine name, any valid user on that machine would be allowed user equivalence (except `root`). The machine is called a *trusted* host.

Unfortunately, this type of access poses considerable security problems, so it should be used only under stringently controlled or very reliable conditions. A major problem is that a user can log in as any other valid user on the remote system without using a password. A sample `hosts.equiv` file looks like this:

```
# hosts.equiv for brutus.com
merlin tparker
pepper
freya rmaclean
```

In this example, any user on the remote system (`pepper`) could log in as any valid user (except `root`) on the local machine, without using a password. Only the user `tparker`, on the remote machine `merlin`, could log in as any valid system user (except `root`) on the local machine. The potential for misuse of user equivalence with this type of access is high, although it can be handy for access to specific utilities or applications.

If both `.rhosts` and `hosts.equiv` exist with entries for the same machine and user ID, the entry from the `hosts.equiv` file is used for determining the user's equivalence. Remember that for both `.rhosts` and `hosts.equiv`, matching user entries must exist in the `/etc/passwd` file.

User equivalence configuration can cause problems for system administrators that are frequently blamed on the network software. Also, some users might want to allow specific entries by a user on a remote system without having the system administrator grant open privileges.

To illustrate the entries more clearly, a concrete example might help. Assume user `ychow`, on the machine `pepper`, wants to access machine `merlin` as both `ychow` and `shortie` without using passwords. (In other words, `ychow` on `pepper` is equivalent to `ychow` and `shortie` on `merlin`.) There are several methods of configuring the system to allow this. The system administrator can create an `.rhosts` file in the root directory that has the following entries:

```
pepper ychow
pepper shortie
```

This allows only `ychow` (on `pepper`) to log in as `ychow`, with no access as `shortie` unless `shortie` is logged in to `pepper`, too. This isn't what is required. An entry in the `hosts.equiv` file like this

```
pepper ychow
```

doesn't solve the problem either because ychow can now log in as any valid user on merlin. Solving this requires each user that wants to allow ychow to access their directories to place an .rhosts file in their home directories. On the sample network, both ychow's and shortie's home directories on merlin would have the same entries.

User ychow can now log in to merlin using one of the following commands:

```
rlogin merlin
```

or

```
rlogin merlin -l shortie
```

The latter command logs ychow in as the user equivalent shortie. The first retains the same login ID. Note that the .rhosts file resides in the home directories of the users who want to allow remote user access.

Anonymous FTP

Anonymous FTP enables users from other locations to access a system without logging on. They obtain the FTP prompt as usual but enter anonymous as the user name. In most systems, a password can be anything, although convention dictates that the user's login name be supplied for tracking purposes. There is no check of the names, however. Once logged in to anonymous FTP, users can browse through public directories and retrieve files that reside there. Anonymous FTP is excellent for distributing information to the general public, but its open access has accompanying security concerns.

When a user logs in to the anonymous FTP account, UNIX invokes a process called chroot, which restricts the user from moving out of the home directory. The dependence on chroot requires that some system configuration files (including a copy of the /etc/passwd and /etc/group files) reside in the anonymous FTP directories.

Configuring a UNIX system for anonymous FTP involves establishing a public directory system and changing file permissions to prevent unwanted access to other parts of the file system. Also, an anonymous account is created using the user name ftp. Anonymous FTP usually uses the user ftp's home directory created when the user is generated.

To set up anonymous FTP access, create a user called ftp. With UNIX systems, this is usually performed with a script called mkuser or a system utility. Alternatively, the user can be added to the /etc/passwd file. A group called ftp should exist or be created. Once the home directory for the user ftp exists, change its user and group identities to ftp (using the chown and chgrp commands).

Assuming the user ID ftp has been created and the home directory is /usr/ftp, the steps to follow are shown here. (Comments shown after the pound sign are for description purposes only and need not be entered.)

```
$ cd /usr/ftp    # change to the home directory
$ chmod 555 .    # set file permissions to r-x
$ chown ftp .    # change the owner to ftp
$ chgrp ftp .    # change the group to ftp
$ mkdir pub      # create public directory (see below)
$ chmod 777 pub  # set pub dir permissions as rwx
$ mkdir bin      # create bin dir for executables
$ cd bin
$ chmod 555 bin  # set bin dir to r-x
$ cp /bin/sh /bin/ls .
$ cd ..
$ mkdir etc      # create etc dir for passwd file
$ chmod 555 etc  # set etc dir to r-x
$ cd etc
$ cp /etc/passwd /etc/group .
$ chmod 444 passwd group
$ cd ..
```

If you want to create subdirectories beneath the home directory for the anonymous user to access, ensure that they have the correct ownerships, as well. It is common practice to create a directory called ftp/pub for uploading files to the system. Set file permissions so that the user cannot exit the home directory structure. In the previous example, all the directories except pub are set to read and execute only. The example copied the shell and listing utilities into the FTP directory structure so the anonymous user can access them. Other utilities can be copied if desired.

The /etc/passwd and /etc/group files must be copied into a directory called etc (below the ftp user's home directory) to enable chroot to function properly. It is strongly recommended that these files be edited to remove any other user information; it is conceivable that an anonymous user could access and analyze the files for information about the local system, leading to an unwelcome break-in. Remove all users from the /etc/passwd file except for root, daemon, uucp, and the ftp entries. Similarly, prune the /etc/group file to remove all but these entries.

To help prevent unwanted access, the file etc/ftpusers can be created to contain user names that result in immediate disconnection. This file should have entries for root and uucp as a minimum.

Windows NT Server enables anonymous FTP through a different mechanism (because it isn't UNIX). To enable anonymous FTP on the Windows NT server on the sample network, you have to enable the FTP server. The software for the server should be installed as shown earlier. During the installation you will probably receive a warning about the insecurity of using FTP to transfer passwords over your network. However, unless you can install an authentication scheme for your passwords, this is a necessary evil to enable FTP access to the Windows NT machine.

To configure the FTP server software, you select the FTP server item from the Network Settings window shown in Figure 9.2 and then click the Configure button. This displays the FTP Service window shown in Figure 9.7. You can adjust the number of sessions allowed as well as the time-out interval using the options at the top of this window.

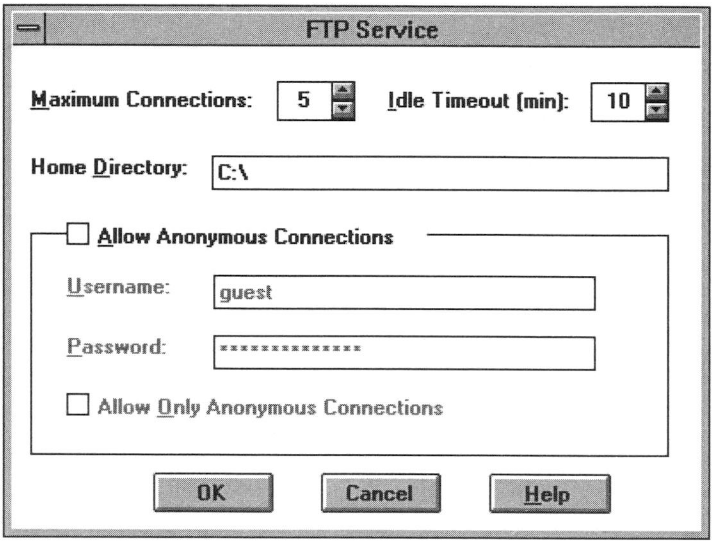

Figure 9.7.

Use this window to alter the behavior of the FTP server.

You might notice that the bottom part of the screen lets you set the FTP server to enable anonymous connections. You can set the anonymous login and password if you want. This enables users who are not on the authorized Windows NT Users' list to transfer files from the Windows NT machine. It is a good idea to restrict access to a subdirectory where there are no sensitive files available.

You can monitor the behavior of the FTP server system through the FTP Server icon on the Control Panel. This displays a window like the one shown in Figure 9.8, which lists all active users. The Disconnect and Disconnect All buttons at the bottom of the window can be used to force users off the Windows NT machine.

Figure 9.8.

The FTP Server window shows users who are currently using FTP.

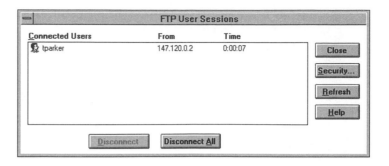

Some security settings can be controlled through the FTP Server window by clicking the Security button. This displays the window shown in Figure 9.9. The Read and Write options enable you to control access to entire drives (all floppy and hard drives, as well as any mounted drives such as CD-ROMs and optical or removable media).

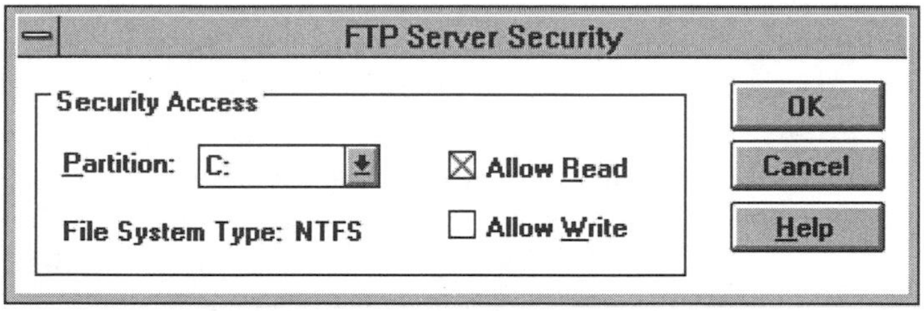

Figure 9.9.

The FTP Server Security window lets you set broad access rights to drives.

Configuring SLIP and PPP

Serial Line Internet Protocol (SLIP) and Point-to-Point Protocol (PPP) operate over serial lines and require some additional information. Because SLIP and PPP connections are between two machines, the source and destination IP addresses are needed. Also, the serial port identifier is needed, including the interrupt vector it uses. Serial lines must be properly configured with their baud rate. This is usually set within another file on the system. SLIP connections also require a netmask setting, although this is not needed for PPP.

PPP is more versatile than SLIP. SLIP supports asynchronous communications only, whereas PPP enables synchronous and asynchronous. SLIP must have a dedicated line that is always tied up, whereas PPP can share the line with other programs like UUCP and free the line on command. SLIP lacks any error detection, whereas PPP implements it. Given the choice, PPP is the better serial-line TCP protocol, although it is not available with all operating system implementations.

SLIP and PPP connections are usually established in the same manner as the Ethernet drivers. SCO UNIX, for example, uses the `netconfig` utility, mentioned previously. When adding a SLIP or PPP chain, the system prompts for the serial line to be used, the baud rate, the address of the local and destination machines, and the remote machine's name. It then configures the system to use that serial port. After relinking the kernel and rebooting, the serial line is available for either SLIP or PPP (depending on the way it was configured).

Remote Printing

Remote printing is a useful feature that enables a user on one machine to send print jobs to other machines that have attached printers. The system is called Remote Line Printing (RLP) and is commonly used to share printers in a workgroup. It is also useful for enabling access to specialty printers such as color lasers and plotters. RLP does not support printer classes, and some operating systems impose restrictions on supported print command-line options. Remote administration of printers is not supported.

RLP functions differently than normal UNIX printing. When a print request is issued, the system consults the printer configuration file (usually `/etc/printcap`) to determine if the printer is local or remote. If the print request is for a local printer, the usual process applies. If the request is for a remote printer, the local system spools the print request and invokes the `lpd` daemon, which packages the print request and sends it to the remote machine, where it is spooled for the printer. A user can set a remote printer as the default destination, as is commonly done in workgroups that share a single printer.

Several versions of RLP are available with support for different operating systems on a network. SCO UNIX, for example, supports two kinds of clients: SCO-based systems and 4.3BSD systems. This enables workstations running Berkeley's 4.3BSD to queue print requests to SCO print servers. SCO clients use RLP with the same commands as a local printer would (`lp` and `cancel`), but 4.3BSD clients have special versions of the commands (`lpr` and `lprm`).

Assuming that RLP is available with your operating system (some versions of UNIX do not support it), it is usually installed and activated with a script or utility program. With SCO UNIX, a `mkdev rlp` command initiates the installation script. Other operating systems use a similar utility. During the installation process, a number of directories are created to handle the spooling, and modifications are made to the printer configuration files. The old printing commands are archived to a directory, and new versions that support RLP are copied into their place.

Remote printing requires a special entry in the printer configuration file (`/etc/printcap`). Some operating systems (such as SCO UNIX) have a script that edits the file for you,

9

prompting for the configuration information. A sample line in the file for a remote printer would look like this:

```
hplaser::lp=:rm=main_hplaser:rp=hplaser:sd=/usr/spool/lpd/hplaser
```

The first field is the name used by the local machine to refer to the printer. The second field is usually empty. It defines the name of an error log file but is not used on most systems. The third field is the device name for a local printer. Remote printers leave the field as `lp=` with no specified printer. The fourth field is the network name for the printer. It can be the same as the local name. The fifth field is the name the print server uses for the printer (usually the same as the local name). Finally, the sixth field is the name of the spooling directory for the printer. This is where print requests are spooled before being sent to the remote printer.

In order for machines on the network to access the Hewlett-Packard LaserJet that is attached to the main machine on the sample network, the three remote machines should have entries for the printer in their `/etc/printcap` files. The main machine also has an entry for it, but as a local printer.

Administering a remote printer is done either by logging into the console of the machine to which the printer is attached or by using several RLP utilities from another machine. The utilities differ with each operating system.

Windows NT Server has remote TCP/IP printing capabilities available as part of the TCP/IP suite.

Configuring SNMP

Most TCP/IP networks use the Simple Network Management Protocol (SNMP) to monitor the network for problems. It enables a system to examine and alter networking information maintained by other machines on the network. SNMP is a simple protocol that uses UDP as a transport.

Many UNIX operating systems use a daemon to run SNMP. When the system is running, SNMP listens on its dedicated port for incoming requests. Three configuration files are also usually involved.

The file `/etc/snmpd.conf` contains basic information required by SNMP. The file contains identifiers for the types of SNMP and TCP/IP software, as well as the contact name of the system administrator and the location of the system. A sample file looks like this:

```
# snmpd.conf configuration file for tpci.com
# the first two fields are default value
descr=SNMPD Version 4.0 for SCO UNIX
objid=SCO.1.0
contact=Tim Parker x53153
location=Network Room
```

If SNMP is set to send trap messages (asynchronous event messages), it sends introductory packets (called *cold-start* traps) to other systems that it is functioning. It reads the names of the systems to send cold-start traps to from the file /etc/snmpd.trap, which lists names, IP addresses, and port numbers:

```
# sample snmpd.trap file for tpci.com
# lists symbolic name, IP address, and port
test1   128.212.64.99   162
merlin  147.120.0.2     162
```

The file snmpd.comm is a list of community and IP address pairs that specifies from whom the agent can accept queries. Each line in the file has the name of the community (sometimes called a session), the IP address of the site (a value of 0.0.0.0 enables any address to communicate), and the privileges that site is allowed. If the privilege is set to READ, only read operations are permitted; WRITE enables read and write operations; and NONE restricts all access.

```
# Copyrighted as an unpublished work.
# (c) Copyright 1989 INTERACTIVE Systems Corporation
# All rights reserved.
#       @(#)snmpd.comm    3.1 INTERACTIVE SNMP   source
test1 128.212.64.99 READ
test2 128.212.64.15 WRITE
test3 128.212.64.15 READ
public 0.0.0.0 read
beast 0.0.0.0 read
excaliber 0.0.0.0 read
```

Configuration of SNMP is usually through an interactive shell script. During the script, the user is prompted for all the information needed for the three configuration files. SCO UNIX uses the command mkdev snmp to install the system.

Summary

This chapter has shown how to install and configure several servers with TCP/IP. These methods have been tested and work correctly. In the process, this chapter mentioned several alternative services such as anonymous FTP and remote printing. Whether these are available on your network is up to you (or the system administrator). The next chapter adds client machines to the sample network.

Q&A

Q What information is necessary to configure a machine's TCP/IP software?

A For a complete configuration, TCP/IP requires the domain name, system name, IP address, driver type, broadcast address, netmask, and hardware network card settings. Some systems enable configuration with only some of this information.

Q What does the network mask do?

A The network mask removes the network identifier from an IP address, leaving only the local machine's address. For example, an IP address of 146.120.94.4 can have the network mask 146.120 applied to leave the local machine address as 94.4.

Q What role does the /etc/inetd.conf file play?

A The file /etc/inetd.conf indicates the processes started by the inetd daemon when a system boots.

Q Explain user equivalence.

A User equivalence lets a user access another machine without requiring a password during the login process. It is controlled by a set of files controlled by the system or individual users.

Quiz

1. How many devices are enabled on a Class B network (the most common)?

2. What is the difference between the BSD UNIX TCP/IP broadcast address setting and the one normally used?

3. What is a pseudo tty?

4. What does the following .rhosts file do?

```
# .rhosts
artemis tparker
artemis goof
artemis aarmenakis
mig rmaclean
```

5. What is anonymous FTP and why would you use it?

Chapter 10

Setting up a Sample Network: Clients

Yesterday, you configured the servers on the sample network. All three UNIX servers followed the same procedure and had similar configuration files. The Windows NT server was configured using the built-in TCP/IP stack. Today you configure some clients for the network. The clients communicate with the server through a TCP/IP stack loaded on each machine. You configure three clients: one DOS, one Windows 3.x, and one Windows 95. Any of the operating systems you configured yesterday as servers can also act as clients on the sample network.

Windows 95 includes TCP/IP client software as part of the distribution software package, but it is not configured when Windows 95 is installed. This is because Windows 95 installs NetWare's IPX/SPX network protocols as the default. Today you see how to change the default protocol to TCP/IP. For the DOS and Windows 3.x machines, several products are available that offer TCP/IP protocols. I have selected two of the most popular packages to configure on these systems. The DOS machine is configured using ftp Software's PC/TCP software product. The Windows 3.x machine, running Microsoft Windows for Workgroups 3.11, is configured with NetManage's ChameleonNFS.

Configuring DOS and Windows machines is different than configuring UNIX systems because of the changes in file systems, operating system architecture, and the individual software vendor's approaches. However, the same basic information is required, and the steps to add DOS machines are analogous to those for a UNIX system.

Although today I use two specific commercial packages for the DOS and Windows 3.11 machines, the process is similar to other vendors' TCP/IP products. The names of files and the exact configuration information might differ, but the same general principles apply.

DOS-Based TCP/IP: ftp Software's PC/TCP

PC/TCP from ftp Software has been available for several years and has become a *de facto* standard for DOS machines that want to connect with a TCP/IP network. PC/TCP runs under both DOS and Windows. It lets a user perform all the TCP/IP functions, such as `ftp` and `telnet`, and includes software for several members of the TCP family of protocols, including SNMP. Other machines can also access a PC running PC/TCP, copying its files (assuming access has been granted). Bear in mind that we are configuring this machine as a DOS platform only, even though PC/TCP offers some Windows icons. The machine might be an older device that doesn't support Windows, for example, or the user might not want to install Windows 3.x on this machine. Some DOS-based applications might not work with a Windows-based TCP/IP stack—hence the need for a DOS-only TCP/IP configuration.

PC/TCP can run TCP/IP as the sole network protocol on the PC, or it can piggy-back on top of other networks, such as Windows for Workgroups (NetBEUI and NetBIOS) or Novell NetWare (IPX/SPX). Your system administrator can decide the best configuration for your machine, depending on the nature of the network. For example, if a large Windows for Workgroups network already exists but a user wants access to a TCP/IP UNIX server, it might not make sense to convert the entire network to TCP/IP. In that case, either a second network card can be added specifically for the TCP/IP network, or TCP/IP can coexist with the Windows for Workgroups system. (Remember that TCP/IP isn't particular about the network transport type.)

The sample network you are configuring is TCP/IP-based, so PC/TCP is installed to run on that network protocol only. However, because it would be useful to be able to run Windows for Workgroups over the network between the DOS and Windows 3.11 machines, the installation process you take is designed so that both NetBEUI and TCP/IP can reside simultaneously on the network.

10

One approach is to set the PC/TCP system to enable Windows for Workgroups and TCP/IP packets on the same network. With this approach, TCP/IP sends out IP packets, and Windows for Workgroups sends out NetBEUI packets (the default type). Both protocols use NDIS (Network Device Interface Specification) device drivers to communicate with the network card. The problem with this approach is that other machines receiving the packets might get confused because of two different packet types, and the system does not work well if an external network is to be accessed (such as the Internet) because routers do not handle NetBEUI packets.

The alternative approach is to configure Windows for Workgroups to encapsulate its message within IP packets, which can then be sent across the internetwork and the local network between TCP/IP machines with no problems. This approach has a couple of useful advantages. The network is completely IP-based, so routers can handle the traffic through internetworks. Also, a Windows for Workgroups computer on another network can communicate through the router, hence making the Windows for Workgroups services more widely available. A receiving Windows for Workgroups machine has to extract the information from the IP packet, but otherwise the system works well.

The sample network you are installing is configured to enable both PC/TCP and Windows for Workgroups to coexist using NDIS drivers. This results in two software stacks—one for PC/TCP and one for Windows for Workgroups—coexisting and communicating with the NDIS driver. This structure is shown in Figure 10.1. This is probably not the best choice for the sample network, because all the other machines on the network prefer TCP/IP packet formats, but this approach shows how PC/TCP can be configured for dual protocols on other networks.

Figure 10.1.
PC/TCP and Windows for Workgroups stacks using NDIS.

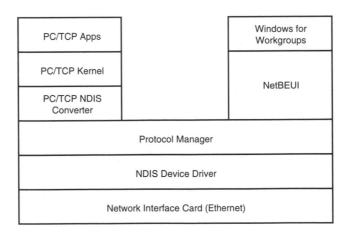

10

PC/TCP uses a kernel that is loaded into memory when DOS boots. The kernel is a Terminate and Stay Resident (TSR) program. To ensure that the network is available at all times, the kernel load command is usually added to the AUTOEXEC.BAT file. The sample network uses a kernel called ETHDRV.EXE, which is the Ethernet driver supplied with PC/TCP. (A different kernel must be used if the network is IEEE 802.3 Ethernet, which differs from the normal DIX Ethernet.) In addition, an NDIS Converter must be loaded in the AUTOEXEC.BAT file as a device driver to provide NDIS-format packets to the protocol manager.

Installing PC/TCP

PC/TCP includes an automated installation procedure that copies the distribution media to the hard disk and sets up some of the configuration files. Today, most of the system is configured manually to show the necessary steps and to enable you to verify the changes made to system files by the installation program. In practice, you would allow PC/TCP to install itself and perform the configuration automatically, then check the files for proper content.

Installation of PC/TCP requires the same basic information as TCP/IP under UNIX: the device driver, the system's name and IP address, and the names and IP addresses of other systems to be accessed. The process begins with a properly installed network card. The IRQ and memory address of the card must be known, and a device driver for it must be present for inclusion in the CONFIG.SYS file. Device drivers are usually supplied by the network card vendor, but generic drivers are also included with the PC/TCP software disks. They include drivers for the most popular types of network systems but might not include all possible cards.

After copying all the distribution files to the hard drive, the configuration can begin. The sample machine is running DOS 6.22 and Windows for Workgroups 3.11, although you are configuring the DOS operating system in particular in this section. Changes in the DOS software release number might affect the following details, but the PC/TCP installation instructions are updated for new releases. When installing PC/TCP with Windows for Workgroups, the Windows network must be installed, configured, and running properly before PC/TCP modifies the Windows files to enable both DOS and Windows to work over the network.

During the installation process, PC/TCP requires a lengthy serial number and authentication key. These verify the software and prevent a network from using many copies of the same software when only one license has been purchased.

Four files are involved in the initial configuration:

☐ AUTOEXEC.BAT: Starts the PC/TCP kernel

☐ CONFIG.SYS: Starts the device drivers for the network and PC/TCP

10

☐ PROTOCOL.INI: Defines the type of network and drivers

☐ PCTCP.INI: Kernel parameters for PC/TCP

In yesterday's material, UNIX kernel parameter configuration was mentioned in passing as a way to fine-tune the behavior of the operating system with TCP/IP. In some cases, this is necessary with the DOS PC/TCP system as well. A utility program called KAPPCONF enables the kernel parameters to be altered. The settings for the kernel are saved in a configuration file called PCTCP.INI.

The AUTOEXEC.BAT File

The AUTOEXEC.BAT file requires environment variables to be properly set for PC/TCP and two instructions to be added to the file. One instruction starts the network, and the other loads the Ethernet driver. The sample machine already had Windows for Workgroups installed, so a line in the AUTOEXEC.BAT file reads

```
C:\WINDOWS\NET START
```

This line starts the network. The NET START command can remain in place or be replaced with a PC/TCP command called NETBIND, which accomplishes the same thing for NDIS drivers. If both commands are in the AUTOEXEC.BAT file, an error message results when the second network startup command is executed. (The drive assignments for all the examples today might be different on other systems, as might the installation directories. Installation defaults were used throughout this chapter for both PC/TCP and Windows for Workgroups. Change their values as needed to match your system.)

After the NET START or NETBIND command, the following line must be added to the AUTOEXEC.BAT file:

```
C:\PCTCP\ETHDRV
```

This starts the PC/TCP Ethernet driver. If another network system is being used, this would be replaced with the device driver for that network (such as IEEEDRV for IEEE 802.3 Ethernet or SLPDRV for SLIP).

It is useful to define two environment variables in the AUTOEXEC.BAT file for the PC/TCP software to use when searching for files. One is a simple addition to the PATH command, adding the PCTCP installation directory to the search path. The second is an environment variable that points to the PCTCP.INI file. The two declarations look like this:

```
SET PCTCP=C:\PCTCP\PCTCP.INI
SET PATH=C:\PCTCP;%PATH%
```

The latter change to the PATH command adds C:\PCTCP to an already defined PATH. An alternative would be to edit the PATH command to include the directory on the same line as the rest of the declaration. The PC/TCP software can be run without these environment variables defined, but problems with file locations can result if commands are not executed from the installation directory.

Therefore, on the DOS machine, the completed AUTOEXEC.BAT file should have one of the following four-line combinations in it:

```
SET PCTCP=C:\PCTCP\PCTCP.INI
SET PATH=C:\PCTCP;%PATH%
C:\WINDOWS\NET START
C:\PCTCP\ETHDRV
```

or

```
SET PCTCP=C:\PCTCP\PCTCP.INI
SET PATH=C:\PCTCP;%PATH%
C:\PCTCP\NETBIND
C:\PCTCP\ETHDRV
```

When these lines are executed during the system boot process, the system displays status messages when each command is completed. The NETBIND command displays this message if it loads successfully:

```
MS-DOS LAN Manager v2.1 Netbind
Microsoft Netbind version 2.1
```

A third line might display a status message about the interrupt vector used by the system. If NETBIND couldn't load correctly, it generates a message like this:

```
MS-DOS LAN Manager v2.1 Netbind
Error: Making PROTMAN IOCTL call.
```

This usually is generated when the network is already running (such as from issuing a NET START command before the NETBIND command; you might recall that only one of these two should be in the AUTOEXEC.BAT file).

The ETHDRV command displays a message with status information when it loads successfully. It looks like this:

```
MAC/DIS converterFTP Software PC/TCP Resident Module 2.31   01/07/94 12:38
Copyright (c) 1986-1993 by FTP Software, Inc.  All rights reserved.
Patch level 17637
Patch time: Fri Jan 07 14:25:09 1994
Kernel interrupt vector is 0x61
Code Segment occupies 49.0K of conventional memory
Data Segment occupies 19.5K of conventional memory
Packet Driver found at vector 0x60
        name:
        version: 30, class: 1, type: 57, functionality: 6
ifcust (PC/TCP Class 1 packet driver - DIX Ethernet) initialized
5 free packets of length 1514, 5 free packets of length 160
The Resident Module occupies 68.7K of conventional memory
```

10

If there is an error when the ETHDRV program loads, it generates an error message (of varying utility for debugging purposes). A sample error is shown here:

```
FTP Software PC/TCP Resident Module 2.31    01/07/94 12:38
Copyright (c) 1986-1993 by FTP Software, Inc.  All rights reserved.
Patch level 17637
Patch time: Fri Jan 07 14:25:09 1994
PC/TCP is already loaded (interrupt 0x61). Use 'inet unload' to unload it.
```

This error occurred because a PC/TCP driver had been loaded prior to the ETHDRV command.

Some DOS users like to leave these commands out of the AUTOEXEC.BAT file and issue them manually. This has the advantage of reducing the amount of memory chewed up when the machine boots and the network is not required. A useful compromise is to create a small batch file that has these two commands and then run the batch file only if the network is used. Both NETBIND and ETHDRV do not seem to be critical as far as when they are loaded in the startup sequence (as opposed to some software that insists on being loaded first or last in the AUTOEXEC.BAT file).

The CONFIG.SYS File

The CONFIG.SYS file has to have drivers loaded for the protocol manager, the NDIS packet converter, and the network card driver. Systems running Windows for Workgroups might require additional drivers. The CONFIG.SYS file must have an entry setting the number of files open at one time to at least 20. If this doesn't exist, PC/TCP crashes. Add this line:

```
FILES=20
```

to the CONFIG.SYS file. Depending on the amount of memory available, the number could be readily increased. With 8MB RAM or more, a value of 40 is satisfactory. Numbers above this setting tend to be counterproductive because RAM is wasted for no reason.

The protocol manager is supplied as part of Windows for Workgroups, and one is included with the PC/TCP software package. The choice of which to use is yours or your system administrator's. If Windows for Workgroups 3.1 (not 3.11) was already loaded and functional, CONFIG.SYS has a line similar to this:

```
DEVICE=C:\WINDOWS\PROTMAN.DOS /I:C:\WINDOWS
```

The protocol manager is not always used with the Windows for Workgroups 3.11 release because it is included with other drivers within the CONFIG.SYS file (such as IFSHLP.SYS). If there is no protocol manager started at boot time, one should be added from the PC/TCP software. The entry within the CONFIG.SYS file is

```
DEVICE=C:\PCTCP\PROTMAN.DOS \I:C:\PCTCP
```

This loads the PC/TCP protocol manager. The \I at the end of the command tells the driver where to look for files (in this case, the PC/TCP installation directory).

A network card driver should appear next in CONFIG.SYS. This differs for each network card, but for the sample network DOS machine's Intel EtherExpress 16 network card, the line is

```
DEVICE=C:\WINDOWS\EXP16.DOS
```

This loads the EXP16 driver for the Intel network card. This was included with the Windows for Workgroups software, but it is also available as a generic driver. Some machines with Windows for Workgroups already installed might have this command already in the CONFIG.SYS file.

The final step is to load the PC/TCP NDIS Packet Converter. The current release of PC/TCP uses a packet converter called DIS_PKT.GUP. The line looks like this:

```
DEVICE=C:\PCTCP\DIS_PKT.GUP
```

Some systems running Windows for Workgroups 3.1 (and a few that have upgraded to 3.11) have the line

```
DEVICE=C:\WINDOWS\WORKGRP.SYS
```

in the CONFIG.SYS file. This is for Windows for Workgroups use and is not necessary if PC/TCP is to be used as a DOS-based system only. If the file was not installed by Windows for Workgroups and the system works properly without it, there is no need to add it.

When the system boots, the device drivers are loaded in turn. Each displays a short message showing its version number. Any errors that occur are also displayed. Usually the device drivers don't cause any problems.

The properly configured CONFIG.SYS file for the DOS machine should have these lines in it

```
DEVICE=C:\WINDOWS\PROTMAN.DOS /I:\C:\WINDOWS
DEVICE=C:\WINDOWS\EXP16.DOS
DEVICE=C:\PCTCP\DIS_PKT.GUP
```

if it is using the Windows for Workgroups protocol manager. It should have the following lines if it is using the PC/TCP protocol manager:

```
DEVICE=C:\PCTCP\PROTMAN.DOS /I:\C:\PCTCP
DEVICE=C:\WINDOWS\EXP16.DOS
DEVICE=C:\PCTCP\DIS_PKT.GUP
```

As noted earlier, the network interface driver (EXP16) is different if your machine does not use the Intel EtherExpress 16 board.

The position of these lines within the CONFIG.SYS file isn't critical, although there might be problems if they are loaded into high memory with other drivers. Experimentation is the only way to find the most memory-efficient sequence.

The PROTOCOL.INI File

Windows for Workgroups has a PROTOCOL.INI file as part of its setup. The file tells the system about the network cards and drivers in use. The PC/TCP PROTOCOL.INI file does the same, but it resides in the PCTCP directory.

The contents of the PROTOCOL.INI file are different for each network card and driver configuration. There must be a section labeled [PKTDRV] (all in uppercase) that defines the driver name, the binding to the network card, and any configuration information needed. The sample network's PROTOCOL.INI file looks like this:

```
[PKTDRV]
drivername=PKTDRV$
bindings=MS$EE16
intvec=0x60

[MS$EE16]
DriverName=EXP16$
IOADDRESS=0x360
IRQ=11
IOCHRDY=Late
TRANSCEIVER=Thin Net (BNC/COAX)
```

This PROTOCOL.INI file defines the packet driver as PKTDRV$, the default driver with PC/TCP. The binding to the Intel EtherExpress 16 card used on the DOS machine refers to another section in the file that lists the address, IRQ, and some specifics of the EtherExpress card. These lines could have been included in the [PKTDRV] section but were separated for compatibility with the Windows for Workgroups PROTOCOL.INI file, which is similar in layout. The EtherExpress 16 card is set to use IRQ 11, memory address 360, and the Thin Ethernet cable connector. The intvec line in the [PKTDRV] section does not define the IRQ for the network card; instead, it is an interrupt for the driver.

A PROTOCOL.INI file for a system using a simpler network card than the EtherExpress can be shorter. A sample PROTOCOL.INI file for such a card might look like this:

```
[PKTDRV]
drivername=PKTDRV$
binding=MS$ELNKII
intvec=0x65
chainvec=0x67
```

Finding the proper settings for the variables in the PROTOCOL.INI file can be a harrowing experience. If Windows for Workgroups is installed and running, the Windows PROTOCOL.INI file is a good source of information and can sometimes be copied without modification. Otherwise, the network card documentation can sometimes help.

10

The PCTCP.INI File

The PCTCP.INI file holds the kernel configuration information for PC/TCP. In most cases, it can be left as supplied with the software. Tweaking the kernel parameters should be performed only after the network is installed and has been operating properly for a while. The PCTCP.INI file is quite lengthy, and care should be taken to avoid accidental changes, which can render the system inoperative.

If the supplied installation script is not used to install PC/TCP, a minimum PCTCP.INI file must be created manually. Examples are included with the distribution media, usually under the name TEMPLATE.INI. There are two ways to create the PCTCP.INI file and configure it properly. The first is to use an editor and modify the template file. The alternative is to run the kernel configuration utility KAPPCONF.

A minimum PCTCP.INI file needs to have the software serial number and activation key, the IP address, broadcast address, router address, a subnet mask, and information about the system in general. The minimum PCTCP.INI file would look like this:

```
[pctcp general]
domain                  = tpci.com
host-name               = sinbad
time-zone               = EST
time-zone-offset        = 600
user                    = tparker

[pctcp kernel]
serial-number           = 1234-5678-9012
authentication-key      = 1234-5678-9012
interface               = ifcust 0
low-window              = 0
window                  = 2048

[pctcp ifcust 0]
broadcast-address       = 255.255.255.255
ip-address              = 147.120.0.11
router                  = 147.120.0.1
subnet-mask             = 255.255.0.0

[pctcp addresses]
domain-name-server      = 147.120.0.1
mail-relay              = 147.120.0.1
```

This configuration assumes that the SCO UNIX server (147.120.0.1) is the primary server for the network. The DOS machine's name (sinbad) and IP address (147.120.0.11) are shown in the PCTCP.INI file. As different features of PC/TCP are enabled (such as SNMP and Kerberos), new sections are added to the PCTCP.INI file.

10

The Windows SYSTEM.INI File

If Windows for Workgroups is to be used on the DOS machine and you are going to use the PC/TCP drivers instead of a dedicated Windows for Workgroups TCP/IP package, the Windows for Workgroups SYSTEM.INI file requires modification. The Windows for Workgroups SYSTEM.INI file must be set to use the Windows for Workgroups driver instead of the PC/TCP driver.

When the PC/TCP automatic installation process detects a copy of Windows, it makes changes to the SYSTEM.INI file for you. Some of these changes must be checked and modified to enable Windows to boot properly with the PC/TCP drivers. One of the most important changes is the commenting out of the Windows for Workgroups network driver and its replacement with the PC/TCP driver:

```
network.drv=C:\PCTCP\PCTCPNET.DRV
```

For Windows for Workgroups 3.1, confirm that the SYSTEM.INI file has these three sections, with these commands shown:

```
[boot]
network.drv=wfwnet.drv

[boot.description]
network.drv=Microsoft Windows for Workgroups (version 3.1)

[386Enh]
device=c:\pctcp\vpctcp.386
device=c:\pctcp\wfwftp.386
```

Windows for Workgroups 3.11 has a slightly different SYSTEM.INI. It should look like this:

```
[boot]
network.drv=wfwnet.drv

[boot.description]
network.drv=Microsoft Windows Network (version 3.11)

[386Enh]
device=c:\pctcp\vpctcp.386
```

At the bottom of the Windows for Workgroups SYSTEM.INI file, PC/TCP sometimes adds a block of information that looks like this:

```
[vpctcp]

; These option settings may be added to SYSTEM.INI, in a
;   new section "[vpctcp]".

; The next line tells VPCTCP how much copy space memory to request.
;   It is in units of kilobytes (x1024).  This value is only a bid,
;   as Windows may choose to reduce your allocation arbitrarily.
;   This value should be increased if using Windows applications which
;   call the PC/TCP DLL from another DLL; suggested value in such
;   instances is at least 28.
MinimumCopySpace=12
```

```
; The next line tells VPCTCP the segment (paragraph) number of the
;   beginning of memory reserved for devices, BIOS, and upper-
;   memory blocks (which could contain TSRs).  All calls below the
;   PSP of Windows or above this parameter are not processed by
;   the VxD but rather are passed-thru to the kernel untouched.
HiTSRFenceSegment=A000h

; eof
```

For most installations, this block can be left as it is. The comment lines (those beginning with a semicolon) are ignored by Windows, whereas the two variables established in these sections are used by PC/TCP. There is no need to delete this information. However, as the first note indicates, users of PC/TCP might have to increase the values to account for heavy usage.

If the target system is running Windows 3.1 (not Windows for Workgroups), there are more changes to be made, because the SYSTEM.INI file and network-dependent initialization files do not have the proper format yet. To configure a Windows system, changes must be made to the PROGMAN.INI and SYSTEM.INI files.

Windows 3.1's PROGMAN.INI file controls the startup of the Windows Program Manager. Normally, this is modified by the PC/TCP installation script, but if a manual installation has been performed, changes must be made with a text editor. The PROGMAN.INI file must have the following lines added:

```
[Groups]
GROUP16 = C:\PCTCP\PCTCPDOS.GRP
GROUP17 = C:\PCTCP\PCTCPWIN.GRP
```

The numbers next to GROUP should be higher than any existing number, usually listed sequentially for convenience. In this example, the list of groups ran to number 15.

Changes to the Windows 3.1 SYSTEM.INI file must be made in a few sections. In the [386Enh] section, add a line for the PC/TCP device driver:

```
device=c:\pctcp\vpctcp.386
```

A [vpctcp] section must be added with the following entries:

```
[vpctcp]
MinimumCopySpace=12
HiTSRFenceSegment=A000h
```

See the discussion of the Windows for Workgroups SYSTEM.INI file for more information on these variables.

Some additional entries might be necessary if the network driver is located in high memory, if there is a conflict with the default serial port IRQs or if a Token Ring network is used. See the PC/TCP installation manual for complete change information in these cases.

Windows for Workgroups using NetBIOS

As mentioned earlier, Windows for Workgroups can be set to use IP packets. This requires a NetBIOS driver for both Windows for Workgroups and PC/TCP. The architecture of such as system is shown in Figure 10.2. The Windows for Workgroups packets are sent through PC/TCP's NetBIOS and then into the normal PC/TCP stack.

Figure 10.2.

Windows for Workgroups with NetBIOS.

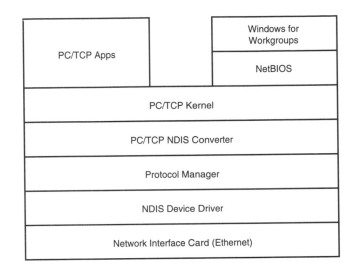

10

To install Windows for Workgroups in this manner, Windows must first be set up to use the Microsoft LAN Manager option. This is usually a matter of selecting the LAN Manager option from the Network window if it is not already the default setting. (Consult the Windows for Workgroups documentation for more information.)

The configuration files must also be changed to reflect the new architecture. The AUTOEXEC.BAT file has the network initiation command, the network kernel driver, and a NETBIOS command:

```
C:\WINDOWS\NET START
C:\PCTCP\ETHDRV
C:\PCTCP\NETBIOS.COM
```

A NETBIND can be performed instead of a NET START command, although the latter is preferable. The NETBIOS command must come after the NETBIND or NET START command.

The CONFIG.SYS file is similar to that seen earlier, with the same drivers. A sample CONFIG.SYS file for this type of architecture looks like this:

```
DEVICE=C:\WINDOWS\PROTMAN.DOS /I:\C:\WINDOWS
DEVICE=C:\WINDOWS\EXP16.DOS
DEVICE=C:\PCTCP\DIS_PKT.GUP
```

This starts the protocol manager, the card driver, and the NDIS packet converter. This example uses the Intel EtherExpress 16 card driver.

The PROTOCOL.INI file is the same as the previous example. A sample PROTOCOL.INI file for the Intel EtherExpress 16 card looks like this:

```
[PKTDRV]
drivername=PKTDRV$
bindings=MS$EE16
intvec=0x60

[MS$EE16]
DriverName-EXP16$
IOADDRESS=0x360
IRQ=11
IOCHRDY=Late
TRANSCEIVER=Thin Net (BNC/COAX)
```

Finally, the SYSTEM.INI file requires that the Windows for Workgroups network driver be used and not the PC/TCP network driver. This might require editing the SYSTEM.INI file, as noted earlier. The SYSTEM.INI file should contain the following lines:

```
[boot]
network.drv=wfwnet.drv

[boot.description]
network.drv=Microsoft Windows for Workgroups (version 3.1)

[386Enh]
device=c:\pctcp\vpctcp.386
device=c:\pctcp\wfwftp.386
TimerCriticialSection=50000
```

The last line in the [386Enh] section might have to be added manually. The version number in the [boot.description] section changes to (version 3.11) with the later version of Windows for Workgroups.

Testing PC/TCP

After making all the changes previously mentioned, the DOS machine is rebooted for testing. If no error messages are displayed when the new commands are executed, the system is ready for testing the TCP/IP protocol stack. The simplest test is to use ping to ensure that the TCP/IP software is talking to the local machine, and then use it to test the remote machines.

Machine name information for other machines hasn't yet been added to the PC/TCP DOS system, so IP addresses must be used with ping. The following is an example of a ping command for the local machine (147.120.0.11), the SCO UNIX server (147.120.0.1), and the Windows 95 machine (147.120.0.10) on the sample network (which has not yet been installed and hence should not communicate):

10

```
C:\> ping 147.120.0.11
host responding, time = 25 ms

Debugging information for interface ifcust  Addr(6): 00 aa 00 20 18 bf
interrupts: 0 (2 receive, 0 transmit)
packets received: 2, transmitted: 3
receive errors: 0, unknown types: 0
     runts: 0, aligns: 0, CRC: 0, parity: 0, overflow: 0
     too big: 0, out of buffers: 0, rcv timeout: 0, rcv reset: 0
transmit errors: 0
     collisions: 0, underflows: 0, timeouts: 0, resets: 0
     lost crs: 0, heartbeat failed: 0
ARP statistics:
arps received: 1 (0 requests, 1 replies)
     bad: opcodes: 0, hardware type: 0, protocol type: 0
arps transmitted: 2 (2 requests, 0 replies)
5 large buffers; 4 free now; minimum of 3 free
5 small buffers; 5 free now; minimum of 4 free
C:\>
C:\> ping 147.120.0.1
host responding, time = 25 ms

Debugging information for interface ifcust  Addr(6): 00 aa 00 20 18 bf
interrupts: 0 (5 receive, 0 transmit)
packets received: 5, transmitted: 6
receive errors: 0, unknown types: 0
     runts: 0, aligns: 0, CRC: 0, parity: 0, overflow: 0
     too big: 0, out of buffers: 0, rcv timeout: 0, rcv reset: 0
transmit errors: 0
     collisions: 0, underflows: 0, timeouts: 0, resets: 0
     lost crs: 0, heartbeat failed: 0
ARP statistics:
arps received: 2 (0 requests, 2 replies)
     bad: opcodes: 0, hardware type: 0, protocol type: 0
arps transmitted: 3 (3 requests, 0 replies)
5 large buffers; 4 free now; minimum of 3 free
5 small buffers; 5 free now; minimum of 4 free
C:\>
C:\> ping 147.120.0.10
ping failed: Host unreachable: ARP failed

Debugging information for interface ifcust  Addr(6): 00 aa 00 20 18 bf
interrupts: 0 (5 receive, 0 transmit)
packets received: 5, transmitted: 7
receive errors: 0, unknown types: 0
     runts: 0, aligns: 0, CRC: 0, parity: 0, overflow: 0
     too big: 0, out of buffers: 0, rcv timeout: 0, rcv reset: 0
transmit errors: 0
     collisions: 0, underflows: 0, timeouts: 0, resets: 0
     lost crs: 0, heartbeat failed: 0
ARP statistics:
arps received: 2 (0 requests, 2 replies)
     bad: opcodes: 0, hardware type: 0, protocol type: 0
arps transmitted: 4 (4 requests, 0 replies)
5 large buffers; 4 free now; minimum of 3 free
5 small buffers; 5 free now; minimum of 4 free
```

10

The message ping failed: Host unreachable for the last attempt is expected. PC/TCP provides the user with diagnostic messages with each ping command. To suppress these messages and simply get a success or fail message, the -z option can be used:

```
C:\> ping -z 147.120.0.11
host responding, time = 25 ms
C:\>
C:\> ping -z 147.120.0.1
host responding, time = 25 ms
C:\>
C:\> ping -z 147.120.0.10
ping failed: Host unreachable: ARP failed
```

If the ping command is not successful with the local address, either the network interface card is configured incorrectly, or the software installation has incorrect parameters. Check the network card for the correct IRQ and memory settings and then check the cable to ensure that it is connected properly and network terminators are in place. The software must have the correct drivers loaded, as well as the machine name, IP address, and similar information.

If the local machine responds but the remote machines do not, check the network connections. Try ping from one of the remote machines to ensure that the DOS machine can be reached by the other machines. Experience has shown that PC-based TCP/IP implementations can be quirky when booting. It is not unusual to have a ping command fail four or five times and then start working properly. Repeat the command several times, waiting a few seconds between each attempt.

Once the machines can successfully respond to a ping request, try ftp or telnet from the DOS-based machine. An ftp attempt to log onto the SCO UNIX machine is shown here:

```
FTP Software PC/TCP File Transfer Program 2.31    01/07/94 12:38
Copyright (c) 1986-1993 by FTP Software, Inc.  All rights reserved.
FTP Trying....Open
220 tpci.tpci.com FTP Server (Version 5.60 #1) ready.
Userid for logging in on 147.120.0.1? tparker
331 Password required for tparker.
Password for logging in as tparker on 147.120.0.1? abcdefg
230 User tparker logged in.
ftp:147.120.0.1> ls
.profile
.lastlogin
.odtpref
trash
Initial.dt
XDesktop3
Transferred 265 bytes in 0 seconds
226 Transfer complete.
ftp:147.120.0.1> exit
```

This session, which displayed the listing of files on the SCO UNIX server, shows that the ftp command worked properly. The FTP session was closed with the command exit.

10

Following the DOS-based test, start Windows (if it was installed) and ensure that the applications within the PC/TCP Applications program group are available and working. If problems are encountered with Windows starting, it is likely that an error was made in the SYSTEM.INI file. Check the previous instructions for the correct configuration.

After all that, the ftp Software PC/TCP system is installed and configured properly. The DOS machine can now be used for TCP/IP applications such as ftp and telnet. If some of the more powerful protocol features were installed, they are also usable. The DOS-based machine installation is now completed. The PC/TCP documentation contains instructions for using the system, as well as fine-tuning the kernel. It also helps users create gateways, routers, mail servers, and several other TCP/IP-related features.

Windows-Based TCP/IP: NetManage's Chameleon

10

NetManage produces a line of TCP/IP-based software specifically for Windows, Windows 95, and Windows for Workgroups. These applications are designed to provide full access to TCP/IP utilities through the Windows environment. NetManage's line of products includes a basic TCP/IP stack (called Newt), as well as full TCP/IP application packages in several forms, all called Chameleon. The system is also available for Windows NT. You are installing Chameleon on a Windows for Workgroups 3.11 machine on the sample network.

Chameleon uses the standard NDIS (Network Device Interface Specification) or the ODI (Open Data Link Interface) for communicating with the network interface card. This enables any card that uses either NDIS or ODI to be used with Chameleon.

Prior to installation of Chameleon, the same steps are performed as for the DOS-based TCP/IP package. The network interface card must be installed with suitable IRQ and memory address settings. If Chameleon is being added to an existing Windows for Workgroups system, the network card should already be installed and properly configured. The same information is required as for all TCP/IP installations: the host name, IP address, broadcast mask, subnetwork mask, and any information about gateways or routers that needs to be included.

The version of ChameleonNFS used for the sample network had its installation information slightly jumbled because of updates to both Chameleon and Windows for Workgroups. The information supplied today applies to Windows for Workgroups 3.1 and 3.11 and ChameleonNFS version 4.0, although other versions should be similar.

Installing Chameleon

Chameleon can be installed over a fully functioning Windows or Windows for Workgroups system. If Windows for Workgroups is used, ensure that the network performs properly (if possible) when talking to other NetBEUI-compatible machines. In this case, that's not possible because the sample network uses only TCP/IP.

The installation procedure for Chameleon is simple. From the Program Manager's File menu, select Run, and then execute the SETUP.EXE program from the first Chameleon disk. As with most Windows applications, this starts the installation program.

WARNING

> The changes made to the system files might cause problems, affecting Windows capability to boot. Before installing the Chameleon software, make copies of the AUTOEXEC.BAT, CONFIG.SYS, PROTOCOL.INI, WIN.INI, and SYSTEM.INI files. If problems are encountered, these files can return the system to its original state. You should consider making a full system backup before any major changes to software, of course.

The Chameleon installation program requires a lengthy serial number and an activation key to ensure that there is only one such version on a network. (This locks out multiple installations using the same serial number and activation key.) The installation script prompts for the distribution disks in order and copies all the necessary files.

Following the installation process, Chameleon builds the program group with the Chameleon applications included. The ChameleonNFS program group is shown in Figure 10.3. After creating the program group, Chameleon starts a customization screen that lets you specify your IP address, host name, network mask, and broadcast address. Save this information and then exit out of Windows to the DOS prompt to complete the check of the installation.

Figure 10.3.

The ChameleonNFS program group.

Because of the different installation variables encountered with different network drivers, it is advisable to check the following configuration files manually:

```
AUTOEXEC.BAT
CONFIG.SYS
PROTOCOL.INI
SYSTEM.INI
```

The following sections discuss each of these files in more detail. If the files do not have the information specified in them, add them with a text editor. Failure to check the files properly can result in Windows being unable to boot properly. If this happens, copy the backup files in place of the newly modified files, restart Windows, and reinstall or reconfigure as necessary.

The AUTOEXEC.BAT File

The changes to the AUTOEXEC.BAT file necessary to enable Chameleon to run are the inclusion of the installation directory in the PATH environment variable and a network startup command. If Chameleon is installed on a Windows for Workgroups system, the network startup command should already exist.

The PATH environment variable must be modified to include the Chameleon installation directory, which by default is C:\NETMANAG. An existing PATH statement can be altered, or a new line can be added below the existing PATH statement that looks like this:

```
PATH=C:\NETMANAG;%PATH%
```

Of course, the correct drive and subdirectory should be substituted. This chapter assumes default values throughout.

The command

```
C:\WINDOWS\NET START
```

is already in the AUTOEXEC.BAT file if a Windows for Workgroups system is used (either version 3.1 or 3.11). If Chameleon is installed on a Windows (not Windows for Workgroups) system, the NETBIND command included with the distribution software should be called as well:

```
C:\NETMANAG\NETBIND
```

Chameleon might install a SHARE command in the AUTOEXEC.BAT file if one does not exist. If one doesn't exist, it is advisable to add it if others can access the machine. SHARE is a DOS utility that activates file-sharing and record-locking. If other machines will be accessing the machine, SHARE is necessary to prevent error messages and potential system freezes when file conflicts occur.

The completed AUTOEXEC.BAT file looks like this for a Windows for Workgroups 3.1 or 3.11 installation:

```
PATH=C:\NETMANAG;%PATH%
C:\WINDOWS\NET START
SHARE
```

and like this for a Windows installation:

```
PATH=C:\NETMANAG;%PATH%
C:\NETMANAG\NETBIND
SHARE
```

If the NET START or NETBIND command is not executed properly, Windows displays an error message when it loads. In some cases, Windows can lock up when it tries to access the network drivers.

The CONFIG.SYS File

The CONFIG.SYS file might be considerably different for each installation. The HIMEM memory device driver is required, and the SMARTDRIVE caching system is recommended. All installations should have adequate values for the FILES and BUFFERS settings, which are normally set by Windows when it is installed. The CONFIG.SYS should have these values as a minimum:

```
BUFFERS=30
FILES=30
LASTDRIVE=Z
STACKS=9,256
```

This creates enough file and buffer settings to enable multiple files to be opened at once. Higher values are better, although there is a trade-off of efficiency once the values exceed a certain value (depending on the amount of RAM in a system). The LASTDRIVE setting enables more drives to be open than are physically connected to the system. This is necessary when remote drives are mounted, either through Windows for Workgroups or Chameleon.

For a Windows or Windows for Workgroups 3.1 system, Chameleon adds the following commands to the CONFIG.SYS file:

```
DEVICE=C:\NETMANAG\PROTMAN.DOS /I:C:\NETMANAG
DEVICE=C:\NETMANAG\EXP16.DOS
DEVICE=C:\NETMANAG\NETMANAG.DOS
```

These load the device drivers for the protocol manager, the network interface card, and the specific protocol for Chameleon. The protocol manager and network interface card device drivers were discussed in the DOS section earlier today.

Windows for Workgroups 3.11 usually has a command in the CONFIG.SYS file that looks like this:

```
DEVICE=C:\WINDOWS\IFSHLP.SYS
```

This automatically loads all the necessary drivers. In some cases, Chameleon adds the command for the Windows for Workgroups 3.1 device drivers to the end of the CONFIG.SYS file, even if the IFSHLP.SYS driver exists. Comment out the added device drivers and try the system without them. The IFSHLP.SYS device driver should be sufficient.

The SYSTEM.INI File

The Windows SYSTEM.INI file requires a few changes to ensure that Chameleon is loaded properly. These should be effected by the installation script, but check the lines carefully anyway.

The [boot] section of the SYSTEM.INI file should have the following two lines:

```
[boot]
shell=progman.exe
network.drv=C:\NETMANAG\MULT400.DRV
```

The shell line might be different if the system uses a replacement program manager (such as Central Point PC Tools for Windows Desktop Manager). The MULT400 driver supports several networks at a time. The order of these lines in the SYSTEM.INI file is not important, as long as they appear in the proper section. The MULT400 driver takes care of loading all the necessary drivers for each network. Windows for Workgroups should have this line

```
network.drv=wfwnet.drv
```

either commented out with a semicolon at the start of the line or removed entirely. The WFWNET driver is the Windows for Workgroups network driver, which must be replaced by MULT400.

The [boot.description] section of the SYSTEM.INI file is changed to

```
[boot.description]
network.drv=NetManage ChameleonNFS
```

or a similar line if another NetManage product is installed.

The [386Enh] section has several changes made. These are as follows:

```
[386Enh]
device=C:\netmanag\nmredir.386
network=*vnetbios,*vwc,vnetsup.386,vredir.386,vserver.386
netmisc=ndis.386,ndis2sup.386
netcard=
transport=nwlink.386,nwnblink.386,netbeui.386
InDOSPolling=FALSE
```

The order of the lines in the section doesn't matter. They load the correct network device drivers into the Windows kernel.

10

Finally, the [network drivers] section should have these lines:

```
[network drivers]
netcard=elnk3.dos
devdir=C:\WINDOWS
LoadRMDrivers=YES
transport=ndishlp.sys,c:\netmanag\netmanag.dos,*netbeui
```

The netcard line changes depending on the network interface card used. The LoadRMDrivers line should be changed from the Windows for Workgroups default value of NO to YES.

The PROTOCOL.INI File

The PROTOCOL.INI file for a Windows for Workgroups installation doesn't require many changes. The driver information should already exist. A new section added by Chameleon should look like this:

```
[NETMANAGE]
DRIVERNAME=netmng$
BINDINGS=MS$ELNK3
```

The BINDINGS line changes depending on the network interface card. It is easiest to copy the line from another section of the PROTOCOL.INI file.

Configuring Chameleon

Once Chameleon has been installed and the startup files checked for proper content, you can configure the software for the sample machine. This is done through the Chameleon CUSTOM application. When started, CUSTOM displays a status screen as shown in Figure 10.4.

Figure 10.4.

The Chameleon Custom screen.

If the installation routine didn't add the machine's name and IP address to the Custom screen, use the Setup menu item to select the different aspects of the configuration that must be specified. You should provide a machine name, IP address, subnet mask, and domain name, as well as the interface if not already added (Ethernet, in this case).

10

To enter the names of the other machines on the network and their IP addresses, select the Services menu Host Table option to display the Host Table dialog box. To add the other machines on the sample network, enter a name in the top portion of the window in the field titled Official Name and click the Add button. This shows a window for the IP address, which should be filled in completely. Then click OK. The IP address and the machine name are now entered into the host table. This window is shown in Figure 10.5 with the address for the machine megan added. If a machine has more than one name, the different names can be added as aliases through this screen, as well.

Figure 10.5.

Chameleon's Host Table
IP Address dialog box.

Testing Chameleon

After the changes to the four configuration files are completed, reboot the system and start Windows. Watch for error messages as the Chameleon lines in the CONFIG.SYS and AUTOEXEC.BAT files are executed. If Windows for Workgroups was installed and working prior to installing Chameleon, there should not be any errors.

The easiest way to test the new TCP/IP system is to use the ping utility within the Chameleon program group. When selected, it displays a small dialog box. Select the Start option, which displays another dialog box waiting for a machine name. Enter the name of the local machine. This is shown in Figure 10.6 for the sample network Windows machine pepper.

Figure 10.6.

Using ping to test the
local host.

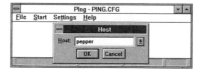

The ping window should show a successful result. This is indicated by a message showing the number of bytes received, as well as time information. A sample output from a successful attempt to ping the local machine is shown in Figure 10.7.

Figure 10.7.

ping *diagnostic messages.*

If the ping attempt is not successful, Chameleon displays a message about the network drivers not installed or about unreachable hosts. Upon receipt of such a message, check the network card settings and all the configuration information through the CUSTOM program.

The next step is to use ping to send to another machine on the network. Figure 10.8 shows the output from a ping attempt on freya, the sample network's Linux server and to whitney, the Windows 95 machine that is not booted (and hence should fail). The system timed out on the whitney attempt, as you would expect.

Figure 10.8.

ping *across a network.*

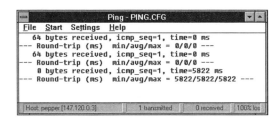

If the ping attempts across the network fail on all machines, the problem is likely with the configuration. Check all the configuration information (as previously noted), as well as the network cables and cards. Make sure the machines to be pinged are up and running TCP/IP.

If the network is operating properly, try the ftp and telnet applications from the Chameleon program group. Full instructions for these utilities are in the documentation. As long as a host table entry has been created and ping succeeded, the other utilities should function properly. Both provide a graphical interface that Windows users will find familiar, instead of the character-based line interface found with DOS. To configure more elaborate functions within Chameleon (such as SNMP, mail, and Gateway routing), consult the Chameleon documentation.

Configuring Windows 95 for TCP/IP

The final client on the sample network that requires configuration is the machine called whitney, with IP address 147.120.0.10. Windows 95 is the easiest of the three clients to configure because everything you need to set up TCP/IP under Windows 95 is included with the software distribution. Windows 95 is configured by default to use NetWare IPX/SPX as the network protocol, but switching to TCP/IP is quite easy.

Begin the Windows 95 configuration process by installing the network adapter card. In some cases when you restart Windows 95, the operating system automatically recognizes the addition of the network card and proceeds to the configuration routines for you. In many cases, though, you have to instruct Windows 95 to look for the network adapter card.

To install a network adapter card, open the Windows 95 Control Panel and double-click the Add New Hardware icon. This calls the Add New Hardware Wizard. After you click the Next button on the introductory dialog, Windows 95 gives you the option of having the operating system try to detect the new hardware automatically.

It is usually best to let Windows 95 try to find the network adapter by itself, especially if the new card is a plug-and-play type. If Windows 95 can identify the hardware automatically, it saves you having to provide configuration information. If you want Windows 95 to go ahead and look for the network adapter, select the Yes button on this dialog (the default value) and click the Next button. Windows 95 begins searching the system for new hardware. If Windows 95 detects a new network card, it displays a screen showing the parameters it detected and lets you confirm the selection. After a reboot, the network card should be properly recognized and active.

If Windows 95 didn't detect the network adapter, you have to install and configure it manually. Windows 95 shows a dialog like the one in Figure 10.9. Clicking the Next button displays the dialog shown in Figure 10.10, which asks for the type of new hardware device you are installing. In this case, you double-click the Network adapters option.

Figure 10.9.

This dialog is displayed if Windows 95 couldn't detect a new network adapter card.

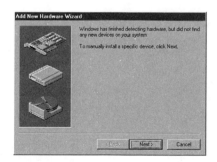

The next dialog to appear shows a list of network adapter card manufacturers on the left side and a more detailed list of network card models from the selected manufacturer on the right. Select the proper manufacturer of the network adapter card in the list at left by single-clicking the manufacturer's name, and then select the name in the right-side list that matches the specific card.

Figure 10.10.

This dialog asks for the type of hardware you are installing.

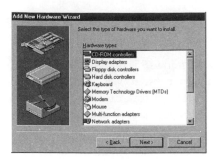

WARNING

You must be careful that you match the name of the adapter card exactly with the list, because some drivers do not work on other cards from the same manufacturer. If you select the wrong adapter card, you won't cause any damage to either the card or Windows 95, but the network will not be found properly by Windows 95. If you can't find the particular model name of the network adapter card you are using but you have a driver supplied on disk, use the Have Disk button to read the driver into Windows 95.

Once you have selected the proper network card name, Windows 95 displays a window with configuration information shown in it. This dialog is shown in Figure 10.11. The amount of configuration information shown in this dialog and the settings it shows are different for each network adapter card.

Figure 10.11.

Windows 95 uses this dialog to ask for the configuration settings of the network card.

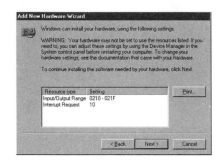

If the network adapter was found by autodetection, the settings shown in this dialog are the ones Windows 95 assumed are correct for the card. If Windows 95 couldn't find the network card, the settings shown are the default values usually used by the manufacturer. Check the

10

documentation supplied with the network adapter card to confirm the settings. After you confirm that the displayed values are correct, Windows 95 installs the software necessary to drive the network adapter card.

Installing TCP/IP

You can install the TCP/IP drivers included with Windows 95 by displaying the Network dialog. Click the Network icon in the Control Panel to display the Network dialog shown in Figure 10.12. The dialog should show a few basic entries created when Windows 95 installed itself, as well as the network hardware card. By default, the NetBEUI or NetWare (IPX) protocols might already be loaded.

Figure 10.12.

The Network window shows all configured hardware and protocols.

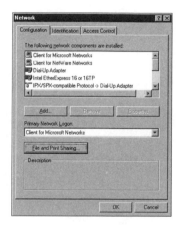

To add the TCP/IP protocol drivers to Windows 95, select the Add button below the list of installed components to display the Select Network Component Type dialog shown in Figure 10.13. This window asks for the type of component (adapter card, protocol, service, or client) you want to install. Because you want to install the TCP/IP protocol drivers, choose Protocol. The Select Network Protocol dialog, shown in Figure 10.14, is displayed.

Figure 10.13.

The Select Network Component Type dialog lets you add a protocol, client, service, or adapter card.

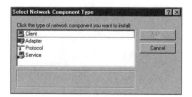

Figure 10.14.

*The Select Network
Protocol dialog lets you
choose the type of protocol
to add.*

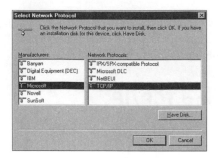

From the Select Network Protocol window, select Microsoft in the left scroll list and then move to the right window, which lists all the Microsoft protocols supplied with Windows 95. Choose the TCP/IP entry. You are returned to the Network dialog, and TCP/IP is listed as a supported protocol.

To start the configuration process, either double-click the TCP/IP protocol entry in the Network dialog list, or select the TCP/IP protocol entry and click the Properties window. The TCP/IP Properties dialog appears, as shown in Figure 10.15.

Figure 10.15.

*The TCP/IP Properties
dialog has six pages
of configuration infor-
mation.*

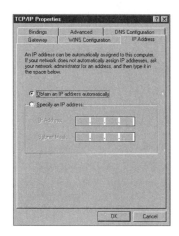

From the TCP/IP Properties dialog, six pages of information are available by choosing one of the tabs across the top of the dialog. For most installations you have to supply only a small part of this information. You can start with the IP Address page, which is the first page shown whenever the TCP/IP Properties window is displayed. Enter the IP address and subnet mask in the spaces provided, making sure to keep the four parts of the dotted-quad notation separate.

10

NOTE

Some larger corporate networks are set up to assign IP addresses to connecting clients automatically using a special protocol. This protocol, called Dynamic Host Configuration Protocol (DHCP) servers, is usually used for machines that connect to a TCP/IP network only occasionally. If your network uses DHCP, you can select the first button on the IP Address page and let Windows 95 obtain your IP address and subnet mask for you. Most networks do not use DHCP.

Next, you move to the Advanced page of the TCP/IP Properties dialog by selecting the Advanced tab. This dialog lets you specify that TCP/IP is the default protocol used by the Windows 95 machine by clicking the option at the bottom of the page, as shown in Figure 10.16. If your Windows 95 system is attached to a TCP/IP network and uses TCP/IP most of the time, make sure that you select this option; otherwise, Window 95 tries to use NetBIOS or IPX/SPX on the TCP/IP network.

Figure 10.16.

Select the default option from the Advanced page of the TCP/IP Properties dialog.

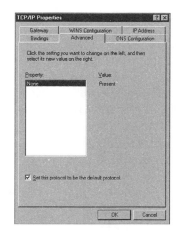

For many simple TCP/IP networks, that's all the information you need to supply. Windows 95 now loads the proper drivers into the operating system, using the values supplied for the IP address and subnet mask. After the software has been properly loaded, Windows 95 must be restarted to make the TCP/IP drivers effective.

Further TCP/IP Configuration

Some TCP/IP systems require extra configuration to provide Windows 95 with the name of the servers, gateways, or other details. You can make many of these configuration steps at any time, but some services might not be available to you until you do. All of these changes are made through the TCP/IP Properties dialog used to set the IP address and subnet mask.

The WINS Configuration page of the TCP/IP Properties window is used to instruct your Windows 95 system how to talk to a Windows Internet Naming Service (WINS) server. WINS lets you use the NetBIOS protocol on a TCP/IP network. Most networks don't use WINS, so you can probably ignore this page completely unless you know you will need to use WINS on your network. If WINS is required on your network, enter the IP address of the primary (and secondary, if used) WINS server, as well as the Scope ID. If WINS is not used on your network, make sure the Disable WINS Resolution option is selected.

The Gateway page lets you specify where your network's gateways are. Gateways are used to connect to other networks, including the Internet. If your network uses a gateway, enter the IP address of the primary network gateway machine and click the Add button. You can enter many gateways into Windows 95, but you should always provide the primary gateway IP address first (because Windows 95 searches the list of gateways in order).

The DNS Configuration page must be completed if your network uses the Domain Name System (DNS). DNS performs a conversion between an IP address and a symbolic name. DNS requires a special network configuration and server, so small networks are unlikely to use DNS. If your network is running DNS, you can enter your machine's symbolic name, the domain name (the name of your workgroup or entire company), and the IP address of your DNS server on this page. After Windows 95 has connected to the DNS server and told it your IP address and symbolic name, other users of the network can connect to your machine using your symbolic name. Similarly, if you know the symbolic name of a remote machine, you can use that to connect to it instead of the IP address.

The final page of the TCP/IP Properties window is the Bindings page. This page lists all the network components that use the TCP/IP protocol. If you have installed other networking protocols on your Windows 95 system, there might be more entries in the Bindings list. Select only those that use the TCP/IP protocol. Minimizing the number of bindings for each protocol helps improve the efficiency of the Windows 95 networking software.

Testing TCP/IP

Once you have installed the network card and software, you can test the new TCP/IP protocol. The best utility for a quick check of your TCP/IP network connection is ping. The ping utility supplied with Windows 95 is a DOS application, not Windows 95, so it should be launched in a DOS window. It usually resides in the same directory as Windows 95 files (usually \windows).

To use ping, enter the name or address after the ping command at the DOS prompt. The ping utility then sends and receives packets of information. If messages such as Bad IP Address, Request Timed out, or Unknown host are displayed, ping can't connect or resolve the name or IP address you supplied.

At this point, if you successfully sent and received packets, all is well with the TCP/IP connection. If ping displayed error messages or couldn't send and receive packets over the network, you should verify that the IP address is valid. If it is, try another machine on the network to ping the Windows 95 machine. If you can't, then the network adapter or protocol on the Windows 95 machine is not loaded properly.

Winsock

10

For some Windows and Windows 95 users, Winsock is the easiest method to get into TCP/IP because it is available from many public domain, BBS, and online service sites. There are several versions of Winsock, some of which are public domain or shareware. We will look at two versions of Winsock, one for Windows 3.x and another for Windows 95. We have chosen the popular Trumpet Winsock implementations for both operating systems because they are shareware, readily available, and well supported.

Winsock is short for Windows Sockets, originally developed by Microsoft. Released in 1993, Windows Sockets is an interface for network programming in the Windows environment. Microsoft has published the specifications for Windows Sockets, hence making it an open application programming interface (API). The Winsock API (called WSA) is a library of function calls, data structures, and programming procedures that provide this standardized interface for applications. The second release of Winsock, called Winsock version 2, was released in mid 1995.

Trumpet Winsock

Trumpet Winsock is a shareware implementation of Winsock produced by Trumpet Software International. Trumpet Winsock is available for Windows 3.x and Windows 95 systems. Registration of the Winsock package, developed in Australia, is $25 US. Trumpet Winsock lets you use several different protocols including PPP and SLIP for connection to the Internet or remote networks, direct connection using TCP/IP, and the BOOTP protocol. Trumpet Winsock allows dynamic IP addressing, which is necessary with many Internet Service Providers.

The Trumpet Winsock files are usually provided in an archive Zip file and should be extracted into a new subdirectory on your system. The primary files in the Trumpet Winsock distribution are

- ☐ WINSOCK.DLL: The primary protocol stack for Winsock
- ☐ TCPMAN.EXE: Manages the communications between WINSOCK.DLL and the network
- ☐ TRUMPWSK.INI: Contains Winsock variable settings
- ☐ HOSTS: A list of hosts that Winsock is aware of
- ☐ SERVICES: A list of services supported by Winsock
- ☐ PROTOCOL: A list of protocols supported by Winsock

There are a number of sample configuration files included in the archive, as well as utilities such as PING and HOP. Some of the files in the Winsock archive, such as HOSTS, PROTOCOL, and SERVICES, mirror UNIX files of the same name.

Installing Trumpet Winsock

The installation process for Trumpet Winsock is the same whether you are using SLIP/PPP for connection or a packet driver for LAN-based operations. Begin the installation by adding the directory holding the Trumpet Winsock files to your PATH. The files should, of course, be extracted from the Zip file they are usually supplied in. After the path has been modified, reboot your machine to effect the change.

You can create a Windows program group for the Trumpet Winsock system by adding a new program group from the Program Manager menus. (Select File menu, the New menu item, and then Program Group.) Create a title, such as Trumpet Winsock, for the new program group.

Next, create a Program Icon for the TCPMAN program (the primary Trumpet Winsock program) by either creating a new Program Item from the Program Manager or opening the File Manager and dragging the TCPMAN.EXE entry from its directory to the Trumpet Winsock program group. Windows will prompt you for any information it needs. The program icon is read from the distribution files if the path is properly set.

To test the installation of the path and the Windows icon, click the TCPMAN icon. If you receive error messages, either the PATH is not set properly, or the program icon has not been properly defined. Because you are primarily interested in using Winsock on a TCP/IP network, ignore configuring PPP and SLIP and concentrate on the TCP/IP stack.

Configuring the TCP/IP Packet Driver

Trumpet Winsock relies on a program called WINPKT to provide TCP/IP packet capabilities under Windows. After you create a program group for Winsock, you need to set up the packet driver information in the network files.

You will need a packet driver for your system, which is not included with most Trumpet Winsock distributions. In many cases, the network card vendor includes a disk with a packet driver on it. If not, one of the best sources for a packet driver is the Crynwr Packet Driver collection, a library of different packet drivers available from many online, BBS, FTP, and WWW sites. The packet driver specifications are added to your network startup batch file, usually AUTOEXEC.BAT for DOS-based systems.

 NOTE

> To obtain a Crynwr packet driver, use a Web browser to connect to http://www.crynwr.com. There are several dozen public domain drivers available from this site.

The process for configuring Trumpet Winsock for LAN operation is quite simple. Set the IRQ and I/O address of the packet driver and add the packet driver to your system. A typical entry in the network batch file looks like this:

```
ne2000 0x60 2 0x300
WINPKT 0x60
```

This sets the network to use an NE2000 (Novell) type card, with I/O address of 300H, IRQ of 2, and a vector of 60. Several configurations are usually provided with the Trumpet Winsock distribution, although it is easy to derive your own from the network interface card manufacturer's documentation.

To set up Trumpet Winsock for a packet driver, use the Setup screen that appears when TCPMAN is first launched, or use the menus within TCPMAN to display the Setup screen. Deselect both Internal SLIP and Internal PPP settings. If either of them are checked, the packet driver will not launch properly.

Enter the IP address, netmask, name server IP address, and domain name information. You may also modify the entries for Demand Load Time-out, MTU, TCP RWIN, TCP MSS, and TCP RTO MAX. See the section on SLIP/PPP configuration above for more details on any of these settings. The default values used for a packet driver are different than those for a SLIP/PPP setting. If you are using BOOTP or RARP to determine your machine IP address, enter the proper protocol name in the IP address field.

The Packet Vector field should be set to the vector you used in the network card description, or you can leave it as 00 to let Trumpet Winsock search for the packet driver. After the configuration is saved, restart TCPMAN and the network will be available (if the configuration and packet drivers are properly set). A ping command or similar utility will verify that the packet driver operation is correct.

Summary

Today you learned how to install and configure three PC-based systems: one for DOS and two specifically for Windows versions. They are now connected to the sample network, and files can be transferred between the machines quickly and easily. The DOS machines can also run Windows for Workgroups piggy-backed on the TCP/IP network.

Adding other machines usually follows the same procedure. For example, to add a Macintosh running Mac TCP/IP, follow the installation guide to install and configure the software, and then use ping to verify that everything is working correctly.

10

Chapter 11

DNS

TCP/IP uses a 32-bit address to route a datagram to a destination. It is useful to forget these 32-bit addresses and use common names instead, because names are much easier to remember. There are several methods used for this. The most common is examined on Day 7, "TCP/IP Configuration and Administration Basics," employing an ASCII file on the sending machine that had names and corresponding addresses (`/etc/hosts` on a UNIX device). One major limitation to this system is that the machine can route only to other machines that have an entry in this file, which can be impossible to maintain when there are many target machines or you want to access all the devices on your network.

Another approach is to off-load the address resolution to another process that acts like a directory service. There are two such schemes in common use today: Domain Name Service (DNS) and Network Information Service (NIS), which is now part of NFS. Today I look at DNS in more detail. On Day 12, "NFS and NIS," I examine NFS in depth.

Also today I look at the BOOTP protocol, a system that is becoming widely adopted as diskless workstations and client/server systems become more common. BOOTP relies on TCP/IP. Anyone working with TCP/IP can eventually expect to run across the BOOTP protocol, so an explanation of it is useful at this stage.

Finally, the day closes with a quick look at the Network Time Protocol (NTP), which is used to ensure synchronization of timestamps between machines.

Domain Name Service (DNS)

A symbolic name is a character string that is used to identify a machine. A symbolic name can be straightforward (`bills_machine` or `tpci_server1`) or more complex, as is often the case in large organizations where the name identifies the type of machine and its location (such as `hpws510`, where hpws identifies an HP workstation on the fifth floor, room 10).

When sending information to remote machines, IP addresses or Internet addresses must be used. Instead of requiring the user to memorize the remote machine's numbers, it is common to use a symbolic name. After all, a simple name is much easier to remember than a 32-bit Internet address.

As you saw earlier in this book, the conversion from a symbolic name to an actual IP address is usually performed within the sending machine, using a file such as UNIX's `/etc/hosts` file. This type of approach works well within a small network, where a limited number of destination machines are involved. When dealing with the entire Internet, however, it is unreasonable to expect an ASCII file to contain all possible symbolic names and their addresses.

The sheer size of a file required to hold all possible symbolic domain names and their corresponding unique network addresses is not the only problem. Large networks tend to change constantly, especially on an internetwork the size of the Internet. Hundreds of additions and modifications to existing entries must be performed daily. The time required to update each machine (or even selected gateways to autonomous networks) on the internetwork would be huge.

The solution to the problem is to offer a method of moving the management of the lookup tables away from the Network Information Center (NIC), which governs the Internet, and toward the participants and their autonomous networks in such a manner that the load on the network is small but flexibility is not compromised. This is what the Domain Name Service (DNS) does. DNS is sometimes also called the Internet directory service, although the name is somewhat of a misnomer.

UNIX implements DNS through a daemon called `named`, which runs on a *name server*, a machine that handles the resolution of symbolic names using DNS methods. Part of the system is a library of functions that can be used in applications to perform queries on the name server. This query routine is called the *resolver* or *name resolver* and can reside on another machine. The name server and resolver are examined in more detail shortly.

11

DNS Structure

The Domain Name Service, as its name implies, works by dividing the internetwork into a set of domains, or networks, that can be further divided into subdomains. This structure resembles a tree, as shown in Figure 11.1, using some arbitrarily chosen domain names. The first set of domains is called the *top-level domains.* There are six top-level domains in regular use:

- ☐ ARPA: For Internet-specific organizations
- ☐ COM: For commercial enterprises
- ☐ EDU: For educational organizations
- ☐ GOV: For governmental bodies
- ☐ MIL: For military organizations
- ☐ ORG: For noncommercial organizations

Figure 11.1.

The Internet domain structure.

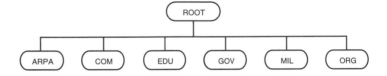

In addition to these top-level domains, there are dedicated top-level domains for each country that is connected. These are usually identified by a short form of the country's name, such as .ca for Canada and .uk for the United Kingdom. These country top-level domains are usually left off diagrams of the Internet structure for convenience (otherwise there would be hundreds of top-level domains). The domain breakdown is sometimes repeated beneath the country domain, so there could be a .com extension coupled with .ca to show a Canadian commercial domain, or an .edu with .uk for a British university.

Beneath the top-level domains is another level for the individual organizations within each top-level domain. The domain names are all registered with the Network Information Center (NIC) and are unique to the network. Usually the names are representative of the company or organization, but a few "cute" names do work their way in (usually because of historical reasons).

There are two ways to name a target. If the target is on the internetwork, the *absolute name* is used. The absolute name is unique and unambiguous, specifying the domain of the target machine. A *relative name* can be used either within the local domain, where the name server knows that the target is within the domain and hence doesn't need to route the datagram onto the internetwork, or when the relative name is known by the name server and can be expanded and routed correctly.

The Name Server

Each DNS name server manages a distinct area of a network (or an entire domain, if the network is small). The set of machines managed by the name server is called a *zone*. Several zones can be managed by one name server. Almost every zone has a designated secondary or backup name server, with the two (primary and secondary) name servers holding duplicate information. The name servers within a zone communicate using a *zone transfer protocol.*

DNS operates by having a set of nested zones. Each name server communicates with the one above it (and, if there is one, the one below it). Each zone has at least one name server responsible for knowing the address information for each machine within that zone. Each name server also knows the address of at least one other name server. Messages between name servers usually use the User Datagram Protocol (UDP) because its connectionless method provides for better performance. However, TCP is used for database updates because of its reliability.

When a user application needs to resolve a symbolic name into a network address, a query is sent by the application to the resolver process, which then communicates the query to the name server. (I examine the resolver in more detail in the next section, "Resource Records.") The name server checks its own tables and returns the network address corresponding to the symbolic name. If the name server doesn't have the information it requires, it can send a request to another name server. This process is shown in Figure 11.2. Both the name servers and the resolvers use database tables and caches to maintain information about the machines in the local zone, as well as recently requested information from outside the zone.

Figure 11.2.
Resolving symbolic names.

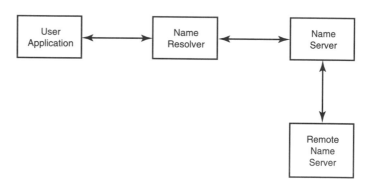

When a name server receives a query from a resolver, there are several types of operations the name server can perform. Name resolver operations fall into two categories: *recursive* and *nonrecursive.* A recursive operation is one in which the name server must access another name server for information.

Nonrecursive operations performed by the name server include a full answer to the resolver's request, a referral to another name server (which the resolver must send a query to), or an error message. When a recursive operation is necessary, the name server contacts another name server with the resolver's request. The remote name server replies to the request with either a network address or a negative message, indicating failure. DNS rules prohibit a remote name server from sending a referral to yet another name server.

Resource Records

The information required to resolve symbolic names is maintained by the name server in a set of *resource records*, which are entries in a database. Resource records (often abbreviated RR) contain information in ASCII format. Because ASCII is used, it is easy to update the records. The format of resource records is shown in Figure 11.3.

Figure 11.3.

The resource record format.

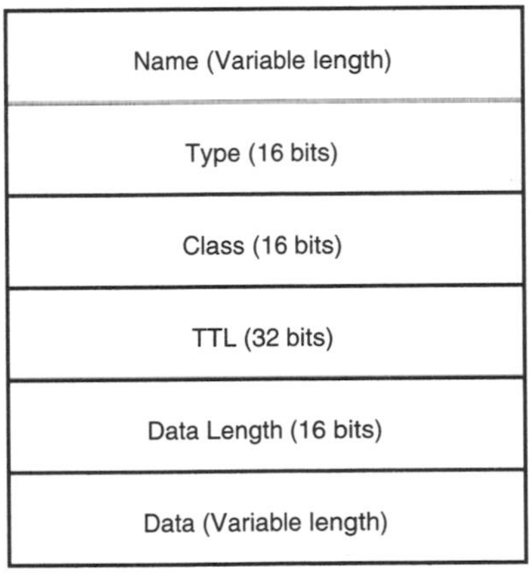

| Name (Variable length) |
| Type (16 bits) |
| Class (16 bits) |
| TTL (32 bits) |
| Data Length (16 bits) |
| Data (Variable length) |

The Name field is the domain name of the machine the record refers to. If no name is specified, the previously used name is substituted.

The Type field identifies the type of resource record. Resource records are used for several purposes, such as mapping names to addresses and defining zones. The type of resource record is identified by a mnemonic code or a number. These codes and their meanings are shown in Table 11.1. Some of the resource record types are now obsolete (3 and 4), and others are considered experimental at this time (13 and 17–21).

Table 11.1. Resource record types.

Number	Code	Description
1	A	Network address
2	NS	Authoritative name server
3	MD	Mail destination; now replaced by MX
4	MF	Mail forwarder; now replaced by MX
5	CNAME	Canonical alias name
6	SOA	Start of zone authority
7	MB	Mailbox domain name
8	MG	Mailbox member
9	MR	Mail rename domain
10	NULL	Null resource record
11	WKS	Well-known service
12	PTR	Pointer to a domain name
13	HINFO	Host information
14	MINFO	Mailbox information
15	MX	Mail exchange
16	TXT	Text strings
17	RP	Responsible person
18	AFSDB	AFS-type services
19	X.25	X.25 address
20	ISDN	ISDN address
21	RT	Route through

The Class field in the resource record layout contains a value for the class of record. If no value is specified, the last class used is substituted. Internet name servers usually have the code IN.

The Time to Live (TTL) field specifies the amount of time in seconds that the resource record is valid in the cache. If a value of 0 is used, the record should not be added to the cache. If the TTL field is omitted, a default value is used. Usually this field tells the name server how long the entry is valid before it has to ask for an update.

The data section of the resource record contains two parts, consisting of the length of the record and the data itself. The Data Length field specifies the length of the data section. The data is a variable-length field (hence the need for a length value) that describes the entry somehow. The use of this field differs with the different types of resource records.

11

Some resource record types have a single piece of information in the data area, such as an address, or at most three pieces of information. The only exception is the Start of Authority resource record. The contents of the resource record data areas (except SOAs) are given in Table 11.2.

Table 11.2. The contents of the resource record data areas.

RR Type	Fields in Data Area
A	Address: A network address
NS	NSDNAME: The domain name of host
MG	MGNAME: The domain name of mailbox
CNAME	CNAME: An alias for the machine
HINFO	CPU: A string identifying CPU type OS: A string identifying operating system
MINFO	RMAILBX: A mailbox responsible for mailing lists EMAILBOX: A mailbox for error messages
MB	MADNAME: Now obsolete
MR	NEWNAME: Renames the address of a specific mailbox
MX	PREFERENCE: Specifies the precedence for delivery EXCHANGE: The domain name of the host that acts as mail exchange
NULL	Anything can be placed in the data field
PTR	PTRDNAME: A domain name that acts as a pointer to a location
TXT	TXTDATA: Any kind of descriptive text
WKS	Address: A network address Protocol: The protocol used Bitmap: Used to identify ports and protocols

11

The Start of Authority (SOA) resource record format is used to identify the machines within a zone. There is only one SOA record in each zone. The format of the SOA data field is shown in Figure 11.4. The fields in the SOA resource record are used mostly for administration and maintenance of the name server.

The MNAME field is the domain name of the source of data for the zone. The RNAME (responsible person name) field is the domain name of the mailbox of the administrator of the zone. The Serial field contains a version number for the zone. It is incremented when the zone is changed; otherwise, it is maintained as the same value for all such messages.

Figure 11.4.

The SOA resource record format.

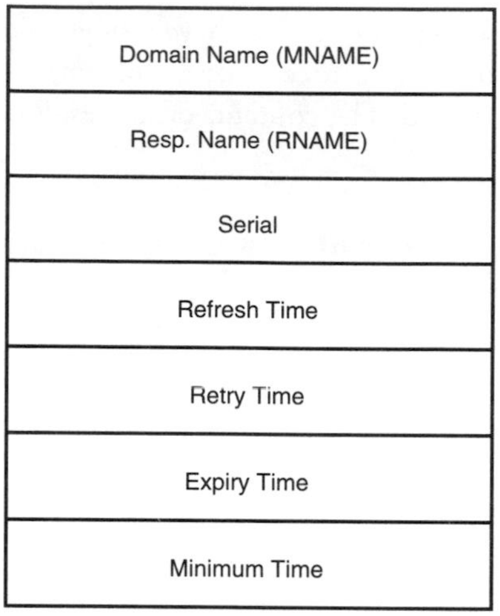

Domain Name (MNAME)
Resp. Name (RNAME)
Serial
Refresh Time
Retry Time
Expiry Time
Minimum Time

The Refresh Time is the number of seconds between data refreshes for the zone. The Retry Time is the number of seconds to wait between unsuccessful refresh requests. The Expiry Time is the number of seconds after which the zone information is no longer valid. Finally, the Minimum Time is the number of seconds to be used in the Time to Live field of resource records within the zone.

Some sample resource records show the simple format used. Address resource records consist of the machine name, the type of resource record indicator (A for Address RRs, for example), and the network address. A sample Address resource record would look like this:

```
TPCI_SCO_4     IN     A     143.23.25.7
```

The IN tags the resource record as an Internet class. This format makes it easy to locate a name and derive its address. (The reverse, going from address to name, is not as easy and requires a special format called IN-ADDR-ARPA, which is examined in the next section, "IN-ADDR-ARPA.")

For Well-Known Service resource records (WKS, or type 11), the data field of the record contains three fields used to describe the services supported at the address the record refers to. A sample WKS resource record might look like this:

```
TPCI_SCO.TPCI.COM     IN     WKS     143.23.1.34.
                                      FTP  TCP  SMTP  TELNET
```

The full domain name and Internet address are shown, as is the IN to show the Internet class of resource records. The type of record is indicated with the WKS. The protocols supported by the machine at that address are listed after the address. In reality, these are bitmaps that correspond to ports. When the port bit is set to a value of 1, the service is supported. The list of ports and services is defined by an Internet RFC.

11

IN-ADDR-ARPA

The address fields, such as in the Address resource record type, use a special format called IN-ADDR-ARPA. This enables reverse mapping from the address to the host name as well as host-to-address mapping. To understand IN-ADDR-ARPA, it is useful to begin with a standard-format resource record. Earlier it was mentioned that resource records are maintained in ASCII format. One of the simplest types of resource record is for the address (type A), as seen earlier. An extract from an address file is shown here:

```
TPCI_HPWS1      IN    A      143.12.2.50
TPCI_HPWS2      IN    A      143.12.2.51
TPCI_HPWS3      IN    A      143.12.2.52
TPCI_GATEWAY    IN    A      143.12.2.100
                IN    A      144.23.56.2
MERLIN          IN    A      145.23.24.1
SMALLWOOD       IN    A      134.2.12.75
```

Each line of the file represents one resource record. In this case, they are all simple entries that have the machine's symbolic name (alias), the class of machine (IN for Internet), A to show it is an Address resource record, and the Internet address. The entry for the machine TPCI_GATEWAY has two corresponding addresses because it is a gateway between two networks. The gateway has a different address on each of the networks, so it has two resource records in the same file. (As with most other code fragments in this book, these example addresses are hypothetical.)

This type of file makes name-to-address mapping easy. The name server simply searches for a line with the symbolic name requested by the application and returns the Internet address at the end of that line. The databases are indexed on the name, so these searches proceed very quickly.

Searching from the address to the name is not quite as easy. If the resource record files are small, time delays for a manual search are not appreciable, but with large zones there can be thousands or tens of thousands of entries. The index is on the name, so searching for an address can be a slow process. To solve this reverse-mapping problem, IN-ADDR-ARPA was developed. IN-ADDR-ARPA uses the host address as an index to the host's resource record information. When the proper resource record is located, the symbolic name can be extracted.

IN-ADDR-ARPA uses the PTR resource record type (see Table 11.1) to point from the address to the name. There might be one of these pointer indexes maintained on each name server. An example of a number-to-name file follows:

```
23.1.45.143.IN-ADDR-ARPA.    PTR    TPCI_HPWS_4.TPCI.COM
1.23.64.147.IN-ADDR-ARPA.    PTR    TPCI_SERVER.MERLIN.COM
3.12.6.123.IN-ADDR-ARPA.     PTR    BEAST.BEAST.COM
23.143.IN-ADDR-ARPA          PTR    MERLINGATEWAY.MERLIN.COM
```

The Internet addresses are reversed in the IN-ADDR-ARPA file for ease of use. As shown in the sample file, it is not necessary to specify the complete address for a gateway because the domain name provides enough routing information.

Messages

DNS messages are transferred between name servers to update their resource records. The fields of these messages are quite similar to those of the records themselves. The format of a DNS message is shown in Figure 11.5. The header has several subfields that contain information about the type of question or answer being sent. The rest of the message consists of four variable-length fields, which are further subdivided:

- ☐ **Question:** The information required.
- ☐ **Answer:** The answer to the query (from the RR).
- ☐ **Authority:** The name of other name servers that might have the information requested, if it is not readily available on the targeted name server.
- ☐ **Additional information:** Information that can be provided to answer the query, or the addresses of name servers if the Authority field was used.

Figure 11.5.

The DNS message format.

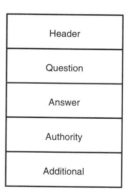

The DNS message header has several different fields itself, as shown in Figure 11.6. The header is present in all DNS messages. The header ID field is 16 bits long and is used to match queries and answers to each other. The single-bit QR field is set to a value of 0 to indicate a query, or a value of 1 to show a response. The OpCode field is 4 bits long and can have one of the values shown in Table 11.3.

11

Figure 11.6.
The DNS message header format.

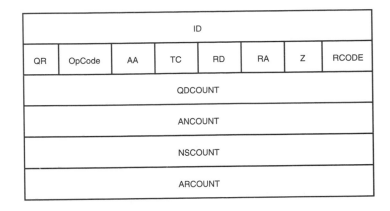

Table 11.3. The DNS message header OpCode values.

OpCode Value	Description
0	Standard query
1	Inverse query
2	Server status request
3–15	Not used

The AA field is the authoritative answer bit. A value of 1 in a response message indicates that the name server is the recognized authority for the queried domain name. The TC (truncation) bit is set to a value of 1 when the message is truncated because of excessive length. Otherwise, the TC bit is set to 0. The RD (recursion desired) bit is set to 1 when the name server is requested to perform a recursive query. The RA (recursion available) bit is set to 1 in a response when the name server can perform recursions.

The Z field is 3 bits long and is not used. The RCODE field is 4 bits long and can be set to one of the values shown in Table 11.4.

Table 11.4. The DNS message header RCODE values.

RCODE Value	Description
0	No errors
1	Format error; name server unable to interpret the query
2	Name server problems have occurred
3	The name server could not find the domain reference in the query

continues

Table 11.4. continued

RCODE Value	Description
4	Name server does not support this type of query
5	Name server cannot perform the requested operation for administrative reasons
6–15	Not used

The QDCOUNT field is a 16-bit field for the number of entries in the Question section. The ANCOUNT field is another 16-bit field for the number of replies in the Answer section (the number of resource records in the answer). The NSCOUNT field is 16 bits and specifies the number of server resource records in the Authority section of the message. The ARCOUNT 16-bit field specifies the number of resource records in the Additional record section.

The Question section of the message has three fields of its own, as shown in Figure 11.7. The Question field carries the query, which is identified by these fields. The QNAME field is the domain name requested. The QTYPE is the type of query, using one of the values shown in Table 11.1. The QCLASS is the class of query, which can be set according to the application's requirements.

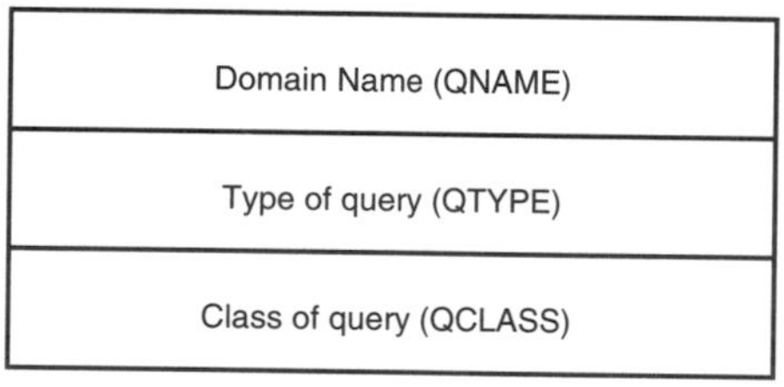

Figure 11.7.

The DNS message Question field format.

```
┌────────────────────────────────┐
│      Domain Name (QNAME)        │
├────────────────────────────────┤
│      Type of query (QTYPE)      │
├────────────────────────────────┤
│     Class of query (QCLASS)     │
└────────────────────────────────┘
```

The last three fields in the DNS message (Answer, Authority, and Additional information) all have the same format, as shown in Figure 11.8. The Name field holds the domain name of the resource record. The Type field has any of the valid resource record type values. (See Table 11.1.)

The Class Field is the class of data in the data field. The Time to Live (TTL) field is the number of seconds the information is valid without an update. The RDLENGTH field is the length of the information in the data field. Finally, the RDATA field is the resource record information or other data, depending on the class and type of the query and reply. There can be many such records in the Answer, Authority, and Additional information sections of the DNS message.

11

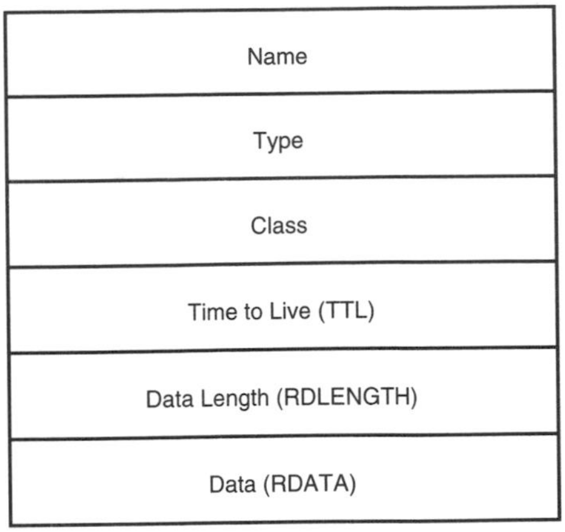

Figure 11.8.

The format for DNS message Answer, Authority, and Additional information fields.

Name
Type
Class
Time to Live (TTL)
Data Length (RDLENGTH)
Data (RDATA)

The Name Resolver

As far as user applications are concerned, resolving the symbolic names into actual network addresses is easy. The process has been mentioned earlier. The application sends a query to a process called the *name resolver,* or *resolver* (which sometimes resides on another machine). The name resolver might be able to resolve the name directly, in which case it sends a return message to the application. If the resolver cannot determine the network address, it communicates with the name server (which might contact another name server).

The resolver is intended to replace existing name resolution systems on a machine, such as UNIX's /etc/hosts file. The replacement of these common mechanisms is transparent to the user, although the administrator must know whether the native name resolution system or DNS is to be used on each machine so the correct tables can be maintained.

When the resolver acquires information from a name server, it stores the entries in its own cache to reduce the need for more network traffic if the same symbolic name is used again (as is often the case with applications that work across networks). The amount of time the name resolver stores these records is dependent on the Time to Live field in the resource records sent, or on a default value set by the system.

When a name server cannot resolve a name, it can send back a message to the resolver with the address of another name server in the Authority field of the message. The resolver must then address a message to the other name server in the hopes of resolving the name. The resolver can ask the name server to conduct the query itself by setting the RD (recursive) bit in the message. The name server can refuse or accept the request.

The resolver uses both UDP and TCP in its query process, although UDP is more common, due to its speed. However, iterative queries or transfers of large amounts of information might resort to TCP because of its higher reliability.

Under the UNIX operating system, several different implementations of the name resolver are in use. The resolver supplied with the BSD versions of UNIX was particularly limited, offering neither a cache nor iterative query capabilities. To solve these limitations, the Berkeley Internet Name Domain (BIND) server was added. BIND provides both caching and iterative query capabilities in three different modes: as a primary server, as a secondary server, or as a caching-only server (which doesn't have a database of its own, only a cache). The use of BIND on BSD systems enables another process to take over the workload of name resolution, a process that might be on another machine entirely.

Configuring a UNIX DNS Server

Configuring a DNS server requires several files and databases to be modified or created. The process is time-consuming, but luckily has to be done only once for each server. The files involved in most DNS setups, and their purposes, are as follows:

named.hosts: Defines the domain with hostname-to-IP mappings

named.rev: Uses IN-ADDR-ARPA for IP-to-hostname mappings

named.local: Used to resolve the loopback driver

named.ca: Lists root domain servers

named.boot: Used to set file and database locations

These filenames are used by convention, but they can be changed to suit your own personal needs. The primary file in the list is named.boot, which is read when the system boots up and defines the other files in the set. Therefore, any filename changes are reflected in named.boot. For simplicity, I use the conventional filenames in this chapter. Each of the files listed here is a database with entries in the form of a resource record.

Entering the Resource Records

For the sample server configuration, I assume a UNIX operating system using fairly standard names and network layouts. DNS lets you get very complex, but it's easier to see what the files and resource records are doing with a simple layout.

An SOA resource record is placed in the named.hosts file. Semicolons in the record are used for comments. This resource record has been formatted as one field per line to make its entries clear, although this is not necessary. This resource record defines an upper boundary of the tpci.com domain, with server.tpci.com the primary name server for the domain, root.merlin.tpci.com the e-mail address of the person responsible for the domain, and the rest of the entries identified by comments:

11

```
tpci.com.   IN   SOA     server.tpci.com
    root.merlin.tpci.com (
    2  ; Serial number
    7200 ; Refresh (2 hrs)
    3600 ; Retry (1 hr)
    151200 ; Expire (1 week)
    86400 ); min TTL
```

Note that the information from the serial number to the expire field is enclosed in parentheses. This is part of the command syntax and must be included to indicate the parameter order.

In addition to the SOA RR, the named.hosts file contains Address (A) records. These records are used for the actual mapping of a hostname to its IP address. A few Address resource records show the format of these entries (refer to earlier sections of this chapter for the meanings of each field if you are not sure):

```
artemis    IN    A    143.23.25.7
merlin     IN    A    143.23.25.9
pepper     IN    A    143.23.25.72
```

The hostnames are not given as fully qualified domain names because the server can deduce the full name. If you want to use the full domain name, you must follow the name with a period. The machines shown in the preceding example would be given like this using fully qualified domain names:

```
artemis.tpci.com.    IN    A    143.23.25.7
merlin.tpci.com.     IN    A    143.23.25.9
pepper.tpci.com.     IN    A    143.23.25.72
```

The Pointer (PTR) resource record is used to map an IP address to a name using IN-ADDR-ARPA. A single PTR RR helps make this clear. The record

```
7.0.120.147.in-addr.arpa IN PTR merlin
```

indicates that the machine named merlin has the IP address 147.120.0.7.

The Name Server resource records point to the name server that has authority for a particular zone. Name Server (NS) records are used when a large network has several subnetworks, each with its own name server. An entry looks like this:

```
tpci.com   IN   NS   merlin.tpci.com
```

This record indicates that the DNS server for the tpci.com domain is called merlin.tpci.com. If there were several subnets used in tpci.com, there would be an NS RR for each subnet.

11

Completing the DNS Files

As you saw earlier, DNS uses several files to hold resource records describing the zones used by DNS. The first file of interest is named.hosts, which contains the SOA, NS, and A resource records. All entries in the named.hosts file must begin in the first character position of each line. Here's a sample named.hosts file with comments added to show the records:

```
; named.hosts files
; Start Of Authority RR
tpci.com.    IN    SOA       merlin.tpci.com
             root.merlin.tpci.com (
             2  ; Serial number
             7200 ; Refresh (2 hrs)
             3600 ; Retry (1 hr)
             151200 ; Expire (1 week)
             86400 ); min TTL
;
; Name Service RRs
tpci.com    IN    NS   merlin.tpci.com
subnet1.tpci.com IN NS goofy.subnet1.tpci.com
;
; Address RRs
artemis      IN    A     143.23.25.7
merlin       IN    A     143.23.25.9
windsor      IN    A     143.23.25.12
reverie      IN    A     143.23.25.23
bigcat       IN    A     143.23.25.43
pepper       IN    A     143.23.25.72
```

The first section sets the SOA record, which defines the parameters for TTL, expiry, refresh, and so on. It sets the name server for the tpci.com domain to merlin.tpci.com. The second section uses the NS resource records to define the name server for the tpci.com domain as merlin.tpci.com (the same as the SOA) and a subnet of tpci called subnet1, for which the name server is goofy.subnet1.tpci.com. The third section has a list of the address-record-name-to-IP-address mapping. There is an entry in this section for each machine on the network.

The named.rev file provides the reverse mapping of IP address to machine name and is composed of Pointer resource records. The same format as the named.hosts file is followed, except for the swapping of name and IP address and the conversion of the IP address to IN-ADDR-ARPA style. The equivalent named.rev file for the named.hosts file shown earlier looks like this:

```
; named.rev files
; Start Of Authority RR
23.143.in-addr.arpa     IN     SOA       merlin.tpci.com
             root.merlin.tpci.com (
             2  ; Serial number
             7200 ; Refresh (2 hrs)
             3600 ; Retry (1 hr)
             151200 ; Expire (1 week)
             86400 ); min TTL
;
```

```
; Name Service RRs
23.143.in-addr.arpa      IN    NS  merlin.tpci.com
100.23.143.in-addr.arpa    IN NS goofy.subnet1.tpci.com
;
; Address RRs
9.25.23.143.in-addr.arpa    IN    PTR merlin
12.25.23.143.in-addr.arpa   IN    PTR windsor
23.25.23.143.in-addr.arpa   IN    PTR reverie
43.25.23.143.in-addr.arpa   IN    PTR bigcat
72.25.23.143.in-addr.arpa   IN    PTR pepper
```

There must be a separate named.rev file for each zone or subdomain on the network. These files can have different names or be placed in different directories. If you have only a single zone, one named.rev file is all that's needed.

The named.local file contains an entry for the loopback driver (which always has the IP address 127.0.0.1). This file must contain information about the IN-ADDR-ARPA mapping of the loopback driver, as well as a domain again (because the named.rev file doesn't cover the 127 subnet). A named.local file looks like this:

```
; named.local files
; Start Of Authority RR
0.0.127.in-addr.arpa      IN      SOA      merlin.tpci.com
            root.merlin.tpci.com (
            2  ; Serial number
            7200 ; Refresh (2 hrs)
            3600 ; Retry (1 hr)
            151200 ; Expire (1 week)
            86400 ); min TTL
;
; Name Service RR
0.0.127.in-addr.arpa    IN    NS  merlin.tpci.com
;
; Address RR
1.0.0.127.in-addr.arpa    IN    PTR localhost
```

This file then provides the mapping from the machine named localhost to the IP address 127.0.0.1.

The named.ca file is used to specify name servers that the system can resort to. The machines specified in the named.ca file should be stable and not subject to rapid change. A sample named.ca file looks like this:

```
; named.ca
; servers for the root domain
;
.  99999999   IN   NS  ns.nic.ddn.mil.
   99999999   IN   NS  ns.nasa.gov.
   99999999   IN   NS  ns.internic.net
; servers by address
;
ns.nic.ddn.mil   99999999    IN   A  192.112.36.4
ns.nasa.gov      99999999    IN   A  192.52.195.10
ns.internic.net  99999999    IN   A  198.41.0.4
```

In this file only three DNS servers have been specified. A normal `named.ca` file can have a dozen or so name servers, depending on their proximity to your system. You can get a full list of valid root domain name servers through anonymous FTP to `nic.ddn.mil`, in the file `/netinfo/root-servers.txt`. This file can be pasted into `named.ca`. The servers specified in the `named.ca` file are each identified by two entries. One gives the root domain (the period) followed by the name server name; the other has the name server IP address. The Time to Live field is set very large because these servers are expected to be always available.

The `named.boot` file is used to trigger the loading of the DNS daemons and to specify the primary and secondary name servers on the network. A sample `named.boot` file looks like this:

```
; named.boot
directory     /usr/lib/named
primary     tpci.com      named.hosts
primary     25.143.in-addr.arpa      named.rev
primary     0.0.127.in-addr.arpa      named.local
cache    .    named.ca
```

The first line of the `named.boot` file has the keyword `directory` followed by the directory of the DNS configuration files. Each following line with the keyword `primary` tells DNS the files that it should use to find configuration information. The first line, for example, sets `named.hosts` as the file for locating the primary server of `tpci.com`. The `IN-ADDR-ARPA` information is kept in the file `named.rev` for the `143.25` subnet. The localhost information is in `named.local`, and finally the server and name cache information are in `named.ca`.

A secondary name server is configured only slightly differently than a primary server. The difference is in the `named.boot` file, which points back to the primary server.

Starting the DNS Daemons

The final step in the DNS configuration is to ensure that the DNS daemon called `named` is loaded when the UNIX system boots. This is usually done through the rc startup scripts. Most versions of UNIX have the routines for DNS startup already entered in the startup script, usually in the form of a check for the file `named.boot`. If `named.boot` exists, the DNS daemon `named` starts. The code usually looks like this:

```
# Run DNS server if named.boot exists
if [ -f /etc/inet/named.boot -a -x /usr/sbin/in.named ]
then
    /usr/sbin/in.named
fi
```

The exact directory paths and options might be different in your rc script, but the command should check for the `named.boot` file and start `named` if it exists.

Configuring a Client

Configuring a UNIX machine to use a primary DNS server for resolution is a quick process. First, the `/etc/resolv.conf` file is modified to include the primary server's address. For example, a `resolv.conf` file might look like this:

```
domain tpci.com
nameserver   143.25.0.1
nameserver   143.25.0.2
```

The first line establishes the domain name, which is followed by the IP addresses of available name servers. This file points to two name servers on the `143.25` subnet.

BOOTP Protocol

TCP/IP needs to know an Internet address before it can communicate with other machines. This can cause a problem when a machine is initially loaded or has no dedicated disk drive of its own. On Day 2, "TCP/IP and the Internet," you saw how Reverse Address Resolution Protocol (RARP) can be used to determine an IP address, but an alternative is in common use: the *bootstrap protocol* or BOOTP. BOOTP uses UDP to enable a diskless machine to determine its IP address without using RARP.

Diskless machines usually contain start-up information in their PROMs. Because these must be kept small and consistent between many models of diskless workstations to reduce costs, it is impossible to pack a complete protocol such as TCP/IP into a chip. It is also impossible to embed an IP address, because the chip can be used in many different machines on the same network. This forces a newly booted diskless workstation to determine its own IP address from the other machines on the network. (In practice, the diskless machine also must determine the IP address of the network server it will use, as well as the address of the nearest IP gateway.)

BOOTP overcomes a few of RARP's problems. RARP requires direct access to the network hardware, which can cause problems when dealing with servers. Also, RARP supplies only an IP address. When large packets must be sent, this wastes a lot of space that could be used for useful information. BOOTP was developed to use UDP and can be implemented within an application program. BOOTP also requires only a single packet of information to provide all the information a new diskless workstation requires to begin operation. Therefore, BOOTP is more efficient and easier to develop applications for, making it popular.

To determine a diskless workstation's IP address, BOOTP uses the broadcast capabilities of IP. (You might recall that IP enables several special network addresses that are broadcast to all machines on the network.) This lets the workstation send a message even when it doesn't know the destination machine's address or even its own.

NOTE

IP broadcast addresses such as 255.255.255.255 enable a message to be sent to all machines on a network despite having no source or destination network address.

BOOTP puts all the communications tasks on the diskless workstation. It specifies that all UDP messages sent over the network use checksums and that the Do Not Fragment bit is set. This tends to reduce the number of lost, misinterpreted, or duplicated datagrams.

To handle the loss of a message, BOOTP uses a simple set of timers. When a message has been sent, a timer starts. If no reply has been received when the timer runs out, the message is resent. The protocol stipulates that the timer is set to a random value, which increases each time the timer expires until it reaches a maximum value, after which it is randomized again. This prevents massive traffic after several machines fail at once and try to broadcast BOOTP messages at the same time.

BOOTP uses the terms *client* and *server* to refer to machines. The client is the machine that initiates a query, and the server is the machine that replies to that query. From these definitions, it is easy to see that client and server have no physical relation to any workstation, because the role of each workstation can change with message traffic. Because most systems can handle multiple traffic threads at a time, it is possible for a machine to be both a client and a server simultaneously.

NOTE

When considering client/server roles in BOOTP, remember that the machine that sends the first message is the client and the machine that replies is the server. There is no relationship to client/server architecture terms.

BOOTP Messages

BOOTP messages are kept in fixed formats for simplicity and to enable the BOOTP software to fit in a small space within a PROM. The format of BOOTP messages is shown in Figure 11.9. The OpCode field is used to signal either a request (set to a value of 1) or a reply (set to a value of 2). The HTYPE field indicates the network hardware type. The HLEN field indicates the length of a hardware address. (These last two fields are the same as in ARP.)

Figure 11.9.

The BOOTP message format.

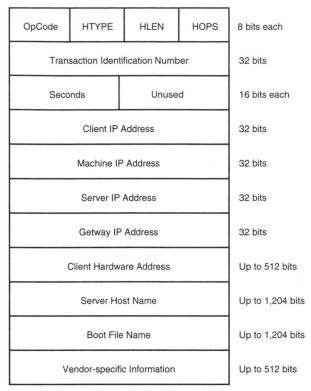

OpCode	HTYPE	HLEN	HOPS	8 bits each
Transaction Identification Number				32 bits
Seconds		Unused		16 bits each
Client IP Address				32 bits
Machine IP Address				32 bits
Server IP Address				32 bits
Getway IP Address				32 bits
Client Hardware Address				Up to 512 bits
Server Host Name				Up to 1,204 bits
Boot File Name				Up to 1,204 bits
Vendor-specific Information				Up to 512 bits

The HOPS field keeps track of the number of times the message is forwarded. When the client sends the request message, a value of 0 is put in the HOPS field. If the server decides to forward the message to another machine, it increments the HOPS count. (Forwarding is necessary when bootstrapping a machine across more than one gateway.)

The Transaction Identification Number field is an integer assigned by the client to the message and is unchanged from request to reply. This enables matching the replies to the correct request. The Seconds field is the number of seconds the client has been booted, assigned by the client when the message is sent.

The Client IP Address field is filled in as much as possible by the client. This might result in a partial network address or no information at all, depending on the client's knowledge of the network it is in. Any information that is unknown is set to 0 (so the field might be 0.0.0.0 if nothing is known about the network address). If the client wants information from a particular server, it can put the address of the server in the Server IP Address field. Similarly, if the client knows the server's name, it puts it in the Server Host Name field. The same applies for the other address fields. If the fields are set to 0, any server can respond. If a specific server or gateway is given, only that machine responds to the message.

The Vendor-specific Information field is used, as the name suggests, for implementation information that is specific to each vendor. This field is optional. The first 32 bits define the format of the remaining information. These first bits are known as the *magic cookie* and have a standard value of 99.120.83.99. Following the magic cookie are sets of information in a three-field format: a type, a length, and a value. There are several types identified by the Internet RFC, as shown in Table 11.5. The Length field is not used for types 0 and 255, but it must be present for types 1 and 2. The length can vary depending on the number of entries in the other types of messages.

Table 11.5. BOOTP vendor-specific types.

Type	Code	Length	Description
Padding	0	—	Used only for padding messages
Subnet Mask	1	4	Subnet mask for local network
Time of Day	2	4	Time of day
Gateways	3	Number of entries	IP addresses of gateways
Time Servers	4	Number of entries	IP addresses of time servers
IEN116 Server	5	Number of entries	IP addresses of IEN116 servers
Domain Name Server	6	Number of entries	IP addresses of Domain Name Servers
Log Server	7	Number of entries	IP addresses of log servers
Quote Server	8	Number of entries	IP addresses of quote servers
LPR Servers	9	Number of entries	IP addresses of lpr servers
Impress	10	Number of entries	IP addresses of impress servers
RLP Server	11	Number of entries	IP addresses of RLP servers
Hostname	12	Number of bytes	Client hostname in hostname
Boot size	13	2	Integer size of boot file
Unused	128–254	—	Not used
End	255	—	End of list

You might remember that a machine can obtain the subnet mask from an ICMP message, but BOOTP is the recommended method of obtaining this value.

11

The Boot Filename field can specify a filename from which to obtain a memory image that enables the diskless workstation to boot properly. This might be vendor-set or supplied by the server. This enables the memory image to be obtained from one machine while the actual addresses are obtained from another. If this field is set to 0, the server selects the memory image to send.

The process of booting follows two steps. The first is to use BOOTP to obtain information about the network addresses of the client and at least one other machine (a gateway or server). The second step uses a different protocol to obtain a memory image for the client.

NOTE   A two-step process using two different protocols is used to separate the configuration and operating system load of the machine. The use of two protocols enables optimization for each task. Two steps are also used because the machine that replies to the BOOTP client message might not be the machine that downloads the memory image.

Network Time Protocol (NTP)

Timing is very important to networks, not only to ensure that internal timers are maintained properly, but also for synchronization of clocks for sending messages and timestamps within those messages. Some systems rely on time for routing. Ensuring that time clocks are consistent and accurate is a task often overlooked, but it remains important enough to have a formal procedure defined by an Internet RFC. The protocol that maintains time standards is called the Network Time Protocol, or NTP. NTP can use either TCP or UDP; port 37 is dedicated to it.

The operation of NTP relies on obtaining an accurate time from a query to a primary time server, which itself gets its timing information from a standard time source (such as the National Institute of Standards and Technology in the U.S.). The time server queries the standard clock (also called a *master clocking source*) and sets its own times to the standard.

Once the primary time server has an accurate time, it sends NTP messages to secondary time servers further out on the internetwork. Secondary time servers can communicate with more secondary time servers using NTP, although accuracy is lost with each communication due to latency in the networks. Eventually, these time messages can be sent to gateways and individual machines within a network, if the administrator so decides. Usually each network has at least one primary time server and one secondary server, although large networks might have several of each.

The format of NTP messages is simple, as shown in Figure 11.10. Several control fields are used for synchronization and updating procedures, but the details of these fields are not important to this discussion. The Sync Distance to Primary field is an estimate of the round-trip delay incurred to the primary clock. The ID of the primary time server is the address of the primary.

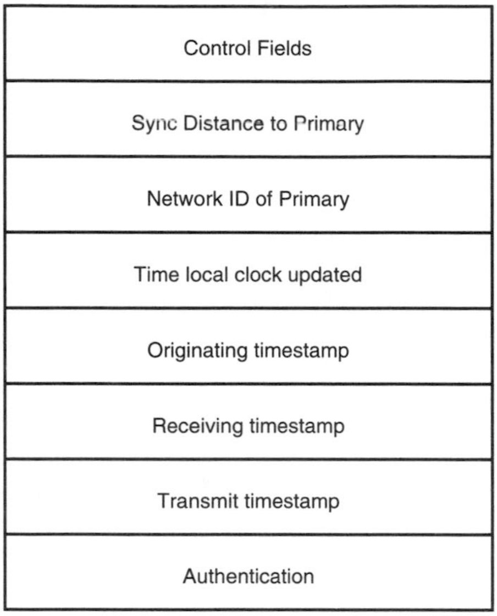

Figure 11.10.

The NTP message format.

| Control Fields |
| Sync Distance to Primary |
| Network ID of Primary |
| Time local clock updated |
| Originating timestamp |
| Receiving timestamp |
| Transmit timestamp |
| Authentication |

There are several timestamps in the NTP message. The Time local clock updated is the time the message originator's local clock was updated. The Originate timestamp is the time the message was sent. The Receive timestamp is the time it was received. The Transmit timestamp is the time the message was transmitted after reception.

All timestamps are calculated from an offset of the number of seconds since January 1, 1900. The timestamp fields are 64 bits, the first 32 bits for a whole number and the last 32 for a fraction. The final Authentication field is optional and can be used to authenticate the message.

Summary

You have now seen how the Domain Name Service works. DNS is an integral and important part of most TCP/IP installations, enabling symbolic names to be resolved properly across networks. The use of name servers was explained, as well as the manner in which records are stored within the servers. Associated with DNS is the ARP and IN-ADDR-ARPA name resolution process.

Today I also looked at the BOOTP protocol, necessary to enable many diskless terminals and workstations to connect to the network and load their operating system. Without BOOTP, you would all need full-featured computers or workstations.

Q&A

Q What are the top-level domain names and what are their purposes?

A The top level domains are .arpa (Internet-specific), .com (commercial), .edu (educational institutions), .gov (governmental), .mil (military), and .org (non-commercial organizations).

Q What does a DNS server do?

A The DNS server manages a zone of machines and provides name resolution for all machines within that zone.

Q If a name server cannot resolve a name using its own tables, what happens?

A Queries can be sent from the machine receiving the query to other name servers to search for a resolution. If another machine does have the answer, it is not returned to the inquiring machine, however. Only the address of the name resolver with the answer is returned. The inquiring machine must then send a specific query to the resolver with the answer.

Q What is the advantage of the IN-ADDR-ARPA format?

A IN-ADDR-ARPA enables a mapping from the IP address to the symbolic hostname. Sometimes this is a fast way to obtain the symbolic name of a destination machine.

Q Why does BOOTP use UDP?

A Simply because it is smaller to code. To embed TCP code in a PROM would take much more room than the simple code needed for UDP.

Quiz

1. What protocol is used by DNS servers? Why is that a good choice?
2. What is a DNS resource record?
3. Show a sample entry in an IN-ADDR-ARPA file and explain what the fields mean.
4. BOOTP helps a diskless workstation boot. How does it get a message to the network looking for its IP address and the location of its operating system boot files?
5. What is the Network Time Protocol? Why is it used?

Chapter 12

NFS and NIS

Today I look at the Network File System (NFS), a set of protocols and products in wide use with TCP/IP-based networks. NFS is especially popular with UNIX networks, but it is now available for many platforms and works well across a local area network. I also look at several protocols that are closely associated with NFS, such as Network Information Service (NIS), and the Remote Execution Service (REX).

Today's text concentrates on the UNIX versions of these protocols, simply because they serve as an excellent illustration. For other operating systems, names of files and procedures might change, but the fundamentals are compatible. I show some examples of using PC machines for NFS and NIS as appropriate.

Network File System (NFS)

The move to distributed processing and client/server architectures has meant that many users have small, powerful machines on their desk that communicate with a larger server somewhere on a network. The applications the user needs are often located in places other than on their desktop, so some method of accessing remote files (applications and data) is required. Although both Telnet and rlogin enable a user to use a remote machine, neither system takes advantage of the user's desktop machine. Peripheral sharing has also become important as local area networks grow. To help integrate workstations into local area networks, as well as to simplify remote file access and peripheral sharing, Sun Microsystems introduced the Network File System (NFS).

Sun designed NFS so that it would enable machines from different vendors to work together, even if they used different operating systems. Sun published the NFS specifications, enabling other vendors to adopt their own hardware and software to work smoothly with NFS. This results in a completely homogeneous network. Since Sun's introduction, NFS has become a de facto standard among UNIX environments, with strong support in other operating systems, as well.

NFS actually refers to both a product and a protocol. There is an NFS product that consists of a set of protocols for different tasks (these are examined in the section titled "NFS Protocols"). The NFS protocol is the one protocol of the NFS product that deals with file access. To avoid confusion, you should think of the NFS protocol specifically (instead of the entire product set) when NFS is mentioned today.

NFS is now intimately tied with UNIX, and it is shipped as part of the System V Release 4 software version. It is also tied to TCP/IP, which remains the communications protocol of choice for UNIX networks. For other operating systems, NFS is usually an extension that is added at the system administrator's option. UNIX systems use the process nfsd to manage NFS access, with the process started automatically when the UNIX system boots after NFS has been properly configured.

NFS enables an application to read and write files that reside on NFS servers, with the access to the NFS server completely transparent to the application and the user. For developers, NFS requires no extra coding or special handling, which makes it especially attractive. This transparent access to another machine's file structure is achieved by logically attaching the NFS server to the client, a process called *mounting*.

The NFS server's file system can be attached as a whole, or just a portion of it can be mounted. The directory at which the mount occurs is called the *mount point*. The concept of shared files similar to that encountered with NFS is sometimes called a *distributed file system*, although this is a misnomer with NFS.

NOTE UNIX has had the capability to mount or attach another file system for a long time. This type of mounting can occur across networks and is transparent to the application and user, as long as filenames take into account the full pathname of the mounted file system. The NFS mount is similar to the UNIX mount process.

NFS uses the term *client* to represent any machine that requests a file from another machine, which is the *server*. Multitasking operating systems can act as both client and server simultaneously, with processes on the machine accessing files on another machine while others on the network access its own hard disk. Usually, restrictions are imposed as to the files or portions of a file system that can be shared, both for security and speed considerations. Typical NFS installations use personal computers or diskless workstations as clients accessing a more powerful server system. Because personal computer operating systems such as MS-DOS are single-tasking, PCs usually act only as clients, unless they run a multitasking operating system such as Windows NT or OS/2. It is possible to have an entire network of multitasking computers sharing their drives with each other, although in practice this works well only for small networks because of the high density of network traffic required to support all the mounted filesystems.

Because of the need to transfer files quickly, network speed becomes vitally important. When it was designed, the original goal for an NFS-mounted file system was to provide performance equivalent to 80 percent of the performance expected from a locally mounted hard disk. This puts the performance emphasis on both the NFS disk drive and the network system. Typically, NFS disk drives are among the fastest available, specifically to reduce bottlenecks at the drive end. The network hardware and software must be chosen to enable the fastest possible throughput.

Because NFS is UNIX-based, the security offered is rudimentary. For this reason, Sun has introduced Secure NFS, which implements an encrypted messaging protocol for added protection against unauthorized access to NFS-mounted file systems.

NFS Protocols

The NFS product comprises several protocols, only one of which is called the NFS protocol. The NFS product protocols are designed as a set of layers, similar to the OSI model. The layers of the NFS product are compared to the OSI layers in Figure 12.1. Each protocol in the NFS product has an Internet RFC dedicated to its specification.

Figure 12.1.

NFS protocol layers.

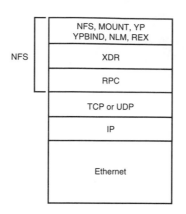

The NFS product is based on the OSI layered model, resulting in protocols that are independent (in theory, at least) from each other and protocols in different layers. The design philosophy is that any single-layer protocol could be replaced with any other one, assuming the functionality of the protocol was the same. To date there are no common alternatives for the two lower-layer products, RPC and XDR, although there are several for the top layer.

NOTE The source code for both the Remote Procedure Call (RPC) and External Data Representation (XDR) protocols is available free of charge from Sun Microsystems.

Figure 12.1 introduces the RPC (Remote Procedure Call) and XDR (External Data Representation) protocols that I look at now in more detail.

Remote Procedure Call (RPC)

The Remote Procedure Call (RPC) protocol acts as the session layer and as the message exchanger for all NFS-based applications. RPC is composed of a set of procedures that can be incorporated into high-level applications to handle any required network access. The remote procedures are no more complicated to use than local procedures.

NOTE RPC was specially developed for NFS but has since found use in other protocol suites. The principles covered here apply to those RPC products, as well.

Application developers can create their own RPC procedures between a client (the one that issues the request) and a server (the one that processes the request). A group of procedures is called a *service*. Each server can use only one service, so each service is assigned a *program number* to identify itself to both the client and the server.

RPC functions over the network between a client and a server. The process followed by an RPC is shown in Figure 12.2. It begins with the activation of the procedure by the client, from which a request message is sent to the server. After receiving the message and extracting the request, the server executes the requested procedure and assembles a response message with the results. Upon receipt of the reply, the client disassembles the message and continues with the application's normal execution. Every step of the procedure is controlled by routines within the RPC library (which is linked into the applications).

Figure 12.2.

The execution of an RPC.

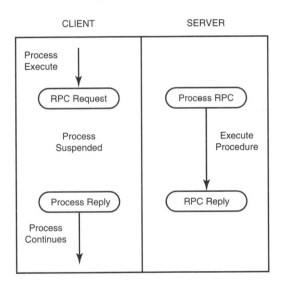

RPC messages can be sent using either TCP or UDP (or for that matter, any other protocol that provides the same functionality). Typically, RPC is used with UDP because a connection-based protocol is not necessary and UDP is usually faster. However, UDP does impose a maximum packet size, which can cause some problems with procedures. Also, UDP does not guarantee delivery, so an application that uses UDP must handle reliability issues (usually with a retransmission timer).

The use of TCP offers the capability not only to ignore reliability concerns (leaving that to the TCP software), but also to batch requests. With a batch connection, the client and server agree that the client can send several RPC requests one after another without waiting for acknowledgment or a reply to each. This can be a useful feature with some applications.

The RPC protocol is used to send requests and replies. The format of the RPC protocol packet header is shown in Figure 12.3, with all fields coded in the External Data Representation (XDR) format (see the section titled "External Data Representation (XDR)" later today). The Transaction ID field is used to match requests and replies and is changed (usually incremented) by the client with each new request. The Direction Indicator field shows whether the message originated with the client (a value of 0) or with the server (a value of 1). The first Version Number is the version of RPC used and the second Version Number identifies the version of the program. The Program Number identifies the service (set of procedures) to use, as mentioned earlier. The Procedure Number identifies the particular procedure in the service.

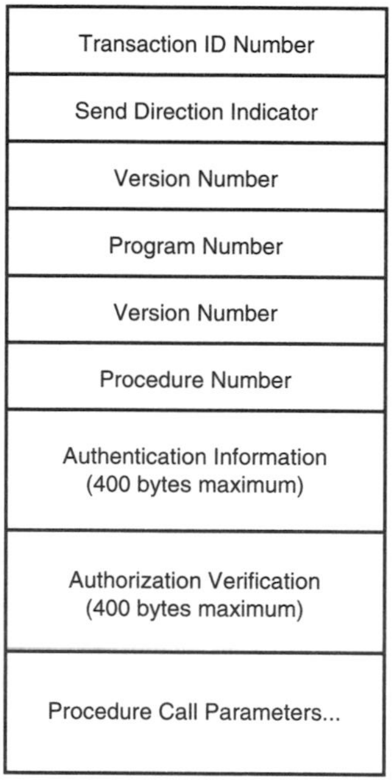

Figure 12.3.

The RPC protocol header.

Transaction ID Number
Send Direction Indicator
Version Number
Program Number
Version Number
Procedure Number
Authentication Information (400 bytes maximum)
Authorization Verification (400 bytes maximum)
Procedure Call Parameters...

Some procedures might require a client to authenticate itself to the server, both for identification purposes and for security reasons. The RPC protocol header contains two fields for authentication. The Authorization Information field is for information itself, and the Authorization Verification field is used for the validation. The RPC RFC does not define how authentication is to be performed, leaving it up to the application developer, but it does specify two fields with a maximum size of 400 bytes each. There are currently four types of authentication predefined for use:

12

- [ ] **None:** No authentication is used. Both authentication fields have zero length.
- [ ] **UNIX:** Uses UNIX permissions (group and user IDs). This type of authentication is used by the NFS protocol. There is no authentication information.
- [ ] **Short:** Short authentication process. The client generates an authentication sequence, which is returned by the server (usually a reference to a previous RPC request for convenience).
- [ ] **DES:** Authentication is a character string with a Data Encryption Standard (DES) encoded timestamp used as the verification. The DES authentication is used by the secure NFS product.

The only authentication system that is really secure is the DES method. The other three systems can be readily broken by a knowledgeable developer.

Each service that uses RPC has a program number that uniquely identifies it to the protocol. RPC keeps track of connections using a program number for each, which can be mapped to a program name. In UNIX, this mapping is performed in the file /etc/rpc. A sample /etc/rpc file follows:

```
portmapper      100000  portmap sunrpc
rstat_svc       100001  rstatd rstat rup perfmeter
rusersd         100002  rusers
nfs             100003  nfsprog
ypserv          100004  ypprog
mountd          100005  mount showmount
ypbind          100007
walld           100008  rwall shutdown
yppasswdd       100009  yppasswd
etherstatd      100010  etherstat
rquotad         100011  rquotaprog quota rquota
sprayd          100012  spray
3270_mapper     100013
rje_mapper      100014
selection_svc   100015  selnsvc
database_svc    100016
rexd            100017  rex
alis            100018
sched           100019
llockmgr        100020
nlockmgr        100021
x25.inr         100022
statmon         100023
status          100024
bootparam       100026
ypupdated       100028  ypupdate
keyserv         100029  keyserver
ypxfrd          100069  ypxfr
pcnfsd          150001  pcnfsd
```

12

This file shows the program name and its corresponding program number. The third column, when present, shows a program name that corresponds with the process name in the first column. The program numbers shown in this file are assigned by the RPC RFC and should be consistent across all implementations of RPC.

Port Mapper

Connections between a client and server are over ports, each with its own number (port numbers are used in TCP/IP to define a connection). To prevent problems with port allocation using RPC, a *port mapper* was developed. Without the port mapper, a server could easily run out of available ports with only a few RPC connections active.

The port mapper controls a table of ports and RPC programs using those ports. The port mapper itself has a dedicated port number (port 111 with both UDP and TCP). The ports available to RPC connections are assigned when the RPC program is initiated, at which time these port numbers are sent to the port mapper.

When a client wants to use RPC, it sends a request to the server. This request follows the RPC header format seen in Figure 12.3 and includes the version number of RPC, the service number, and the protocol to be used. The port mapper can then allocate a suitable port number and return that number in a reply message to the client. Once a port number has been assigned for that client, it is maintained, so that all procedure requests come over that port until the application terminates. The port numbers might be maintained over several processes, so the port inquiry needs to be conducted only once between system power cycles.

This procedure does have a drawback: the client must know the server's address. It cannot simply send out a generic request for a server with the services it is looking for. This has been overcome with some newly developed network file systems, although not NFS.

External Data Representation (XDR)

The External Data Representation (XDR) is the method by which data is encoded within an RPC message (or other protocol systems, as well). There is no formal message header or protocol system for XDR, although the XDR RFC does define the method of encoding data.

XDR is used to ensure that data from one system is compatible with others. It might seem that no formal definition is required, but consider the case of an EBCDIC-based machine communicating with an ASCII-based machine. XDR enables both ends to convert from their local data representation to a common format, removing any doubts about the meaning of the data. (EBCDIC to ASCII is not the major conversion problem. Some systems use high bits as significant, and others use low bits. Also, formats for defining types of numbers differ considerably.)

12

The XDR format uses sequential bits written into a buffer, then formatted into a message and sent to the lower protocol layers. XDR relies on an 8-bit byte, with the lower bytes being the most significant. The RFC defines all integer data types, which are converted to 4-byte integers, with an extended 64-bit *hyperinteger* format available. IEEE 32-bit formats are used for floating-point numbers, where the mantissa is the lower 23 bits, the exponent takes 8 bits, and the sign of the number is 1 bit. Where data takes less than 4 bytes for any type, padding is added to ensure 4-byte lengths.

NOTE

A special C-like language called XDR has been developed to simplify the handling of XDR-format data. It can be used from within other programming languages.

Network File System Protocol

The NFS protocol is composed of a set of RPC procedures. It is not a protocol in the conventional sense of defining a complex handshaking process between two machines. Instead, it is a method of communicating information about a procedure to be run. NFS uses UDP and has a port number of 2049 assigned. This port number is nonsense; it arises from an error in the original implementation that could not be corrected subsequently because of compatibility issues. Because the port numbers are assigned by the port mapper, this number has no real meaning.

NFS was designed to be a *stateless* protocol, meaning that the machines using NFS would not have to maintain state tables to use the protocol. Also, it was designed to be robust, meaning that after failures (of a connection or a machine) the system could recover quickly and easily.

The NFS protocol is difficult to describe without introducing some programming, because the system is described in terms of the XDR language. This type of discussion is beyond the scope of this book; for more information, refer to the RFCs. However, it is possible to convey a sense of the protocol's contents through an overview of its capabilities and features.

To understand the NFS procedures that comprise the protocol, it is necessary to examine the data structures and objects in the protocol. NFS defines a set of constants that are used to establish various parameters, such as the number of bytes in a pathname, the maximum number of bytes in a read or write request, or the size of an NFS pointer. These are called *protocol constants* and should be the same for all implementations of NFS.

12

NOTE

> A *data object* is a set of variables or values that are combined in one entity, much as an entry in a telephone book is actually composed of a name, address, and telephone number. All three variables or values combine to form a single entry or object.

Several data objects are used by NFS to define files and their attributes. Because NFS deals specifically with files, these objects are important to the protocol. One data object is the file handle (or `fhandle`), which uniquely identifies a file on the server. File handles are provided in all NFS messages that refer to the file. As with most NFS data types, the file handle is a 32-byte field of free format that is understandable by the server. For example, a UNIX file is uniquely defined by its device major and minor numbers and its inode number. The filename itself is not used.

A data object is used for the file type (called `ftype`), which defines all the kinds of files known by NFS. These mimic the UNIX file types, including a regular file (any kind of data), a directory (which is a file entry in UNIX), links (which are several pointers under different names to the same file) and both block and character mode files.

Also used is a data structure for the file attributes, called `fattr`. This defines the permissions of the file, the times of access, the owner, and several other parameters. This is necessary whenever a file read or write is performed, because the attributes must be correct to allow the procedure to continue. (The attributes can be changed by another NFS procedure called set attributes or `sattr`.)

These data objects can be combined into a larger entity using a discriminating union. A *discriminating union* is a combination of several data objects that are given a single label. These discriminating unions can be thought of as a label followed by data, which might differ depending on the outcome of a procedure. For example, after a procedure has been executed, a discriminating union might be a label followed by either an error message or the result of the procedure, if it executes properly. The union, though, is referred to by the label and doesn't care about the contents in the data area. This type of structure is used to simplify programming.

Seventeen procedures (and a `Null` procedure) are defined within the NFS protocol. These procedures are summarized in Table 12.1. This book doesn't go into detail about the procedures, as they are not relevant to the level of discussion. The RFC covers them all in exhaustive detail.

Table 12.1. NFS procedures.

Name	Description
Null	Null procedure
Fetch file attributes	Returns the attributes of a file
Set file attributes	Sets the attributes of a file
Read file system root	Not used; now obsolete
Lookup filename	Returns the file handle corresponding to a filename
Read contents of link	Returns details of symbolic links to a file
Read file	Reads a file
Write to cache	Not used
Write to file	Writes a file
Create file	Creates a new file and returns the new file's handle
Delete file	Deletes a file
Rename file	Renames a file
Generate link	Creates a link to a file (same file system)
Generate symbolic link	Generates a symbolic link (across file systems)
Create directory	Creates a new directory
Delete directory	Removes a directory
Read directory	Returns a list of files in the directory
Read file system attributes	Returns information about the file system

Programmers might have noticed the lack of any open and close file functions within NFS. This arises from the stateless nature of the protocol. When a file must be opened, the local NFS process handles it, not the remote process. This allows for better control of files and ports after failure of a machine or a connection.

Mount Protocol

In today's introduction I mentioned that NFS works by mounting an NFS server file system onto a client file system. As you have just seen, however, the NFS protocol is actually about file access and information, not connecting file systems. This file system mounting procedure is dealt with as a separate issue by the NFS product, using the Mount protocol. Mount uses UDP.

12

The Mount protocol is involved in returning a file handle from the server to the client, enabling the client to access an area on the server file system. The protocol returns not only the file handle but also the name of the file system in which the requested file resides. Mount consists of a number of procedures that facilitate communications between the client and server, designed especially for dealing with files.

A process called `mountd` takes care of handling the mount protocol at both ends of a connection. The `mountd` process maintains a list of machines and path names that are involved in a mount operation. Once a mount has been performed, NFS can continue operating without referring back to Mount at all. This lets Mount continue to modify its internal tables without affecting ongoing sessions. This can cause a problem if a client crashes and reconnects. The server still has the original connections listed in its internal Mount tables. To correct this problem, most NFS clients send a command (called `UMNTALL`, or unmount all) to all NFS servers when they boot.

NOTE

The Mount protocol is involved only during the original connection between a client and a server. The `mountd` process keeps track of connections, but once the connection is established, the Mount protocol relinquishes all control to NFS. All NFS needs to access a file system is a valid file handle (which Mount provides when the connection is made).

As mentioned earlier, the Mount protocol consists of a set of procedures. These are summarized in Table 12.2 and are self-explanatory.

Table 12.2. Mount protocol procedures.

Name	Description
NULL	Null
MNT	Mounts a file system and returns the file handle and file system name
UMNT	Unmounts a server file system, deleting the entry from the Mount table
UMNTALL	Unmounts all server file systems used by the client and updates the Mount table
EXPORT	Provides a list of exported file systems
DUMP	Provides a list of the file systems on the server that are currently mounted on the client

Some versions of NFS enable an automount capability, in which the remote file systems are mounted only when required. This prevents them from being attached for extended periods of time and simplifies administration. The process of automounting is completely transparent to the user.

The automount capability is built upon NFS's procedures, but it performs a few clever tricks. The automounter is not part of NFS but is an application that sits on top of it. Symbolic links are the key to the automounter's operation.

File Locking

Occasionally a system administrator wants to prevent access to an NFS-available file system. Such instances occur regularly during maintenance, software updates, or to protect data during a particular process. UNIX has the capability to lock a particular file by changing permissions, and the same can be done for file systems to some extent, but it would seem intuitive that locking a file system is more involved than simply locking a file or two. The capability to lock file systems from access was not developed with the original NFS product but was implemented as a parallel service after NFS became more widely available.

NOTE

> Separating functionality (such as file locking) into separate protocols or procedures is consistent with both the OSI and NFS philosophies. This also enables better portability and compatibility across platforms.

File system locking is handled by several protocols and procedures, involving a few daemon processes. In the original file locking system developed by Sun Microsystems, a lock daemon called lockd was used. This requires that every RPC activity that involves a lock communicates with the process, even when it is on another machine. The communications between RPC and lockd use a protocol called Kernel Lock Manager (KLM), which rides on UDP.

Whenever a lock procedure is called, lockd decides whether it can handle the task on the local machine or whether messages have to be sent to remote lockd processes (on other machines). Communications between different lockd processes are through another protocol called the Network Lock Manager (NLM). There are several versions of both KLM and NLM in use, with implementations available for most hardware platforms.

A process called statd (status monitor) monitors the state of locks and handles queries against a locked file system. This is necessary so that a new query against a locked file system can be queued (if it is locked for a short time) or rejected (if the file system is locked for a while).

12

There are several built-in protection systems for file locking, such as automatic timers to prevent infinite locking after a machine crash, conflicting requests for locks, and a short period for completion of existing procedures before a lock is completed. These are all defined and explained in the RFC.

Remote Execution Service (REX)

The Remote Execution Service (REX) is designed to enable a user to run commands on another machine with full environment variables, without incurring the overhead of processes such as Telnet, rlogin, or rsh. REX uses a daemon called rexd that runs on the server and employs NFS's services. (Remember that each machine can be both client and server, so most multitasking machines on a network can run rexd.) REX is commonly used when some applications are installed on only a few machines but should be available to all users.

REX has an important advantage over the other UNIX utilities for this type of service. It enables access to the local machine's data while executing the command on the remote. This enables a user to run an application on another machine while accessing data files on the local machine. It also enables another machine's resources to be used without starting a user shell process or logging into the remote machine.

To run an application or execute a command on a remote machine, the REX on command is used. The syntax adds the name of the machine on which the command is to be executed and the command to run. The following code gives an example of this:

```
$ hostname
tpci_hpws4
$ cat file1
This is the file "file1" on "tpci_hpws4".
This is the client machine.
$ on merlin hostname
merlin
$ rsh merlin cat file1
cat: cannot open file1
$ on merlin cat file1
This is the file "file1" on "tpci_hpws4".
This is the client machine.
```

This example shows the remote machine executing a cat command on a local file. When the remote machine runs commands using on, an identical environment to the client is established on the remote, including user and group IDs and environment variables. So, if the remote machine in the previous example had a file called file1, but it was not in the search path of the process running the command, the system would still refer back to the client for the file.

12

rusers **and** spray

Two utilities available to NFS users are simple examples of RPC programs. They are also useful to the user who wants to check the status of connections and the load on a remote machine.

The spray program is similar to ping in that it sends a batch of messages across the network and waits for replies. Several supported options can configure the use of spray. When the spray command is issued with the -c option, it sends a supplied number of datagrams to the remote machine and times the results. A typical use is shown here:

```
$ spray -c 200 beast
sending 200 packets of length 86 to beast...
   in 18.3 seconds elapsed time,
   4 packets (2.00%) dropped by beast
Sent:  10 packets/sec, 912 bytes/sec
Recd:   9 packets/sec, 862 bytes/sec
```

The rusers program gives you an idea of who is logged into remote machines. A typical output is the following:

```
$ rusers
beast.tpci.com       tparker  bsmallwood  rmaclean
merlin.tpci.com      ychow  etreijs  tgrace
tpci_hpws3.tpci.com  tparker  sysadm
tpci_hpws4.tpci.com  pepper
```

As shown, the output from the rusers program includes the machine name and the list of users on that machine. Some implementations support options for rusers, whereas some have slightly differing output.

Configuring NFS

Many people love using the NFS service when they are faced with it as a user but are scared to configure it when acting as a system administrator. The general assumption is that the process must be convoluted, complex, and require a lot of knowledge about the operating systems. For this reason, many people don't bother with NFS, which is a shame because it is one of the most useful services TCP/IP has to offer. As you see in this section, it is not difficult to implement an NFS network.

I configure NFS on two different operating systems to show the general process. I use an SCO UNIX machine as an example of a UNIX installation, and a Windows for Workgroups system to show setting up a client and server NFS PC system. I start with the UNIX machine, because UNIX is most often associated with NFS servers.

12

Configuring UNIX as an NFS Server

The NFS service makes extensive use of the RPC service. For this reason, the RPC server daemon must be running for NFS to be implemented. On some UNIX systems you can check whether RPC is active by issuing this command at the shell prompt:

```
rpcinfo -p
```

You should see a list of all the RPC servers currently running on your machine. If RPC is running properly, you see four rpcbind listings (two for UDP and two for TCP) and an entry for pcnfsd, the NFS daemon. This command doesn't show all this output for some versions of UNIX, including SCO UNIX.

For SCO UNIX, NFS is started and stopped by a script called /etc/nfs. This can be linked into the startup routines to load NFS automatically when the system boots by linking the /etc/nfs file to the file /etc/rc2.d/Sname. To shut down NFS properly, you also need to link /etc/nfs to the file /etc/rc0.d/Kname. (On other UNIX implementations the filenames change, but the general approach is the same.) If you want to start and stop the NFS daemon manually, you can do this with these commands:

```
/etc/nfs start
/etc/nfs stop
```

The /etc/nfs command starts up and shuts down the NFS server daemon when the appropriate command is issued. When you issue the start command, the daemons that are activated are echoed to the screen:

```
$ /etc/nfs start
Starting NFS services: exportfs mountd nfsd pcnfsd biod(x4)
Starting NLM services: statd lockd
```

With a stop command, you see a message that the daemons and server are shut down:

```
$ /etc/nfs stop
NFS shutdown: [NFS Shutdown Complete]
```

For a filesystem on a SCO UNIX machine to be available to NFS clients on other machines, the filesystem must be listed in the UNIX file /etc/exports. With some versions of UNIX, the NFS daemons are started automatically if the /etc/exports file exists during boot time. This invokes a program called exportfs that sets the filesystem as available for NFS use. If any changes are made to the /etc/exports file while the system is running, you can issue another exportfs command, or simply reboot the machine, to make the changes effective.

The format of the /etc/exports file is as follows:

```
directory [ -option, option ... ]
```

The directory is the pathname of the directory or file to be shared (exported, in NFS terminology) by NFS, and the options are one of the following:

   ro: Export the directory as read-only. (The default value is to export as read-write.)

   rw=hostnames: Export the directory as read-mostly, which means read-only to most machines but read-write to machines specifically identified.

   anon=uid: If an NFS request comes from an unknown user, use uid as the effective user ID for ownership and permissions.

   root=hostnames: Gives root access to the root users from a specified machine.

   access=client: Gives mount access to each client listed. A client can be a host name or a net group.

An example of an /etc/exports file helps show the use of these options. A pound sign (#) on a line means a comment. Here's a sample /etc/exports file:

```
/usr/stuff -ro            # export as read-only to anyone
/usr   -access=clients    # export to the group called clients
/usr/public               # export as read-write to anyone
```

NFS is now ready for use on the SCO UNIX server. You might notice that SCO UNIX creates a new file called /etc/xtab that contains the filesystem information from the exports file. You should not modify the contents of the /etc/xtab file or the NFS server cannot function properly. The /etc/xtab file is generated by the exportfs command.

Some versions of UNIX use the share command to set up a directory for export. (SCO UNIX does not support the share command because the functions are duplicated in the /etc/exports file.) The syntax of the share command is as follows:

```
share -F nfs -o options -d description path
```

The -F option indicates that the directory or files given in the path are to be set as NFS filesystems. The options following -o set the type of access in the same way as the SCO UNIX options for the /etc/exports file shown earlier. The -d option can be followed by a descriptive statement used by clients to describe the export filesystem. For example, to share the directory /usr/public as read-write (the default), you could issue this command:

```
share -F nfs -d "Server public directory" /usr/public
```

Options can be combined, as shown in this example:

```
share -F nfs -o ro=artemis,anon=200 -d "Book material" /usr/tparker/book
```

This command shares the directory /usr/tparker/book, which is tagged with the description "Book material", with everyone as read-write except for a machine called artemis, for which it is read-only. Any anonymous users accessing the system use UID 200.

The share command by itself usually shows a list of all filesystems that are exported.

12

Setting Up a UNIX NFS Client

UNIX can mount an NFS exported filesystem from another machine with the `mount` command. The syntax for mounting an NFS filesystem is as follows:

```
mount -F nfs -o options machine:filesystem mount-point
```

The `-F` option tells the `mount` command the filesystem is an NFS filesystem; `machine:filesystem` is the name of the remote machine and the filesystem to be mounted; and `mount-point` is the location in the current filesystem where the remote filesystem is to be mounted. Some versions of UNIX change the syntax a little. For example, SCO UNIX uses a lower case `f` and uppercase `NFS` to indicate the type. Check the man pages for the exact syntax on your version.

In use, `mount` is easy to work with. For example, the command

```
mount -F nfs artemis:usr/public /usr/artemis
```

mounts the filesystem `/usr/public` on the remote machine called `artemis` onto the local machine in the directory called `/usr/artemis`. The mount-point (in this case `/usr/artemis`) must exist for the mount to succeed.

The `-o` optional component of the `mount` command can be used to set options from the following list:

> `rw`: Sets the mount to read-write (the default value)
>
> `ro`: Sets the mount to read-only
>
> `timeo=x`: Gives a timeout value in tenths of a second to attempt the mount before giving up
>
> `retry=x`: Retries x times before giving up
>
> `soft`: Forces the client to give up the `mount` attempt if an acknowledgment is not received from the remote machine
>
> `hard`: The client continues trying to mount the filesystem until successful
>
> `intr`: Enables the keyboard to interrupt the `mount` request; otherwise, the attempts go on forever

Any of these options can be combined in one `mount` command, as they could be for the `share` command. For example, the command line

```
mount -F nfs -o soft,ro artemis:usr/public /usr/artemis
```

tries to mount the `/usr/public` directory on `artemis` as read-only, but it gives up if the mount attempt is not acknowledged by `artemis`. The `mount` command by itself usually shows all mounted filesystems.

Setting Up Windows-Based NFS

Several TCP/IP suites and application packages for Windows 3.x, Windows 95, and Windows NT provide NFS support. One of the widest used is NetManage's ChameleonNFS, which can be used under any of the Windows operating system versions. ChameleonNFS enables a Windows machine to act as both client and server for NFS file access. In other words, another machine can access files on the ChameleonNFS machine, and the ChameleonNFS machine can access files on other NFS-equipped machines.

Implementing NFS access on a Windows machine can vary from very complex to very easy, depending on the software package that provides the NFS capabilities. Some available NFS products don't offer server capabilities, enabling only NFS client behavior on the installation machine. Carefully check the software before you purchase or install it to ensure you are getting a product that meets your NFS requirements. In this section I continue with ChameleonNFS as the example NFS software, because it is relatively easy to install, configure, and use. I use Windows 3.11 as the operating system example.

ChameleonNFS relies on a software daemon called Portmapper, which maintains a list of all currently registered network services (including NFS). Portmapper is loaded automatically when the Windows machine boots in most installations. ChameleonNFS is set to record mounted drives to the WIN.INI file (for Windows 3.x at least) whenever a Windows session is saved. This enables currently mounted drives to be remounted automatically when the next Windows session is started.

ChameleonNFS server activities such as administration and configuration are conducted through the NFS icon in the NetManage program group. The sole exception is printer handling for network devices, which is handled through the Printer icon on the Control Panel. NFS client activities are done through normal Windows applications, such as the File Manager and Control Panel. Drives are mounted and unmounted through the File Manager, whereas all other options are handled through the Network panel in the Control Panel.

Once installed, ChameleonNFS lets you mount a remote directory on an NFS server from the File Manager. Select the Network Connections option from the Disk pull-down menu. This displays the Network Connections dialog shown in Figure 12.4. The remote machine name and the directory to be mounted are specified in this dialog. The mounted filesystem is usually mounted as another drive, not as part of an existing drive's filesystem.

12

Figure 12.4.

The Network Connections dialog lets you mount a remote filesystem using NFS.

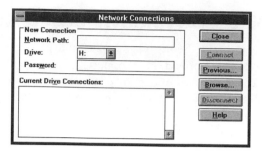

If you want to see all the filesystems that are available for mounting on a remote machine, use the Browse button. The remote machine name and all the filesystems available are listed, as shown in Figure 12.5. In Figure 12.5 the only filesystem that is showing as available on the machine called tpci is the root filesystem, which means the entire filesystem on the remote. You can't tell from this window whether it is set for special access rights such as read-only.

Figure 12.5.

When you specify the host name in the Browse dialog, all that remote's NFS filesystems are listed.

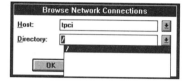

Clicking the OK button after the remote machine name and directory name are filled in mounts the remote filesystem at the location you indicate in the window, as shown in Figure 12.6. This mounts the remote machine's root directory as drive H on the local machine. When you click OK to close the NFS dialog, the remote machine's filesystem is available from the File Manager. The drive icon shows that it is a network drive.

Figure 12.6.

This window shows that tpci's root directory is to be mounted as drive H on the local machine.

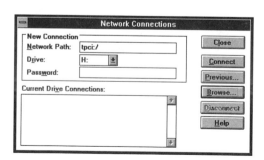

12

To disconnect an NFS-mounted drive, use the Disconnect button on the Network Connections dialog. The drive icon should be removed from the File Manager to show that the mount is no longer in effect.

Sharing a Windows Directory

ChameleonNFS can be used to share PC drives or directories with other users on the network. To share a drive, create a list of users who have access to the drive, unless everyone can mount the drives. The user access list is maintained under the NFS icon with ChameleonNFS. Start the NFS server process by clicking the NFS icon in the Chameleon program group. This displays the NFS main window. Clicking the Users menu item on the NFS window opens the Server Users window, shown in Figure 12.7. From here you can add and manage all access to your NFS available drives. To enter a user, type the name, any password you want them to use (if you want a password), and a group and user ID number. Click the Add button, and the entry appears as part of the user list.

Figure 12.7.

The Server Users window lets you set access rights to your NFS drives.

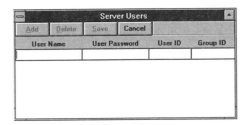

When you have entered all the users, click the Save button to write the entries to the disk. If you don't save the table, any changes are lost. Figure 12.8 shows two users on the access table.

Figure 12.8.

Two users are allowed to access the local machine's NFS drives.

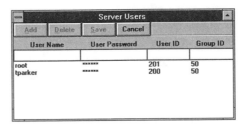

Next, you need to set the drives and directories that can be exported by other clients. Use the Exports menu item in the NFS window to display the Server Exports window. Use the directory browser to move between the drives and directories, selecting the ones you want to export. Click the Add button to enter the drive and directory combination to the export list.

12

Figure 12.9 shows the Server Exports window with two specific directories and one entire drive set to be exported. For each drive or directory you can set access rights by clicking the Access button. This displays the Access dialog, which you can use to select the proper permissions and access rights.

Figure 12.9.

The Server Exports window with directories and drives defined for NFS access.

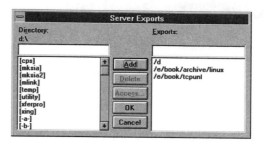

Once the access permissions are set, a remote client can access your NFS drives. The remote user is prompted for a password if you have set your system to require one.

Network Information Service (NIS)

The Yellow Pages (YP) protocol is an RPC application layer service (like NFS) that provides a versatile directory service. Because of copyright restrictions, Yellow Pages was renamed to Network Information Service (NIS), although both terms are in common use. NIS was developed for several reasons, but the one that affects users the most is access permissions. The effect these permissions have on users is generally transparent except for one major advantage.

If you are a user on a large network and you tend to connect to other machines frequently (through Telnet or FTP, for example), you must maintain accounts on each machine you connect to. Thus, you would need user accounts on every machine you could conceivably want to access. Maintaining the passwords on a large number of machines is awkward, because you must log into each one and perform password changes. NIS was developed to enable one single, central user file to be shared over the network, requiring only a single entry to enable access to all machines (unless specific restrictions are imposed), and simplifying a password change on all machines to one step.

In RPC terms, this combination of user ID and password works on the RPC authentication procedures. RPC uses the user and group IDs to grant access to files, so it is necessary for the client and server's user and group IDs to match. Without NIS this could be very difficult to implement because each machine's user file might have the same names, but their user IDs might not coincide. Worse, another user with a matching user ID on another machine could access files on your machine as though he or she were logged in as you.

12

NIS is a distributed access system in that each machine on the network that uses NIS accesses a central server, called the *NIS master* or *ypmaster* (depending on the version), for access information. On larger networks, to spread the load, and for all networks as a backup contingency, several other machines are designated as *slaves* or *ypslaves* that maintain up-to-date access information. In case of a failure of the master server, a slave takes up the functions. NIS uses both TCP and UDP for communications.

NOTE   There are two versions of NIS in general use. The first release (Version 1) had serious problems under certain circumstances, so Version 2 was quickly released. However, some systems still use the older version.

The NIS protocol has a set of procedures defined within the RFC. These enable a search for master servers, access to the user files, and system management functions. Another procedure is used to transfer copies of the master files. Several machines are grouped together into one NFS subnetwork, called a *domain* (not to be confused with the Internet domain). Each domain has master and slave machines.

NIS keeps the access information in a set of *maps,* each map corresponding to a particular area or domain of a network. This allows for several groups to use the same NIS master but have different access permissions. The NIS maps do not have to correspond to DNS domains, enabling more versatility in configuration. Maps consist of a set of records in ASCII format, each with an *index key* for fast lookup. The index key is usually the user name. The records have the same structure as normal user files (such as UNIX's /etc/passwd), both for compatibility and for simplicity.

NOTE   The use of NIS does not negate the need for a complete set of access files on each machine, because NIS is loaded after the machine has been booted (and these files are read). The stand-alone files should have access for a system administrator at least, although it is good practice to also include the most frequent users in case of a network crash preventing access to the NIS directories.

NIS is not restricted to the users of a system. Any file can be set up to use NIS, such as the list of machines on a network (UNIX's /etc/hosts file). Thus, only one change needs to be made to these files on any network. A set of aliases also can be managed by NIS.

12

Several NIS-specific commands are involved with the protocol, although most system administrators set up aliases to minimize the impact on users. For most users, only one command is necessary on a regular basis. For UNIX systems, this is the command yppasswd to change a user's password. This is usually aliased to passwd, the normal password change command. Application developers might have to examine the NIS protocol in more detail when writing client/server code that runs on an NIS-based system, but the effects of the distributed system are usually transparent.

Configuring NIS

Earlier today you saw how NIS can be used to provide network-wide access to files that would normally be local, offering greatly improved access for users and administrators. With NIS active, you don't need to maintain a separate current /etc/passwd file on each UNIX system; instead, you can use the NIS master password files to enable global access to any machine on the network.

In this section I look at how to set up NIS on a simple UNIX network. There are many variations of network architecture and configurations, some of which get awfully complex for a network administrator. Although the principles of setting up NIS and NIS domains are the same for all networks, some extra steps are required on very complex setups. For the most part, I look at the basics only. The files that are normally handled by NIS are as follows:

/etc/ethers	Ethernet MAC to IP address mappings
/etc/group	Group access information
/etc/hosts	IP address to hostname mappings
/etc/netmasks	IP network masks
/etc/passwd	User access information
/etc/protocols	Network protocol and number mappings
/etc/rpc	RPC numbers
/etc/services	Port number to TCP/IP protocol mappings

I look at the most commonly used files as I set up the NIS master and NIS slave, as well as looking at what has to be changed on any client machines that want to use NIS.

Setting Up the NIS Domain

NIS domains are usually assigned to group machines together with an NIS master and one or more NIS slaves as backup. An NIS domain doesn't have to be the same as an Internet domain, although for most networks they are identical (in other words, the entire network is the NIS domain). The NIS domain has to have a name, which can also correspond with

12

your Internet domain name. Alternatively, you can set up subsidiary domains for small logical groups in a large corporation, such as domains for accounting, research and development, and marketing.

To set up an NIS domain, you need to decide on the domain name and know the IP address of the NIS master and any NIS slaves. If you have more than one NIS domain established, you need to know which machines are handled by which NIS master. Each machine on the domain (whether one or many domains are established) must be entered into a configuration file to enable the client machine to use NIS.

To set up the NIS domain, you need to log into each client machine on the network and set up the domain name with the following command:

```
domainname domain
```

domain is the domain name the machine uses. You need to be logged in as root or an administrative account with access to the root utilities to set these values. Because this type of command is effective only until the machine is rebooted, it is better to enter the domain name in one of the startup rc scripts. These differ for each version of UNIX, so you should check your rc commands to find out where to embed the domain name. Usually it is in a file under the /etc/rc.d directory.

NIS Daemons

NIS uses several daemons on the server and on all clients to enable the NIS system. On the NIS master and any NIS slaves, the daemon is usually called ypserv. The ypserv daemon waits for incoming client requests for service, then handles them.

On the clients, the process ypbind is used. This is responsible for connecting with the NIS master when the machine boots and determining any resolution steps necessary to handle logins and other network configuration information handled by NIS. The process of having ypbind connect to the NIS master and establish procedures is called a binding, because the client is bound to the master for requests.

The binding process begins with ypbind sending out a broadcast message for any NIS masters on the network to respond with their IP address and the port number to send requests on. If more than one NIS master responds to the request, only the first received reply is used. If for some reason ypbind finds it isn't getting replies from the NIS master, it assumes that the master has crashed and retransmits a request for a master.

You can find out which NIS master any client machine is bound to with the command ypwhich. It usually responds with the name of the NIS master, as shown here:

```
$ ypwhich
merlin
```

Setting Up an NIS Master

Setting up an NIS master is usually straightforward. Begin by verifying the existing files on the master machine, such as /etc/passwd and /etc/group, to ensure that the information is accurate and current. You should remove any expired or unwanted accounts, for example, and verify that all the login directories and commands are correct. While you are examining the /etc/passwd file, check to make sure that all accounts have passwords. If they don't, either assign a password or remove the account. With a network-wide NIS system in place, anyone can exploit these security holes to gain access to any machine on the network, including the NIS master and gateway machines.

Once the files are ready for NIS map generation, make sure you are logged in as root (to set the proper ownerships and ensure full access to the filesystem). The NIS maps are generated from the standard UNIX files, using the ypinit command with the -m option. The -m option indicates that this machine is the NIS master. From the root prompt, issue the following command:

```
/usr/sbin/ypinit -m
```

The path to the ypinit program might be different on your UNIX system. Check the path if the command produces an error message when trying to execute.

When the ypinit command executes, it scans all the NIS files named in the file /var/yp and produces the NIS maps that are used by the client processes. The /var/yp file might have a different directory name on some systems, such as SCO UNIX, which uses /etc/yp as a directory for all NIS files. Check your UNIX system documentation or man pages for proper file locations. The /var/yp file contains a list of all the maps to be generated, and usually you do not have to make any changes to this file.

A new directory (usually called /var/yp/domainname, where domainname is the NIS domain name) is created. The maps are placed in this new directory. If you are setting up more than one domain all handled by the same NIS master machine, the maps for each domain are beneath the domain name's subdirectory.

As the last step in ypinit, you are asked which machines are NIS slave servers, at which point you should enter their names. The slave names are saved in a file in the domain directory.

After the maps have been generated properly, you can start the ypserv daemon. It is best to automate the startup by editing the startup rc files to do this for you when the machine boots. There is a section in an rc file (usually the one that starts RPC) that looks like this:

```
if [ -f /etc/yp/ypserv -a -d /var/yp/'domainname' ]
then
  /etc/yp/ypserv
fi
```

This script checks for the existence of the directory /var/yp/domainname, where domainname is the domain name for your NIS domain. The entry on the first line where domainname is located must be in single back quotes, which means the shell should execute the `domainname` command and use the results. If the directory exists, the `ypserv` daemon is started. You should replace the directory paths with those used by your UNIX system.

To manually start the `ypserv` daemon, log in as root and issue the command

```
/etc/yp/ypserv
```

or whatever the path to your `ypserv` daemon is.

Next, you need to start the `ypbind` daemon on the server, too (otherwise, `ypserv` can't find the maps). Again, this is usually done through the rc startup scripts with an entry like this:

```
if [ -d /var/yp ]
then
  /etc/yp/ypbind
fi
```

Again, you should verify that the directory path is correct. You can start the `ypbind` daemon manually by issuing it on the command line when logged in as root. Make sure the directory path is correct when you do so.

If you want to perform a quick test of the NIS daemons, issue a command like this one at the command line:

```
ypmatch tparker passwd
```

The `ypmatch` command asks NIS to use the maps to match up the next argument with the map of the third argument's name. In this example, `ypmatch` is instructed to look in the `passwd` file (`passwd` is the alias to `passwd.byname`) for the entry for `tparker`. You should get back the line that matches. You can use any combination of map alias and entry that you know exists to test the NIS server daemon.

Setting Up NIS Slaves

To set up an NIS slave, the NIS master must be configured and running. When you are sure the master is operational, log in as root to the machine to be set up as the NIS slave. The domain name of the slave must be properly set before the configuration can proceed, so check the startup rc commands for the entry that sets the `domainname` variable or use the `domainname` command to set the domain name.

To set up the NIS slave and propagate the NIS files from the master to the slave, issue the command

```
/etc/yp/ypbind
```

substituting for whatever path is correct on your system. Check that the binding to the master is correct by issuing the `ypwhich` command. It should return the NIS master name.

12

Finally, issue the command

```
/etc/yp/ypinit -s servername
```

where the path is correct and *servername* is the name of your NIS master. The `ypbind -s` option sets the local machine up as a slave. The `ypbind` command sets up directories on the local machine and transfers all the maps from the master to the slave.

After the setup is complete, you can test the slave setup with the `ypmatch` command, as shown in the previous section.

To update the maps on the slaves at regular intervals, the `ypxfr` command is used on the slave, followed by the name of the map to be transferred. For example the command

```
ypxfer passwd.byname
```

transfers the `passwd.byname` file from the master to the slave. Most administrators create a set of `cron` entries for transferring all the NIS files at regular intervals (such as nightly). You can also use a script file executed by a network administrator.

Setting Up NIS Clients

Setting up an NIS client requires that you have the `domainname` set properly, either with the `domainname` command or an entry in the rc startup files, and that the `ypbind` command has been issued properly and the NIS client is bound to the NIS server.

As mentioned earlier, when an entry in the `/etc/passwd` or `/etc/group` file must be searched for a match, the local files are examined first, then the server is queried if no match is found. To instruct your client to go to the NIS master to match a login, you need to add the following entry to the bottom of the `/etc/passwd` file:

```
+:*:0:0:::
```

If you know the format of the `/etc/passwd` file entries, you will recognize this as a legal entry with no information specified. The plus sign in the username field is to instruct `ypbind` to query the NIS master. This is called a marker entry. The plus sign entry can be anywhere in the file. When it is reached, NIS is used, then the file is read as before if no match has been found.

RPC and NFS Administration

RPC and NFS have two primary administration tools available for providing status updates and indications of trouble within the system: `rpcinfo` and `nfsstat`. Usually these tools are not available to end users, although it is useful to know of their existence and their role in monitoring NFS and RPC.

Running any single tool is usually not sufficient to isolate a problem. Often one tool reports a problem with a port, but upon closer examination it is found that the port is functioning but the process at the other end died. Therefore, these tools are designed to be used as a complement to each other until an accurate diagnosis can be reached.

rpcinfo

The rpcinfo program monitors the port mapper of the machine on which it is running, and through the network, the port mappers of servers. Because the port mapper is the program that controls access to RPCs, this type of information is important in tracking problems. The rpcinfo program can display the contents of the mapping tables, showing the port and program numbers for each connection, and can activate remote servers for testing a connection.

Typically, rpcinfo is called with the -p option to show the list of RPC programs that are currently tracked by the port mapper. An optional machine name can be added to display only connections with one machine. A typical output from the rpcinfo program is shown here:

```
$ rpcinfo -p
   program vers proto   port
    100000    2   tcp    111  portmapper
    100000    2   udp    111  portmapper
    100008    1   udp   1026  walld
    150001    1   udp   1027  pcnfsd
    150001    2   udp   1027  pcnfsd
    100002    1   udp   1028  rusersd
    100002    2   udp   1028  rusersd
    100024    1   udp   1029  status
    100024    1   tcp   1024  status
    100020    1   udp   1034  llockmgr
    100020    1   tcp   1025  llockmgr
    100021    2   tcp   1026  nlockmgr
    100021    1   tcp   1027  nlockmgr
    100021    1   udp   1038  nlockmgr
    100021    3   tcp   1028  nlockmgr
    100021    3   udp   1039  nlockmgr
```

In case of a problem contacting the port mapper, rpcinfo returns an error message. In such a case, the port mapper is not functioning correctly and there may be no contact with other machines. A check using ping verifies this. An example of this kind of fatal error message is shown here:

```
$ rpcinfo -p
rpcinfo: can't contact port mapper:
RFC: Remote system errer -125
```

12

Specific connections can be tested with rpcinfo by using the machine and process name, as the following example shows:

```
$ rpcinfo -u merlin walld
program 100008 version 1 is ready and waiting
```

Note that the -u option is used for UDP connections, whereas -t must be used with TCP connections. In this example, the client rpcinfo sent a request to the program specified and waited for a reply. A successful reply results in the message shown here. If a reply is not received before a timer expires, an error message is displayed.

In the previous sample output, there is a process called pcnfsd, which is an RPC server developed for use with MS-DOS based machines. It handles access rights and spooling services for the DOS side, while simplifying the DOS machine's access to NFS services.

nfsstat

The nfsstat program, as its name suggests, provides statistics about the number and type of RPC requests that are made. It is usually called without an option, although several exist (depending on the implementation and version) to show specific statistics or sample only certain parts of the connection.

The output from nfsstat is shown here for a typical small network:

```
Server rpc:
calls       badcalls    nullrecv    badlen      xdrcall
10465       0           0           0           0

Server nfs:
calls       badcalls
10432       0
null        getattr     setattr     root        lookup      readlink    read
1 0%        24 0%        1 0%       0 0%        10123 0%    0 0%        5 0%
wrcache     write       create      remove      rename      link        symlink
0 0%        2 0%        0 0%        1 0%        0 0%        1 0%        0 0%

Client rpc:
calls       badcalls    retrans     badxid      timeout     wait        newcred
8273        2           0           0           0           0           0

Client nfs:
calls       badcalls
8263        0
null        getattr     setattr     root        lookup      readlink    read
1 0%        24 0%        1 0%       0 0%        10123 0%    0 0%        5 0%
wrcache     write       create      remove      rename      link        symlink
0 0%        2 0%        0 0%        1 0%        0 0%        1 0%        0 0%
```

12

The output from nfsstat is useful for diagnosing connection problems. The value shown as badcalls shows the number of defective RPC message processed by the system. The values for nullrecv and badlen show the number of empty or incomplete messages. The value for xdrcall shows the number of errors in understanding messages.

For the client side, badxid shows the number of received messages that did not match with a sent request (based on the identification numbers). The timeout and retrans values show the number of times a message had to be resent. If these numbers are high, it usually means the connection is too slow or there is a fault with UDP. The wait value shows the number of times a process had to be delayed because of a lack of available ports.

These types of statistics are useful for configuring RPC properly. System administrators can adjust (tweak) values for the NFS system and monitor their effects on performance over time.

Summary

The Network File System has a reputation for being complex and ornery. It is neither. Instead, NFS is an elegant solution to a problem and one in common usage. Today I have examined the concept and basic architecture of NFS, hopefully without getting bogged down in the details.

I have also shown you how NIS works, and how to set it up on a network. Although every network is not necessarily a target for NIS, it is a very handy service that is part of the TCP/IP family.

Q&A

Q What does NFS do, in one sentence?

A NFS enables an application to read and write files residing on remote machines as though they were on the local filesystem.

Q Define client and server as used in NFS.

A Despite complex definitions from the computer industry, this one is really easy. A client issues a request. A server answers it.

Q What is the role of RPC in NFS?

A The Remote Procedure Call protocol handles message exchange between NFS-based systems. It is a set of procedures that can be called by clients.

Q What does a port mapper do?

A The port mapper provides a correlation between the ports on a machine and the applications that use them.

12

Q What does the Kernel Lock Manager do?

A The Kernel Lock Manager is involved in file locking, preventing access to files or filesystems. A file lock request is issued by clients when they want exclusive access to a file. The Kernel Lock Manager handles file lock requests.

Quiz

1. Show how the NFS layers compare to the OSI Reference Model.
2. Explain how a port mapper assigns ports.
3. What is External Data Representation?
4. What does the Mount protocol do?
5. What is REX? What advantage does REX offer other similar utilities?

Chapter 13

Managing and Troubleshooting TCP/IP

Today you will not learn how to configure and manage a network. The reason is simple: network management and configuration is a very complex issue that can be only briefly examined in a single chapter. If you are assigned the task of network administrator, there are a few good books available that help a little, but the only real teacher of network administration and troubleshooting is experience. The more you work with networks, the more you learn. Today's text presents an overview of network topologies and configuration issues and examines the basic steps in troubleshooting faulty TCP/IP systems. Remember that this is an overview only, intended to provide you with the background to the administration process.

Traditionally, network management means two different tasks: monitoring and controlling the network. *Monitoring* means watching the network's behavior to ensure that it is functioning smoothly and watching for potential troublespots. *Controlling* means changing the network while it is running, altering the configuration in some manner to improve performance or affect parts that are not functioning correctly.

On Day 1, "Open Systems, Standards, and Protocols," I looked at the ISO standards; ISO addresses networks, as well. ISO goes further than just two aspects of network administration, however, dividing network management into five parts defined within the Open Systems Interconnection Reference Model (OSI-RM). These five parts are called Specific Management Functional Areas (SMFAs) in the standard. The five aspects are as follows:

- **Accounting management:** Providing information on costs and account usage.
- **Configuration management:** Managing the actual configuration of the network.
- **Fault management:** Detecting, isolating, and correcting faults, including maintaining error logs and diagnostics.
- **Performance management:** Maintaining maximum efficiency and performance, including gathering statistics and maintaining logs.
- **Security management:** Maintaining a secure system and managing access.

The five groups have some overlap, especially between performance and fault management. However, the division of the network management tasks can help account for all the necessary aspects. In some cases, large organizations have dedicated people for each group. For many smaller LANs, the role of handling all the problems usually falls to one person, who seldom worries about whether his or her actions are ISO-compliant.

Network Management Standards

The Internet Advisory Board (IAB) has developed or adopted several standards for network management. These have been, for the most part, specifically designed to fit TCP/IP requirements, although they do, whenever possible, meet the OSI architecture. An Internet working group responsible for the network management standards adopted a two-stage approach to provide for current and future needs.

The first step involves the use of the Simple Network Management Protocol (SNMP), which was designed and implemented by the working group. SNMP is currently used on many Internet networks, and it is integrated into many commercially available products. As technology has improved, SNMP has evolved and become more encompassing.

The second step involves OSI network management standards, called the Common Management Information Services (CMIS) and Common Management Information Protocol (CMIP), both to be used in future implementations of TCP/IP. The IAB has published *Common Management Information Services and Protocol over TCP/IP* (*CMOT*) as a standard for TCP/IP and OSI management.

Both SNMP and CMOT use the concept of network managers exchanging information with processes within network devices such as workstations, bridges, routers, and multiplexers.

13

The primary management station communicates with the different management processes, building information about the status of the network. The architecture of both SNMP and CMOT is such that the information collected is stored in a manner that enables other protocols to read it.

The SNMP manager handles the overall software and communications between the devices using the SNMP communications protocol. Support software provides a user interface, enabling a network manager to observe the condition of the overall system and individual components and monitor any specific network device.

SNMP-managed devices all contain the SNMP agent software and a database called the Management Information Base (MIB). I look at the SNMP protocol and MIB layout later today, but for now a quick overview should help you understand how SNMP is used for network management. The MIB has 126 fields of information about the device status, performance of the device, its connections to different devices, and its configuration. The SNMP manager queries the MIB through the agent software and can specify changes to the configuration. Most SNMP managers query agents at a regular interval, such as 15 minutes, unless instructed otherwise by the user.

The SNMP agent software is usually quite small (typically less than 64KB) because the SNMP protocol is simple. SNMP is designed to be a polling protocol, meaning that the manager issues messages to the agent. For efficiency and small size of executable programs, SNMP messages are enclosed within a UDP datagram and routed via IP (although many other protocols could be used). There are five message types available in SNMP:

- **Get request:** Used to query an MIB.
- **Get next request:** Used to read sequentially through an MIB.
- **Get response:** Used for a response to a get request message.
- **Set request:** Used to set a value in the MIB.
- **Trap:** Used to report events.

UDP port 161 is used for all messages except traps, which arrive on UDP port 162. Agents receive their messages from the manager through the agent's UDP port 161.

Despite its widespread use, SNMP has some disadvantages. The most important might also be an advantage, depending on your point of view: the reliance on UDP. Because UDP is connectionless, there is no reliability inherent in the message sending. Another problem is that SNMP provides only a simple messaging protocol, so filtering messages cannot be performed. This increases the load on the receiving software. Finally, SNMP uses polling, which consumes a considerable amount of bandwidth. The trade-offs between SNMP and its more recent successor, CMIP, will make decisions regarding a management protocol more difficult in the future.

13

SNMP enables proxy management, which means that a device with an SNMP agent and MIB can communicate with other devices that do not have the full SNMP agent software. This proxy management lets other devices be controlled through a connected machine by placing the device's MIB in the agent's memory. For example, a printer can be controlled through proxy management from a workstation acting as an SNMP agent, which also runs the proxy agent and MIB for the printer.

Proxy management can be useful to off-load some devices that are under heavy load. For example, it is common under SNMP to use proxy to handle authentication processes, which can consume considerable resources, by passing this function to a less heavily used machine. Proxy systems can also affect the processing that needs to be performed at a bridge, for example, by having a proxy reformat the datagrams arriving, again to off-load the bridge from that time-consuming task.

After providing a quick overview, I can now look at SNMP in more detail. If you are satisfied with the overview, you can skip the next section, because most users never need to know about the make-up and layout of SNMP and MIB. If you want to know what's going on in a network, though, this information is invaluable.

What Is SNMP?

The Simple Network Management Protocol (SNMP) was originally designed to provide a means of handling routers on a network. SNMP, although part of the TCP/IP family of protocols, is not dependent on IP. SNMP was designed to be protocol-independent (so it could run under IPX from Novell's SPX/IPX just as easily, for example), although the majority of SNMP installations use IP on TCP/IP networks.

SNMP is not a single protocol but three protocols that together make up a family, all designed to work toward administration goals. The protocols that make up the SNMP family and their roles follow:

- ☐ **Management Information Base (MIB):** A database containing status information
- ☐ **Structure and Identification of Management Information (SMI):** A specification that defines the entries in an MIB
- ☐ **Simple Network Management Protocol (SNMP):** The method of communicating between managed devices and servers

Peripherals that have SNMP capabilities built-in run a management agent software package, either loaded as part of a boot cycle or embedded in firmware in the device. These devices with SNMP agents are called by a variety of terms depending on the vendor, but they are known as SNMP-manageable or SNMP-managed devices. SNMP-compliant devices also have the code for SNMP incorporated into their software or firmware. When SNMP exists on a device, it is called a managed device.

13

SNMP-managed devices communicate with SNMP server software located somewhere on the network. The device talks to the server in two ways: polled and interrupt. A polled device has the server communicate with the device, asking for its current condition or statistics. The polling is often done at regular intervals, with the server connecting with all the managed devices on the network. The problem with polling is that information is not always current, and network traffic rises with the number of managed devices and frequency of polling.

An interrupt-based SNMP system has the managed device send messages to the server when some conditions warrant. This way, the server knows of any problems immediately (unless the device crashes, in which case notification must be from another device that tried to connect to the crashed device). Interrupt-based devices have their own problems. Primary among the problems is the need to assemble a message to the server, which can require a lot of CPU cycles, all of which are taken away from the device's normal task. This can cause bottlenecks and other problems on that device. If the message to be sent is large, as it is if it contains a lot of statistics, the network can suffer a noticeable degradation while the message is assembled and transmitted.

If there is a major failure somewhere on the network, such as a power grid going down and uninterruptible power supplies kicking in, each SNMP-managed device might try to send interrupt-driven messages to the server at the same time to report the problem. This can swamp the network and result in incorrect information at the server.

A combination of polling and interruption is often used to get by all these problems. The combination is called trap-directed polling, and it involves the server polling for statistics at intervals or when directed by the system administrator. In addition, each SNMP-managed device can generate an interrupt message when certain conditions occur, but these tend to be more rigorously defined than in a pure interrupt-driven system. For example, if you use interrupt-only SNMP, a router might report load increases every 10 percent. If you use trap-directed polling, you know the load from the regular polling and can instruct the router to send an interrupt only when a significant increase in load is experienced. After receiving an interrupt message with trap-directed polling, the server can further query the device for more details, if necessary.

An SNMP server software package can communicate with the SNMP agents and transfer or request several types of information. Usually, the server requests statistics from the agent, including number of packets handled, status of the device, special conditions associated with the device type (such as out-of-paper indications or loss of connection from a modem), and processor load.

The server can also send instructions to the agent to modify entries in its database (the Management Information Base). The server can also send thresholds or conditions under which the SNMP agent should generate an interrupt message to the server, such as when CPU load reaches 90 percent.

13

Communications between the server and agent occur in a fairly straightforward manner, although they tend to use abstract notation for message contents. For example, the server might send a What is your current load message and receive back a 75% message. The agent never sends data to the server unless an interrupt is generated or a poll request is made. This means that some long-standing problems can exist without the SNMP server knowing about them, simply because a poll wasn't conducted or an interrupt generated.

Management Information Base (MIB)

Every SNMP-managed device maintains a database that contains statistics and other data. These databases are called a Management Information Base, or MIB. The MIB entries have four pieces of information in them: an object type, a syntax, an access field, and a status field. MIB entries are usually standardized by the protocols and follow strict formatting rules defined by Abstract Syntax Notation One (ASN.1).

The object type is the name of the particular entry, usually as a simple name. The syntax is the value type, such as a string or integer. Not all entries in an MIB have a value. The access field is used to define the level of access to the entry, normally defined by the values read-only, read-write, write-only, and not accessible. The status field contains an indication of whether the entry in the MIB is mandatory (which means the managed device must implement the entry), optional (the managed device can implement the entry), or obsolete (not used).

There are two types of MIB in use, called MIB-1 and MIB-2. The structures are different. MIB-1 was used starting in 1988 and has 114 entries in the table, divided into groups. For a managed device to claim to be MIB-1 compatible, it must handle all the groups that are applicable to it. For example, a managed printer doesn't have to implement all the entries that deal with the Exterior Gateway Protocol (EGP), which is usually implemented only by routers and similar devices.

MIB-2 is a 1990 enhancement of MIB-1, made up of 171 entries in ten groups. The additions expand on some of the basic group entries in MIB-1 and add three new groups. As with MIB-1, an SNMP device that claims to be MIB-2 compliant must implement all those groups that are applicable to that type of device. You will find many devices that are MIB-1 compliant but not MIB-2.

In addition to MIB-1 and MIB-2, several experimental MIBs in use add different groups and entries to the database. None of these have been widely adopted, although some show promise. Some MIBs have also been developed by individual corporations for their own use, and some vendors offer compatibility with these MIBs. For example, Hewlett-Packard developed an MIB for their own use that some SNMP-managed devices and software server packages support.

Simple Network Management Protocol

The Simple Network Management Protocol (SNMP) has been through several iterations. The most commonly used version is called SNMP v1. Usually SNMP is used as an asynchronous client/server application, meaning that either the managed device or the SNMP server software can generate a message to the other and wait for a reply, if one is expected. These are packaged and handled by the network software (such as IP) as any other packet would be. SNMP uses UDP as a message transport protocol. UDP port 161 is used for all messages except traps, which arrive on UDP port 162. Agents receive their messages from the manager through the agent's UDP port 161.

☐ The first major release of SNMP, SNMP v1, was designed for relatively simple operations, relatively easy implementation by device manufacturers, and good portability to operating systems.

When a request is sent, some of the fields in the SNMP entry are left blank. These are filled in by the client and returned. This is an efficient method of transferring the question and answer in one block, eliminating complex look-up algorithms to find out what query a received answer applies to.

The get command, for example, is sent with the Type and Value fields in the message set to NULL. The client sends back a similar message with these two fields filled in (unless they don't apply, in which case a different error message is returned).

SNMP v2 adds some new capabilities to the older SNMP version, the most handy of which for servers is the get-bulk operation. This lets a large number of MIB entries be sent in one message, instead of requiring multiple get-next queries with SNMP v1. In addition, SNMP v2 has much better security than SNMP v1, preventing unwanted intruders from monitoring the state or condition of managed devices. Both encryption and authentication are supported by SNMP v2. SNMP v2 is a more complex protocol and is not as widely used as SNMP v1.

Despite its widespread use, SNMP has a few disadvantages. The most important is its reliance on UDP. Because UDP is connectionless, there is no reliability inherent in messaging between server and agent. Another problem is that SNMP provides only a simple messaging protocol, so filtering messages cannot be performed. This increases the load on the receiving software. Finally, SNMP almost always uses polling to some degree, which consumes a considerable amount of bandwidth.

Setting Up SNMP Under UNIX

Although many operating systems support SNMP and enable you to configure its use, SNMP remains a very UNIX-oriented protocol. Chances are, if there's a UNIX box on your network, SNMP is based on the UNIX machine. Other operating systems such as Windows NT support SNMP client and server software—and they are usually very easy to set up and manage— but for this section I bow to the majority and look only at UNIX.

Most UNIX versions include both the client and server software as part of the operating system. The client software is executed through the `snmpd` daemon, which usually runs all the time when SNMP is used on the network. Normally, the `snmpd` daemon is started automatically when the system boots; it is controlled through the `rc` startup files. When SNMP starts, the daemon reads several configuration files. On most SNMP agents, the files that `snmpd` reads are as follows:

```
/etc/inet/snmpd.conf

/etc/inet/snmpd.comm

/etc/inet/snmpd.trap
```

The directories these files are under might be different for each UNIX version, so you should check the filesystem for their proper location.

The `snmpd.conf` file contains four system MIB objects. Most of the time these objects are set during installation, but you might want to verify their contents. A sample `snmpd.conf` file is shown here:

```
#       @(#)snmpd.conf    6.3 8/21/93 - STREAMware TCP/IP  source
#
# Copyrighted as an unpublished work.
# (c) Copyright 1987-1993 Lachman Technology, Inc.
# All rights reserved.
descr=SCO TCP/IP Runtime Release 2.0.0
objid=SCO.1.2.0.0
contact=Tim Parker  tparker@tpci.com
location=TPCI Int'l HQ, Ottawa
```

In many `snmpd.conf` files you have to fill out the `contact` and `location` fields yourself (which define the contact user and physical location of the system), but the `descr` and `objid` fields should be left as they are. The variables defined in the `snmpd.conf` file correspond to MIB variables as shown in Table 13.1.

Table 13.1. `snmpd.comf` **and MIB variables.**

`snmpd.comf` Variables	MIB Variables
descr	sysDescr
objid	sysObjectID
contact	sysContact
location	sysLocation

The snmpd.comm (community) file is used to provide authentication information and a list of hosts that have access to the local database. Access by a remote machine to the local SNMP data is provided by including the remote machine's name in the snmpd.comm file. A sample snmpd.comm file looks like this:

```
#       @(#)snmpd.comm    6.5 9/9/93 - STREAMware TCP/IP  source
accnting    0.0.0.0       READ
r_n_d       147.120.0.1   WRITE
public      0.0.0.0       READ
interop     0.0.0.0       READ
```

Each line in the snmpd.comm file has three fields: the community name, the IP address of the remote machine, and the privileges the community has. If the IP address is set to 0.0.0.0, any machine can communicate with that community name. The privileges can be READ for read-only, WRITE for read and write, and NONE to prevent access by that community. Read and write access are references to capabilities to change MIB data, not filesystems.

The snmpd.trap file specifies the name of hosts to whom a trap message must be sent when a critical event is noticed. A sample snmpd.trap file looks like this:

```
#       @(#)snmpd.trap    6.4 9/9/93 - STREAMware TCP/IP  source
superduck  147.120.0.23   162
```

Each line in the snmpd.trap file has three fields: the name of the community, its IP address, and the UDP port to use to send traps.

SNMP Commands

UNIX offers several SNMP-based commands for network administrators to obtain information from an MIB or an SNMP-compliant device. The exact commands vary a little depending on the implementation, but most SNMP systems support the commands shown in Table 13.2.

Table 13.2. SNMP commands.

Command	Description
getone	Uses the SNMP get command to retrieve a variable value
getnext	Uses the SNMP getnext command to retrieve the next variable value
getid	Retrieves the values for sysDescr, sysObjectID, and sysUpTime
getmany	Retrieves an entire group of MIB variables
snmpstat	Retrieves the contents of SNMP data structures
getroute	Retrieves routing information
setany	Uses the SNMP set command to set a variable value

13

Most of the SNMP commands require an argument that specifies the information to be set or retrieved. The output from some of the commands given in Table 13.2 is shown in the following extract from an SNMP machine on a small local area network:

```
$ getone merlin udpInDatagrams.0
Name: udpInDatagrams.0
Value: 6
$ getid merlin public
Name: sysDescr.0
Value: UNIX System V Release 4.3
Name: sysObjectID.0
Value: Lachman.1.4.1
Name: sysUpTime.0
Value: 62521
```

None of the SNMP commands can be called user-friendly, because their responses are terse and sometimes difficult to analyze. For this reason, many GUI-based network analyzers are becoming popular, offering menu-based access to many SNMP functions and better presentation of data. The use of a GUI-based SNMP tool can present full-color graphical displays of network statistics in a real-time manner. However, these GUI tools tend to cost a considerable amount.

Network Topologies

I briefly examined both LAN and WAN topologies on Day 1, looking at bus and ring networks and the connections between LANs to make a WAN, so that material should be somewhat familiar to you. You can now extend your attention from the LAN topology to the larger internetworked topology by using TCP/IP. To do that, I must tie the role of routers, bridges, and similar devices into the network topology and show their role in a TCP/IP system.

One useful concept to keep in mind is the 80/20 rule, which states that 80 percent of most network traffic is for local machines, and 20 percent needs to move off the LAN. In reality, the ratio of local traffic is usually much higher, but planning for an 80/20 split helps establish workable limits for connections to network backbones.

LANs are tied to a larger network backbone (either a WAN or an internetwork such as the Internet) through a device that handles the passage of datagrams between the LAN and the backbone. In a simple setup, a router performs this function. This is shown in Figure 13.1. Routers connect networks that use different link layer protocols or Media Access Control (MAC) protocols. Routers examine only the headers of datagrams that are specifically sent to them or are broadcast messages, but there is a lot of processing involved within the router.

Figure 13.1.

A router connects a LAN to the backbone.

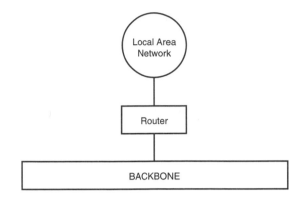

If two or more LANs are involved in one organization and there is the possibility of a lot of traffic between them, it is better to connect the two LANs directly with a bridge instead of loading the backbone with the cross-traffic. This is shown in Figure 13.2. Bridges can also connect two WANs using a high-speed line, as shown in Figure 13.3.

Figure 13.2.

Using a bridge to connect two LANs.

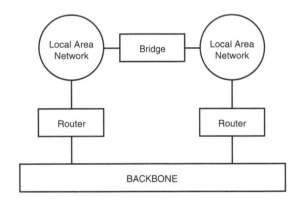

Figure 13.3.

Using a bridge to connect two WANs.

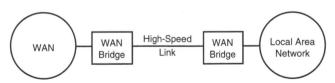

You might recall that bridges are used when the same network protocol is on both LANs, although the bridge does not care which physical media is used. Bridges can connect twisted-pair LANs to coaxial LANs, for example, or act as an interface to a fiber optic network. As long as the Media Access Control (MAC) protocol is the same, the bridge functions properly.

Many high-end bridges available today configure themselves automatically to the networks they connect and learn the physical addresses of equipment on each LAN by monitoring traffic. One problem with bridges is that they examine each datagram that passes through them, checking the source and destination addresses. This adds overhead and slows the routing through the bridge. (As mentioned earlier, routers don't examine each datagram.)

In a configuration using bridges between LANs or WANs, traffic from one LAN to another can be sent through the bridge instead of onto the backbone, providing better performance. For services such as Telnet and FTP, the speed difference between using a bridge and going through a router onto a heavily used backbone can be appreciable. If the backbone is not under the direct administration of the LAN's administrators (as with the Internet), having a bridge also provides a method for the corporation or organization to control the connection.

The use of a bridge has one other advantage: if the backbone fails, communications between the two LANs are not lost. The same applies, of course, if the bridge fails, because the backbone can be used as a rerouting path. For critical networks, backbones are usually duplicated for redundancy. In the same manner, most organizations have duplicate routers and bridges in case of failure.

Bridges can be used when splitting a large LAN into smaller networks. This is often necessary when a LAN continues to expand as new equipment is added. Eventually the network traffic becomes bottlenecked. A useful and relatively easy solution is to divide the larger LAN into smaller LANs connected over a backbone. This helps conform to the 80/20 rule, while simplifying the traffic and administration overhead. This is shown in Figure 13.4. If the backbone is carefully chosen with lots of excess capacity, this type of topology can account for sizable future growth.

Figure 13.4.

Dividing a large LAN into several smaller LANs.

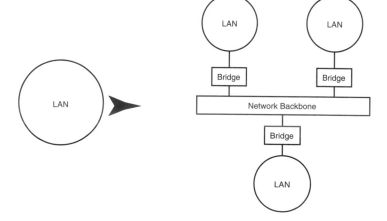

Routers, too, can be used to control large networks. This is an advantage when broadcasts are frequently used, because the router can filter out broadcasts that apply only to a specific LAN. (Most bridges propagate broadcasts across the network.) The use of a single *switching router* or *hub router* is becoming popular for joining different LANs within an organization, as shown as in Figure 13.5.

Figure 13.5.
Using a hub router to connect LANs.

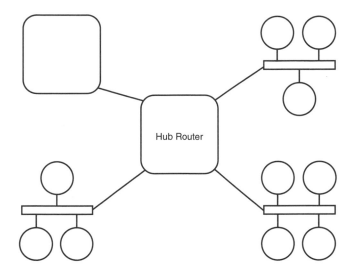

When large networks are necessary, several routers can be used to split the load. Intelligent network routers can optimize the routing of datagrams, as well as monitor and control network traffic and bottlenecks at any location.

On many occasions the advantages of a bridge and a router together are ideal. These combined devices, called *brouters,* are now making an appearance. Brouters can perform routing with some messages and bridging with others by examining incoming datagrams and using a filter mask to decide which function is performed. Brouters have the capability to handle multiple protocols, much like routers.

Configuring a Network

Equipment available today is much more capable than was available when TCP/IP began its development cycle. In some ways, this has simplified the task of adding to or configuring a network, but it has also posed some problems of its own. Most equipment can be added to a network by simply attaching the network medium (such as a coaxial or twisted-pair cable) and configuring the interface with the IP address and domain name.

13

Of course, the more complicated the network, the more work must be done. Configuring a bridge, for example, can be as simple as connecting it to the networks it serves. Most bridges can autoconfigure themselves and watch the network traffic to build a table of network addresses. However, adding filters to restrict traffic or limiting access through blocking ports requires more detailed configuration processes.

Configuring a network and TCP/IP is not difficult, but it can be time-consuming. Different operating systems approach the task in a variety of ways. UNIX, for example, uses a large number of small configuration files scattered throughout the file system. IBM mainframes use a single large file. Configurations on some systems use a menu-driven interface that guides the user through all the necessary steps, ensuring that no errors are made.

For most networks and their interface cards, the following information is required:

☐ **Physical address:** Usually provided by the interface manufacturer.

☐ **IP address:** Optional with serial-line interfaces.

☐ **Subnet mask:** Specifies the network address.

☐ **Protocol:** IP, if TCP/IP or UDP is used.

☐ **Routing protocols:** Whether ARP or RARP is used.

☐ **Broadcast address:** Format to use for broadcasts, usually all 1s.

Secondary IP addresses can be used for devices such as routers, which can handle two logical networks. As noted, serial interfaces do not need an IP address, although they can be supplied. Serial interfaces also require a setting to indicate whether the device is configured to act as Data Terminal Equipment (DTE) or Data Communications Equipment (DCE), the serial port's baud rate and parity, and settings for the maximum size of a transmission.

Whatever equipment is used on a network, they all have a physical connection to the network transport medium. Typically this is a network card in a workstation, desktop PC, or printer. Software supplied with the device controls the interface, eliminating most of the worries of matching hardware, software, and protocols. After deciding on an IP address, the setting can be programmed either by switches or software, and the device is ready to talk to the network.

IP addresses can be chosen at random by the system administrator, but this can cause problems when the datagrams are released to a larger internetwork such as the Internet. Ideally, a network mask is assigned by the Network Information Center (NIC). This is then combined with the administrator's own numbering scheme in the LAN to produce the full IP address.

The IP addresses are assigned by the NIC based on the *class* of network, which reflects the size of the organization and the number of local equipment addresses required. As shown in Figure 13.6, there are four NIC-approved IP address structures. Class A addresses are for very large networks that need 24 bits available for local addresses, reducing the network address

13

to 7 bits. Class B assigns 16 bits locally and 14 bits for the network address, whereas Class C enables only 8 bits for local addresses and 21 bits for the network address. Class C networks are for small companies only, because only 256 local addresses can be created. Class D addresses are used for special systems not usually encountered by users.

Figure 13.6.

The four IP address class structures.

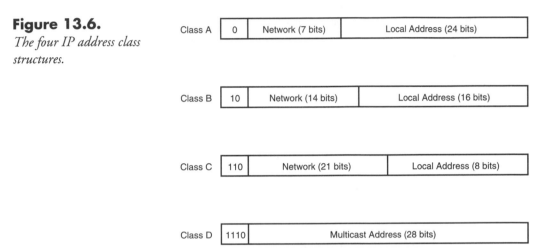

| Class A | 0 | Network (7 bits) | Local Address (24 bits) |

| Class B | 10 | Network (14 bits) | Local Address (16 bits) |

| Class C | 110 | Network (21 bits) | Local Address (8 bits) |

| Class D | 1110 | Multicast Address (28 bits) |

Numbering schemes within a network are left to the administrator's whim, although a convention of assigning low numbers to routers and bridges is usually followed. It is also useful to use Address Resolution Protocol (ARP) on local servers or routers to provide for faster startup when machines query for their IP addresses. This prevents system-wide broadcasts. The manner in which user equipment starts up (whether it uses BOOTP, ARP, or RARP) can affect the configuration of the local servers and routers.

Physical addresses of network connectors seldom have to be changed from their default settings. Most vendors guarantee a unique physical setting for their hardware, so these can usually be maintained with no change. For the conversion of IP address to physical address, this information must be stored in a routing table.

Routing tables for small networks are often created and maintained by hand. Larger networks might involve too many changes for the manual approach to be effective, so a routing protocol such as Routing Information Protocol (RIP) is used. Several routing protocols are available, including RIP and Open Shortest Path First (OSPF). The choice of the routing protocol can be important and usually depends on the size of the network and the connections between subnetworks and external systems. Routing protocols should be started automatically when the network is booted.

13

Configuring the network includes setting the domain name and network IP mask, following the formats approved by the NIC. Many operating systems have utilities that help configure the domain name and network IP mask. The *Domain Administrator's Guide,* which describes the process of forming a domain name, is available from the NIC (RFC 1032). These steps apply only if the network is to connect to the Internet or a similar internetwork. If the network is autonomous with no outside connections, the administrator can choose any network IP mask and domain name (although future connections might force a complete reconfiguration of the network if an NIC-consistent scheme is not used).

Connections to the Internet require an Autonomous System (AS) number from the NIC, which provides other systems with your border router address. Gateway protocols such as the Exterior Gateway Protocol (EGP) or newer Border Gateway Protocol (BGP) must be installed and configured to provide Internet routing.

Also involved in naming are the name-to-address resolution tables, which convert a symbolic name to an IP address. These are usually configured manually, although some automated formatting tools are offered with different operating systems. If the Domain Name System (DNS) is to be implemented, that adds another level of complexity to the name configuration, the details of which are best left to more specialized texts.

Some routers can be configured to filter message traffic. In these cases, the masks used to restrict or enable datagrams must be added to the router tables, as well as any limitations or exceptions to requests for socket services (such as Telnet). Setting ARP tables in routers can help bring up newly started machines more quickly than if a broadcast is sent network-wide to the primary ARP server. Several routers can be configured for priority routing, enabling priority based on the protocol, type of service, or a selected criterion such as IP address or socket.

Router software can be accessed either locally through a dedicated terminal or over the network. The latter enables a system administrator to log in using Telnet from a machine on the network and then run configuration or maintenance utilities. It is advisable to make access to these utilities extremely limited.

After the network addresses have been established, TCP can be configured. This is normally performed on a per-machine basis using an interface utility. In the TCP software configuration are settings for default window sizes and maximum segment size. If changes over the standard TCP port assignments are required, the configuration files must be edited. Processes that start TCP and monitor ports for connections (such as inetd, described on Day 6, "Telnet and FTP,") must be added to the system startup files. Other services such as electronic mail (which might use a dedicated protocol such as SNMP) must be installed and properly configured.

13

Monitoring and Basic Troubleshooting Utilities

On Days 6 and 7 I looked at TCP/IP network utilities such as ping, finger, ruptime, and netstat, which help determine the status of connections and interfaces. I mention them here again briefly and also introduce some new commands. Several software vendors now offer talented network monitoring products that provide excellent information about the network, its connections, and the traffic it carries. Many of these products also enable dynamic configuration of the system.

The ping (Packet Internet Groper) command is the easiest method for checking a machine's connection to the network. It uses the Internet Control Message Protocol (ICMP) to send a request for response. The ping command is useful with routers, because it can check each interface. Different versions of ping are available, some with different options.

The following output shows a character-based system using ping to check on another machine on the network. The command line uses the -c option to limit the number of packets sent. As you can see, an IP address was used to indicate the destination machine, and the machine translated this to the symbolic name pepper based on the host table.

```
# ping -c5 205.150.89.2
PING 205.150.89.2 (205.150.89.2): 56 data bytes
64 bytes from pepper (205.150.89.2): icmp_seq=0 ttl=32 time=40 ms
64 bytes from pepper (205.150.89.2): icmp_seq=1 ttl=32 time=0 ms
64 bytes from pepper (205.150.89.2): icmp_seq=2 ttl=32 time=0 ms
64 bytes from pepper (205.150.89.2): icmp_seq=3 ttl=32 time=0 ms
64 bytes from pepper (205.150.89.2): icmp_seq=4 ttl=32 time=0 ms

--- 205.150.89.2 ping statistics ---
5 packets transmitted, 5 packets received, 0% packet loss
round-trip min/avg/max = 0/8/40 ms
```

A GUI-based ping utility is shown in Figure 13.7. This shows the ChameleonNFS ping utility sending a single packet to a remote device (in this case a network printer with the IP address 205.150.89.200) and getting a positive response.

Figure 13.7.

ping *can also be used on GUI systems, although usually with fewer options than on UNIX.*

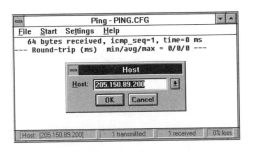

13

A similar utility is spray, which uses a Remote Procedure Call (RPC, discussed on Day 9, "Setting Up a Sample Network: Servers") to send a constant stream of datagrams or ICMP messages. The difference between ping and spray is that spray sends the datagrams constantly, whereas ping has an interval between datagrams. This can be useful for checking burst-mode capabilities of the network. The output of a spray command on a BSD UNIX system looks like this:

```
$ spray -c 5 tpci_sun2
sending 5 packets of lnth 86 to tpci_sun2 ...
   in 0.3 seconds elapsed time,
   1 packets (20.00%) dropped by tpci_sun2
Sent: 19 packets/sec, 1.8K bytes/sec
Rcvd: 16 packets/sec, 1.6K bytes/sec
```

Day 7, "TCP/IP Configuration and Administration Basics," covered the netstat command in some detail. It is useful for checking the status of the network. The implementations of netstat vary widely depending on the operating system version.

Some systems have a utility called traceroute (available as public domain software), which sends a series of UDP datagrams to the target. The datagrams are constructed slightly differently depending on their location in the stream. The first three datagrams have the Time to Live (TTL) field set to 1, meaning the first time a router encounters the message it is returned with an expired message. The next three messages have the TTL field set to 2, and so on, until the destination is reached.

The traceroute output shows the round-trip time of each message (which is useful for identifying bottlenecks in the network) and the efficiency of the routing algorithms (through a number of routers that might not be the best route). A sample output from a traceroute command (all machine names and IP addresses are invented) follows:

```
$ traceroute black.cat.com
1   TPCI.COM (127.01.13.12)            51ms    3ms     4ms
2   BEAST.COM (143.23.1.23)            60ms    5ms     7ms
3   bills_machine.com (121.22.56.1)    121ms   12ms    12ms
4   SuperGateway.com (130.12.14.2)     75ms    13ms    10ms
5   black.cat.com  (122.13.2.12)       45ms    4ms     6ms
```

When dealing with RPC, a utility called rpcinfo can determine which RPC services are currently active on the local or any remote system that supports RPC. The options supported by rpcinfo vary with the implementation, but all enable flags to decide which type of service to check. For example, the -p option displays the local portmapper. The following example shows the options supported on the SCO UNIX version of rpcinfo, as well as the output for the portmapper:

```
$ rpcinfo
Usage: rpcinfo [ -n portnum ] -u host prognum [ versnum ]
       rpcinfo [ -n portnum ] -t host prognum [ versnum ]
       rpcinfo -p [ host ]
       rpcinfo -b prognum versnum
```

13

```
$ rpcinfo -p
   program vers proto   port
    100000   2   tcp     111  portmapper
    100000   2   udp     111  portmapper
    150001   1   udp    1026  pcnfsd
    150001   2   udp    1026  pcnfsd
    100008   1   udp    1027  walld
    100002   1   udp    1028  rusersd
    100002   2   udp    1028  rusersd
    100024   1   udp    1029  status
    100024   1   tcp    1024  status
    100020   1   udp    1034  llockmgr
    100020   1   tcp    1025  llockmgr
    100021   2   tcp    1026  nlockmgr
    100021   1   tcp    1027  nlockmgr
    100021   1   udp    1038  nlockmgr
    100021   3   tcp    1028  nlockmgr
    100021   3   udp    1039  nlockmgr
```

Monitoring NFS (an RPC service) can be more complicated. A few utility programs are available. The snfsstat command displays information about recent calls:

```
$ nfsstat
Server rpc:
calls       badcalls    nullrecv    badlen      xdrcall
458         0           1           2           0

Server nfs:
calls       badcalls
412         2
null        getattr     setattr     root        lookup      readlink    read
0 0%        200 49%     0 0%        0 0%        120 29%     75 18%      126 31%
wrcache     write       create      remove      rename      link        symlink
0 0%        0 0%        0 0%        0 0%        0 0%        0 0%        0 0%
mkdir       rmdir       readdir     fsstat
0 0%        0 0%        52 13%      12 3%

Client rpc:
calls       badcalls    retrans     badxid      timeout     wait        newcred
1206        1           0           0           3           0           0
peekeers    badresps
0           1

Client nfs:
calls       badcalls    nclget      nclsleep
1231        0           1231        0
null        getattr     setattr     root        lookup      readlink    read
0 0%        0 0%        0 0%        0 0%        562 46%     134 11%     137 11%
wrcache     write       create      remove      rename      link        symlink
0 0%        0 0%        0 0%        0 0%        0 0%        0 0%        0 0%
mkdir       rmdir       readdir     fsstat
0 0%        0 0%        239 19%     98 8%
```

The mount program shows which directories are currently mounted, and the command showmount shows the current NFS servers on the system:

13

```
$ mount
pepper:/                /server             nfs ro,bg,intr
pepper:/apps            /server/apps        nfs ro,bg,intr
pepper:/usr             /server/usr         nfs rw,bg,intr
pepper:/u1              /server/u1          nfs rw,bg,intr
$ showmount
m_server.tpci.com
merlin.tpci.com
sco_gate.tpci.com
tpti.tpci.com
```

The mount output shows the directories on the machine named pepper that were mounted onto the local /server directory when the system booted. The permissions for each mounted directory are shown at the end of each line, where ro means read-only and rw means read-write. The bg in the status lines means background, indicating that if the mount fails, the system tries again periodically. The intr option means that keyboard interrupts can be used to halt the reconnection attempts.

Also available as public domain software are nfswatch and nhfsstone. The nfswatch utility monitors all NFS traffic on a server and updates status information at predetermined intervals. This can be useful for watching the load change during the day. The nhfsstone utility is for benchmarking, generating an artificial load, and measuring the results.

A fast method to verify a port's proper functioning is to connect to it with Telnet or FTP. Both programs enable the user to specify the port to use instead of the default. In the following example, port 25 (usually used for mail) is tested:

```
$ telnet tpci_hpws4 25
Trying 127.12.12.126 ...
Connected to tpci_hpws4.
Escape shcracter is '^]'.
220 tpci_hpws4 Sendmail 3.1 ready at Sat, 2 July 94 12:16:54 EST
HELO TPCI_SERVER_1
250 tpci_hpws4 This is garbage typed to force a closed connections as it doesn't
understand this stuff
QUIT
221 tpci_hpws4 closing connection
Connection closed by foreign host.
```

In this example, port 25 received the connection request properly and waited for the mail protocol messages. Because it didn't get any, it closed the connection. This short session establishes that port 25 is functioning properly as far as connections are concerned. It doesn't convey any information about the integrity of the mail transfer protocol, though.

All of these utilities can be combined to provide a troubleshooting checklist for basic problems. These tell you at least where the problem is, if not more. A diagnostic procedure is assembled from the utilities, such as the following:

13

☐ If DNS is on the system, use a DNS utility such as `nslookup` to ensure that DNS is active.

☐ If NFS is used, check it with the `mount` utility.

☐ Use `ping` to check whether a remote machine is alive.

☐ Use `traceroute` to ensure that a routing problem is not occurring. Check all ports of the routers if `traceroute` fails (use the Telnet login process shown previously).

☐ Use `netstat` to examine ICMP messages recently generated.

☐ Try logging into the remote directly with FTP or Telnet.

☐ If RPCs appear to be the problem, use `rpcinfo`.

Of course, if better tools are available from commercial sources, use them to their full advantage. It is important to know that you don't have to spend thousands of dollars on a network monitoring tool, because the utilities supplied with the operating system are often quite capable (if not as fancy or graphically oriented).

Troubleshooting the Network Interface

The physical connection to the network is a suitable starting point for troubleshooting when a problem is not obvious. Because there are many popular network interfaces, each of which must be dealt with in a slightly different manner, some generalizations must be made. The overall approach remains the same, however.

Assuming that the network itself is functional, the most common problems with the network interface are a faulty network card or a bad connector. Checking each is easily done by simple replacement. If the problem persists, the fault is most likely higher in the architecture.

Faulty network transport media (usually cables) are not uncommon. If a device at the end of a cable is not functioning, it is worthwhile to check the cable itself to ensure that a communication path exists. This can be done with a portable computer or terminal, or in some cases a conductivity tester, depending on the network. A systematic testing process can narrow down a network cabling problem to a specific segment.

One overlooked problem arises, not because of a real fault with the network interface or the network itself, but because one device on the network is transmitting a different protocol. This can foul up the entire network and grind it to a halt. (For example, an Ethernet network might have one or more devices set to transmit IEEE 802.3 frames, which are not the same as Ethernet.)

If there is a conversion from one protocol to another, that can be suspect. For example, it is common to find AppleTalk networks running TCP/IP. The IP messages are encapsulated in AppleTalk frames. If the conversion between the two formats (which can occur at a

13

gateway or router) is not clean, some faulty packets might be passed. This can cause network problems.

If the network connections and network interface cards appear to be working (which can be verified with a network analyzer or board swapping), the problem is in a higher layer.

Troubleshooting the Network (IP) Layer

The network layer (where IP resides) can be the most trouble-prone aspect of the network if configuration rules are not followed scrupulously. Because this layer handles routing, any mistakes can cause lost packets, making it appear that a machine on the network is not communicating with the others. ICMP can be a useful tool for troubleshooting this layer.

One of the most common mistakes, especially with large networks, is a duplication of IP addresses. This can be an accident, as a new address is programmed, or a user can move his or her machine and in the process jumble the IP address. It is not uncommon for users to change the IP address by mistake when investigating the software. The network mask must also be correct.

Addressing of packets within the IP layer (where the source and destination IP addresses are encapsulated in the IP header) is another source of problems. Determining destination IP addresses requires communications with another machine, which should hold the necessary information. If the Domain Name Service (DNS) is active, it can contribute to the confusion if the server has faulty tables.

It is necessary for the IP address to be mapped to the physical address. Both ARP and RARP require this table to direct packets over the network. If a network card is changed for any reason, the unique physical address on the board no longer corresponds to the IP address, so messages are rerouted elsewhere. Network administrators must keep close track of any changes to the network hardware in all devices.

Problems can also occur with devices that handle intermediary routing, such as bridges, routers, and brouters. These must be aware of all changes to the network, as well as physical and logical addresses for the devices they are connected to. Specialized protocols such as Routing Information Protocol (RIP) and Open Shortest Path First (OSPF) handle much of this maintenance, but somewhere in the network a manual notation of changes must be made.

There are many potential sources of trouble with the network layer. Even processes that should work without trouble, such as packet fragmentation and reassembly, can cause problems.

Connectivity between machines at both the transport and network levels can be tested using utilities such as ping. A systematic check of machines along a network and out over an

13

internetwork can help isolate problems, not just in the source and destination machines but also in intermediate processors such as routers. The `traceroute` utility can be used for this, also, if it is available.

Troubleshooting TCP and UDP

Assuming the network layer is functioning correctly, the host-to-host software might be a problem. If the software is correctly installed and started (which might sound obvious but is a common cause of failure), a process to isolate the problem must be followed. There are many files involved with both TCP and UDP, differing with each operating system version, so the documentation accompanying the TCP or UDP software should be consulted.

The protocol in use must be determined first: Is the machine using TCP or UDP, and if both, are both failing? Problems such as too many retransmissions or no timeout values can make UDP appear as if it is failing, but TCP would not be affected (unless it uses the same port or too many processes are active).

Port addresses can be problematic, especially with TCP. Each port on a machine can be sent a `ping` message from a remote machine to verify that it is communicating properly. If a port request fails, it might indicate an improper or missing entry in a configuration file. The `finger` utility might also be useful. If messages are passing correctly from one machine to another, the problem is in the configuration of the software, or a higher-level application.

Incorrect configuration parameters can cause TCP or UDP failures. For example, if the send and receive window values for TCP are set to low levels, there might be no opportunity for applications to pass enough information. In this case, it might appear that TCP is at fault. Carefully check all configuration files and settings.

Troubleshooting the Application Layer

Assuming that both IP and TCP or UDP are functioning properly, the application layer is suspect. It is in this layer that higher-level protocols such as the File Transfer Protocol (FTP), Telnet, and SMTP are based. It can be difficult to find problems within the application layer, although a few simple tests help eliminate obvious solutions. Several commercial utilities are available to monitor reception within the application layer.

Assuming that data is getting to the right application (which can be checked with some diagnostic tools or simple programming routines), the problem might be in interpretation. Verify that the communications between two applications are both the same format. More than one application has expected ASCII and received EBCDIC. Diagnostics show the messages moving into the application properly, but they are total gibberish to the application when it tries to interpret them.

13

Assuming that is not the problem, there could be a fault with the applications at either end. Although you might assume that a Telnet program from one vendor would talk to one from another vendor, this is not true in an unfortunately large number of cases. If there are no identical software packages or versions known to work with the other package, this can be difficult to troubleshoot. This kind of cross-application problem is particularly prevalent with mixed-platform systems, such as a PC-based FTP or TCP/IP software package trying to access services on a UNIX host.

Some readily available utilities can be used to monitor the application layer. Some of these utilities are distributed with operating systems, and others are distributed as public domain software. The utility snmpwatch is a network monitoring program that reports on any SNMP variables that change their values. This can be helpful in diagnosing communications problems within SNMP.

The Internet Rover is a network monitoring program that enables testing of several protocols, including Telnet, FTP, and SMTP. Unfortunately, it doesn't work with all operating system variants. Another tool for SMTP testing is mconnect, which verifies connections.

Security

This is not the place for a long discourse on computer security. Instead, I touch on the impact security has on TCP/IP-based networks only in the slightest terms. Security is an important issue and one often overlooked, usually to the administrator's rue. Taking the steps to set up a proper security policy and protecting the system as well as possible should be a mandatory task for every system administrator.

Routers can be significant in a network's security plan. Most routers enable the system administrator to restrict traffic through the router in some manner, either in one direction or both. A router can be set, for example, to prohibit Telnet or rlogin requests from outside the network, but enable through file transfer requests such as FTP. Routers can also prevent traffic into a local network through the router from anywhere outside the network, cutting down on access into (and through) a network.

Routers usually perform this type of traffic filtering by simply looking at the datagram headers for the requested port. If one of the restricted ports is requested, the datagram can be returned to the sender or discarded. Setting the proper access filters from a network router can be an effective and simple manner of restricting outside access.

Unfortunately, the Internet and most networks were simply not designed to prevent unauthorized access or monitoring. These features were usually added as an afterthought, and as such have some problems. Watching network traffic and trapping addresses, user IDs, and passwords is ridiculously easy, so MIT developed Kerberos security protocols to help.

13

Kerberos (named after the three-headed dog guarding the gates of Hades) uses an encryption key and server introduction method to enable access. Kerberos is slowly being adopted as a standard among Internet users (despite some governmental protests), and it works well with the TCP/IP family of protocols. For more information on Kerberos, connect to ATHENA.MIT.EDU over the Internet or send e-mail to that site requesting information.

Summary

I took a brief look at the network management and troubleshooting tools available with TCP/IP. As mentioned in the introduction, both subjects are complex, potentially demanding, and still considered by many to be an art. There are many excellent books on network management, so you are encouraged to scour your library or bookstore for ones that interest you if you want to know more about this subject.

The tools provided within the TCP/IP family give you enough diagnostic resources to isolate the source of practically any software or hardware problem. Sometimes the solution to a problem is simple and can be easily managed through a configuration change. Often, though, a problem is outside the bounds of TCP/IP's protocol, requiring more powerful diagnostic procedures. It is useful to follow the steps outlined in this chapter first, and resort to other systems only when the TCP/IP diagnostics have been unable to help.

System administration and network troubleshooting are both curious tasks. They require a lot of work at times, but there is an undeniable sense of accomplishment when a network runs smoothly or you have tracked down and fixed a problem. Although only a few users in every group are called upon to perform either task, those that do are in for quite an adventure!

Q&A

Q According to the OSI Reference Model, what is the role of fault management?

A Fault management is the detection, isolation, and correction of faults. It also includes the maintenance and checking of error and diagnostic logs. Fault management is one of five Specific Management Functional Areas defined by the ISO as part of the OSI-RM.

Q What are CMIP and CMIS? How do they relate to SNMP?

A CMIP is the Common Management Information Protocol. CMIS is the Common Management Information Service. Both are part of the OSI network management proposal for use as a replacement for SNMP.

13

Q With SNMP, what is proxy management?

A Proxy management is when a device that cannot hold the full SNMP agent software and management information base (MIB) has that information controlled by another machine (its proxy). The proxy communicates with the device being managed. A typical example is a printer attached to a workstation. The workstation acts as the printer's proxy because the printer has no controlling software with it.

Q What four utilities provide the basic TCP/IP troubleshooting information?

A The four utilities most commonly used for troubleshooting a TCP/IP network are `ping`, `finger`, `ruptime`, and `netstat`.

Q When would you use the utility `traceroute`?

A The `traceroute` utility is used to send UDP datagrams to a target machine, one hop at a time. The output from `traceroute` shows each machine that forwards the message, enabling you to follow the route to isolate a problem.

Quiz

1. What are the five parts of the OSI Reference Model dealing with network management (called the Specific Management Functional Areas)?

2. What is a Management Information Base (MIB)?

3. What is `ping`?

4. Assume a LAN has some machines using Ethernet and others using IEEE 802.3. Can they communicate?

5. What is Kerberos?

Chapter 14

The Socket Programming Interface

Today I look at the last remaining aspect of TCP/IP this course covers: the socket interface for programming. This information is intended to convey the process needed to integrate an application with TCP/IP and as such involves some basic programming functions. It is not necessary to understand programming to understand this information. The functions involved in the socket programming interface help you understand the steps TCP/IP goes through when creating connections and sending data.

Understanding the socket interface is helpful even if you never intend to write a line of TCP/IP code, because all the applications you will work with use these principles and procedures. Debugging or troubleshooting a problem is much easier when you understand what is going on behind the user interface. Today I don't attempt to show the complete socket interface. Instead I deal only with the primary functions necessary to create and maintain a connection. This chapter is not intended to be a programming guide, either.

Because the original socket interface was developed for UNIX systems, today's text has a decidedly UNIX-based orientation. However, the same principles apply to most other operating systems that support TCP/IP.

Development of the Socket Programming Interface

TCP/IP is fortunate because it has a well-defined application programming interface (API), which dictates how an application uses TCP/IP. This solves a basic problem that has occurred on many other communications protocols, which have several approaches to the same problem, each incompatible with the other. The TCP/IP API is portable (it works across all operating systems and hardware that support TCP/IP), language-independent (it doesn't matter which language you use to write the application), and relatively uncomplicated.

The Socket API was developed at the University of California at Berkeley as part of their BSD 4.1c UNIX version. Since then the API has been modified and enhanced but still retains its BSD flavor. Not to be outdone, AT&T (BSD's rival in the UNIX market) introduced the Transport Layer Interface (TLI) for TCP and several other protocols. One of the strengths of the Socket API and TLI is that they were not developed exclusively for TCP/IP but are intended for use with several communications protocols. The socket interface remains the most widespread API in current use, although several newer interfaces are being developed.

The basic structure of all socket programming commands lies with the unique structure of UNIX I/O. With UNIX, both input and output are treated as simple pipelines, where the input can be from anything and the output can go anywhere. The UNIX I/O system is sometimes referred to as the *open-read-write-close* system, because those are the steps that are performed for each I/O operation, whether it involves a file, a device, or a communications port.

Whenever a file is involved, the UNIX operating system gives the file a *file descriptor,* a small number that uniquely identifies the file. A program can use this file descriptor to identify the file at any time. (The same holds true for a device; the process is the same.) A file operation uses an open function to return the file descriptor, which is used for the read (transfer data to the user's process) or write (transfer data from the user process to the file) functions, followed by a close function to terminate the file operation. The open function takes a filename as an argument. The read and write functions use the file descriptor number, the address of the buffer in which to read or write the information, and the number of bytes involved. The close function uses the file descriptor. The system is easy to use and simple to work with.

TCP/IP uses the same idea, relying on numbers to uniquely identify an end point for communications (a socket). Whenever the socket number is used, the operating system can resolve the socket number to the physical connector. An essential difference between a file descriptor and a socket number is that the socket requires some functions to be performed prior to the establishment of the socket (such as initialization). In techno-speak, "a file descriptor binds to a specific file or device when the open function is called, but the socket can be created without binding them to a specific destination at all (necessary for UDP), or bind them later (for TCP when the remote address is provided)." The same open-read-write-close procedure is used with sockets.

The process was actually used literally with the first versions of TCP/IP. A special file called /dev/tcp was used as the device driver. The complexity added by networking made this approach awkward, though, so a library of special functions (the API) was developed. The essential steps of open, read, write, and close are still followed in the protocol API.

Socket Services

There are three types of socket interfaces defined in the TCP/IP API. A socket can be used for TCP *stream communications,* in which a connection between two machines is created. It can be used for *UDP datagram communications,* a connectionless method of passing information between machines using packets of a predefined format. Or it can be used as a *raw* datagram process, in which the datagrams bypass the TCP/UDP layer and go straight to IP. The latter type arises from the fact that the socket API was not developed exclusively for TCP/IP.

The presence of all three types of interfaces can lead to problems with some parameters that depend exclusively on the type of interface. You must always bear in mind whether TCP or UDP is used.

There are six basic communications commands that the socket API addresses through the TCP layer:

- ☐ open: Establishes a socket
- ☐ send: Sends data to the socket
- ☐ receive: Receives data from a socket
- ☐ status: Obtains status information about a socket
- ☐ close: Terminates a connection
- ☐ abort: Cancels an operation and terminates the connection

14

All six operations are logical and used as you would expect. The details for each step can be quite involved, but the basic operation remains the same. Many of the functions have been seen in previous days when dealing with specific protocols in some detail. Some of the functions (such as open) comprise several other functions that are available if necessary (such as establishing each end of the connection instead of both ends at once).

Despite the formal definition of the functions within the API specifications, no formal method is given for how to implement them. There are two logical choices: synchronous, or *blocking,* in which the application waits for the command to complete before continuing execution; and asynchronous, or *nonblocking,* in which the application continues executing while the API function is processed. In the latter case, a function call further in the application's execution can check the API functions' success and return codes.

The problem with the synchronous or blocking method is that the application must wait for the function call to complete. If timeouts are involved, this can cause a noticeable delay for the user.

Transmission Control Block

The Transmission Control Block (TCB) is a complex data structure that contains details about a connection. The full TCB has over 50 fields in it. The exact layout and contents of the TCB are not necessary for today's material, but the existence of the TCB and the nature of the information it holds are key to the behavior of the socket interface.

Creating a Socket

The API lets a user create a socket whenever necessary with a simple function call. The function requires the family of the protocol to be used with the socket (so the operating system knows which type of socket to assign and how to decode information), the type of communication required, and the specific protocol. Such a function call is written as follows:

```
socket(family, type, protocol)
```

The *family* of the protocol actually specifies how the addresses are interpreted. Examples of families are TCP/IP (coded as AF_INET), Apple's AppleTalk (AF_APPLETALK), and UNIX filesystems (AF_UNIX). The exact protocol within the family is specified as the protocol parameter. When used, it specifically indicates the type of service that is to be used.

The *type* parameter indicates the type of communications used. It can be a connectionless datagram service (coded as SOCK_DGRAM), a stream delivery service (SOCK_STREAM), or a raw type (SOCK_RAW). The result from the function call is an integer that can be assigned to a variable for further checking.

14

Binding the Socket

Because a socket can be created without any binding to an address, there must be a function call to complete this process and establish the full connection. With the TCP/IP protocol, the socket function does not supply the local port number, the destination port, or the IP address of the destination. The bind function is called to establish the local port address for the connection.

Some applications (especially on a server) want to use a specific port for a connection. Other applications are content to let the protocol software assign a port. A specific port can be requested in the bind function. If it is available, the software allocates it and returns the port information. If the port cannot be allocated (it might be in use), a return code indicates an error in port assignment.

The bind function has the following format:

```
bind(socket, local_address, address_length)
```

socket is the integer number of the socket to which the bind is completed; local_address is the local address to which the bind is performed; and address_length is an integer that gives the length of the address in bytes. The address is not returned as a simple number but has the structure shown in Figure 14.1.

Figure 14.1.

Address structure used by the socket API.

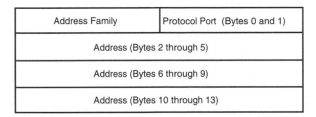

Address Family	Protocol Port (Bytes 0 and 1)
Address (Bytes 2 through 5)	
Address (Bytes 6 through 9)	
Address (Bytes 10 through 13)	

The address data structure (which is usually called sockaddr for *socket address*) has a 16-bit Address Family field that identifies the protocol family of the address. The entry in this field determines the format of the address in the following field (which might contain other information than the address, depending on how the protocol has defined the field). The Address field can be up to 14 bytes in length, although most protocols do not need this amount of space.

14

NOTE

> The use of a data structure instead of a simple address has its roots in the UNIX operating system and the closely allied C programming language. The formal structure of the socket address enables C programs to use a union of structures for all possible address families. This saves a considerable amount of coding in applications.

TCP/IP has a family address of 2, following which the Address field contains both a protocol port number (16 bits) and the IP address (32 bits). The remaining eight bytes are unused. This is shown in Figure 14.2. Because the address family defines how the Address field is decoded, there should be no problem with TCP/IP applications understanding the two pieces of information in the Address field.

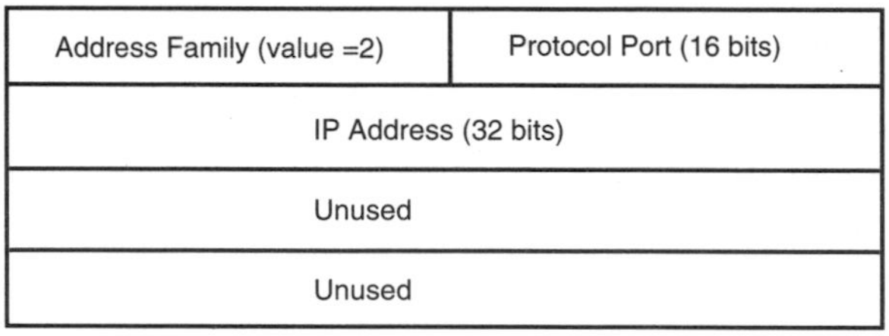

Figure 14.2.

The address structure for TCP/IP.

Address Family (value =2)	Protocol Port (16 bits)
IP Address (32 bits)	
Unused	
Unused	

Connecting to the Destination

After a local socket address and a port number have been assigned, the destination socket can be connected. A one-ended connection is referred to as being in an *unconnected state,* whereas a two-ended (complete) connection is in a *connected state.* After a bind function, an unconnected state exists. To become connected, the destination socket must be added to complete the connection.

 NOTE

> Connectionless protocols such as UDP do not require a connected state to function. They can, however, be connected to enable transfer between the two sockets without having to specify the destination address each time. Connection-based protocols such as TCP require both ends of the connection to be specified.

To establish a connection to a remote socket, the connect function is used. The connect function's format is

```
connect(socket, destination_address, address_length)
```

The *socket* is the integer number of the socket to which to connect; the *destination_address* is the socket address data structure for the destination address (using the same format as shown in Figure 14.1); and the *address_length* is the length of the destination address in bytes.

The manner in which connect functions is protocol-dependent. For TCP, connect establishes the connection between the two endpoints and returns the information about the remote socket to the application. If a connection can't be established, an error message is generated. For a connectionless protocol such as UDP, the connect function is still necessary but stores only the destination address for the application.

The open **Command**

The open command prepares a port for communications. This is an alternative to the combination of the functions shown previously, used by applications for specific purposes. There are really three kinds of open commands, two of which set a server to receive incoming requests and the third used by a client to initiate a request. With every open command, a TCB is created for that connection.

The three open commands are an unspecified passive open (which enables a server to wait for a connection request from any client), a fully specified passive open (which enables a server to wait for a connection request from a specific client), and an active open (which initiates a connection with a server). The input and output expected from each command are shown in Table 14.1.

Table 14.1. Open command parameters.

Type	Input	Output
Unspecified passive open	Local port Optional: timeout, precedence, security, maximum segment size	Local connection name Local connection name
Fully specified passive open	Local port, remote IP address, remote port Optional: timeout, precedence, security, maximum segment size	Local connection name

14

continues

Table 14.1. continued

Type	Input	Output
Active open	Local port, destination IP address, destination port Optional: timeout, precedence, security, maximum segment size	Local connection name

When an open command is issued by an application, a set of functions within the socket interface is executed to set up the TCB, initiate the socket number, and establish preliminary values for the variables used in the TCB and the application.

The passive open command is issued by a server to wait for incoming requests. With the TCP (connection-based) protocol, the passive open issues the following function calls:

- [ ] socket: Creates the sockets and identifies the type of communications.
- [ ] bind: Establishes the server socket for the connection.
- [ ] listen: Establishes a client queue.
- [ ] accept: Waits for incoming connection requests on the socket.

The active open command is issued by a client. For TCP, it issues two functions:

- [ ] socket: Creates the socket and identifies the communications type.
- [ ] connect: Identifies the server's IP address and port; attempts to establish communications.

If the exact port to use is specified as part of the open command, a bind function call replaces the connect function.

Sending Data

There are five functions within the Socket API for sending data through a socket. These are send, sendto, sendmsg, write, and writev. Not surprisingly, all these functions send data from the application to TCP. They do this through a buffer created by the application (for example, it might be a memory address or a character string), passing the entire buffer to TCP. The send, write, and writev functions work only with a connected socket because they have no provision to specify a destination address within their function call.

The format of the send function is simple. It takes the local socket connection number, the buffer address for the message to be sent, the length of the message in bytes, a Push flag, and an Urgent flag as parameters. An optional timeout might be specified. Nothing is returned as output from the send function. The format is

```
send(socket, buffer_address, length, flags)
```

The sendto and sendmsg functions are similar except they enable an application to send a message through an unconnected socket. They both require the destination address as part of their function call. The sendmsg function is simpler in format than the sendto function, primarily because another data structure is used to hold information. The sendmsg function is often used when the format of the sendto function would be awkward and inefficient in the application's code. Their formats are

```
sendto(socket, buffer_address, length, flags, destination, address_length)
```

```
sendmsg(socket, message_structure, flags)
```

The last two parameters in the sendto function are the destination address and the length of the destination address. The address is specified using the format shown in Figure 14.1. The *message_structure* of the sendmsg function contains the information left out of the sendto function call. The format of the message structure is shown in Figure 14.3.

Figure 14.3.
The message structure used by sendmsg.

Pointer to Socket Address
Size of Socket Address (in bytes)
Pointer to iovector List (Message)
Length of iovector List
Destination Address
Length of Destination Address

The fields in the sendmsg message structure give the socket address, size of the socket address, a pointer to the iovector, which contains information about the message to be sent, the length of the iovector, the destination address, and the length of the destination address.

NOTE
The sendmsg function uses the message structure to simplify the function call. It also has another advantage: the recvmsg function uses the same structure, simplifying an application's code.

14

The `iovector` is an address for an array that points to the message to be sent. The array is a set of pointers to the bytes that comprise the message. The format of the `iovector` is simple. For each 32-bit address to a memory location with a chunk of the message, a corresponding 32-bit field holds the length of the message in that memory location. This format is repeated until the entire message is specified. This is shown in Figure 14.4. The `iovector` format enables a noncontiguous message to be sent. In other words, the first part of the message can be in one location in memory, and the rest is separated by other information. This can be useful because it saves the application from copying long messages into a contiguous location.

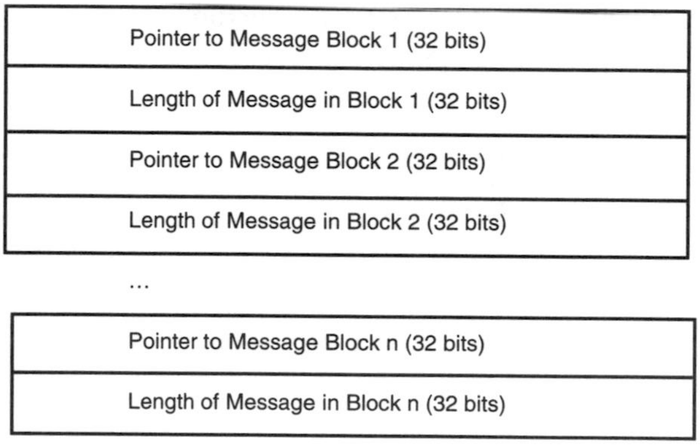

Figure 14.4.

The `iovector` *format.*

Pointer to Message Block 1 (32 bits)
Length of Message in Block 1 (32 bits)
Pointer to Message Block 2 (32 bits)
Length of Message in Block 2 (32 bits)

...

Pointer to Message Block n (32 bits)
Length of Message in Block n (32 bits)

The `write` function takes three arguments: the socket number, the buffer address of the message to be sent, and the length of the message to send. The format of the function call is

write(*socket*, *buffer_address*, *length*)

The `writev` function is similar to `write` except it uses the `iovector` to hold the message. This lets it send a message without copying it into another memory address. The format of `writev` is

writev(*socket*, *iovector*, *length*)

where *length* is the number of entries in `iovector`.

The type of function chosen to send data through a socket depends on the type of connection used and the level of complexity of the application. To a considerable degree, it is also a personal choice of the programmer.

Receiving Data

Not surprisingly, because there are five functions to send data through a socket, there are five corresponding functions to receive data: `read`, `readv`, `recv`, `recvfrom`, and `recvmsg`. They all accept incoming data from a socket into a reception buffer. The receive buffer can then be transferred from TCP to the application.

The `read` function is the simplest and can be used only when a socket is connected. Its format is

```
read(socket, buffer, length)
```

The first parameter is the number of the socket or a file descriptor from which to read the data, followed by the memory address in which to store the incoming data, and the maximum number of bytes to be read.

As with `writev`, the `readv` command enables incoming messages to be placed in noncontiguous memory locations through the use of an `iovector`. The format of `readv` is

```
readv(socket, iovector, length)
```

`length` is the number of entries in the `iovector`. The format of the `iovector` is the same as mentioned previously and shown in Figure 14.4.

The `recv` function also can be used with connected sockets. It has the format

```
recv(socket, buffer_address, length, flags)
```

which corresponds to the `send` function's arguments.

The `recvfrom` and `recvmsg` functions enable data to be read from an unconnected socket. Their formats include the sender's address:

```
recvfrom(socket, buffer_address, length, flags, source_address, address_length)
```

```
recvmsg(socket, message_structure, flags)
```

The message structure in the `recvmsg` function corresponds to the structure in `sendmsg`. (Refer to Figure 14.3.)

Server Listening

A server application that expects clients to call in to it has to create a socket (using `socket`), bind it to a port (with `bind`), then wait for incoming requests for data. The `listen` function handles problems that could occur with this type of behavior by establishing a queue for incoming connection requests. The queue prevents bottlenecks and collisions, such as when a new request arrives before a previous one has been completely handled, or two requests arrive simultaneously.

The `listen` function establishes a buffer to queue incoming requests, thereby avoiding losses. The function lets the socket accept incoming connection requests, which are all sent to the queue for future processing. The function's format is

14

```
listen(socket, queue_length)
```

where `queue_length` is the size of the incoming buffer. If the buffer has room, incoming requests for connections are added to the buffer and the application can deal with them in the order of reception. If the buffer is full, the connection request is rejected.

After the server has used `listen` to set up the incoming connection request queue, the `accept` function is used to actually wait for a connection. The format of the function is

```
accept(socket, address, length)
```

`socket` is the socket on which to accept requests; `address` is a pointer to a structure similar to Figure 14.1; and `length` is a pointer to an integer showing the length of the address.

When a connection request is received, the protocol places the address of the client in the memory location indicated by the address parameter, and the length of that address in the length location. It then creates a new socket that has the client and server connected together, sending back the socket description to the client. The socket on which the request was received remains open for other connection requests. This enables multiple requests for a connection to be processed, whereas if that socket was closed down with each connection request, only one client/server process could be handled at a time.

One possible special occurrence must be handled on UNIX systems. It is possible for a single process to wait for a connection request on multiple sockets. This reduces the number of processes that monitor sockets, thereby lowering the amount of overhead the machine uses. To provide for this type of process, the `select` function is used. The format of the function is

```
select(num_desc, in_desc, out_desc, excep_desc, timeout)
```

`num_desc` is the number of sockets or descriptors that are monitored; `in_desc` and `out_desc` are pointers to a bit mask that indicates the sockets or file descriptors to monitor for input and output, respectively; `excep_desc` is a pointer to a bit mask that specifies the sockets or file descriptors to check for exception conditions; and `timeout` is a pointer to an integer that indicates how long to wait. (A value of 0 indicates forever.) To use the `select` function, a server creates all the necessary sockets first, then calls `select` to determine which ones are for input, output, and exceptions.

Getting Status Information

Several status functions are used to obtain information about a connection. They can be used at any time, although they are typically used to establish the integrity of a connection in case of problems or to control the behavior of the socket.

14

The status functions require the name of the local connection, and they return a set of information, which might include the local and remote socket names, local connection name, receive and send window states, number of buffers waiting for an acknowledgment, number of buffers waiting for data, and current values for the urgent state, precedence, security, and timeout variables. Most of this information is read from the Transmission Control Block (TCB). The format of the information and the exact contents vary slightly, depending on the implementation.

The function `getsockopt` enables an application to query the socket for information. The function format is

```
getsockopt(socket, level, option_id, option_result, length)
```

`socket` is the number of the socket; `level` indicates whether the function refers to the socket itself or the protocol that uses it; `option_id` is a single integer that identifies the type of information requested; `option_result` is a pointer to a memory location where the function should place the result of the query; and `length` is the length of the result.

The corresponding `setsockopt` function lets the application set a value for the socket. The function's format is the same as `getsockopt` except that `option_result` points to the value that is to be set, and `length` is the length of the value.

Two functions provide information about the local address of a socket. The `getpeername` function returns the address of the remote end. The `getsockname` function returns the local address of a socket. They have the following formats:

```
getpeername(socket, destination_address, address_length)
```

```
getsockname(socket, local_address, address_length)
```

The addresses in both functions are pointers to a structure of the format shown in Figure 14.1.

Two host name functions for BSD UNIX are `gethostname` and `sethostname`, which enable an application to obtain the name of the host and set the host name (if permissions allow). Their formats are as follows:

```
sethostname(name, length)
```

```
gethostname(name, length)
```

The `name` is the address of an array that holds the name, and the `length` is an integer that gives the name's length.

A similar set of functions provides for domain names. The functions `setdomainname` and `getdomainname` enable an application to obtain or set the domain names. Their formats are

```
setdomainname(name, length)
```

```
getdomainname(name, length)
```

14

The parameters are the same as with the sethostname and gethostname functions, except for the format of the name (which reflects domain name format).

Closing a Connection

The close function closes a connection. It requires only the local connection name to complete the process. It also takes care of the TCB and releases any variable created by the connection. No output is generated.

The close function is initiated with the call

```
close(socket)
```

where the socket name is required. If an application terminates abnormally, the operating system closes all sockets that were open prior to the termination.

Aborting a Connection

The abort function instructs TCP to discard all data that currently resides in send and receive buffers and close the connection. It takes the local connection name as input. No output is generated. This function can be used in case of emergency shutdown routines, or in case of a fatal failure of the connection or associated software.

The abort function is usually implemented by the close() call, although some special instructions might be available with different implementations.

UNIX Forks

UNIX has two system calls that can affect sockets: fork and exec. Both are frequently used by UNIX developers because of their power. (In fact, forks are one of the most powerful tools UNIX offers, and one that most other operating systems lack.) For simplicity, I deal with the two functions as though they perform the same task.

A fork call creates a copy of the existing application as a new process and starts executing it. The new process has all the original's file descriptors and socket information. This can cause a problem if the application programmer didn't take into account the fact that two (or more) processes try to use the same socket (or file) simultaneously. Therefore, applications that can fork have to take into account potential conflicts and code around them by checking the status of shared sockets.

The operating system itself keeps a table of each socket and how many processes have access to it. An internal counter is incremented or decremented with each process's open or close function call for the socket. When the last process using a socket is terminated, the socket is permanently closed. This prevents one forked process from closing a socket when its original is still using it.

Summary

Today you have seen the basic functions performed by the socket API during establishment of a TCP or UDP call. You have also seen the functions that are available to application programmers. Although the treatment has been at a high level, you should be able to see that working with sockets is not a complex, confusing task. Indeed, socket programming is surprisingly easy once you have tried it.

Not everyone wants to write TCP or UDP applications, of course. However, understanding the basics of the socket API helps in understanding the protocol and troubleshooting. If you are interested in programming sockets, one of the best books on the subject is *UNIX Network Programming,* by W. Richard Stevens (Macmillan).

Q&A

Q What is the socket interface used for?

A The socket interface enables you to write applications that make optimal use of the TCP/IP family of protocols. Without it, you would need another layer of application to translate your program's calls to TCP/IP calls.

Q What is the difference between blocking and nonblocking functions?

A A blocking function waits for the function to terminate before enabling the application to continue. A nonblocking function enables the application to continue executing while the function is performed. Both have important uses in applications.

Q What does binding do?

A Binding makes a logical connection between a socket and the application. Without it, the application couldn't access the socket.

14

Q What happens when an active open command is executed?

A An active open command creates a socket and binds it, then issues a connect call to identify the IP address and port. The active open command then tries to establish communications.

Q What is the difference between an abort and a close operation?

A A close operation closes a connection. An abort abandons whatever communications are currently underway and closes the connection. With an abort, any information in receive buffers is discarded.

Quiz

1. What are the six basic socket commands?
2. A Transmission Control Block performs what function?
3. What is the difference between an unspecified passive open and a fully specified passive open?
4. What command displays status information about a socket?
5. What is a fork?

14

APPENDIX A

Acronyms and Abbreviations

Table A.1. Acronyms and abbreviations, and what they mean.

Acronym	Explanation
ACB	Access Control Block
ACK	Acknowledgment
AF	Address Family
ANSI	American National Standard Institute
API	Application Programming Interface
ARP	Address Resolution Protocol
ARPA	Advanced Research Projects Agency
AS	Autonomous System
ASA	American Standards Association
ASCII	American National Standard Code for Information Interchange
ASN.1	Abstract Syntax Notation One
BBN	Bolt, Beranek, and Newman, Incorporated
BER	Basic Encoding Rules
BGP	Border Gateway Protocol
BSD	Berkeley Software Distribution
CMIP	Common Management Information Protocol
CMIS	Common Management Information Services
CMOT	Common Management Information Services and Protocol over TCP/IP
CRC	Cyclic Redundancy Check
CSMA/CD	Carrier Sense Multiple Access with Collision Detection
DARPA	Defense Advanced Research Projects Agency
DCA	Defense Communications Agency
DCE	Distributed Computing Environment
DCE	Data Circuit-Terminating Equipment (also called Data Communications Equipment)
DDN	Defense Data Network
DES	Data Encryption Standard
DFS	Distributed File Service
DISA	Defense Information Systems Agency
DIX	Digital, Intel, and Xerox Ethernet Protocol

Acronym	Explanation
DME	Distributed Management Environment
DNS	Domain Name Service
DSA	Directory System Agent
DSAP	Destination Service Access Point
DTE	Data Terminal Equipment
DUA	Directory User Agent
EBCDIC	Extended Binary Coded Decimal Interchange Code
EGP	Exterior Gateway Protocol
EOF	End of File
EOR	End of Record
FCS	Frame Check Sequence
FDDI	Fiber Distributed Data Interface
FIN	Final Segment
FTAM	File Transfer, Access, and Management
FTP	File Transfer Protocol
GGP	Gateway to Gateway Protocol
GOSIP	Government Open Systems Interconnection Profile
GTF	Generalized Trace Facility
HDLC	High-Level Data Link Control Protocol
IAB	Internet Architecture Board
IAB	Internet Activities Board
IAC	Interpret as Command
IANA	Internet Assigned Numbers Authority
ICMP	Internet Control Message Protocol
ID	Identifier
IEEE	Institute of Electrical and Electronic Engineers
IEN	Internet Engineering Notes
IESG	Internet Engineering Steering Group
IETF	Internet Engineering Task Force
IGMP	Internet Group Management Protocol
IGP	Interior Gateway Protocol
IP	Internet Protocol

continues

Table A.1. continued

Acronym	Explanation
IRTF	Internet Research Task Force
ISDN	Integrated Services Digital Network
ISN	Initial Sequence Number
ISO	International Organization for Standardization
ISODE	ISO Development Environment
LAN	Local Area Network
LAPB	Link Access Procedures Balanced
LAPD	Link Access Procedures on the D-Channel
LLC	Logical Link Control
MAC	Media Access Control
MAN	Metropolitan Area Network
MIB	Management Information Base
MSS	Maximum Segment Size
MTA	Message Transfer Agent
MTU	Message Transfer Unit
MTU	Maximum Transmission Unit
MX	Mail Exchanger
NETBIOS	Network Basic Input/Output System
NFS	Network File System
NIC	Network Interface Card
NIS	Network Information System
NREN	National Research and Education Network
NSAP	Network Service Access Point
NSFNET	National Science Foundation Network
NVT	Network Virtual Terminal
OSF	Open Software Foundation
OSI	Open Systems Interconnect
OSPF	Open Shortest Path First
PAD	Packet Assembly/Disassembly
PDU	Protocol Data Unit
PI	Protocol Interpreter

Acronym	Explanation
PING	Packet Internet Groper
POP	Post Office Protocol
PPP	Point-to-Point Protocol
RARP	Reverse Address Resolution Protocol
RFC	Request For Comment
RIP	Routing Information Protocol
RMON	Remote Network Monitor
RPC	Remote Procedure Call
RST	Reset
RTT	Round Trip Time
SDLC	Synchronous Data Link Communication
SLIP	Serial Line Interface Protocol
SMDS	Switched Multimegabit Data Service
SMTP	Simple Mail Transfer Protocol
SNA	Systems Network Architecture
SNMP	Simple Network Management Protocol
SONET	Synchronous Optical Network
SPF	Shortest Path First
SSAP	Source Service Access Point
SSCP	System Services Control Point
SYN	Synchronizing Segment
TCB	Transmission Control Block
TCP	Transmission Control Protocol
TCU	Trunk Coupling Unit
TELNET	Terminal Networking
TFTP	Trivial File Transfer Protocol
TLI	Transport Layer Interface
TP4	OSI Transport Class 4
TSAP	Transport Service Access Point
TTL	Time-to-Live
UA	User Agent
UDP	User Datagram Protocol

continues

Table A.1. continued

Acronym	Explanation
ULP	Upper Layer Protocol
WAN	Wide Area Network
XDR	External Data Representation
XNS	Xerox Network Systems

APPENDIX

B

Glossary

10Base2 An Ethernet term meaning a maximum transfer rate of 10 Megabits per second that uses baseband signaling, with a contiguous cable segment length of 100 meters and a maximum of 2 segments.

10Base5 An Ethernet term meaning a maximum transfer rate of 10 Megabits per second that uses baseband signaling, with 5 continuous segments not exceeding 100 meters per segment.

10BaseT An Ethernet term meaning a maximum transfer rate of 10 Megabits per second that uses baseband signaling and twisted-pair cabling.

Abstract Syntax Notation One (ASN.1) An OSI language used to define datatypes for networks. It is used within TCP/IP to provide conformance with the OSI model.

Access Control A process that defines each user's privileges on a system.

Acknowledgment (ACK) A positive response returned from a receiver to the sender indicating success. TCP uses acknowledgments to indicate the successful reception of a packet.

Active Open An operation performed by a client to establish a TCP connection with a server.

Address A memory location in a particular machine's RAM. A numeric identifier or symbolic name that specifies the location of a particular machine or device on a network, and a means of identifying a complete network, subnetwork, or a node within a network.

Address Mask (also called the subnet mask) A set of rules for omitting parts of a complete IP address in order to reach the target destination without using a broadcast message. The mask can, for example, indicate a subnetwork portion of a larger network. In TCP/IP, the address mask uses the 32-bit IP address.

Address Resolution Mapping of an IP address to a machine's physical address. TCP/IP uses the Address Resolution Protocol (ARP) for this function.

Address Resolution Protocol (ARP) See *Address Resolution*. ARP is a protocol used to correlate an IP address to a machine's physical address. The reverse operation is performed by Reverse Address Resolution protocol (RARP).

Address Space A range of memory addresses available to an application program.

Advanced Research Project Agency (ARPA) DARPA's former name. ARPA was an agency funded by the U.S. federal government originally for pure research. When it was changed to DARPA, the funding became part of the defense budget.

Agent In TCP/IP, an agent is an SNMP process that responds to get and set requests. Agents can also send trap messages.

American National Standards Institute (ANSI)   The U.S. body responsible for setting standards.

Application Layer   The highest layer in the OSF model. It establishes communications rights and can initiate a connection between two applications.

Application Programming Interface (API)   A set of routines available to developers and applications to provide specific services used by the system, usually specific to the application's purpose. They act as access methods into the application.

ARPANET (Advanced Research Projects Agency Network)   A packet-switched network that later became known as the Internet.

ASCII (American National Standard Code for Information Interchange)   An 8-bit character set defining alphanumeric characters.

Assigned Numbers   Used in Request For Comment (RFC) documents to specify values used by TCP/IP.

Asynchronous   Communications without a regular time basis, enabling transmission at unequal rates.

Autonomous System   A collection of routers that are under the control of a single management body. The system usually uses a common Interior Gateway Protocol.

Backbone   A set of nodes and links connected together comprising a network, or the upper layer protocols used in a network. Sometimes the term is used to refer to a network's physical media.

Bandwidth   The range of frequencies transmitted on a channel, or the difference between the highest and lowest frequencies transmitted across a channel.

Baseband   A type of channel where data transmission is carried across only one communications channel, supporting only one signal transmission at a time. Ethernet is a baseband system.

Baseband Signaling   A type of transmission that has a continuous encoded signal. Only one node at a time can send data over this type of transmission technology. Used in Local Area Networks.

Basic Encoding Rules (BER)   The rules for encoding datatypes using ASN.1.

Baud   The number of times a signal changes state in one second.

Berkeley Software Distribution (BSD)   A version of the UNIX operating system that first included TCP/IP support. The UNIX operating systems that included TCP/IP are referred to as 4.2BSD or 4.3BSD.

Bit Error Rate (BER)   The number of errors expected in a transmission.

Bit Rate   The rate that bits are transmitted, usually expressed in seconds.

BITNET (Because It's Time Network)   An electronic mail network connecting over 200 universities. It merged with the CSNET network to produce CREN.

Block Mode   A string of data recorded or transmitted as a unit. Block mode transmission is usually used for high-speed transmissions and in large, high-speed networks.

Border Gateway Protocol (BGP)   A protocol that provides information about the devices that can be reached through a router (into an autonomous network). BGP is newer than EGP.

Bridge   A network device capable of connecting networks that use similar protocols.

Broadband (also known as wideband)   A range of frequencies divided into several narrower bands. Each band can be used for different purposes.

Broadband Signaling   The type of signaling used in Local Area Networks that enables multiplexing of more than one transmission at a time.

Broadcast   The simultaneous transmission of the same data to all nodes connected to the network.

Brouter   A network device that is a combination of the functions of a bridge and a router. It can function as a bridge while filtering protocols and packets destined for nodes on different networks.

BSD   See *Berkeley Software Distribution*.

Buffer   A memory area used for handling input and output.

Burst Mode   A transmission mode where data is transmitted in bursts rather than in continuous streams.

Bus   In network topology, a linear configuration. Also used to refer to part of the electronic layout of network devices.

Cache   A memory location that keeps frequently requested material ready. Usually the cache is faster than a storage device. It is used to speed data and instruction transfer.

Carrier Sense   A signal generated by the physical network layer to inform the data link layer that one or more nodes are transmitting on the network medium.

Carrier Sense Multiple Access with Collision Detection (CSMA/CD)   A network media access control protocol wherein a device listens to the medium to monitor traffic. If there is no signal, the device is allowed to send data.

Cheapernet   A reduced-cost Ethernet variant where the maximum length of the network is 200 feet. It uses inexpensive 75-ohm coaxial cable, simple connectors, and no transceivers.

Client   A program that tries to connect to another program (usually on another machine) called a server. The client calls the server. The server listens for calls.

Client/Server Architecture   A catch-all term used to refer to a distributed environment where one program can initiate a session and another program can answer its requests. The origin of client/server designs is closely allied with the TCP/IP protocol suite.

CMIP   See Common Management Information Protocol.

CMOT   The TCP/IP implementation of CMIP.

Collision   An event that occurs when two or more nodes broadcast packets at the same time—the packets collide.

Collision Detection   A device's capability to detect whether a collision has occurred.

Common Management Information Protocol (CMIP)   A network management protocol usually associated with OSI. When used with TCP/IP, CMIP is called CMOT.

Common Management Information Service (CMIS)   Management services provided by CMIP.

Connection   A link between two or more processes, applications, machines, networks, and so forth. Connections can be logical, physical, or both.

Connection Oriented   A type of network service where the transport layer protocol sends acknowledgments to the sender regarding incoming data. This type of service usually provides for retransmission of corrupted or lost data.

Connectionless   A type of network service that does not send acknowledgments to the sender upon receipt of data. UDP is a connectionless protocol.

Consortium for Research and Education Network (CREN)   The name for the body arising from the combination of CSNET and BITNET.

Contention   A condition occurring in some LANs where the Media Access Control (MAC) sublayer allows more than one node to transmit at the same time, risking collisions.

Core Gateway   A router operated by the Internet Network Operations Center to distribute routing information.

Crosstalk   Signals that interfere with another signal.

CSNET (Computer Science Network)   An electronic mail network that merged with BITNET to form CREN.

Cyclic Redundancy Check (CRC)   A mathematical function performed on the contents of an entity that is then included to enable a receiving system to recalculate the value and compare to the original. If the values are different, corruption of the contents has occurred.

B

Daemon   A UNIX process that operates continuously and unattended to perform a service. TCP/IP uses several daemons to establish communications processes and provide server facilities.

DARPA (Defense Advanced Research Project Agency)   The governmental body that created the DARPANET for widespread communications. DARPANET eventually became the Internet.

Data Circuit-Terminating Equipment (DCE)   Required equipment to attach Data Terminal Equipment (DTE) to a network or serial line. A modem is a DCE device. Also called Data Communications Equipment and Data Circuit Equipment.

Data Encryption Standard (DES)   An encryption standard officially sanctioned in the U.S.

Data Link   The part of a node controlled by a data link protocol. It is the logical connection between two nodes.

Data Link Protocol (DLP)   A method of handling the establishment, maintenance, and termination of a logical link between nodes. Ethernet is one example of a Data Link Protocol.

Data Terminal Equipment (DTE)   The source or destination of data, usually attached to a network by DCE devices. A terminal or computer acting as a node on a network is usually a DTE device.

Datagram   A basic unit of data used with TCP/IP.

Defense Communications Agency (DCA)   The governmental agency responsible for the Defense Data Network (DDN).

Defense Data Network (DDN)   Refers to military networks such as MILNET and ARPANET and the communications protocols (including TCP/IP) that they employ.

Destination Address   The destination device's address.

Directory System Agent (DSA)   A program that accepts queries from a directory user agent (DUA).

Directory User Agent (DUA)   A program that helps a user to send a query to a directory server.

Distributed Computing Environment (DCE)   A set of technologies developed by the Open Software Foundation (OSF) supporting distributed computing.

Distributed File Service (DFS)   An Open Software Foundation (OSF) fileserver technology sometimes used with TCP/IP.

Distributed Management Environment (DME)   A system and network management technology developed by the Open Software Foundation (OSF).

Distributed Processing   When a process is spread over two or more devices, it is distributed. It is usually used to spread CPU loads among a network of machines.

Domain Name Service (DNS)   A service that converts symbolic node names to IP addresses. DNS is frequently used with TCP/IP. DNS uses a distributed database.

Dotted Decimal Notation   A representation of IP addresses. Also called "dotted quad notation" because it uses four sets of numbers separated by decimals (for example, 255.255.255.255).

Double Byte Character Set   A character set where alphanumeric characters are represented by two bytes, instead of one byte as with ASCII. Double byte characters are often necessary for Asian languages, which have more than 255 symbols.

Drop Cable   In Ethernet networks it refers to the cable connecting the device to the network, sometimes through a transceiver.

Dumb Terminal   A terminal with no significant processing capability of its own, usually with no graphics capabilities beyond the ASCII set.

Emulation   A program that simulates another device. For example, a 3270 emulator emulates an IBM 3270 terminal, sending the same codes as the real device would.

Encapsulation   Including an incoming message into a larger message by adding information at the front, back, or both. Encapsulation is used by layered network protocols. With each layer, new headers and trailers are added.

Enterprise Network   A generic term usually referring to a Wide Area Network providing services to all of a corporation's sites.

Ethernet   A data link level protocol comprising the OSI model's bottom two layers. It is a broadcast networking technology that can use several different physical media, including twisted-pair cable and coaxial cable. Ethernet usually uses CSMA/CD. TCP/IP is commonly used with Ethernet networks.

Ethernet Address   A 48-bit address commonly referred to as a physical or hard address that uniquely identifies the Ethernet Network Interface Card (NIC) and hence the device the card resides in.

Ethernet Meltdown   A slang term for a situation where an Ethernet network becomes saturated. The condition usually persists for only a short time and is usually caused by a misrouted or invalid packet.

Extended Binary Coded Decimal Interchange Code (EBCDIC)   An alternative to ASCII used extensively in IBM machinery. Some other vendors use it for mainframes. EBCDIC and ASCII are not compatible but are easy to convert between.

Exterior Gateway Protocol (EGP)   A protocol used by gateways to transfer information about devices that can be reached within their autonomous systems.

Fiber Distributed Data Interface (FDDI)   An ANSI-defined standard for high-speed data transfer over fiber-optic cabling.

File Server   A process that provides access to a file from remote devices. Also used to refer to the physical server itself, although the term *server* also implies other services than file provision in most client/server networks.

File Transfer Access Method (FTAM)   A file transfer program and protocol developed by OSI. It includes some basic management functions.

File Transfer Protocol (FTP)   A TCP/IP application used for transferring files from one system to another.

Fragmentation   The breaking of a datagram into several smaller pieces, usually because the original datagram was too large for the network or software.

Frame   Usually refers to the completed Ethernet packet, which includes the original data and all the TCP/IP layers' headers and trailers (including the Ethernet's).

Frame Check Sequence (FCS)   A mathematical function used to verify the integrity of bits in a frame, similar to the Cyclic Redundancy Check (CRC).

Frame Relay   A network switching mechanism for routing frames as quickly as possible.

Gateway   In Internet terms, a gateway is a device that routes datagrams. More recently used to refer to any networking device that translates protocols of one type of network into those of another network.

Gateway-to-Gateway Protocol (GGP)   A protocol used to exchange routing information between core routers.

Gigabyte   One billion bytes, corresponding to decimal 1,073,741,824 (a kilobyte is 1,024 decimal).

Government Open System Interconnection Profile (GOSIP)   A government standard that uses the OSI reference model.

Hardware Address   The low-level address associated with each device on a network, usually corresponding to the unique identifier of the network interface card (NIC). Ethernet addresses are 48 bits.

High Level Data Link Control (HDLC)   An international data communication standard.

Hop Count   The number of bridges that data crosses in a Token Ring network.

IEEE 802.2   An IEEE-approved data link standard used with the 802.3, 802.4, and 802.5 protocol standards.

IEEE 802.3   An IEEE-approved physical layer standard that uses CSMA/CD on a bus network topology.

IEEE 802.4   An IEEE-approved physical layer standard that uses token passing on a bus network topology.

IEEE 802.5   An IEEE-approved physical layer standard that uses token passing on a ring network topology.

Initial Sequence Number (ISN)   A number defined during the startup of a connection using TCP. Used to number datagrams.

Initiate   In TCP/IP, to send a request for something (usually a connection).

Institute of Electrical and Electronic Engineers (IEEE)   A professional organization for engineers that also proposes and approves standards.

Integrated Service Digital Network (ISDN)   A set of standards for integrating multiple services (voice, data, video, and so on).

Interface   A shared point between two software applications or two hardware devices.

Interior Gateway Protocol (IGP)   A protocol used by gateways in an autonomous system to transfer routing information.

International Organization for Standardization (ISO)   An international body composed of individual countries' standards groups that focuses on international standards.

Internet   A collection of networks connected together that span the world and use the NFSNET as its backbone. The Internet is the specific term for a more general internetwork or collection of networks.

Internet Activities Board (IAB)   The Internet group that coordinates the development of the TCP/IP protocol suite.

Internet Address   A 32-bit address used to identify hosts and networks on the Internet.

Internet Control Message Protocol (ICMP)   A control and error message protocol that works in conjunction with the Internet Protocol (IP).

Internet Engineering Notes (IEN)   Documents that discuss TCP/IP, available through the Network Information Center (NIC).

Internet Engineering Steering Group (IESG)   The executive party of the IETF.

Internet Engineering Task Force (IETF)   Part of the IAB responsible for short-term engineering needs relating to the TCP/IP protocol suite.

Internet Protocol (IP)   The part of TCP/IP that handles routing.

Internet Research Task Force (IRTF)   A part of the IAB that concentrates on research and development of the TCP/IP protocol suite.

IP Address   A 32-bit identifier that is unique to each network device.

IP Datagram   The basic unit of information passed through a TCP/IP network. The datagram header contains source and destination IP addresses.

IS-IS (Intermediate System to Intermediate System Protocol)   A routing protocol that performs routing functions with IP and OSI data.

ISO Reference Model   The seven-layer ISO networking model. It isolates specific functions within each layer.

ISODE (ISO Development Environment)   An attempt to develop software that enables OSI protocols to run on TCP/IP.

Jam   An Ethernet term for communicating with all devices on a network on which a collision has occurred.

Jitter   A term used with 10BaseT (twisted-pair Ethernet) networks where signals are out of phase with one another.

Kerberos   An authentication scheme developed at MIT used to prevent unauthorized monitoring of logins and passwords.

LAN (Local Area Network)   A collection of devices connected to enable communications between themselves on a single physical medium.

Learning Bridge   A network bridge device that has the function of a bridge and the capability to monitor the network in order to determine which nodes are connected to it, and adjust routing data accordingly.

Leased Line   A dedicated communication line between two points. Usually used by organizations to connect computers over a dedicated telephone circuit.

Link   A generic term referring to a connection between two end points.

Logical   Conveys an abstract concept in a simpler manner, such as using a logical machine name instead of its physical address.

Logical Link Control (LLC)   The upper part of the data link sublayer protocol that is responsible for governing the exchange of data between two end points.

Mail Exchanger   A system used to relay mail into a network.

Management Information Base (MIB)   A database used by SNMP containing configuration and statistical information about devices on a network.

Maximum Segment Size   The maximum permissible size for the data part of a packet.

Maximum Transmission Unit (MTU)   The largest datagram that can be handled by a specific network. The MTU can change over different networks, even if the transport is the same (such as Ethernet).

Media Access Control (MAC)   The lower half of the data link sublayer that is responsible for framing data and controlling the physical link between two end points.

Medium Access Unit (MAU)   A MAU handles the connection of a device operating on a network.

Message Transfer Agent (MTA)   A process that moves messages between devices.

Metropolitan Area Network (MAN)   An IEEE-approved network that supports high speeds over a metropolitan area.

MILNET (Military Network)   A network that was originally part of ARPANET, now designated for exclusive military use in installations that require reliable network services.

Modem (Modulator-Demodulator)   A device that converts digital signals into analog signals and vice versa. Used for conversion of signals for transmission over telephone lines.

Modem Eliminator   A device that functions as two modems to provide service for data terminal equipment (DTE) and data communications equipment (DCE).

Multihomed Host   A device attached to two or more networks.

Multiplex   Simultaneously transmitting multiple signals over one channel.

Name Resolution   The process of mapping aliases to an address. The Domain Name Service (DNS) is one system that does this.

National Institute of Standards and Technology (NIST)   A U.S. standards body previously called the National Bureau of Standards that promotes communications-oriented standards.

National Research and Education Network (NREN)   A network backbone supporting large capacities planned for future Internet use.

National Science Foundation Network (NFSNET)   The network that acts as part of the Internet backbone.

NetBIOS (Network Basic Input/Output Operating System)   A network programming interface typically used to connect PCs together.

Network   A number of devices connected to enable the device to communicate with any other device over a physical medium.

Network Address   For TCP/IP, the 32-bit IP address of a device.

Network File System (NFS)   A protocol developed by Sun MicroSystems that enables clients to mount remote directories onto their own local filesystem.

Network Information Center (NIC)   The Internet administration facility that controls the naming of networks accessible over the Internet.

B

Network Information Service (NIS)   A set of protocols developed by Sun Microsystems used to provide directory services for network information.

Network Interface Card (NIC)   A generic term for a networking interface board used to connect a device to the network. The NIC is where the physical connection to the network occurs.

Network Management   Any aspect of monitoring or controlling a network, including all administration details.

Network Service Access Point   Used to identify an OSI device and point to the transport layer.

Network Virtual Terminal (NVT)   Protocols that govern virtual terminal emulation.

Node   A generic term used to refer to network devices.

Open Shortest Path First (OSPF)   The basic Internet routing protocol for sending data over multiple paths. It uses the network's topology for routing decisions.

Open Software Foundation (OSF)   A consortium of hardware and software vendors collaborating to produce technologies for device-independent operation.

Open Systems Interconnection (OSI)   A family of ISO-developed standards relating to data communications.

Optical Fiber   A plastic or glass cable that uses light as a communications medium.

Packet   In TCP/IP, a term referring to the data passing between the Internet layer and the data link layer. Also a generic term used to refer to data transferred through a network.

Passive Open   An action taken by a server daemon to prepare it to receive requests from clients.

PING (Packet Internet Groper)   A utility program used to test a system's TCP/IP software by sending an ICMP echo request and then waiting for a response.

Point-to-Point   Transmission directly between two points without any intervening devices.

Point-to-Point Protocol (PPP)   A TCP/IP protocol that provides host-to-network and router-to-router connections. Can be used to provide a serial line connection between two machines.

Port   A number used to identify TCP/IP applications. Generally a port is an entry or exit point.

Protocol   Rules governing the behavior or method of operation of something.

Protocol Conversion   The process of changing one protocol to another.

Protocol Data Unit (PDU)   A term used in TCP/IP to refer to a unit of data, headers, and trailers at any layer in a network.

Protocol Interpreter (PI)   A process that carries out FTP functions. FTP uses one Protocol Interpreter for the server and another one for the user.

Proxy   A mechanism whereby one system functions for another when responding to protocol requests.

Push Service   A service provided by TCP to enable an application to specify when data must be transmitted as soon as possible.

RARP   See *Reverse Address Resolution Protocol.*

Receive Window   A range of sequence numbers that a sender can transmit at a given time.

Remote Network Monitor (RMON)   A device (such as a workstation) that collects and maintains information about network traffic.

Remote Procedure Call (RPC)   A TCP/IP protocol that provides a routine which calls a server that returns output and status (return) codes to the client.

Repeater   A network device that boosts the power of incoming signals to enable the length of a network to be extended.

Requests for Comment (RFCs)   Documents containing specifications for TCP/IP protocols. RFCs are also used to propose new protocols. RFCs are available from the Network Information Center (NIC).

Resolver   Software that enables clients to access the Domain Name Service (DNS) database and acquire an address.

Resource   Usually refers to application programs, but also used generally to refer to system capabilities such as memory, networks, and so on.

Retransmission Timeout   Occurs when data has been sent to a destination but no acknowledgment has been received when a timer has expired. When a retransmission timeout occurs, the protocol usually resends the data.

Reverse Address Resolution Protocol (RARP)   A TCP/IP protocol that enables a device to acquire its IP address by performing a broadcast on the network.

RIP (Routing Information Protocol)   A TCP/IP protocol used to exchange information about routing. Usually used when only a small number of computers are in use.

rlogin   Remote login service that enables a user on one machine to log in as a user on another. It is similar to Telnet.

Round Trip Time   The time for a TCP segment to be sent and its acknowledgment received.

Router   A device that connects LANs into an internetwork and routes traffic between them.

Routing   The process of determining a path to use to send data to its destination.

Routing Information Protocol (RIP)   A protocol used to exchange information between routers.

Routing Table   A list of valid paths through which data can be transmitted.

RS232C   A physical layer specification for connecting devices. Commonly used for serial lines.

SAP (Service Access Point)   The location at which two applications can exchange information.

Segment   A protocol data unit (PDU) that consists of a TCP header and (optional) data. Also used to refer to parts of a network that is divided into smaller parts (segments).

Send Window   A range of sequence numbers that can be received.

Sequence Number   A 32-bit field in the IP header that identifies the datagram.

Serial   A sequence of events occurring one after another.

Serial Line Internet Protocol (SLIP)   A protocol used to utilize TCP/IP over serial lines.

Server   An application that answers requests from other devices (clients). Also used as a generic term for any device that provides services to the rest of the network, such as printing, high-capacity storage, and network access.

Simple Mail Transfer Protocol (SMTP)   In TCP/IP, an application providing electronic mail services.

Socket   In TCP/IP, an addressable point that consists of an IP address and a TCP or UDP port number that provides applications with access to TCP/IP protocols.

Socket Address   The complete designation of a TCP/IP node consisting of a 32-bit IP address and a 16-bit port number.

Socket Descriptor   An integer used by an application to identify the connection.

Source   The originating device.

Source Routing   A routing method determined by the source device.

Subnet   In TCP/IP, part of a TCP/IP network identified by a portion of the Internet address.

Subnet Address   The part of the IP address that identifies the subnetwork.

Subnet Mask   A set of bits that excludes networks from having a system-wide broadcast, instead restricting the broadcast to a subnetwork.

Switched Connection A data link connection that is established on demand (like a telephone call).

SYN A segment used in the start of a TCP connection to enable both devices to exchange information defining characteristics about the session. It is also used to synchronize the target and destination devices.

Synchronous Data Transfer The transfer of data between two nodes at a timed rate (as opposed to asynchronously).

TCP/IP Transmission Control Protocol/Internet Protocol.

Telnet A TCP/IP application that enables a user to log in to a remote device.

Terminal Server A network device that provides physical access for dumb terminals, usually using an abbreviated TCP/IP protocol to enable a dumb terminal to remotely log on.

Terminator A resistor that must be on both ends of thick and thin Ethernet networks.

Throughput The amount of data that can be transferred through a medium within a certain time period.

Time-to-Live (TTL) The amount of time a datagram can remain on the internetwork. It is usually specified as the number of hops to permit.

Token Ring A lower-layer, connection-based networking protocol using a token-passing method to control data traffic.

Topology The configuration of network devices.

Traffic A general term used to describe the amount of data on a network back-bone.

Transceiver A network device required in baseband networks that takes a digital signal and puts it on the analog baseband medium. Transceivers can sense collisions.

Transmission Class 4 An OSI transport layer protocol similar to TCP. Often referred to as OSI TP4.

Transmission Control Block (TCB) A data structure that holds information about TCP and UDP connections.

Transmission Control Protocol (TCP) A transport layer protocol that is part of the TCP/IP protocol suite and provides a connection-based, reliable data stream.

Trivial File Transfer Protocol (TFTP) A mechanism for remote logons similar to Telnet but that uses UDP as a transport layer protocol instead of TCP.

UDP (User Datagram Protocol) A connectionless transport layer protocol. It does not perform retransmission of data.

User Agent   An electronic mail program that helps end users manage messages.

User Service   A service provided by TCP permitting an application to specify that data being transmitted is urgent and should be processed as soon as possible.

Well-Known Port   In TCP/IP, an address for an agreed upon purpose.

Wide Area Network (WAN)   Usually used to refer to a network spanning large geographic distances.

X.400   A protocol defining standards for electronic mail in an open network.

X.500   A protocol defining standards for directory services in an open network.

X Series   A collection of widely accepted standards, including data communications.

X Window   A software protocol developed at MIT for a distributed windowing system. X uses TCP for a transport protocol.

XNS (Xerox Networking Standard)   Networking protocols developed by Xerox, similar to TCP/IP.

APPENDIX

C

Commands

The commands associated with the TCP/IP utilities mentioned in this book are summarized in the following list. Refer to the Index for their occurrences throughout the text.

arp	View or update the Address Resolution Protocol tables
finger	View the list of users logged on the network
ftp	Invoke the file transfer protocol program
ifconfig	View or configure network interface parameters
mount	Mount a directory or filesystem onto the local file structure, or view a list of mounted directories or filesystems
netstat	Display network statistics
nfsstat	View statistics on NFS usage and configuration
nslookup	Look up IP addresses and associated information through a Domain Name Service Server
ping	Send an ICMP echo message to a remote system to test connectivity
rlogin	Log in to a remote host
rpcinfo	Display information about active processes
ruptime	Display the total time a system has been functioning and its current load
showmount	View all servers currently mounted
spray	Send a batch of UDP datagrams to a remote system to check connectivity and throughput
telnet	Log in to a remote host
traceroute	Display messages from routers along the path of a set of test datagrams
ypcat	Display the contents of a Network Information Service database
ypmatch	Look up an entry in a Network Information Service database

APPENDIX D

Well-Known Port Numbers

Both TCP and UDP use well-known ports, also known as *service contact ports*. The port names reflect the specific TCP and UDP applications. Ports are the end points of a connection, providing a convenient method for accessing and addressing the connection end.

The following list does not include all TCP and UDP ports, but it does include all those you are likely to encounter. The rest are assigned for historical or experimental reasons.

Port	Name	Description
1	TCPMUX	TCP Port Service Multiplexer
5	RJE	Remote Job Entry
7	ECHO	Echo
9	DISCARD	Discard
11	USERS	Active Users
13	DAYTIME	Daytime
17	Quote	Quote of the Day
19	CHARGEN	Character Generator
20	FTP-DATA	File Transfer (Data Channel)
21	FTP	File Transfer (Control Channel)
23	TELNET	TELNET
25	SMTP	Simple Mail Transfer
27	NSW-FE	NSW User System FE
29	MSG-ICP	MSG-ICP
31	MSG-AUTH	MSG Authentication
33	DSP	Display Support Protocol
35		Private Printer Server
37	TIME	Time
39	RLP	Resource Location Protocol
41	GRAPHICS	Graphics
42	NAMESERVER	Host Name Server
43	NICNAME	Who Is
49	LOGIN	Login Host Protocol

Port	Name	Description
53	DOMAIN	Domain Name Service
67	BOOTPS	Bootstrap Protocol Server
68	BOOTPC	Bootstrap Protocol Client
69	TFTP	Trivial File Transfer Protocol
79	FINGER	Finger
101	HOSTNAMENIC	Host Name Server
102	ISO-TSAP	ISO TSAP
103	X400	X.400
104	X400SND	X.400 SND
105	CSNET-NSCSNET	Mailbox Name Server
109	POP2	Post Office Protocol v2
110	POP3	Post Office Protocol v3
111	SUNRPC	SUN RPC Portmap
137	NETBIOS-NS	NETBIOS Name Service
138	NETBIOS-DGMNET	BIOS Datagram Service
139	NETBIOS-SSNNET	BIOS Session Service
146	ISO-TP0	ISO TP0
147	ISO-IP	ISO IP
150	SQL-NET	SQL-NET
153	SGMP	SGMP
156	SQLSRV	SQL Service
160	SGMP-TRAP5	SGMP TRAPS
161	SNMP	SNMP
162	SNMPTRAP	SNMPTRAP
163	CMIP-MANAGE	CMIP/TCP Manager
164	CMIP-AGENT	CMIP/TCP Agent
165	XNS-COURIER	Xerox Network
179	BGP	Border Gateway Protocol

APPENDIX

E

RFCs

Most of the information about the TCP/IP protocol family is published as Requests For Comments (RFCs). RFCs define the various aspects of the protocol, its use, and management as a set of loosely coordinated notes.

The RFCs contain a lot of useless information (mostly because it is system-specific or considerably outdated), but they also contain a wealth of detail for those who want to take TCP/IP to its limits. Unexpectedly, there is quite a bit of interesting and humorous reading in the RFCs, including several classic works such as "'Twas the Night Before Start-up" (RFC 968), "ARPAWOCKY" (RFC 527), and "Telnet Randomly—Lose Option" (RFC 748).

This appendix lists the important (or, as just mentioned, interesting or humorous) RFCs that readers might want to refer to. Instructions for accessing the RFCs are also included. This list is not complete. Where possible, old and outdated RFCs have been dropped from the list. However, thinning the list of RFCs is a time-consuming process, involving reading each of the documents in turn. Because there are almost 1,500 RFCs, I have relied on other users' comments, notes from the NIC, and other reference works for a suitable pruning.

Accessing RFCs

RFCs can be obtained in several ways, the easiest of which is electronically. Paper copies are available upon request. Electronic copies are usually in ASCII format, although some are in PostScript format and require a PostScript interpreter to print them. Most RFCs obtained electronically do not have diagrams, figures, or pictures.

Accessing RFCs Through FTP

RFCs can be obtained using FTP through the Internet Network Information Center (NIC). Use FTP to access the NIC archive NIC.DDN.MIL. Use the user name guest and the password anonymous. RFCs can then be retrieved by using the FTP get command with the following format:

```
<RFC>RFC527.txt
```

Replace the RFC527 portion with the number of the RFC required. You can FTP into the NIC archive only if you have access to a machine with Internet access.

Accessing RFCs Through E-Mail

RFCs can be requested through electronic mail. Both the NIC and the NFSNET Network Service Center provide automated responses, returning the requested RFC. Both services read incoming electronic mail for keywords that indicate which RFC is required as well as the sender's e-mail address, then send back the RFC requested.

To obtain an RFC from the NIC, send a message with the subject field set to the RFC you want. Mail it to `service@nic.ddn.mil`. If you want more information on obtaining information through the NIC e-mail system, send mail with the word `help` as the subject.

To obtain RFCs from the NFSNET Network Service Center, send a message with the first two lines like this:

```
REQUEST: RFC
TOPIC: 527
```

The first line specifies that you want an RFC, and the second line gives the RFC number. Send the mail to `info-server@sh.cs.net`. For more information, set the topic to `help`.

Accessing Printed Copies of RFCs

If you do not have access to electronic communications, you can request a preprinted copy of an RFC. To obtain a printed copy of any RFC, call the Network Information Center at 1-800-235-3155.

It is considered bad manners to make the NIC staff wait while you find which RFCs you want. Make a list of them first, so your telephone conversation is short and succinct. They must answer many calls a day and are usually quite busy.

Useful RFCs Sorted by Category

Following are categorized lists of available RFCs.

General Information

RFC1360	"IAB Official Protocol Standards," Postel, J.B.; 1992
RFC1340	"Assigned Numbers," Reynolds, J.K.; Postel, J.B.; 1992
RFC1208	"Glossary of Networking Terms," Jacobsen, O.J.; Lynch, D.C.; 1991
RFC1180	"TCP/IP Tutorial," Socolofsky, T.J.; Kale, C.J.; 1991
RFC1178	"Choosing a Name for Your Computer," Libes, D.; 1990
RFC1175	"FYI on Where to Start: A Bibliography of Inter-networking Information," Bowers, K.L.; LaQuey, T.L.; Reynolds, J.K.; Reubicek, K.; Stahl, M.K.; Yuan, A.; 1990
RFC1173	"Responsibilities of Host and Network Managers: A Summary of the Oral Tradition of the Internet," vanBokkelen, J.; 1990

RFC1166	"Internet Numbers," Kirkpatrick, S.; Stahl, M.K.; Recker, M.; 1990
RFC1127	"Perspective on the Host Requirements RFCs," Braden, R.T.; 1989
RFC1123	"Requirements for Internet Hosts—Application and Support," Braden, R.T., ed; 1989
RFC1122	"Requirements for Internet Hosts—Communication Layers," Braden, R.T., ed; 1989
RFC1118	"Hitchhiker's Guide to the Internet," Krol, E., 1989
RFC1011	"Official Internet Protocol," Reynolds, J.R.; Postel, J.B.; 1987
RFC1009	"Requirements for Internet Gateways," Braden, R.T.; Postel, J.B.; 1987
RFC980	"Protocol Document Order Information," Jacobsen, O.J.; Postel, J.B.; 1986

TCP and UDP

RFC1072	"TCP Extensions for Long-Delay Paths," Jacobson, V.; Braden, R.T.; 1988
RFC896	"Congestion Control in IP/TCP Internetworks," Nagle, J.; 1984
RFC879	"TCP Maximum Segment Size and Related Topics," Postel, J.B.; 1983
RFC813	"Window and Acknowledgment Strategy in TCP," Clark, D.D.; 1982
RFC793	"Transmission Control Protocol," Postel, J.B.; 1981
RFC768	"User Datagram Protocol," Postel, J.B.; 1980

IP and ICMP

RFC1219	"On the Assignment of Subnet Numbers," Tsuchiya, P.F.; 1991
RFC1112	"Host Extensions for IP Multicasting," Deering, S.E.; 1989
RFC1088	"Standard for the Transmission of IP Datagrams over NetBIOS Networks," McLaughlin, L.J.; 1989
RFC950	"Internet Standard Subnetting Procedure," Mogul, J.C.; Postel, J.B.; 1985
RFC932	"Subnetwork Addressing Schema," Clark, D.D.; 1985

RFC922	"Broadcasting Internet Datagrams in the Presence of Subnets," Mogul, J.C.; 1984
RFC919	"Broadcasting Internet Datagrams," Mogul, J.C.; 1984
RFC886	"Proposed Standard for Message Header Munging," Rose, M.T.; 1983
RFC815	"IP Datagram Reassembly Algorithms," Clark, D.D.; 1982
RFC814	"Names, Addresses, Ports, and Routes," Clark, D.D.; 1982
RFC792	"Internet Control Message Protocol," Postel, J.B.; 1981
RFC791	"Internet Protocol," Postel, J.B.; 1981
RFC781	"Specification of the Internet Protocol (IP) Timestamp Option," Su, Z.; 1981

Lower Layers

RFC1236	"IP to X.121 Address Mapping for DDN," Morales, L.F. Jr.; 1991
RFC1220	"Point-to-Point Protocol Extensions for Bridging," Baker, F., ed.; 1991
RFC1209	"Transmission of IP Datagrams over the SMDS Service," Piscitello, D.M.; Lawrence, J.; 1991
RFC1201	"Transmitting IP Traffic over ARCNET Networks," Provan, D.; 1991
RFC1188	"Proposed Standard for the Transmission of IP Datagrams over FDDI Networks," Katz, D.; 1990
RFC1172	"Point-to-Point Protocol Initial Configuration Options," Perkins, D.; Hobby, R.; 1990
RFC1171	"Point-to-Point Protocol for the Transmission of Multiprotocol Datagrams over Point-to-Point Links," Perkins, D.; 1990
RFC1149	"Standard for the Transmission of IP Datagrams on Avian Carriers," Waitzman, D.; 1990
RFC1055	"Nonstandard for Transmission of IP Datagrams over Serial Lines: SLIP," Romkey, J.L.; 1988
RFC1044	"Internet Protocol on Network System's HYPERchannel: Protocol Specification," Hardwick, K.; Lekashman, J.; 1988
RFC1042	"Standard for the Transmission of IP Datagrams over IEEE 802 Networks," Postel, J.B.; Reynolds, J.K.; 1988

E

RFC1027	"Using ARP to Implement Transparent Subnet Gateways," Carl-Mitchell, S.; Quarterman, J.S.; 1987
RFC903	"Reverse Address Resolution Protocol," Finlayson, R.; Mann, T.; Mogul, J.C.; Theimer, M.; 1984
RFC895	"Standard for the Transmission of IP Datagrams over Experimental Ethernet Networks," Postel, J.B.; 1984
RFC894	"Standard for the Transmission of IP Datagrams over Ethernet Networks," Hornig, C.; 1984
RFC893	"Trailer Encapsulations," Leffler, S.; Karels, M.J.; 1984
RFC877	"Standard for the Transmission of IP Datagrams over Public Data Networks," Korb, J.T.; 1983

Bootstrapping

RFC1084	"BOOTP Vendor Information Extensions," Reynolds, J.K.; 1988
RFC951	"Bootstrap Protocol," Croft, W.J.; Gilmore, J.; 1985
RFC906	"Bootstrap Loading Using TFTP," Finlayson, R.; 1984

Domain Name Service

RFC1101	"DNS Encoding of Network Names and Other Types," Mockapetris, P.V.; 1989
RFC1035	"Domain Names—Implementation and Specification," Mockapetris, P.V.; 1987
RFC1034	"Domain Names—Concepts and Facilities," Mockapetris, P.V.; 1987
RFC1033	"Domain Administrators Operations Guide," Lottor, M.; 1987
RFC1032	"Domain Administrators Guide," Stahl, M.K.; 1987
RFC974	"Mail Routing and the Domain System," Partridge, C.; 1986
RFC920	"Domain Requirements," Postel, J.B.; Reynolds, J.K.; 1984
RFC799	"Internet Name Domains," Mills, D.L.; 1981

File Transfer and File Access

RFC1094	"NFS: Network File System Protocol Specification," Sun Microsystems, Inc.; 1989
RFC1068	"Background File Transfer Program (BFTP)," DeSchon, A.L.; Braden, R. T.; 1988
RFC959	"File Transfer Protocol," Postel, J.B.; Reynolds, J.K.; 1985
RFC949	"FTP Unique-Named Store Command," Padlipsky, M.A.; 1985
RFC783	"TFTP Protocol (Revision 2)," Sollins, K.R.; 1981
RFC775	"Directory Oriented FTP Commands," Mankins, D.; Franklin, D.; Owen, A.D.; 1980

Mail

RFC1341	"MIME (Multipurpose Internet Mail Extensions) Mechanisms for Specifying and Describing the Format of Internet Message Bodies," Borenstein, N.; Freed, N.; 1992
RFC1143	"Q Method of Implementing Telnet Option Negotiation," Bernstein, D.J.; 1990
RFC1090	"SMTP on X.25," Ullmann, R.; 1989
RFC1056	"PCMAIL: A Distributed Mail System for Personal Computers," Lambert, M.L.; 1988
RFC974	"Mail Routing and the Domain System," Partridge, C.; 1986
RFC822	"Standard for the Format of ARPA Internet Text Messages," Crocker, D.; 1982
RFC821	"Simple Mail Transfer Protocol," Postel, J.B.; 1982

Routing Protocols

RFC1267	"A Border Gateway Protocol 3 (BGP-3)," Lougheed, K.; Rekhter, Y.; 1991
RFC1247	"OSPF version 2," Moy, J.; 1991
RFC1222	"Advancing the NSFNET Routing Architecture," Braun, H.W.; Rekhter, Y.; 1991
RFC1195	"Use of OSI IS-IS for Routing in TCP/IP and Dual Environments," Callon, R.W.; 1990

RFC1164	"Application of the Border Gateway Protocol in the Internet," Honig, J.C.; Katz, D.; Mathis, M.; Rekhter, Y.; Yu, J.Y.; 1990
RFC1163	"Border Gateway Protocol (BGP)," Lougheed, K.; Rekhter, Y.; 1990
RFC1136	"Administrative Domains and Routing Domains: A Model for Routing in the Internet," Hares, S.; Katz, D.; 1989
RFC1074	"NSFNET Backbone SPF-Based Interior Gateway Protocol," Rekhter, J.; 1988
RFC1058	"Routing Information Protocol," Hedrick, C.L.; 1988
RFC911	"EGP Gateway under Berkeley UNIX 4.2," Kirton, P.; 1984
RFC904	"Exterior Gateway Protocol Formal Specification," Mills, D.L.; 1984
RFC888	"STUB Exterior Gateway Protocol," Seamonson, L.; Rosen, E.C.; 1984
RFC827	"Exterior Gateway Protocol (EGP)," Rosen, E.C.; 1982
RFC823	"DARPA Internet Gateway," Hinden, R.M.; Sheltzer, A.; 1982

Routing Performance and Policy

RFC1254	"Gateway Congestion Control Survey," Mankin, A.; Ramakrishnan, K.K, eds.; 1991
RFC1246	"Experience with the OSPF Protocol," Moy, J., ed.; 1991
RFC1245	"OSPF Protocol Analysis," Moy, J., ed; 1991
RFC1125	"Policy Requirements for Inter-Administrative Domain Routing," Estrin, D.; 1989
RFC1124	"Policy Issues in Interconnecting Networks," Leiner, B.M.; 1989
RFC1104	"Models of Policy-Based Routing," Braun, H.W.; 1989
RFC1102	"Policy Routing in Internet Protocols," Clark, D.D.; 1989

Terminal Access

RFC1205	"Telnet 5250 Interface," Chmielewski, P.; 1991
RFC1198	"FYI on the X Window System," Scheifler, R.W.; 1991
RFC1184	"Telnet Linemode Option," Borman, D.A., ed.; 1990
RFC1091	"Telnet Terminal-Type Option," VanBokkelen, J.; 1989

RFC1080	"Telnet Remote Flow Control Option," Hedrick, C.L.; 1988
RFC1079	"Telnet Terminal Speed Option," Hedrick, C.L.; 1988
RFC1073	"Telnet Window Size Option," Waitzman, D.; 1988
RFC1053	"Telnet X.3 PAD Option," Levy, S.; Jacobson, T.; 1988
RFC1043	"Telnet Data Entry Terminal Option: DODIIS Implementation," Yasuda, A.; Thompson, T.; 1988
RFC1041	"Telnet 3270 Regime Option," Rekhter, Y.; 1988
RFC1013	"X Window System Protocol, version 11: Alpha Update," Scheifler, R.W.; 1987
RFC946	"Telnet Terminal Location Number Option," Nedved, R.; 1985
RFC933	"Output Marking Telnet Option," Silverman, S.; 1985
RFC885	"Telnet End of Record Option," Postel, J.B.; 1983
RFC861	"Telnet Extended Options: List Option," Postel, J.B; Reynolds, J.K.; 1983
RFC860	"Telnet Timing Mark Option," Postel, J.B.; Reynolds, J.K.; 1983
RFC859	"Telnet Status Option," Postel, J.B.; Reynolds, J.K.; 1983
RFC858	"Telnet Suppress Go Ahead Option," Postel, J.B,; Reynolds, J.K.; 1983
RFC857	"Telnet Echo Option," Postel, J.B.; Reynolds, J.K.; 1983
RFC856	"Telnet Binary Transmission," Postel, J.B.; Reynolds, J.K.; 1983
RFC855	"Telnet Option Specifications," Postel, J.B.; Reynolds, J.K.; 1983
RFC854	"Telnet Protocol Specification," Postel, J.B.; Reynolds, J.K.; 1983
RFC779	"Telnet Send-Location Option," Killian, E.; 1981
RFC749	"Telnet SUPDUP-Output Option," Greenberg, B.; 1978
RFC736	"Telnet SUPDUP Option," Crispin, M.R; 1977
RFC732	"Telnet Data Entry Terminal Option," Day, J.D.; 1977
RFC727	"Telnet Logout Option," Crispin, M.R.; 1977
RFC726	"Remote Controlled Transmission and Echoing Telnet Option," Postel, J.B.; Crocker, D.; 1977
RFC698	"Telnet Extended ASCII Option," Mock, T.; 1975

E

Other Applications

RFC1196	"Finger User Information Protocol," Zimmerman. D.P.; 1990
RFC1179	"Line Printer Daemon Protocol," McLaughlin, L.; 1990
RFC1129	"Internet Time Synchronization: The Network Time Protocol," Mills, D.L.; 1989
RFC1119	"Network Time Protocol (version 2) Specification and Implementation," Mills, D.L.; 1989
RFC1057	"RPC: Remote Procedure Call Protocol Specification: Version 2," Sun Microsystems, Inc.; 1988
RFC1014	"XDR: External Data Representation Standard," Sun Microsystems, Inc.; 1987
RFC954	"NICNAME/WHOIS," Harrenstien, K.; Stahl, M.K.; Feinler, E.J.; 1985
RFC868	"Time Protocol," Postel, J.B.; Harrenstien, K.; 1983
RFC867	"Daytime Protocol," Postel, J.B.; 1983
RFC866	"Active Users," Postel, J.B.; 1983
RFC8G5	"Quote of the Day Protocol," Postel, J.B.; 1983
RFC8G4	"Character Generator Protocol," Postel, J.B.; 1983
RFC863	"Discard Protocol," Postel, J.B.; 1983
RFC862	"Echo Protocol," Postel, J.B.; 1983

Network Management

RFC1271	"Remote Network Monitoring Management Information Base," Waldbusser, S.; 1991
RFC1253	"OSPE version 2: Management Information Base," Baker, P.; Coltun, R.; 1991
RFC1243	"Appletalk Management Information Base," 1991
RFC1239	"Reassignment of Experimental MIBs to Standard MIBs," Reynolds, J.K.; 1991
RFC1238	"CLNS MIB for Use with Connectionless Network Protocol (ISO 8473) and End System to Intermediate System (ISO 9542)," Satz, G.; 1991
RFC1233	"Definitions of Managed Objects for the DS3 Interface Type," Cox, T.A.; Tesink, K., eds.; 1991

RFC1232   "Definitions of Managed Objects for the DS1 Interface Type,"
               Baker, F.; Kolb, C.P., eds.; 1991

RFC1231   "IEEE 802.5 Token Ring MIB," McCloghrie, K.; Fox, R.;
               Decker, E.; 1991

RFC1230   "IEEE 802.4 Token Bus MIB," McCloghrie, K.; Fox R.; 1991

RFC1229   "Extensions to the Generic-Interface MIB," McCloghrie, K., ed.;
               1991

RFC1228   "SNMP-DPI: Simple Network Management Protocol Distrib-
               uted Program Interface," Carpenter, G.; Wijnen, B.; 1991

RFC1227   "SNMP MUX protocol and MIB," Rose, M.T.; 1991

RFC1224   "Techniques for Managing Asynchronously Generated Alerts,"
               Steinberg, L.; 1991

RFC1215   "Convention for Defining Traps for Use with the SNMP," Rose,
               M.T., ed.; 1991

RFC1214   "OSI Internet Management: Management Information Base,"
               LaBarre, L., ed.; 1991

RFC1213   "Management Information Base for Network Management of
               TCP/IP-based Internets: MiB-II," McCloghrie, K.; Rose, M.T.,
               eds.; 1991

RFC1212   "Concise MIB Definitions," Rose, M.T.; McCloghrie, K., eds.;
               1991

RFC1187   "Bulk Table Retrieval with the SNMP," Rose, M.T.;
               McCloghrie, K.; Davin, J.R.; 1990

RFC1157   "Simple Network Management Protocol (SNMP)," Case, J.D.;
               Fedor, M.; Schoffstall, M.L.; Davin, C.; 1990

RFC1156   "Management Information Base for Network Management of
               TCP/IP-based Internets," McCloghrie, K.; Rose, M.T.; 1990

RFC1155   "Structure and Identification of Management Information for
               TCP/IP-Based Internets," Rose, M.T.; McCloghrie, K.; 1990

RFC1147   "FYI on a Network Management Tool Catalog: Tools for
               Monitoring and Debugging TCP/IP Internets and Intercon-
               nected Devices," Stine, R.H., ed.; 1990

RFC1089   "SNMP over Ethernet," Schoffstall, M.L.; Davin, C.; Fedor, M.;
               Case, J.D.; 1989

E

Tunneling

RFC1241	"Scheme for an Internet Encapsulation Protocol: Version 1," 1991
RFC1234	"Tunneling IPX Traffic through IP Networks," Provan, D.; 1991
RFC1088	"Standard for the Transmission of IP Datagrams over NetBIOS Networks," McLaughlin, L.J.; 1989
RFC1002	"Protocol Standard for a NetBIOS Service on a TCP/UDP Transport: Detailed Specifications," NetBIOS Working Group; 1987
RFC1001	"Protocol Standard for a NetBIOS Service on a TCP/UDP Transport: Concepts and Methods," NetBIOS Working Group; 1987

OSI

RFC1240	"OSI Connectionless Transport Services on Top of UDP: Version 1," Shue, C.; Haggerty, W.; Dobbins, K.; 1991
RFC1237	"Guidelines for OSI NSAP Allocation in the Internet," Gollela, R.; Gardner, E.P.; Callon, R.W.; 1991
RFC1169	"Explaining the Role of GOSIP," Cerf, V.G.; Mills, K.L.; 1990

Security

RFC1244	"Site Security Handbook"
RFC1115	"Privacy Enhancement for Internet Electronic Mail: Part III—Algorithms, Modes, and Identifiers [Draft]," Linn, J.; 1989
RFC1114	"Privacy Enhancement for Internet Electronic Mail: Part II—Certificate-Based Key Management [Draft]," Kent, S.T.; Linn, J.; 1989
RFC1113	"Privacy Enhancement for Internet Electronic Mail: Part I—Message Encipherment and Authentication Procedures [Draft]," Linn, J.; 1989
RFC1108	"Security Options for the Internet Protocol," 1991

Miscellaneous

RFC1251   "Who's Who in the Internet: Biographies of IAB, IESG, and IRSG Members," Malkin, G.S.; 1991

RFC1207   "FYI on Questions and Answers: Answers to Commonly Asked 'Experienced Internet User' Questions," Malkin, G.S.; Marine, A.N.; Reynolds, J.K.; 1991

RFC1206   "FYI on Questions and Answers: Answers to Commonly Asked 'New Internet User' Questions," Malkin, G.S.; Marine, A.N.; 1991

E

APPENDIX

F

Answers to Quizzes

Chapter 2

1. Draw the layered architectures of both the OSI Reference Model and TCP/IP. Show how the layers correspond in each diagram.

   The layered architecture of both the OSI-RM and TCP/IP are shown in Figure 2.2.

2. Show the layered Internet architecture, explaining each layer's purpose.

   The layers of the Internet architecture are shown in Figure 2.5.

3. Show how a datagram is transferred from one network, through one or more gateways, to the destination network. In each device, show the layered architecture and how high up the layered structure the datagrams goes.

This process is shown in Figure 2.6.

4. Draw the IP header and an Ethernet frame, showing the number of bits used for each component. Explain each component's role.

   The IP header and Ethernet frame structure is shown in Figure 2.8. The text in that section explain the role of each component.

5. Explain what an ARP Cache is. What is its structure and why is it used?

The ARP cache is used to hold IP addresses and physical addresses The layout of an ARP cache is shown in Figure 2.10. Each row corresponds to one device, with four pieces of information for each device.

Chapter 3

1. Explain why IP is important to the proper transmission of data.

   IP's primary task is the addressing of datagrams. Without IP, routing information would have to be constructed at a higher layer in the architecture.

2. Show the construction of the IP header and the meaning of each element within the header structure.

   The IP header is shown in Figure 3.1. The meaning of each field within the header is explained in the text accompanying the figure.

3. ICMP headers are quite small. Show the structure of a typical message header and the meaning of the bits within it.

   The ICMP header is shown in Figure 3.4. The meaning of each field and their valid values are explained in the accompanying text.

4. Explain the different EGP message formats and when they are used.

There are four EGP message formats in use: neighbor acquisition and neighbor reachability (both of which indicate the presence and status of neighbor devices); poll (to verify that a neighbor is active); and error (for reporting error conditions).

5. Show the EGP message format, explaining the contents of the header and the network reachability information.

The format of the EGP message headers is shown in Figures 3.6 and 3.7. The text accompanying the figures explains the meaning of the fields within the header.

Chapter 4

1. Draw a diagram showing the binding of port tables when three machines are sending information to each other.

This is shown in Figure 4.3.

2. Draw the TCP protocol data unit (PDU) and explain the meaning of each field.

The TCP PDU is shown in Figure 4.5. The fields are all explained in the accompanying text.

3. Use a diagram to show the signals involved with two machines establishing a TCP connection. Then, show how data is transferred. Finally, show the termination process.

The diagrams for all three steps are shown in Figures 4.6, 4.7, and 4.8.

4. What is a TCP connection table? How is it used?

TCP uses a connection table to keep track of all the active connections. Each existing connection has an entry in the table that shows information about the end-to-end connection. The layout of the TCP connection table is shown in Figure 4.9.

5. Draw the UDP header and explain the fields it contains.

The UDP header is shown in Figure 4.10. The accompanying text explains the purpose of each field.

6. What are the advantages of using UDP over TCP? When would you not want to use UDP?

UDP is connectionless, hence a little faster. It is not as reliable as TCP, though, so it is not useful for applications when a connection must be maintained for long periods or when reliability of transfer is important.

Chapter 5

1. Define the role of gateways, routers, bridges, and brouters.

   A gateway performs routing functions between networks and can translate protocols. A bridge connects two or more networks using the same protocol. A router is a network device that forwards datagrams around the network. A brouter performs the functions of both the bridge and the router.

2. What is a packet-switched network?

   A packet-switched network is one where all transfers of information are based on self-contained packets (like TCP/IP's datagrams).

3. What is the difference between interior and exterior neighbor gateways?

   Interior gateways connect LANs of one organization, whereas exterior gateways connect the organization to the outside world.

4. What are the advantages and disadvantages of the three types of routing tables?

   The three types of routing tables are fixed, dynamic, and fixed central. The fixed table must be manually modified every time there is a change. A dynamic table changes its information based on network traffic, reducing the amount of manual maintenance. A fixed central table lets a manager modify only one table, which is then read by other devices. The fixed central table reduces the need to update each machine's table, as with the fixed table. Usually a dynamic table causes the fewest problems for a network administrator, although the table's contents can change without the administrator being aware of the change.

5. What is the HELLO protocol used for?

   The HELLO protocol uses time instead of distance to determine optimal routing. It is an alternative to the Routing Information Protocol.

Chapter 6

1. Explain what a network virtual terminal is.

   A network virtual terminal (NVT) is used to define both ends of a connection. It has a logical keyboard and a logical printer (display). NVTs are necessary to allow a connection to exist.

2. Draw diagrams showing two- and three-party FTP sessions, indicating the port numbers used by each machine.

   These diagrams are shown in Figures 5.4 and 5.5.

3. Why would you want to enable anonymous FTP access? Are there any reasons for disallowing it?

   Anonymous FTP access enables users to upload and download files to your system without having to log in. This can be useful when you want to share information without worrying about user IDs. Anonymous FTP should be disabled if you do not plan to share information globally, because there are several possible security concerns with a poorly administered anonymous FTP setup.

4. TFTP enables files to be transferred without logging in. What problems can this cause?

   TFTP's capability to transfer files without a login can enable a remote user to transfer a file to or from your system without your specific knowledge, as long as the security system and file permissions are set to enable this. A well-run system controls TFTP's access considerably.

5. What are the Berkeley Utilities?

   The Berkeley Utilities are a set of useful utility programs developed for TCP/IP at the University of California at Berkeley. The tools are known as the Berkeley Utilities in honor of their developers.

Note

Chapters 7 and 10 don't have quizzes.

Chapter 8

1. What components make up a Medium Attachment Unit (MAU) and what are their roles?

   The MAU is composed of the Physical Medium Attachment (PMA) and the Medium Dependent Interface (MDI). The MAU manages the connection of the machine to the network medium itself.

2. What is FDDI? Why is it popular?

   FDDI is Fiber Distributed Data Interface, popular because it provides very high transmission speeds over a fiber optic cable.

3. What is the role of the Discard service?

   The Discard service discards everything it receives, returning nothing back to the sender.

4. The Time protocol is often used by network devices. What is its role?

   The Time protocol is used to synchronize devices on a network so their clocks are consistent. If they were not consistent, some packet information involving actual times would be meaningless.

5. Does the presence of a second network protocol (like IPX) affect the basic TCP/IP protocol suite's operations?

   TCP/IP can function over other network protocols (like IPX) by replacing parts of the TCP/IP layered architecture with the other network protocol's layers. Some duplication and crossover of functionality can be expected, but TCP/IP can function properly with many different networks.

Chapter 9

1. How many devices are enabled on a Class B network (the most common)?

   Class B networks use two bytes for the device portion of the IP address. This enables 65,534 different devices.

2. What is the difference between the BSD UNIX TCP/IP broadcast address setting and the one normally used?

   The BSD UNIX TCP/IP broadcast address uses all 0s, whereas the Internet standard (and most other TCP/IP implementations) uses all 1s. The Internet system is the most widely used except in locations that have run BSD UNIX for many years and have not made the switch.

3. What is a pseudo tty?

   A pseudo tty or false terminal enables external machines to connect through Telnet or rlogin. Without a pseudo tty, no connection can take place.

4. What does the following .rhosts file do?

   ```
   # .rhosts
   artemis tparker
   artemis goof
   artemis aarmenakis
   mig rmaclean
   ```

   This file enables three users from the system artemis and one user from the system mig to log in to the host system without using passwords. The user IDs that can be used are specified after the machine name.

5. What is anonymous FTP and why would you use it?

Anonymous FTP enables users to connect to a host without using a valid login and password. Usually, anonymous FTP uses a login called anonymous or guest, with the password usually requesting the user's ID for tracking purposes only. Anonymous FTP is used to enable a large number of users to access files on the host without having to go to the trouble of setting up logins for them all. Anonymous FTP systems usually have strict controls over the areas an anonymous user can access.

Chapter 11

1. What protocol is used by DNS servers? Why is that a good choice?

DNS uses UDP for communication between servers. It is a better choice than TCP because of the improved speed a connectionless protocol offers. Of course, transmission reliability suffers with UDP.

2. What is a DNS resource record?

A resource record is an entry in a name server's database. There are several types of resource records used, including name-to-address resolution information. Resource records are maintained as ASCII files.

3. Show a sample entry in an IN-ADDR-ARPA file and explain what the fields mean.

An entry in an IN-ADDR-ARPA file would look like this:

```
merlin    IN    A    143.12.2.46
```

The line contains the machine name, the class of machine (IN means Internet), A to show it is an address resource record, and the IP address.

4. BOOTP helps a diskless workstation boot. How does it get a message to the network looking for its IP address and the location of its operating system boot files?

BOOTP sends a UDP message with a subnetwork broadcast address and waits for a reply from a server that gives it the IP address. The same message might contain the name of the machine that has the boot files on it. If the boot image location is not specified, the workstation sends another UDP message to query the server.

5. What is the Network Time Protocol? Why is it used?

The Network Time Protocol is designed specifically to ensure that all internal timers are synchronized and have similar settings.

Chapter 12

1. Show how the NFS layers compare to the OSI Reference Model.

   This is shown in Figure 9.1. The NFS layers comprise the top three layers of the architecture, including the application layer protocols (mount, yp, and so forth), XDR (External Data Representation) in place of the presentation layer, and RPC (Remote Procedure Call) in place of the session layer.

2. Explain how a port mapper assigns ports.

   The port mapper controls assignment of ports based on requests from applications. The port mapper maintains a table of ports and the RPC programs that are using them. When the port mapper receives a request for a port, it checks for an available port, then completes a table entry for the port and application, returning the port number with a status message.

3. What is External Data Representation?

   External Data Representation is a method of encoding data within an RPC message, used to ensure that the data is not system-dependent.

4. What does the Mount protocol do?

   The Mount protocol returns a file handle and the name of the file system in which a requested file resides. The message is sent to the client from the server after reception of a client's request.

5. What is REX? What advantage does REX offer other similar utilities?

   The Remote Execution Service (REX) is designed to enable users to run commands on other machines without logging in and without the overhead of larger utilities like Telnet. Because REX preserves the full shell environment, it is better than other remote procedures.

Chapter 13

1. What are the five parts of the OSI Reference Model dealing with network management (called the Specific Management Functional Areas)?

   The OSI-RM defines the five aspects of network management as accounting, configuration, faults, performance, and security.

2. What is a Management Information Base (MIB)?

   A Management Information Base is part of every SNMP-managed device. Each SNMP agent has the MIB database that contains information about the device's status, its performance, connections, and configuration. The MIB is queried by SNMP.

3. What is ping?

Ping is the Packet Internet Groper. It sends out an ICMP request to a destination and waits for a response. Ping is a simple utility used to check connectivity.

4. Assume a LAN has some machines using Ethernet and others using IEEE 802.3. Can they communicate?

Not unless there is a translation system in place. The datagrams for Ethernet and IEEE 802.3 are slightly different. This is a common problem because most users think that IEEE 802.3 is Ethernet.

5. What is Kerberos?

Kerberos is a network security system developed at MIT. It provides encryption and validation services that are very difficult to break.

Chapter 14

1. What are the six basic socket commands?

The basic socket commands are open, send, receive, status, close, and abort.

2. A Transmission Control Block performs what function?

A TCB is a complex data structure that contains a considerable amount of information about a connection. There is a TCB for each connection.

3. What is the difference between an unspecified passive open and a fully specified passive open?

An unspecified passive open has the server waiting for a connection request from a client. A fully specified passive open has the server waiting for a connection from a specific client.

4. What command displays status information about a socket?

The command `getsockopt` queries a socket and displays all information returned about the socket.

5. What is a fork?

A fork is a UNIX process that creates a copy of the existing application, then executes it.

INDEX

TCP/IP Unleashed

— Timothy Parker, Ph.D.

This book starts with the installation of the most popular TCP/IP products on each platform, and then proceeds through configuration and troubleshooting each product. Subsequent chapters increase the readers understanding of the theory and practice of TCP/IP, both from an administrative and user point of view.

Covers TCP/IP for DOS, Windows, Macintosh, and UNIX systems.

Includes configuration and troubleshooting information.

CD-ROM includes source code from the book.

Covers TCP/IP.

$45.00 USA/$63.95 CDN   *User Level: New – Casual*
ISBN: 0-672-30603-4   *880 pages*

CGI Developer's Guide

— Eugene Eric Kim

This book is one of the first books to provide comprehensive information on developing with CGI (the Common Gateway Interface). It covers many of the aspects of CGI including, interactivity, performance, portability, and security. After reading this book, the reader will be able to write robust, secure, and efficient CGI programs.

CD-ROM includes source code, sample utilities, and Internet tools.

Covers client/server programming, working with gateways, and using Netscape.

Readers will master forms, image maps, dynamic displays, database manipulation, and animation.

$45.00 USA/$63.95 CDN   *User Level: Accomplished – Expert*
ISBN: 1-57521-087-8   *600 pages*

Client/Server Unleashed

— *Neil Jenkins, et al.*

This book leads the reader through the often confusing client/server world. It defines every aspect of the client/server architecture, and gives an overview of all the products and tools. Readers will be conceptually lead through all the major steps in planning and implementing their C/S architecture.

CD-ROM contains demonstrations of various products and a multimedia client/server product encyclopedia.

Guides the reader through planning projects and evaluating business considerations.

Covers migration from standard systems to C/S systems.

$59.99 USA/$84.95 CDN   *User Level: Accomplished – Expert*
ISBN: 0-672-30726-X   *1,200 pages*

Red Hat Linux Unleashed

— *Kamran Husain, Tim Parker, et al.*

Programmers, users, and system administrators will find this a must-have book for operating the Linux environment. Everything from installation and configuration to advanced programming and administration techniques is covered in this valuable reference.

CD-ROM includes source code from the book and powerful utilities.

Teaches editing, typsetting, and more.

Includes coverage of PPP, TCP/IP, networking, and setting up an Internet site.

Covers Red Hat Linux.

$49.99 USA/$70.95 CDN   *User Level: Accomplished – Expert*
ISBN: 0-672-30962-9   *1,176 pages*

Add to Your Sams Library Today with the Best Books for Programming, Operating Systems, and New Technologies

The easiest way to order is to pick up the phone and call

1-800-428-5331

between 9:00 a.m. and 5:00 p.m. EST.

For faster service please have your credit card available.

ISBN	Quantity	Description of Item	Unit Cost	Total Cost
0-672-30603-4		TCP/IP Unleashed (Book/CD-ROM)	$45.00	
1-57521-087-8		CGI Developer's Guide (Book/CD-ROM)	$45.00	
0-672-30726-X		Client/Server Unleashed (Book/CD-ROM)	$59.99	
0-672-30962-9		Red Hat Linux Unleashed (Book/CD-ROM)	$49.99	
		Shipping and Handling: See information below.		
		TOTAL		

Shipping and Handling: $4.00 for the first book, and $1.75 for each additional book. Floppy disk: add $1.75 for shipping and handling. If you need to have it NOW, we can ship product to you in 24 hours for an additional charge of approximately $18.00, and you will receive your item overnight or in two days. Overseas shipping and handling adds $2.00 per book and $8.00 for up to three disks. Prices subject to change. Call for availability and pricing information on latest editions.

201 W. 103rd Street, Indianapolis, Indiana 46290

1-800-428-5331 — Orders   1-800-835-3202 — FAX   1-800-858-7674 — Customer Service

Book ISBN 0-672-30885-1